# THE IT REVOLUTION AND ITS IMPACT ON STATE, CONSTITUTIONALISM AND PUBLIC LAW

What is the future of constitutionalism, state and law in the new technological age?

This edited collection explores the different aspects of the impact of information and technology revolution on state, constitutionalism and public law. Leading European scholars in the fields of constitutional, administrative, financial and EU law provide answers to fascinating conceptual questions including:

- What are the challenges of information and technological revolution to sovereignty?
- How will information and technology revolution impact democracy and the public sphere?
- What are the disruptive effects of social media platforms on democratic will-formation processes and how can we regulate the democratic process in the digital age?
- What are the main challenges to courts and administrations in the algorithmic society?
- What is the impact of artificial intelligence on administrative law and social and health services?
- What is the impact of information and technology revolution on data protection, privacy and human rights?

# The IT Revolution and its Impact on State, Constitutionalism and Public Law

Edited by
Martin Belov

•HART•
OXFORD • LONDON • NEW YORK • NEW DELHI • SYDNEY

HART PUBLISHING

Bloomsbury Publishing Plc

Kemp House, Chawley Park, Cumnor Hill, Oxford, OX2 9PH, UK

1385 Broadway, New York, NY 10018, USA

29 Earlsfort Terrace, Dublin 2, Ireland



First published in Great Britain 2021



A catalogue record for this book is available from the British Library.

Library of Congress Cataloging-in-Publication data

Names: Belov, Martin, editor.

Title: The IT revolution and its impact on state, constitutionalism, and public law / edited by Martin Belov.

Other titles: Information Technology revolution and its impact on state, constitutionalism, and public law

Description: Oxford, UK ; New York, NY : Hart Publishing, an imprint of Bloomsbury Publishing, 2021 | Includes bibliographical references and index.

Identifiers: LCCN 2020048396 (print) | LCCN 2020048397 (ebook) | ISBN 9781509940875 (hardback) | ISBN 9781509944675 (paperback) | ISBN 9781509940899 (pdf) | ISBN 9781509940882 (Epub)

Subjects: LCSH: Information technology—Law and legislation—European Union countries. | Technology and law—European Union countries. | Constitutional law—European Union countries. | Public law—European Union countries.

Classification: LCC KJE959.5.C65 I825 2021 (print) | LCC KJE959.5.C65 (ebook) | DDC 343.409/944—dc23

LC record available at https://lccn.loc.gov/2020048396

LC ebook record available at https://lccn.loc.gov/2020048397

ISBN: HB: 978-1-50994-087-5
ePDF: 978-1-50994-089-9
ePub: 978-1-50994-088-2

Typeset by Compuscript Ltd, Shannon

# TABLE OF CONTENTS

## PART III
## MONETARY SOVEREIGNTY AND TAXATION IN THE INFORMATION TECHNOLOGY ERA



## PART IV
## THE IMPACT OF INFORMATION AND TECHNOLOGY REVOLUTION ON COURTS AND ADMINISTRATION



## PART V
## THE INFORMATION AND TECHNOLOGY REVOLUTION AND ITS IMPACT ON DATA PROTECTION, PRIVACY AND HUMAN RIGHTS

PART VI
INFORMATION AND TECHNOLOGY REVOLUTION AND HEALTH RELATED RIGHTS

# LIST OF CONTRIBUTORS

**Martin Belov (editor)**

Dr Martin Belov is Professor in Constitutional and Comparative Constitutional Law at the University of Sofia 'St. Kliment Ohridski'. He is Vice Dean of the University of Sofia 'St. Kliment Ohridski' Faculty of Law, responsible for international relations and digitalisation. Martin Belov has been visiting professor at University Paris II Pantheon-Assas, France (2019), University Roma Tre, Rome, Italy (2019), Goethe-University Frankfurt am Main, Germany (2019), University of Girona, Spain (2019), University 'Pompeu Fabra', Barcelona, Spain (2019), Europa-University Viadrina, Frankfurt/Oder, Germany (2017 and 2018), University of Bari, Italy (2018), European Law and Governance School, Athens (2017–2018), University of Södertorn, Stockholm, Sweden (2017), Scuolla Superiore Sant'Anna, Pisa, Italy (2016), University of Warsaw, Poland (2015), University of Lisbon, Portugal (2012), State University of Milan, Italy (2011), University of Cologne, Germany (2007–2009) and others. Martin Belov has been project researcher at the Max-Planck Institute for European Legal History, Frankfurt am Main, Germany (2010–2012) and visiting researcher at the Institute for Federalism, Fribourg, Switzerland (2014). He has specialised at the University of Oxford, UK (2017), Max-Planck Institute for Comparative Public Law and International Law, Heidelberg, Germany (2009) and many other academic institutions. Martin Belov is a member of the European Group of Public Law, the International Association of Legislation, the Advisory Board of the Central and Eastern European Forum of Young Legal, Political and Social Theorists, and other scientific and academic organisations. Martin Belov is member of the scientific boards of many academic journals. He has published 18 books and more than 80 scientific papers.

**Carlo Colapietro**

Carlo Colapietro is Professor of Public Law at the Law Department of Roma Tre University, where he also teaches personal data protection and fundamental rights and is Director of the Postgraduate Maser Program in 'Data protection officer and privacy expert'. He is coordinator of Roma Tre University unit in the European Project SMEDATA. He is Director of the Interdepartmental Research Centre for Political-Constitutional and Comparative Law Studies 'Giorgio Recchia' (CRISPEL) and is a Member of the Management Board of Roma Tre University. In March 2020, he was appointed as a member of the Data-driven Working Group of the Ministry of Innovation.

**Marko Dimitrijević**

Marko Dimitrijević is the Associate Professor (PhD) at the Faculty of Law University of Niš (Serbia) Department of Law and Economics and Vice Dean for Science and Finances. His fields of teaching include European and International Monetary Law, Economic Policy for Lawyers, International Financial Law and Law of the Economic System of the European Union. He is an author of a scientific monograph of national importance entitled 'International Monetary Law Institutions' and is an observer at the European Law Institute (Vienna). He developed scientific research in the field of the monetary law at Saarland University, European Institute (EU Cluster of Excellence for International and European Law), Saarbrücken (Germany), Max Planck Institute for Tax Law and Public Finances, Munich (Germany) and Max Planck Institute for International, European and Regional Procedural Law (Luxembourg).

**Stefano Dorigo**

Stefano Dorigo, PhD in International and EU Law, is Associate Professor of Tax Law at the University of Florence (Italy). A member of the Reviewing Board of the *Tax Law Quarterly* (*Rivista trimestrale di diritto tributario*) and of the *International Tax Law Review* (*Rivista di diritto tributario internazionale*), he has taught tax law and international and European tax law in many universities and in postgraduate courses. He is the author of three monographs and more than 60 essays on national, international and European tax law published in Italian and European scientific journals.

**Guerino Fares**

Guerino Fares is Associate Professor of Public Law at Roma 3 University. He is a lecturer of health and pharmaceutical law in the same university. Guerino Fares is qualified as Full Professor of Constitutional Law. He is Director of Roma 3 Master's course in 'Professional Educator for Special Needs' and in 'Social-Health Services' Law and Management', Director of the Legal Clinic on 'The Healthcare in the Constitution', and the Italian representative at the European Network on Health, Law & Bioethics (HeaLab EuroNet). He is also Scientific Director of *Ius & Law* journal.

**Nadina Foggetti**

Nadina Foggetti is a Senior Fellow of INFN Bari. Since 2006 she has been Assistant Professor in International and EU Law at the University of Bari Aldo Moro, Italy, and since 2010 in Legal Informatics at the University of Milan, Italy. She is a member of the National Society of International and EU Law. Starting from 2005, she carried out research activities in the field of International and EU Law, with particular application in the fields of Biolaw and ICT Law. She has contributed to important projects in the field of cybercrime, cyber-security and data privacy. Nadina Foggetti has participated in many scientific projects, such as PON PRISMA and Cloud for Europe EU PCP, and has participated in several national and international projects concerning ICT law and cloud computing. In the EOSC-Pillar Project, Nadina Foggetti contributes in the WP 6 Task 6.6 'Exploring reference data through existing computing services for the bioinformatics community' to the definition of 'Health data security aspects. Legal and ethics requirements on the storage and handling of health data'.

**Patricia Jonason**

Patricia Jonason is Associate Professor in Public Law at the Law Department of Södertörn University, Stockholm, Sweden. She teaches Constitutional Law (including Human Rights), Administrative Law, European Law and Comparative Law. Her main research interests are in the right to privacy and in the right of access to information. She is interested in both the legal and the ethical aspects of these rights.

**Sascha Hardt**

Sascha Hardt is Assistant Professor of Comparative Constitutional Law at Maastricht University and a fellow of the Montesquieu Institute Maastricht. His current research focuses on the law of parliaments, democratic processes and the effects of populism on liberal democracy (Statesman Thorbecke Grant of the Dutch Royal Academy of Sciences 2018–2020).

**Attila Menyhárd**

Attila Menyhárd is Professor of Civil Law at Eötvös Loránd University, Faculty of Law, Civil Law Department (Budapest). His main research fields are contract law, tort law, property law, company law, human rights and private law, economic analysis of law, and private law in other contexts. He was promoted with a PhD degree in 2003 and habilitated in 2007 in Eötvös Loránd University. He has been a full professor since 2012. Upon the invitation of the Ministry of Justice, he contributed to the project for the new Hungarian Civil Code, being responsible for the provisions on property law, rent law and trusts. He is the Hungarian Fellow of European Tort and Insurance Law (Wien) and also a Fellow of the Institute for Legal Studies at the Centre of Social Sciences of the Hungarian Academy of Sciences (Budapest).

**Daniela Mirante**

Daniela Mirante is a researcher at the Centre on Law and Society of Nova Law School, as well as a doctorate student at Nova Law School (FDUNL), Lisbon, Portugal. She is developing her research mainly in the field of private law (including the intersection between private autonomy and public law) and arbitration.

**Benjamin Moron-Puech**

Benjamin Moron-Puech is an Associate Professor in Law at the Laboratory of Legal Sociology (Paris II Panthéon-Assas University). Besides his work on corporal minorities (intersex, transgender and deaf people), he also has some interest in legal theory and the law of obligation, publishing a book in 2020 on the concept of Legal Act. In this field of research, he also co-organised in 2014 one of the first French conferences on the topic of cybercurrencies, a topic linked to the concept of money, which is in itself part of the French law of obligation. The proceedings of this conference were published in 2015 in the French legal review *Banque & Droit*. The contribution for this book derives from the views he had at that time. It was written with two undergraduate students of his commercial law class: Jérémy Cornaire and Harrison Michael Collins.

**Thu Nguyen**

Thu Nguyen is Policy Fellow for EU Institutions and Democracy at the Jacques Delors Centre in Berlin (Germany). Previously she was Assistant Professor of EU and Comparative Constitutional Law at the Department of Public Law at Maastricht University (the Netherlands). She received her PhD from Maastricht University in 2018 with a thesis on power asymmetries between national parliaments in the EU and holds law degrees from Maastricht University and the College of Europe (Bruges, Belgium). She is a re:constitution Fellow in the academic year 2019/2020.

**Alessandro Puzzanghera**

Alessandro Puzzanghera is a legal assistant at the FIDLAW LLP law office in London and a PhD student at the University for Foreigners 'Dante Alighieri' in Reggio Calabria. His fields of research include: artificial intelligence, international law, intellectual property and personal data rights, in particular about GDPR and business law.

**David Roth-Isigkeit**

David Roth-Isigkeit is the director of the SOCAI Centre for Social Implications of Artificial Intelligence at the Faculty of Law at Würzburg University. His research focuses on the constitutional integration of digital transformation.

**Artur Flamínio da Silva**

Artur Flamínio da Silva is Associate Professor of Universidade Autónoma de Lisboa and researcher at the Centre on Law and Society of Nova Law School, Lisbon, Portugal. He holds a PhD and a master's degree in public law. His main areas of research are constitutional law, administrative law, theory of law and arbitration.

**Angioletta Sperti**

Angioletta Sperti is Associate Professor of Comparative Public Law at the University of Pisa, where she teaches comparative constitutional law and human rights law. Her main research interests include constitutional justice, comparative legal systems and LGBT rights. She has also conducted extensive research on presidential accountability and impeachment in the Italian system of government. She holds an Ll.M from UCLA (USA) and a PhD from Scuola Superiore S. Anna

(Italy). She is the author of three monographs (in Italian) on Italian constitutional court ('Corti supreme e conflitti tra poteri', 2003), presidential accountability ('La responsibilità del Presidente della Repubblica', 2010) and the dialogue among constitutional courts on LGBT rights ('Omosessualità e diritti', 2013). She is also the author of *Constitutional Courts, Gay Rights and Sexual Orientation Equality* (Hart Publishing, 2017). She regularly contributes to articolo29.it, a legal website focusing on the advancement of LGBT rights in Italy' and is managing editor of *GenIUS*, an Italian law review on gender and sexual orientation equality.

**Daniel Valchev**

Daniel Valchev is Professor of Jurisprudence and Dean of the Faculty of Law at Sofia University, Bulgaria. Prof Valchev studied law at Sofia University and had different specialisations. He is Doctor Honoris Causa of Soka University, Tokyo, Japan and Honorary Professor of Shanghai University, China. His research focuses on Theory and Philosophy of Law, Theory of State and Human Rights.

# Introduction

Technological revolutions always trigger massive ruptures in social, political and constitutional orders. They challenge the established order, replacing it with temporal disorder before producing new order. The new order resulting from technological revolutions brings human civilisation to new levels. It not only frames the technological advancement of humanity, but establishes and maintains the pillars of its moral, intellectual and socio-political foundations. This is because technological revolutions are usually paralleled by social revolutions and, with only a slight delay, intellectual, scientific and moral revolutions.[1]

In that regard, technological revolutions are not detached from the intellectual, social, political and economic context. On the contrary – they are deeply embedded in it, triggering spillover effects. Thus, technological revolutions are not just new stages in the natural sciences. They are determinants of overall economic, socio-political, moral and intellectual change. Moreover, technological revolutions bring deconstruction of previously secure concepts, paradigms, structures and identities. They contribute to their critical reassessment in the light of the new stage of technology and social development and their reconstruction in accordance with the novel scientific, social and political context.

Hence, technological revolutions have several main features which are of relevance for constitutionalism and law. They are events producing radical shifts in the socio-legal context. Thus, constitutional and public law orders are usually overwhelmed at a certain point by the necessity to offer proper conceptualisations of technological revolutions, and especially to provide for a reliable, efficient and legitimate legal framework for them. This is true for both the overall constitutional and legal conceptualisation of technological revolutions taken as holistic phenomena and for the provision of a legal foundation for their more concrete shapes and forms.

Technological revolutions usually lead to a structural mismatch between the technological sphere, the legal order and the realm of socio-political relations. They produce structural asymmetries between law and technology in general and constitution, constitutionalism and technological advancement in particular. Thus, they offer strategic advantages to novel political, social and economic elites that particularly benefit from the new level of technology. Technological revolutions usually foster the emergence of technocratic oligarchies which take the lead in the new technology era. These elites determine the codes for inclusion and exclusion in the new political, social and constitutional order. They impose the

[1] See T Kuhn, *The Structure of Scientific Revolutions* (University of Chicago Press, 1970).

rules of the new world resulting from the technological revolution. They determine the normative ideology and the institutional design of the new public, legal and constitutional order.

Such structural asymmetries create great perils for human freedom and the just legal order and society, but also incredible opportunities for social advancement, including for political and constitutional improvement. Hence, technological revolution may endanger the equilibrium between authority, efficiency, legitimacy and liberty established by the socio-political, legal and constitutional order. It may produce misbalances beneficial for some segments of society and especially for innovative technocratic elites in possession of knowledge and skills for power maximisation stemming from and based on new technologies. Technological revolution is paralleled by complex new risks challenging the roots of the world and socio-political coexistence. These risks are multiple and diverse – from moral and political hazards to ecological, economic and financial challenges. And they usually have a cumulative effect, mutually reinforcing their overall impact on society and its constitutional and public order.

At the same time, technological revolution usually triggers multitude of opportunities for liberation of the human being, for advancement of humanity and human civilisation, for establishment of new, more just and free, social, political and constitutional order. Technological revolution is the flooding that nourishes the soil, the tsunami that levels old barriers and impediments for progress and the earthquake that keeps the range of development opportunities alive.

In that regard, the mission of social, political and legal philosophy is to conceptually frame technological revolutions, to produce paradigms, concepts and a scientific toolkit capable of grasping the nature of technological revolution, translating it into the language of social and legal sciences and humanities, and pacifying the inevitable perils it brings with it. The task of public law – especially constitutional and administrative law – is to offer a feasible, comprehensive and coherent, efficient and, last but not least, legitimate legal framework for the unfolding of the technological revolution. Public law must draw the demarcation lines between permissible and forbidden results of technological revolutions. It must reflect the moral and ethical judgement produced by philosophy of law. Especially constitutional law must integrate technological progress in the constitutional civilisation, critically including new levels of technology in new forms of constitutionalism.

Several technological revolutions have deeply marked the history of mankind. Some of them, eg agricultural revolutions, revolutions related to weaponry, new modes of production, the establishment of settled economy and the emergence of money and coins, have occurred in the very remote past. Thus, they do not have immediate impact on constitutionalism and contemporary public law, although they are related to the deep roots of our societies. There have also been technological revolutions which have had local or regional impact. They concerned specific regions of the world or particular segments of the society. These temporally remote or particular and partial technological revolutions are not immediate determinants of contemporary constitutionalism, law and the state.

However, with the augmentation of the modes of common life in recent history and especially with the several waves of globalisation, the last one having the deepest and most profound impact on global social development, technological revolutions have also become global phenomena. They have put their imprint on most, if not all, contemporary societies. Indeed, their impact ranges from society to society, from region to region and from social segment to social segment. However, globalisation has promoted new ways for the spread of technological revolutions and has created the preconditions for their synchronised fulfilment.

We are currently exposed to the ongoing information and technology revolution. This is a massive and complex revolutionary event which is profoundly changing the very essence of our moral, human and social pillars. It is challenging the key concepts of our common life with its economic, social, political and legal basis and underpinnings. The moral, socio-political, economic and legal foundations of our societies are deeply shaken. Their conceptual pillars, entrenched in rationalism and enlightenment, rooted in the national territorial state, in the public–private divide and in foundational concepts for delimitation of good or bad, just and unjust, legitimate and illegitimate, are profoundly challenged by the ongoing information and technology revolution.

Our public orders are witnessing ruptures of a magnitude that has previously been observed only rarely. The impact and magnitude of the current information and technology revolution can be compared only with the industrial revolution experienced during the eighteenth and nineteenth centuries.

Indeed, the information and technology revolution has multiple dimensions. The mobility revolution in is revolutionising the ways we travel for business, for pleasure or to search for a better life. Mobility is one of the central phenomena of our age. In fact, freedom of information and free movement have been the main achievements of what I shall call the 'Second Belle Époque', which has deeply marked our civilisation from the fall of the Berlin wall until COVID-19.

The information revolution has multiple aspects. The new information and communication technologies are revolutionising all sectors of our societies and all aspects of our individual, group or social life. Indeed, we can even realistically start thinking of smart technologies used in communication, transportation, engineering, production, medicine and even law defined in terms of artificial intelligence (AI). Information technologies are revolutionising economy and finance. They are challenging key concepts of public law in general and of constitutional law in particular, serving a strategic role in ordering our societies. The information and technology revolution is impacting sovereignty, democracy and the rule of law. It is simultaneously challenging and promoting the welfare state, destroying traditional patterns of welfare while at the same time allowing new forms of social benefits to be created based on new technologies. Consequently, the information and technology revolution has the potential to reshape the institutional design of constitutional, administrative and other branches of public law, impacting on the constitutional axiology enshrined in it and challenging our traditional concepts of efficiency, legality and legitimacy.

This book is an attempt to critically assess the impact of the information and technology revolution on the state, constitutionalism and public law. It addresses the main challenges to the key concepts of constitutional, administrative, financial, tax and health law, which are of strategic and durable importance for legal science, legal practice and society. The book offers multidiscursive assessment of key issues stemming from the information and technology revolution related to human rights protection, public order, institutional design, and the efficiency and legitimacy of the public law of the twenty-first century.

Several main topics are analysed by the contributors to this edited volume. The challenges to state, sovereignty, humanism, democracy, human rights and institutional design are all objects of thorough and critical exploration by the contributors to the volume. Thus, the book is anchored in public law in all its dimensions – theoretical, legal and socio-legal (practical).

The overall issue framing the book is the impact of the information and technology revolution on the state, constitutionalism and public (especially constitutional and administrative) law. After discussing the broader conceptual issues (Part I), the book offers insightful and multifaceted analysis of the impact of the information and technology revolution on democracy and the public sphere (Part II), on courts and administration (Part IV), and on human rights (Parts V and VI). There are two separate chapters containing human rights issues because this approach allows for better focusing on data protection and privacy (Part V), and to expose the challenges to health-related human rights (Part VI) in the digital age and the algorithmic society.

The other part of the book, Part III, concerns acute and topical issues of monetary sovereignty, and monetary, financial and taxation policy in the context of the information and technology revolution. Special attention is given to an original analysis of cryptocurrencies, the impact of the algorithmic revolution on fair taxation in the context of global governance and the mutations of monetary sovereignty under the conditionality imposed by the information and technology revolution.

Part I of the book comprises contributions aiming to draw a larger picture of the main challenges to the state and constitutional law in the context of the information and technology revolution. Thus, it opens the debate with four chapters devoted to issues that are related to the conceptual foundation and framework of the overall topic of the book.

In the first chapter of the book, I explore the impact of the information and technology revolution on humanism as the central ideology of constitutionalism. My main thesis is that constitutionalism and humanism are deeply intertwined, so post-human constitutionalism is a challenge to the very concept of constitutionalism. I outline the main features of humanism as the normative ideology of constitutionalism. I systematise and critically assess the main challenges to humanism and humanist constitutionalism in the context of the algorithmic society. I differentiate between humanity, animality and technicity as key concepts that may serve as pillars for structuring of different approaches to subjectivity in constitutionalism and in constitutional law. I outline the risks of deconstruction of humanism in the context of the algorithmic society combined with increasing trends of illiberalism – a process which might be triggered in the context of the debates on speciesism, transhumanism, post-humanism and anti-humanism. And I define the concept of algorithmic constitutionalism while presenting the risks it creates for humanism and humanist constitutionalism.

Chapter two, written by Daniel Valchev, is devoted to the constitutional dimensions of the information revolution. The author explores the impact of the information and technology revolution on democracy, defined by him as 'governance founded on elections, which is, for the sake of protecting individual freedom, restrained by procedures, bodies of professional élites, and a normative ideology'. Valchev traces the historical phases of the development of information, the means for its communication and dissemination and their impact on law. He critically assesses the concept of revolution and provides an account of what the current information revolution is. The author explores the influence of information revolution on existing tensions in liberal democratic constitutional paradigms.

In chapter three, Attila Menyhárd offers an account of the impacts of technological revolution on the role of the state. The main issues of concern for the author are the role of the state as regulator and provider of public services, and its obligations to control the private agents in an algorithmic society and in the context of increasing information and technology revolution. Menyhárd critically explores the state's withdrawal from its function of controlling transactions via registration systems. Furthermore, he outlines the allocation of the risks of research and development, stipulating that the cornerstones for such risk allocation are liability and insurance. Other central issues of concern for the author are the emergence of artificial intelligence as a tool for increasing transparency and as a tool for manipulation. Hence, Menyhárd offers an account of issues of global information governance and its perils and challenges to public law in the context of the algorithmic society.

The need for the establishment of a global information law as a response to the global information society and to increasingly algorithmic decision-making is a key issue also for David Roth-Isigkeit. In chapter four, he explores the possibility of creating a global information law which copes with the imperatives of the information and technology revolution, digitalisation and algorithmic society, and at the same time transcends the limits of the increasingly dysfunctional nation states' public law orders. In his account, 'the global law of information refers to the study of ways in which existing, emerging and disruptive technological advances in the area of ICTs [information and communication technologies] interact with existing laws, be it national, supranational or international'. According to the author, the emergence of information and communication technology is a transformative process which leads to digital transformation, resulting in social change that is triggered by the increasing interaction of human existence with ICTs.

Roth-Isigkeit's chapter provides an international legal history of the law of information and sets the emergence of global information law in this context. The author follows the history of information law from international information law to global and transnational information law. He outlines the legitimacy demands of global information law and its impact on individual lives and on the systemic imbalance in the current socio-legal context, especially with regard to the expansion of transnational private power. After outlining the foundational concepts of legitimacy, Roth-Isigkeit explores some administrative concepts as 'second-tier' providers of legitimacy. He also defines the risks and benefits of these 'second-tier' options. The chapter explores internet governance with regard to the eventual emergence of *lex digitalis*. Special importance is given to the risks to democratic governance relying on collective self-determination due to manipulation of choices, echo chambers, targeted advertisement, targeted news, social media trolls and other perils of an algorithmic society.

Part II of the book is devoted to the information and technology revolution and its impact on democracy and the public sphere. It comprises two chapters which are in deep intellectual dialogue, being devoted to very similar problems but explored from the personal viewpoints of their authors. It should be noted that these chapters, authored by Hoai-Thu Nguyen and Sascha Hardt, are in a sense continuation of the problems posed in some of the chapters of Part I, especially those written by Daniel Valchev and David Roth-Isigkeit. This is because the chapters framed by Part II assess the impact of big data and algorithmic technologies on democracy and the public sphere. Thus, they address the need for an appropriate legal, and especially constitutional and administrative law, response to the algorithmic challenges of increasingly global or at least transnational information spread.

In chapter five, Hoai-Thu Nguyen explores the disruptive effects of social media platforms on the free will formation of voters. She demonstrates that 'the rise and use of such platforms have changed not only how we communicate in private but, most importantly, also in public'. The author describes the relationship between mass media and the democratic will-formation process in liberal democracies. She explores the impact of the technological revolution on such processes in general. Furthermore, she analyses the different ways in which the democratic will-formation process can be disrupted through social media platforms. Finally, she outlines the advantages and disadvantages of the technological revolution for democratic processes and offers 'an outlook on how to best mitigate the disruptive effects of social media on democratic will-formation processes'. The author focuses especially on algorithmic procedures and technologies, hate speech, offensive language, fake news, microtargeting practices and filter bubbles.

Furthermore, in chapter six, Sascha Hardt explores the impact of data revolution on the public will-formation process. He investigates how to regulate the democratic processes in the digital age. Hardt expresses similar concerns with Valchev regarding the ability of the digital revolution to trigger a crisis of liberal democracy itself. Like Hoai-Thu Nguyen, he focuses on the contribution of mass data analysis, microtargeting and social media to such a crisis. Hardt pays special attention to big data collection and processing, microtargeting, filter bubbles, closed-group communication and voter segmentation. Thus, he tries to explore the direction in which legal rules should mitigate the adverse effects of mass data analysis and microtargeting in political campaigning. He assesses the possible solutions to the 'loss of societies' capacity to engage in fruitful democratic discourse'.

Part III comprises three chapters devoted to monetary sovereignty and taxation in the information technology era. Chapter seven concerns the monetary sovereignty in conditions of technological revolution; chapter eight, the conceptual and legal challenges to the public order of the states stemming from cybercurrencies; and chapter nine, the algorithmic revolution and its impact on fair taxation, and welfare in the context of global governance.

Chapter seven starts with a historical overview of the main features of monetary sovereignty. Marko Dimitrijević explores the development of *lex monetae* in traditional monetary law and outlines the monetary dimension of *lex contractus*. He then analyses the relationship between monetary sovereignty and technological progress, focusing on electronic money. Special emphasis is put on the relationship between monetary sovereignty and cryptocurrencies. The chapter concludes with the author summing up his reflections on the concept of monetary sovereignty in the context of the ongoing information and technology revolution.

The emergence of digital money, cryptocurrencies and cybercurrencies as the product of technological revolution is the common research interest of Marko Dimitrijević (chapter seven) and Benjamin Moron-Puech, Jérémy Cornaire and Harrison Colins (chapter eight). While Dimitrijević believes that 'the emergence of electronic money … does not substantially modify the monetary prerogatives arising from the monetary sovereignty of the state, but merely adapts them to new economic circumstances', Moron-Puech, Cornaire and Colins come to more radical conclusions. They define cybercurrencies as a legal revolution.

The chapter of Moron-Puech, Cornaire and Colins starts with a brief definition of the nature of cybercurrencies. It traces the history of monetary revolutions, starting from fiat money (paper and metallic), going through divisional money and ending up with electronic money. The authors pay attention to the dissociation between the sign, the entry into an account and the signified – the value associated with it.

Special emphasis is put on the current monetary revolution. It is explored from both an economic and legal viewpoint. The main thesis defended by the authors is that

> states must lead a revolution in the legal concept of money and fully recognise that cybercurrencies are a form of money parallel to fiat money. In other words, it is a matter of admitting that a money can exist even though it is not endowed with a specific guarantee by the state concerning its acceptability (legal tender), its authenticity or the risks of default by the depositary bodies.

The authors explore different generations of cybercurrencies, presenting their main features, advantages and disadvantages. The study of the evolution and nature of the different types of cybercurrencies (with special emphasis on 'Libra' – a currency project led by Facebook) is paralleled with a thorough review of their impact on the monetary sovereignty of states and thus on monetary and financial constitutionalism.

Indeed, the influence of the information and technology revolution on financial constitutionalism is a common feature of all three chapters framed by Part III of the book. In chapter nine, Stefano Dorigo explores the effects of algorithmic revolution (or 'industry 4.0') on fair taxation, social pact and global governance. The chapter starts with a definition of the essential characteristics of the algorithmic revolution. Two main aspects of the algorithmic revolution are outlined. These are 'the digitalisation of the economy, with the preponderance of dematerialised services; and the robotisation of the production processes of material goods'. Furthermore, some general reflection of the impact of algorithmic revolution is provided. Dorigo offers an account on the tax issues of the digital economy, with special emphasis on the case of digital multinationals.

Dorigo exposes the main problems created by both trends in the algorithmic revolution in the domain of financial law and taxation. He proposes a 'third way' as a possible reaction of the tax system that is different from the two extreme solutions – interventionism and laissez faire. This 'third way' is global tax governance based on multilateralism. Finally, he draws up some conclusions regarding the interrelation between the new algorithmic revolution and principles of taxation.

Part IV of the book explores the impact of the information and technology revolution on courts and administrations. It comprises three chapters. The chapters of Angioletta Sperti and of Artur Flamínio da Silva and Daniela Mirante address the effects of the information revolution and the digital age on courts, while Alessandro Puzzanghera focuses on AI as one of the most intriguing elements of this age on administration. In addition, both chapters eleven (da Silva and Mirante) and twelve (Puzzanghera) concern the impact of digital technologies on courts and administration, whereas chapter ten (Sperti) is related to the information context in general and the engagement of constitutional courts in it, and thus does not directly address particular issues of technological advancement per se. In this regard, Sperti's chapter is related to the concerns with the overall process of information advancement reflected also in Daniel Valchev's chapter, while da Silva and Mirante's chapter and that of Puzzanghera explore the impact of new technologies on justice, administration and rights. They thus engage in the discourse on the influence of new technologies, and especially of AI, on human rights (this complex issue is also discussed in detail in the four chapters that form the last two parts of the book).

Angioletta Sperti explores in chapter ten the impact of the information and communication revolution on constitutional courts. The central topic of her research is the analysis of the central trends in the engagement of constitutional courts in political communication and especially their main communication strategies. She explores the shift of constitutional courts from indirect to direct communication and the transition from monologue to dialogue with the public. Moreover, Sperti outlines the reasons behind the communication revolution of constitutional courts. She also offers an account of the risks of politicisation of courts in the context of communication revolution. The chapter is based on rich comparative argumentation exploring the practice of the German and Italian constitutional courts, the French constitutional council and the UK, Canadian and US supreme courts.

Chapter eleven, written by Artur Flamínio da Silva and Daniela Mirante, is focused on the constitutional limits of digital justice. The authors explore, in their own words, the 'modifications produced by globalisation of this brave new digital world'. The chapter revolves around the concept of digital justice and the issues it poses to contemporary constitutional orders. Da Silva and Mirante offer a critical account of the advantages and challenges of digital justice, looking for an equilibrium between digital justice and the main principles of constitutional law. In that regard, they explore the protection of fundamental human rights in a digital justice context, posing the question whether consent can serve as a cornerstone according to the case law of the European Court of Human Rights. Thus, they try to provide a constitutional approach to digital justice through the lens of judicial discretion.

Chapter twelve is devoted to the impact of artificial intelligence on administrative law. Alessandro Puzzanghera explores the introduction of AI in the work of administration, termed by him an 'administrative network'. He researches 'the combination of IT and administrative activity, the electronic processing of administrative measures, the processors that prepare content and the implications that arise, considering the relative aspects and conditions, as well as the jurisdictional safeguards, where applicable'. The author offers an account of what he calls a 'human intelligible computational procedure' and an 'artificial intelligible computational procedure', thus exploring 'the progressive computerisation of administrative procedure'. Puzzanghera outlines the double challenges – technological and legal – for the introduction of AI in administrative activity, focusing predominantly on the latter.

The last two parts of the book are devoted to the impact of the information and technology revolution on human rights. Part V focuses on the influence of the information and technology revolution on data protection and privacy, whereas Part VI concerns its effects on health-related rights.

Carlo Colapietro explores in chapter thirteen the impact of the information and technology revolution on the constitutional rights. He puts special emphasis on personal data protection issues. The chapter opens with analysis of the development of the current technological revolution stretched between datafication and AI. In this context, the author explores the constitutional dimension of AI, the new forms of algorithmic discrimination and the use of the right to privacy for protection against the perils of an algorithmic society. Colapietro considers the personal data to be 'the new digital oil' because 'data represents the essential fuel to develop and train AI'. He outlines the risks for this precious resource and the options for its due protection. The author also explores the implications of new technologies in sensitive sectors such as healthcare, elderly care and education.

Moreover, Colapietro critically assesses the 'risk of creating a dehumanisation effect' produced by the new technologies and AI – a topic that I also discuss in chapter one. In this context, the author presents the perils of the emergence of new forms of discrimination based on the application of new information and communication technologies. He warns us to 'carefully evaluate the choices made for the purpose of the algorithm design' in order to avoid the 'discriminatory logic inside the algorithm'. Colapietro concludes that we should aim not at including technology inside constitutional documents, but instead at transposing constitutional values inside algorithmic systems.

The exploration of the issues of privacy and data protection in the digital age is further accomplished by Patricia Jonason. In chapter fourteen, she devotes her research to the digital revolution and the challenges it imposes to constitutional orders for protection of privacy. She offers a comparative research of two EU Member States – France and Sweden – putting special emphasis on the vertical and horizontal aspects of privacy protection in the context of the information and technology revolution.

Jonason commences by presenting the state of the art of the constitutional protection of privacy against new technologies in Sweden and France. She outlines the similarities and differences in both approaches to privacy protection. Subsequently, she exposes the need to reinforce the constitutional protection of privacy for a better response to the challenges posed by new technologies. She insists on the importance of robust enshrinement of the protection of privacy in the constitution and the enshrinement of multidimensional protection with vertical and horizontal effects. Finally, she makes proposals *de lege ferenda* that aim to meet the challenges of digital society.

In chapter fifteen, Guerino Fares offers insightful analysis of the impact of AI in the sphere of social and health services. He explores the new challenges for public authorities in ensuring constitutional rights. In the words of Fares, his 'chapter aims to propose an analysis of the main constitutional and administrative issues with regard to artificial intelligence'.

The author studies the conceptual and regulatory framework that should be imposed on the use of AI in healthcare and related spheres of socio-political activity. He stresses the importance of observing the main constitutional principles when applying new technologies and especially devices containing elements of AI. According to the author, 'the correct management of those technologies based on AI needs an adaptation of the legal framework related to the welfare state, with the aim of guaranteeing citizens' constitutional rights to the most appropriate extent: from the effectiveness of care to equality in patients' access to medical treatment; from reasonableness of the administrative procedures to the application of data protection regulation.'

Fares analyses the relationship between AI and health and social services with regard to the opportunities offered by the technological development. He provides an outline of the European regulatory framework that is promoting the use of AI in the sphere of social work and healthcare. He devotes special attention to the protection of constitutional rights and human rights in general in the context of use of new technologies and especially of AI. The author explores the relationship between patients' health rights, privacy rights and the processing of digital or digitalised social health data. Special emphasis is put on 'digitalisation of public action connected to the big data phenomenon and the algorithmic procedures (eg e-health, telemedicine, m-health and smart-phone apps for healthcare purposes, robotic surgery)'.

The final chapter of the book, chapter sixteen, is written by Nadina Foggetti and is devoted to gene editing e-machine learning within the international and EU legal framework. Foggetti presents the legal framework concerning gene editing in international law and in EU law. She explores gene editing issues in the context of data protection, human rights, bioethics and bioinformatics. Foggetti devotes special attention to the protection of genomic data and the right to privacy. Thus, she engages in the same debate that is raised in several chapters of this volume, eg the chapters of Guerino Fares, Carlo Colapietro and Patricia Jonason.

The author gives an account on the problem of prohibition of discrimination with regard to gene editing and gives an overview of the principle of non-stigmatisation. She emphasises the fact that in this context 'we pass from the protection of an individual right to the need to protect the rights of an ethnic group'. Foggetti insists that 'non-discrimination, non-stigmatisation and equality are fundamental human rights principles and components of the right to health'.

# PART I

# State and Constitutional Law in the Context of the Information and Technology Revolution

# 1

# Post-human Constitutionalism? A Critical Defence of Anthropocentric and Humanist Traditions in Algorithmic Society

MARTIN BELOV

## I. Introduction

This chapter is devoted to humanism as the key normative ideology of constitutionalism. It critically explores post-human constitutionalism as an integral and composite phenomenon challenging the traditional humanist constitutionalism. The focus of the chapter is on the impact of the IT revolution on humanism as a constitutional ideology. Thus, special attention is devoted to algorithmic constitution and algorithmic constitutionalism as a specific challenge to humanist constitutionalism in the age of artificial intelligence (AI) and the IT revolution.

The proper outlining of post-humanism requires as a precondition a thorough analysis of humanism in all its complexity – an exploration which cannot be reduced to only the challenges of the new technologies on humanism as a pillar of constitutionalism. This is because some of the claims of post-human constitutionalism in the context of the IT revolution have already been raised in other critical discourses directed at the reconsideration and deconstruction of humanism. Moreover, the challenges of the IT revolution on humanism have to be seen in the context of the broader reorganisation of the ideological pillars of contemporary constitutionalism. Last but not least, the engagement with different critical discourses on humanism allows for better exposure of the specifics of technological post-humanism, which is not limited to transhumanism.

The central aim of this chapter is to critically reassess and subsequently confirm the concept of subjectivity in constitutional law, which is directly bound to another issue – delimitation – and the setting of conceptual boundaries. There are several conceptual boundaries which are challenged by post-humanism. These are the boundaries between entitlement to rights or being an object of protection, between being an object or subject of constitutional ontology, teleology and axiology, and between humanity, animality and technicity. The chapter critically reassesses the need to set a clear delimitation between the subject and object of law. It questions the need to reconceptualise this distinction and transform it into a scale of nuanced subjectivity based on a range of upgrading and augmenting subjectivities and identities. The analysis focuses on the question whether the ongoing IT revolution and the moral – post-human and transhuman – turn that we are currently experiencing will transform the problem of boundaries into a problem of scale.

The chapter starts with an outline of the concept of humanist constitutionalism. It explores the elements of humanism as the central normative ideology of modern Western constitutionalism. The emergence and development of humanism is briefly summarised. The core assumptions of humanism are presented. Moreover, the main projections of humanism in constitutional law are enlisted and briefly explained. This is because the chapter is focused on humanism and post-humanism as normative ideologies of constitutionalism and constitutional law, and not as general philosophical paradigms.

The analysis continues with the different functions of humanism in constitutional law. Humanism is understood as a frame-setting paradigm determining important borders in constitutionalism. It is also conceived as the central normative ideology of constitutionalism, and is deeply rooted in constitutional ontology, teleology and axiology.

The chapter briefly systematises the main challenges to humanism. It outlines conceptual philosophical challenges, challenges stemming out of authoritarian regimes based on the concept of order instead of humanism, and challenges coming from an animal law perspective. However, the main attention is devoted to challenges produced by the IT revolution, and especially by algorithmic constitutionalism. Post-humanism is understood as both a general threat to humanism and as a summary of several distinct challenges to humanism. Thus, one has to differentiate between post-humanism in a broader sense – as an all-encompassing normative ideology – and post-humanism in multiple stricter senses triggered by concerns related to the theories of animalism,[1] anti-speciesism,[2] transhumanism,[3] illiberal and authoritarian constitutionalism,[4] algorithmic constitutionalism and the various deconstructivist and critical approaches to traditional humanism.

[1] See S Blatti and P Snowdon (eds), *Animalism: New Essays on Persons, Animals, and Identity* (Oxford University Press, 2016); T Jonah, *The Philosophy of Animalism* (independently published, 2019).

[2] See R Ryder, *Animal Revolution: Changing Attitudes Towards Speciesism* (Berg Publishers, 2000); M Vinding, *Speciesism: Why It Is Wrong and the Implications of Rejecting It CreateSpace* (Independent Publishing Platform, 2015); T Milligan, 'Speciesism as Variant of Anthropocentrism' in R Boddice (ed), *Anthropocentrism. Humans, Animals, Environments* (Brill, 2011) 223ff.

[3] See N Lee (ed), *The Transhumanism Handbook* (Springer, 2019); B Ross, *The Philosophy of Transhumanism: A Critical Analysis* (Emerald Publishing, 2020); L Ferry, *La Revolution Transhumaniste* (Edition Plons, 2016).

[4] See H Alviar Garcia and G Frankenberg (eds), *Authoritarian Constitutionalism: Comparative Analysis and Critique* (Edward Elgar, 2019); F Zakaria, *The Future of Freedom: Illiberal Democracy at Home and Abroad* (WW Norton & Company, 2007); T Drinóczi and A Bień-Kacała,

To sum up, this research has the following main claims. First, it demonstrates the belief that humanism is an indispensable part of constitutionalism. Consequently, the deconstruction of humanism as a pillar of constitutionalism will inevitably change the core of constitutionalism. We may use terms such as 'post-human constitutionalism', 'transhuman constitutionalism' or 'algorithmic constitutionalism' to define different phenomena. However, none of them will be a proper continuation of constitutionalism. This is because constitutionalism is structured around the centrality of the human being, its liberty, dignity and rights.

Secondly, we need to understand the new opportunities and perils which the IT revolution produces for humanist constitutionalism. We must not cover up the deficiencies of humanist constitutionalism. Nor must we reject chances for its improvement. But we must resist deconstitutionalisation of the world by virtue of its dehumanisation. The adequate adjustment of constitutionalism to the IT revolution requires deconstruction of its traditional pillars in order to understand what their core is and what part of them should be preserved in the eventually forthcoming AI era and possibly transhumanist age. Thus, we need a critical defence of humanism in the algorithmic society.

## II. Humanism as Normative Ideology of Constitutionalism

Normative ideologies[5] are the conceptual pillars of the socio-political community. They are intellectual products imposed by intellectual and political elites on society. A pure imposition, however, is not sufficient, since the successful normative ideologies also require wide social acceptance. Hence, they must also comply with the political and cultural anthropology of the socio-political community. This compliance or non-compliance also explains the success or failure of the practical implementation of normative ideologies.

Normative ideologies are central elements of the ideal constitution, comprising the ideal, anthropological and theoretical dimensions of constitutionalism. They are also bridges between rational and symbolic-imaginary constitutionalism. Their main function is to predetermine the socio-political behaviour of the subjects of constitutional law, making them apply constitutional law in a specific

'Illiberal Constitutionalism: The Case of Hungary and Poland' (2019) 20 *German Law Journal* 1140; T Drinóczi, 'Illiberal Constitutionalism – a Remodelled Constitutionalism', https://constitutional-change.com/illiberal-constitutionalism-a-remodelled-constitutionalism/; L-A Thio, 'Constitutionalism in Illiberal Polities' in M Rosenfeld and A Sajó (eds), *The Oxford Handbook of Comparative Constitutional Law* (Oxford University Press, 2012).

[5] For the concept of normative ideology, see also H Dyer, *Moral Order/World Order* (Palgrave Macmillan, 1997) 102–28.

way and in accordance with the prescribed model of life. Normative ideologies produce a specific understanding of constitutionalism by durably and profoundly persuading the members of the constitutionally framed socio-political community to follow their imperatives and by triggering normative beliefs of the constitutional order.

Normative ideologies usually consist of a typical set of normative ideas. The normative ideas explain, frame and influence specific discourses of the broader constitutional object underlying the normative ideology. Both normative ideologies and the normative ideas in which they are further developed predetermine the constitutional design and the constitutional practice of human rights and constitutional duties, as well as those of state institutions. Thus, it is of pivotal importance for a proper understanding of the constitutional civilisation, constitutional tradition and constitutional order to define and understand the main constitutional normative ideologies.

Every constitutional civilisation has its own distinct set of normative ideologies and normative ideas. In other words, liberal constitutionalism differs from illiberal constitutionalism and authoritarian constitutionally based orders, republicanism differs from monarchism, representative democracy differs from the Soviet type of government etc, not only on the basis of their institutional design, but especially with a view to the normative ideologies which are underlying the constitutional ontology, teleology, axiology and pragmatics. Normative ideology is also key to the constitutional epistemology. It offers deep insights into the intellectual pillars of constitutionalism and the specific constitutional order, which have important epistemic value. This is the reason why in one of the subsequent paragraphs of this chapter I will explore the impact of humanism and post-humanism on constitutional ontology, axiology and teleology, where special emphasis will be put on algorithmic constitutionalism.

Despite the huge difference between the constitutional traditions of the world and the abundance of comparative constitutional models, there are two normative ideologies which have gained the status of universally recognised pillars of constitutionalism. These are rationalism and humanism. Both are products of the Age of Enlightenment. Until recently, humanism was a predominantly unchallenged pillar of constitutionalism on the sub-national, national and supranational levels. It was a universally recognised normative ideology not only of constitutionalism, but also of international law, with underlying and paradigmatic importance for international human rights law. Thus, humanism is a pillar of constitutionalism, but also of international law, EU law and public law in general. It even underlies the whole Western legal civilisation.

Humanism has emerged with modernity.[6] Although there are important ancient Greek and Roman, as well as Christian, versions of humanism, the

[6] See HR Jr, Alker, 'The Humanistic Moment in International Studies: Reflections on Machiavelli and Las Casas: 1992 Presidential Address' (1992) 36 *International Studies Quarterly* 347.

modern version of humanism has been triggered and influenced mostly by the Enlightenment. The predominantly secular version of humanism, entrenched in the Enlightenment political and moral philosophy and enriched with elements of humanism inherited from the ancient Greek and Roman thought and the Christian humanist traditions, has become the normative model for the constitutional version of humanism. It has been enshrined in the great declarations and charters of human rights, in the constitutions and constitutional acts, and later on – during the twentieth and early twenty-first centuries – also in the international and EU acts with constitutional importance that address human rights issues.

This constitutionalised version of humanism has become universalised due to the global spread of Western constitutionalism. Indeed, humanism is the normative ideology of Western and modern constitutionalism. However, with the spread of Western legal civilisation in the context of colonisation, decolonisation and globalisation, humanism has also been transformed into a normative ideology of constitutional and international law on the global scale.

It is true that humanism never went beyond mainly formal reception in many non-Western contexts, usually in the form of legal transplantation;[7] rather, it was just adopted as part of the constitutions transplanted as a 'package deal' into many non-Western traditions. Thus, the formal elements of humanism were present in the institutional design of most, if not all, constitutional systems of the world at the end of the twentieth century, while many of its legal and especially socio-political consequences were missing or even non-existent. Humanism has been formally accepted, but its practical implementation has been explicitly or implicitly rejected.

Humanism has several important consequences for constitutionalism and constitutional law. In other words, there are some key elements that frame and compose humanism as the normative ideology of modern constitutionalism. These are anthropocentrism,[8] the belief in the holistic nature of the human person, the concept of free will,[9] the understanding of liberty as ultimate value in the constitutional order, the safeguarding of personal autonomy not least as a precondition of social and legal responsibility, the conceptualisation of human dignity as the ultimate right, the normative belief in natural rights and the subsequent detailed provision of constitutional rights. Each of these components plays a crucial role in the fulfilment of humanism as a pillar of constitutionalism.

[7] See A Watson, *Legal Transplants: An Approach to Comparative Law 2* (University of Georgia Press, 1993).

[8] For the different aspects of anthropocentrism, see R Boddice (ed), *Anthropocentrism. Humans, Animals, Environments* (Brill, 2011); R Ryder, *The Political Animal. The Conquest of Speciesism* (McFarland, 1998).

[9] See R Kane, *A Contemporary Introduction to Free Will* (Oxford University Press, 2005); JM Fisher, R Kane, D Pereboom and M Vargas, *Four Views on Free Will* (John Wiley & Sons, 2007).

Constitutions provide for the basic, fundamental and traditional version of humanism understood as an anthropocentric phenomenon. All constitutions place the human being at their core. Homo sapiens is the institutional centre of the constitutional universe. Thus, the constitutions and constitutional orders have a rather pre-Galilean outlook, prescribing that it is the state and society which should rotate around the man and not vice versa. This anthropocentric structure of the constitution and the constitutional order is the product of political choice backed by massive ethical considerations comprising humanism as the normative ideology of constitutionalism. Thus, a technocratic claim may be raised that if we reverse the system and introduce a 'heliocentric' constitutional scheme with prevalence of the common good and the social order over individualism and humanism, and of efficiency and security over liberty, we may achieve technological and even social progress. Collective progress based on algorithmic society might seem a tempting ideal. But it may also be a Pandora's box. Such a claim, however, has a fundamental impact on constitutionalism. Enlightened technocracy opting for such preferences may be fostered by the IT revolution. But it needs justification for the destruction of the inherited humanist constitutionalism – something which is still not convincingly achieved.

In the anthropocentric order of humanist constitutionalism, the human being is assigned different roles. Homo sapiens is variously institutionalised as human being, citizen, foreigner, asylum seeker, refugee, man or woman, child, economic agent, political player and person at risk (eg incapacitated, minor). Nevertheless, only Homo sapiens has standing as the subject of constitutional law and constitutional rights. Hence, we have humanist, anthropocentric and speciesist constitutions which set firm distinctions between humanity, animality[10] and technicity.

Indeed, there are some constitutions, such as the Constitution of Ecuador and the Constitution of Bolivia, which also institutionalise nature ('Mother Nature', 'Pacha Mama'). But nature is just a source of justification that legitimates specific ecological and presumably post-capitalist policies. Moreover, 'Mother Nature' is an important element of symbolic-imaginary constitutionalism and plays the role of a semiotic code. However, it is still not the subject of rights, and it does not compete with or complement the constitutional standing of Homo sapiens as the ultimate agent of constitutionalism in its different constitutional shapes and manifestations.

Even if some constitutional orders grant protection to non-humans, eg to animals or sacred objects, they still do not give them constitutional rights.[11] The only exception from the monopoly of the human being as the status of rights holder are juridical persons. But these are considered to be proxies of the human

[10] I am borrowing the term from Anne Peters. See A Peters, 'Liberté, Égalité, Animalité: Human–Animal Comparisons in Law' (2016) 5 *Transnational Environmental Law* 25.

[11] ibid.

interest and will, and are purely instrumental devices for the realisation of human freedom and human rights.

Thus, Homo sapiens remains the monopolist of subjectivity as a strategic resource of recognition and the subsequent entitlement to rights in all constitutional orders. Consequently, all constitutional orders have been and still remain extensively anthropocentric. In that regard, all constitutions may be defined as being loaded with speciesism in both the traditional sense, as drawing a clear line between man and animals and animated nature in general, and in the postmodern sense of establishing a visible and non-contestable demarcation line between man and AI.

Furthermore, humanism is preconditioned on the belief in the holistic nature of the human person. Humanism requires full protection of the human being in all its aspects – physical, mental, social, political and, since recently, also digital. The holistic nature of the human being is not distorted by the fact that it has different aspects because those aspects are mutually dependent and mutually reinforcing.

The most recent aspect of the human nature is its projection into the digital sphere. This is to an extent paradoxical, since the new information and communication technologies are artificial and thus 'unnatural' in a traditional sense. However, the digital identity of Homo sapiens may also be considered as the latest stage in its evolution as a species. Thus, humanism has been gradually integrated into the digital constitutionalism.[12] However, the constitutional institutionalisation of the digital identity of the human being is still underdeveloped. This is somewhat problematic because history is abundant with examples of the consequences of delayed constitutionalisation of important social phenomena. There is a need for explicit constitutionalisation of the digital identity of the human being and for determining the boundaries of humanity in the digital sphere.

The digital or virtual identity that most people already possess in a fragmented and semi-institutionalised version is increasingly important. Thus, we need a conceptualisation of the human being that also includes its imprint in the digital reality, its presence in the digital world of the Internet. Precisely because of the holistic nature of the human being, the digital aspect or layer of the human identity cannot be detached from all other aspects of the human essence. Consequently, digital humanism cannot be separated from biohumanism, social humanism, political humanism and the other humanist discourses. Such detachment is possible only for the analytical reasons of exploring the separate aspects of humanism or making political claims, eg in favour of transhumanism.

[12] For more about digital constitutionalism, see E Celeste, 'Digital Constitutionalism: Mapping the Constitutional Response to Digital Technology's Challenges', HIIG Discussion Paper Series 2 (2018); G De Gregorio, 'The Rise of Digital Constitutionalism in the European Union' [2020] *International Journal of Constitutional Law* (forthcoming); D Redeker, L Gill and U Gasser, 'Towards Digital Constitutionalism? Mapping Attempts to Craft an Internet Bill of Rights', Berkman Center Research Publication No 2015-15 (2015).

Thus, digital humanism is indivisible from the overall and holistic nature of humanism. This fact actually implicitly increases the anthropocentric nature of constitutionalism by massively influencing digital constitutionalism. Constitutionalism remains intrinsically related to humans, with humans as the central actors of the constitutional order even when the human nature may be augmented by virtue of new technologies, the human body may be technologically improved and there are enhanced semi-autonomous algorithms defined as AI.

Liberty is a core value of humanism as a philosophical concept and as the normative ideology of constitutionalism and constitutional law. Liberty has many projections in constitutional law, some of which are deeply anchored in humanism. These are the concept of free will and moral autonomy, and the understanding of liberty as ultimate value in the constitutional order. Free will and moral autonomy are key elements of liberal constitutionalism. They predetermine the ability of the person to be an independent and rational citizen, a market agent and a political player.[13] They underline the entrenched rationality of constitutionalism, which is of pivotal importance for moral freedom and all rights based on personal self-determination, for political freedom and democracy, and for economic freedom, capitalism and a market economy. Liberty, free will and moral autonomy also predetermine the whole constitutional foundation of public, criminal and private law in a liberal society.

What is particularly important here is that the complex composed of moral autonomy, free will, capability of personal emancipation, liberty, and morally entrenched and ethically embedded rationality are main factors for distinguishing Homo sapiens from the other species of the living world, but also from AI.[14] The rationality – especially instrumental rationality – of human beings and forms of AI may be comparable, but we are still far away from, and may even never see, robots or algorithmic entities that possess moral autonomy, free will, liberty and morally entrenched rationality.

We need to engage with the constitutional conceptualisation and institutionalisation of digital liberty. Indeed, efforts have been made to protect privacy and personal data. Freedom of expression in the digital sphere and the protection of human rights against their infringement on the Internet[15] are also areas of intense

[13] See M Belov, 'EU Citizen – Market Agent, Political Player or a New Dimension of the Personal Identity. Is There Any Chance of a "Supranational Nation" on the EU Level?' in F Snyder and D Thym (eds), *Europe – a Continent of Immigration? Legal Challenges in the Construction of European Migration Policy* (Bruylant, 2011) 405–31.

[14] According to Livingston and Risse, 'consciousness, intentionality, and free will' are the elements which are defining the human agents. See S Livingston and M Risse, 'The Future Impact of Artificial Intelligence on Humans and Human Rights' (2019) 33 *Ethics & International Affairs* 148.

[15] See O Pollicino and G De Gregorio, 'Privacy or Transparency? A New Balancing of Interests for the "Right to Be Forgotten" of Personal Data Published in Public Registers' (2017) 3 *Italian Law Journal* 647; G De Gregorio, 'Expressions on Platforms: Freedom of Expression and ISP Liability in the European Digital Single Market' (2018) 3 *European Competition and Regulatory Law Review* 203; G De Gregorio, 'The E-Commerce Directive and GDPR: Towards Convergence of Legal Regimes in the Algorithmic Society?', Robert Schuman Centre for Advanced Studies Research Paper No RSCAS

focus. However, the problem of digital liberty must also be assessed from the viewpoints of humanism and anthropocentrism, and their eventual alternatives such as transhumanism and algorithmic constitutionalism, in the age of the IT revolution. More precisely, some of the fundamental concepts such as personality, the private sphere and personal self-determination need reassessment in the context of the algorithmic society. Due to space constraints, I am mentioning them only briefly here.

Human dignity is the cornerstone and main projection of humanism in constitutional law.[16] It is the institutional axis around which the system of human rights is organised. Some constitutional acts, eg the German Constitution or the Charter of the Fundamental Rights of the EU, explicitly provide for human dignity as the ultimate foundation of the constitutional status of the human and of the constitutional order in general.[17] Most of the Western constitutional systems provide, whether explicitly or implicitly, for enhanced protection of human dignity.[18] Our moral criteria, developed in the context of the humanist tradition, allow us to consider ascribing a form of dignity to animals, but it does not reach as far as for AI. Moreover, animal dignity is not a source of rights, but a reason for better treatment, defined in terms of speciesism and anthropocentrism as 'human treatment'.[19] But we have not yet developed any moral and subsequently legal standards for the treatment of robots and AI.

Human dignity is an important criterion for the assessment of new opportunities for enhancement and augmentation of the human body and intelligence.[20] On the basis of humanism, one can reflect on the justification of the achievements of nanotechnologies, transplantology, biotechnologies and 3D printing, but also of the digital technologies for the improvement of the human body and mind.

However, human dignity is not an entirely reliable criterion. This is because very different and even antagonistic understandings of human dignity can be applied. I will demonstrate this with the most obvious, but not exhaustive, conceptual opposition.

2019/36 (2019); B Wagner, M Kettemann and K Vieth, *Research Handbook on Human Rights and Digital Technology: Global Politics, Law and International Relations* (Edward Elgar, 2019); O Lynskey, *The Foundations of EU Data Protection Law* (Oxford University Press, 2015); A Kuczerawy, 'Safeguards for Freedom of Expression in the Era of Online Gatekeeping' (2018) 2017 *Auteurs & Media* 292; A Koltay, *New Media and Freedom of Expression* (Hart Publishing, 2019).

[16] See C McCrudden (ed), *Understanding Human Dignity* (OUP/British Academy, 2014).

[17] See R Alexy, *Theorie der Grundrechte* (Suhrkamp, 1994) 95–97; K-H Ladeur and I Augsberg, *Die Funktion der Menschenwurde im Verfassungsstaat. Humangenetik – Neurowissenscahft – Medien* (Mohr Siebeck, 2008) 5–34; P Wallau, *Die Menschenwurde in der Grundrechtsordnung der Europaischen Union* (Bonn University Press, 2010) 21–35.

[18] See P Becchi and K Mathis (eds), *Handbook of Human Dignity in Europe* (Springer, 2019).

[19] For a critical approach towards the extension of the concept of dignity to animals, see F Zuolo, 'Dignity and Animals. Does It Make Sense to Apply the Concept of Dignity to all Sentient Beings?' (2016) 19 *Ethic Theory and Moral Practice* 1117.

[20] See R Raisamo, I Rakkolainen, P Majaranta, K Salminen, J Rantala and A Farooq, 'Human Augmentation: Past, Present and Future' (2019) 131 *International Journal of Human-Computer Studies* 131.

Originalist humanism may require refraining from all advantages of technological revolution in order to keep humankind and Homo sapiens in its initial version as created by God or by nature. Assisted reproduction and corrective surgery are prohibited. Abortion and euthanasia are both crime and sin. Gene editing, transplants and hybridisation between man and machine are unthinkable. There are both religious and secular versions of originalist humanism.

In contrast, transhumanism highly praises and actively strives for the enhancement of the human body and mind through the use of new technologies. In the context of transhumanism, human dignity is changeable. It is socially and politically negotiable. It is just the starting point, rather than the end, of our journey to the individual and collective self of human beings transcending the boundaries of humanity and reaching a post-human stage. In this context, human dignity is not sacred and of eternal axiomatic value, but is an inherited, limited and rudimentary remnant of the age before the IT revolution. Human dignity must be augmented, enhanced or even replaced with transhumanist and post-humanist dignity.

Thus, one may differentiate between the two extremes, between two radically different versions of dignity. These are the originalist (naturalist or religious – in the Western context, predominantly Christian) human dignity and the transhumanist and post-humanist dignity, the latter even renouncing the use of the concept of 'human' as part of the legal and constitutional construction of dignity. These conceptual antipodes have paradigmatic importance for the counterposition between humanism, transhumanism and post-humanism as normative ideologies of humanist, transhumanist and post-humanist constitutionalism.

Two large, interrelated questions arise from this finding. The first is which of the two extreme versions is not only morally and ethically preferable, but also adequate to the new context that will be produced as a result of the ongoing IT revolution? This question indicates the existence of controversy between traditional legitimacy and some versions of ethical legitimacy and competing versions of ethical legitimacy, combined with concerns of efficiency.

One of the big issues here is whether we should stick to traditional humanist versions of Kantianism, as the theory which has most profoundly influenced our understanding of humanism and human dignity, or think also about the unthinkable, namely to expand humanist Kantianism to animals and especially to forms of AI, thus making them not only instruments of our well-being, but also granting them coequal status as dignified persons (or entities). In the latter case, we must depart from traditional anthropocentric versions of humanism and go beyond the category of humanity as the cornerstone of our constitutionally framed social and political coexistence.

The second question is whether there are intermediary options – 'shades of grey' between the two 'black and white' extremities. The current answer given by constitutional law is that we should stick to a modest originalist version of human dignity. It is originalist because it denies granting of dignity to animals or to technologies (even ones eventually possessing partial equivalence of intelligence, usually termed AI). It is modest because most of the constitutions allow for reasonable use of new technologies for improvement and enhancement of the human being in its mental, physical and intellectual dimensions. Thus, there are shades of grey when it comes to the assessment of the impact of new technologies for improvement of the human intellect, soul and body, but not with regard to the human dignity as such. In other words, the only dignity that is recognised by constitutional law is human dignity.

Last but not least, human rights provided in constitutions in the form of constitutional rights are another very important element of humanism as a constitutional phenomenon and as the normative ideology of constitutionalism. Humanism is based on the normative belief in natural rights and the subsequent detailed provision of constitutional rights. I will not go into further detail here due to space constraints.

## III. Challenges to Humanism as Constitutional Ideology

Currently, humanism is experiencing pressure from many directions. Some of the critics are overlapping, thus producing a cumulative deconstructive effect. Critical deconstruction of humanism seems to be part of deeper ruptures in constitutionalism triggered by the ongoing constitutional transition to a world based on new technologies and the reconceptualisation of constitutional truisms in the context of the IT revolution. In that regard, humanism becomes a point of interception of critical discourses on globalisation, algorithmic society, IT revolution and alternative (non-Western or non-liberal) constitutionalisms.

The first trend of criticism is civilisational and geopolitical. Non-Western constitutional orders have formally adopted humanism as part of the constitutional package they have transplanted. However, with the rise in the economic power and political prominence of non-Western constitutional orders, we may expect pressure on humanism, or at least on humanism in its Western version, with its emphasis on human dignity and human rights, individualism, liberalism, free will and individual responsibility. Thus, some non-Western or anti-Western constitutional orders may reject humanism as a pillar of constitutional ideology or may reshape it in a way which is very different or even incompatible with its traditional Western outlook. Hence, with the partial demise of the attractive force of Western constitutionalism and with the rise of powerful, order-based, etatist and paternalist authoritarian regimes, one may expect the augmentation of challenges to humanism stemming from non-Western orders that value the prevalence of state, order and society over individual liberty, free will, moral autonomy, human dignity and human rights and, thus, over humanism.

Threats to humanism may also be produced in a traditionally Western and liberal context. This is evident with regard to the recent development of paternalism and etatism in the context of the COVID-19 crisis. The eventual development of health Leviathan may trigger a reconsideration of the traditional liberal versions of humanism, especially with a view to their intrinsic bond with free will and free choice.

The danger for humanism increases when such non-humanist normative ideologies get mixed with technocratic authoritarian visions of algorithmic scanning, profiling and tracking technologies, with limitation of privacy for the sake of security and with the use of medicine and technology for transhuman improvement of Homo sapiens. Here we can expect the double denial of humanism, stemming from the overlap between illiberal constitutionalism and authoritarian constitutional orders on the one hand, and technocratic transhumanism, paternalism and post-humanism on the other. Thus, there are suggestions in the doctrine that we are rushing into the age of surveillance capitalism[21] with a 'technocratic Leviathan'[22] as the state ideal and with post-humanism and eventually transhumanism as normative ideologies of technocratic illiberal constitutionalism and authoritarian constitutional orders. The recent developments in the context of the COVID-19 pandemic are assertive of the huge potential for the emergence of surveillance and algorithmic regimes disregarding humanism or interpreting it in paternalistic, illiberal, technocratic and autocratic ways.

The second type of challenge comes from the critical deconstruction of humanism. This is not a novel challenge to humanism. Humanism has been criticised in many trends of moral, social and political philosophy. One trend of criticism in constitutional theory aims at exposing the suggested hypocrisy of humanism, which is not fulfilling its emancipatory promise and is serving as a fig leaf and excuse for violations of human rights in the name of human rights and for the infringement of key principles of constitutional and international law.[23] Another arm of the critics focuses on the excessive anthropocentrism of humanism.[24] Thus, humanism is considered to be justificatory ideology for speciesism, human supremacism, implicit consumerism etc. Furthermore, humanism is denounced as being too Western and biased towards very specific ideological trends in Western modernity. Paradoxically, here humanism is attacked from two directions as being already largely detached from traditional Christian values and as being very much entrenched in the Christian roots of Western society and the Western history of ideas. There are also claims that humanism is not really authentic and does not allow for the fulfilment of the real human capabilities culminating in the concept of Dasein.[25]

[21] S Zuboff, *The Age of Surveillance Capitalism. The Fight for a Human Future at the New Frontier of Power* (Public Affairs, 2019).

[22] For some more traditional concerns regarding the technocratic Leviathan, see MA Centeno, 'The New Leviathan: The Dynamics and Limits of Technocracy' (1993) 22 *Theory and Society* 307, www.jstor.org/stable/657736.

[23] See B Meiches, 'Non-human Humanitarians' (2019) 45 *Review of International Studies* 1.

[24] See Peters (n 10).

[25] This problem has been raised by Jacques Derrida. See P Allender, 'Derrida and Humanism: Some Implications for Post-Humanist Political and Educational Practice' (2013) 5 *Power and Education* 318; E Armour, *Deconstruction, Feminist Theology and the Problem of Difference* (University of Chicago Press, 1999) 141.

The third type of pressure on humanism is produced by the ongoing IT revolution. There is increasing interest in the impact of the new technologies on law in general and on constitution, constitutionalism and constitutional law in particular. Humanism has normative impact on the range of values included in the constitution. It shapes the system of human rights. It also impacts the overall constitutional design, especially when determining the set of constitutionally permissible goals that the state institutions may pursue. These goals are entrenched in humanist constitutional axiology. This profound impact of humanism on constitutionalism and constitutional law triggers a range of issues in the context of the IT revolution. Should AI be granted the status of subject of law? Should this be done in principle or just in a layered manner by assigning only specific rights and duties? Can we compare and thus derive the rights of AI in comparison and conjunction with the rights of animals? Is there a general principle for assigning rights and duties to a non-human being?

The list of questions and issues may be further extended. Is the differentiation between human and non-human a matter of principle or a matter or scale? Should we have a clear-cut differentiation between the rights of man and the protection of objects (animals, robots, algorithms, AI), and a clear demarcation between the subject of law and the object of law, between the holder of rights and the object of protection and duties? Or we should instead construct a scale with many shades of grey? In the latter case, can we create different types of subjectivity and personality, and assign to them different kinds of rights? Indeed, it is not only the people who are in possession of rights – legal persons that are 'persona ficta' also hold rights.

An important argument for the scaling of the status instead of introducing a clear-cut differentiation would be that we will be able soon to increasingly merge man with machine. AI, but also implants, 3D printing and other medical and biotechnologies, as well as other IT revolution achievements, will allow us to heal (recover) or improve man, or human beings. Thus, very soon, maybe even in the forthcoming decade, we will be exposed to the question 'What are the boundaries of the human?' If this is the soul, consciousness and self-awareness, will this not lead to a preference for the mental and psychological capacities of the human over his or her physical capacities, which may be more easily exposed to cyborgisation and transhumanisation? Will this not produce 'fractures' within the very concept of the human being, prioritising the mind over the rest of the body? And if so, what should be the response of the law?

Naturally, most of these questions are rather abstract and still theoretical at the moment. Most of them require multi-discursive and thorough research. That is why the analysis here is limited to just a few problems. More precisely, the impact of humanism on conceptual definitions and delimitations in constitutional law will be explored. Furthermore, the importance of humanism and the perils of post-humanism with a view to constitutional ontology, axiology and teleology will be outlined. Special attention will be devoted to the challenges of algorithmic constitutionalism.

## IV. Humanism and the Problem of the Boundaries and Distinctions in Constitutional Law

The problem of the epistemic value and the subsequent critical, evaluative and emancipatory powers of humanism may actually be reduced to the question of the boundaries that the law in general and the constitutional law in particular impose. It concerns conceptual and paradigmatic differentiations between the subject and the object of law. It reflects the difference between the entitlement to be a holder of rights and the granting of special protected status as an addressee of duties for respect.[26] The law defines the boundaries between human and inhuman, human and anti-human, and human and post-human. It determines, on the basis of socio-political and ethical reflection of objective facts, the differentiation between man and animal and between man and machine.

It seems that the boundaries between humanity, animality and technicity are naturally predetermined. This is not necessarily the case.[27] There is long tradition of denial of full citizenship status to some human beings and thus a historical pattern of discrimination.[28] Thus, they have been degraded to second- or even third-class humans, being granted different clusters of human rights. Slaves and groups politically discriminated on the basis of sex, race, wealth etc are good examples.[29]

The future of technology contains huge opportunities for personal enhancement. It offers a gateway for cross-fertilisation between humanity and technicity, between natural and artificial, between human, post-human and transhuman. At the same time, it brings with it huge challenges which require adequate and innovative responses by law and especially by constitutional law. The current age of the IT revolution has many interrelated manifestations – the AI revolution, the Internet of Things, augmented reality, algorithmic and big data society, and cyborgisation of human beings due to the use of new biotechnologies and medical technologies. Together, they challenge the boundaries between humanity and technicity, between human, post-human, transhuman and artificial (technical). They indirectly redefine the concept of our own animality,[30] and thus of our biological predetermination. If man and machine are getting closer and are even being partially merged, then the relationship between man and other species also needs to be reconsidered.

[26] See Peters (n 10).

[27] See G Steiner, *Anthropocentrism and Its Discontents. The Moral Status of Animals in History of Western Philosophy* (University of Pittsburgh Press, 2005).

[28] See K Kolozova *Capitalism's Holocaust of Animals. A Non-Marxist Critique of Capital, Philosophy and Patriarchy* (Bloomsbury, 2019).

[29] See Peters (n 10).

[30] ibid.

Humanism is an ideology which determines the background for inclusion and exclusion in the realm of subjectivity. It is a gateway to constitutional recognition as part of the privileged realm of subjectivity. Thus, it plays an important role in constitutional biopolitics, especially addressing the differentiation between Homo sapiens, the rest of the living world and AI. Humanism determines who is entitled to rights granting higher levels of legal care, and, further, different types of protection than just being an object of special care. Thus, paradoxically to some extent, humanism is a tool for protection against death, inhuman and degrading treatment, torture, exploitation and exposure to mental and physical risks, whilst conversely being an instrument for allowing death, deconstruction, and forms of degradation and exploitation of animals or entities possessing AI which are purged and excluded from the 'safe island' of human and non-degrading treatment that is reserved only for human beings. This feature of humanism as a tool for drawing the delimitation line between life and destruction, between preservation of dignity and instrumental use, is a result of its typical attachment to anthropocentrism. But, as already mentioned, constitutionalism is human endeavour, at least for the moment. And it also encompasses humanist ontology, teleology and axiology, which are currently entirely anthropocentric, as will soon be explained in more detail.

Humanism is also a historic point of no return. Thus, it draws historical demarcation lines between periods in human history. It is one of the points of no return which divided the Middle Ages from modernity. Indeed, humanist thought existed in the history of ideas in Antiquity and in the Medieval Christian philosophy; however, the modern version of humanism, which was cross-fertilised with rationalism during the Enlightenment, has been the clear marker of modernity. Hence, humanism defines the boundary between the pre-modern and the postmodern ages. To some extent, it also marks the boundary between the modern and postmodern ages, since it is challenged, deconstructed and even rejected by some postmodern trends of thought.[31]

In that regard, one should polemically and critically assess the possibility of emergence of post-humanism, transhumanism and anti-humanism[32] as new points of no return dividing modernity from postmodernity. Allowing a degree of subjectivity to non-human entities such as AI and the deconstruction of the border between pure Homo sapiens and the technologically and medically upgraded Homo sapiens as stages or grades of humanity and subjectivity may mark a departure from humanism as the normative pillar of constitutional modernity.

In other words, the forthcoming decades will most probably produce new division lines between de facto privileged and discriminated classes of people. The line of discrimination will be mostly dependent on capabilities for technological

[31] See J Miernowski, *Early Modern Humanism and Postmodern Antihumanism in Dialogue* (Palgrave Macmillan, 2016).

[32] For more about anti-humanism see ibid.

inclusion consisting in benefiting from the range of achievements for technological augmentation of the human reality. These capabilities will be rather complex and not limited only to financial resources, although the latter will play a central role. A new division will be drawn up between the elite, which will be able to take full or partial advantage of the technological progress by upgrading their biological and intellectual status using new technologies, and the disempowered masses, which will not be allowed to benefit or practically, eg due to financial reasons, will be incapable of benefiting from technological progress.[33] Here, the task of political, social and moral philosophy and of constitutional law will be to set a more or less legitimate framework for the parameters of social benefiting from technological progress and to determine the permissible 'elevators of transhumanity' allowing for personal augmentation via new technological instruments.[34] Thus, humanism or its alternatives – post-humanism, transhumanism etc – will be the keys for drawing these strategic demarcation lines, with conceptual importance not only for the status of the human being and for the protection of human rights, but also for the overall constitutional and political structure of the society in the age of IT revolution.

Humanism as an institutional centre of modern constitutionalism is the key strategic source of distinction between legal and illegal, constitutional and unconstitutional, permissible and non-permissible, desirable or non-desirable, and just or unjust. Anti-humanism in general and challenges to human dignity, human freedom and human rights are defined as anti-constitutional and extra-constitutional phenomena precisely on the basis of the humanist tradition. Thus, humanism is at the same time the core and pillar of constitutionalism, but also a strategic tool for the determination of the ultimate boundaries of constitutionalism.

## V. Humanist, Post-humanist and Transhumanist Constitutional Ontology, Axiology and Teleology: Algorithmic Constitution and Constitutionalism

Humanism is the fundamental ideology of modern political philosophy, with paradigmatic importance for constitutionalism and constitutional law. It predetermines the shapes of the human being as a constitutional phenomenon. It underlines the constitutional framework of human existence, human dignity, human rights and human duties. Humanism predetermines the source of the constitution and constitution making. It dictates the design of the constitutional values and the

[33] See Ferry (n 3).

[34] See J Habermas, *Die Zukunft der menschlichen Natur: Auf dem Weg zu einer liberalen Eugenik?* (Suhrkamp, 2005); M Sandel, *The Case against Perfection: Ethics in the Age of Genetic Engineering* (Belknap Press, 2009); Ferry (n 3).

system of constitutional aims. In that regard, humanism has simultaneously ontological, teleological and axiological dimensions.

Humanist ontology underlines the constitution and constitutionalism as emancipatory projects of mankind. The belief in free will, free choice, the creative power of human intention and the emancipatory power of human rationality predetermines the human capability of autonomous establishment of reasonable political and constitutional order.

The normative ideology of the constituent power of the nation and of the people and the key principles of national and popular sovereignty are preconditioned upon humanism. The human origin of the constitution, the creation of the constitution by the joint and shared rationality of human beings united in a political community, the creative and coordinated use of human reason as an ontological ground and source of the constitution are normative ideas which are deeply rooted in humanism as the pillar of the constitutional ideology of modern constitutionalism. Even if we do not consider the constitution to stem out of a reasonable deliberation and a joint socio-political decision of the whole community based on a social contract, humanism still remains of fundamental importance for legitimation of the constitution as a result of human ingenuity. Imposed constitutions, outsourced by an elitist player and presumably gifted with better capability of reasoning than the mass audience and the people as a whole, are a phenomenon which is still justified via recourse to humanity and human reason. In other words, rational, secular, human constitutionalism is impossible without humanism.

Hence, humanism is deeply rooted in constitutional ontology. It justifies the ability of the human species to self-organise on the basis of a rational, reasonable, systematic and written constitution produced by authoritative leadership, technocratic expertise and the joint, socially coordinated use of public reason. In that regard, humanism seems to emancipate humans and human society from metaphysical forces such as the will of God or other supernatural forces, the sanctity of tradition, etc.

However, this claim is not absolutely fulfilled for several reasons. People feel lost without metaphysical and ideological guidance. They are in dire need of permanently producing metaphysical justifications of the world in general and of their socio-political constitutionally framed coexistence in particular. Thus, while humanism is deeply intertwined with rationalism as pillars of modern constitutionalism, it is also grounded on metaphysical suggestions such as the existence of the nation, humankind, the common will of the people and the common good of the community. Paradoxically, all these secular metaphysical ideologies are produced massively via recourse to rationalism and contain an anti-theological ethos. The religious gods are replaced by new, secular gods.

Moreover, humanism is mainly a product of the Enlightenment. However, it is also deeply rooted in the Christian tradition. The Christian version of humanism has been one of the most powerful models not only in the Middle Ages, but also in Western modernity. Hence, it has also profoundly influenced the constitutional outlook not only of humanism as a constitutional ideology, but also the schemes and explanatory models of constitutional ontology even when their authors strived to emancipate it from religious connotation. The nation as a secular god, the will of the nation or the popular will as a secular version of God's will have shaped the humanist constitutional orders.

Nevertheless, humanism has extensively emancipated the constitution, constitutional law and constitutionalism from dependency on religion and God. The new secular metaphysics of the Enlightenment produced new forms of constitutional ideology which were humanist and anthropocentric. Thus, it was the man and citizen (or the human society comprising free and rational human beings) who was at the centre of the constitutional order.

Humanism allows the construction, development and justification of the constitution and the constitutional order from within. This is due to its anthropocentric ontology, axiology and teleology. The human-being-in-the-constitution, the *Homo constitutionalis*, is the source and at the same time the aim and ultimate justification of the constitution and the constitutional order. This we owe mainly to the Kantian tradition, but also to the broader humanist tradition of the Enlightenment.

In contrast, if the constitutional and political order is derived from an external source – God or other non-human sources – or, to put it differently, sources beyond human control, then the constitutionally framed socio-political community ('We the people') and the single person lose their political and even moral autonomy. AI may eventually become such a source that is beyond human control.

The development of AI may soon technically allow, require or trigger the production of 'algorithmic constitutions'.[35] There might be algorithmic constitutions in a formal and in a material sense. Algorithmic constitutions in a formal sense are constitutions that are developed and designed with the help of new technologies, and especially AI. Algorithmic constitutions in a material sense are constitutions allowing for the use of algorithmic technologies and thus adjusted to the conditionality of the emerging algorithmic society and – possibly – of 'surveillance capitalism'.[36] Due to space constraints, I will discuss here only the algorithmic constitutions in a formal sense.

Algorithmic constitutions may be an extreme expression of technocracy detaching, for the first time in history, constitutional ontology from humanism. Even in authoritarian constitutional orders, the constitution is created and adopted by an authority which is internal to mankind (the realm of human beings as actors of constitutionalism) even though it might be external to the constitutionally framed community, as is the case with constitutions imposed by foreign

[35] For the problems of machine normativity, which are to an extent related to algorithmic constitutionalism, see D Roth-Isigkeit, 'Social Implications of Artificial Intelligence – A Research Programme', SOCAI Research Papers 1 (2019).

[36] See Zuboff (n 21).

powers or a monarch. In all cases, the constitution has been an exclusive product of the human mind, and is thus a revolutionary project for the emancipation of Homo sapiens from external authorities.

Thus, the algorithmic constitution might be the first constitutional prototype which lays the constitution-making authority outside of humanity. God cannot create constitutions alone. Even if you are believer, you need men inspired by God to create the constitution. Animals cannot create constitutions either. Under certain circumstances, however, AI can. Indeed, there is no concrete project for the adoption of such algorithmic constitutions, at least to my knowledge. However, an algorithmic constitution in no longer unthinkable due to the extensive development of an algorithmic society and AI. It is technically possible, although democratically unacceptable and (still) politically unnecessary.

Crisis and risk management constitutionalism may trigger unexpected desires for technocratic governance. Fears from disasters or general anxiety with human leadership in times of disaster may possibly start serving as justificatory devices for technocratic constitutionalism and even for algorithmic constitutionalism. The pure rationality of machines – more precisely, of AI – may seem the proper device for managing humanitarian disasters by providing means going beyond humanity and humanism and even beyond constitutionalism.

The COVID-19 crisis has caused a rise in 'health authoritarianism'.[37] Health authoritarianism is based on the fear, insecurity and desire of people to be saved by a 'technocratic Leviathan'. What will happen if the temptation for salvation goes beyond humanity in search not just for a 'technocratic', but even for a 'technological Leviathan'? Will this mark the end not only of our liberties and liberal constitutionalism, but also of the role of the human being in the socio-political world and in the sphere of law, at least in its current form?

In a world risk society,[38] but also in a neo-nationalist and neo-paternalist statehood context, one can imagine growing temptations for the use of the new technologies, AI included, in drafting, implementing and controlling the implementation of constitutional provisions. It seems that routine procedures, where no moral assessment is needed and which can be sufficiently well typified, may be accomplished in the near future by AI or, to put it in more modest terms, by algorithms. After this becomes technically feasible, it will remain a matter of political decision whether such algorithmic constitution-making, algorithmic law-making and algorithmic constitutional implementation and control should be permitted.

Thus, we may witness the emergence of algorithmic constitutionalism. Such algorithmic constitutionalism may be partial or more extensive. It may spread to many spheres of constitutional law or may be limited to just a few of them.

[37] See K Lachmayer, 'Rule of Law Lacking in Times of Crisis', https://verfassungsblog.de/rule-of-law-lacking-in-times-of-crisis/?fbclid=IwAR1xHbCk9hE25mcejS-YV3o1EQ2dE5DcFWFk5uygvp7AOM-5Mm8hrKg574T4.

[38] See U Beck, *World Risk Society* (Polity, 1999).

However, from a certain point onwards, algorithmic constitutionalism will challenge humanist constitutionalism. A constitutional ontology based on algorithmic constitutionalism seems at the moment contrary to the Enlightenment project of constitutionalism. It departs from the requirement that the constitutions, constitutionalism and constitutional law must be products of the free will of the citizen in order to be legitimate. It contests the requirement that moral autonomy, human rationality and human liberty are at the core of constitutionalism, being deeply entrenched in constitutional ontology, axiology and teleology. That is why algorithmic constitutionalism, especially taken as a project that is broad in scope and holistic in essence, and especially determining constitutional ontology, seems to be in deep conceptual contradiction with humanism as the normative ideology of modern constitutionalism. Thus, algorithmic constitutionalism may eventually prove to be a path towards post-human constitutionalism.

AI may be used for drafting the constitutional text on the basis of criteria which are predetermined by the members of the constituent body. Thus, the algorithmic constitution will be partially a human accomplishment and the ultimate decisions – determination of the framework of the project and the adoption of the final draft – will be deeds of Homo sapiens and consequently of human constituent power. In the case of the partial algorithmic constitution, the AI will remain instrumental, submerged and 'pacified' by the human will. Thus, partial algorithmic constitutions may be considered as still being part of humanist constitutionalism.

The extreme case will be a constitution entirely drafted and adopted in an algorithmic way, especially if constitutional teleology and axiology are provided by the AI. This will be a political choice fully detached from the will of the people. Such an algorithmic constitution will be entirely external to the socio-political community. It will be the end of democracy and humanism as fundamental pillars of constitutional ontology, even if the constitution itself is based on humanist teleology and axiology and provides for a democratic design chosen in an algorithmic way. In the case of full algorithmic constitutions, 'We the people' will be replaced by 'They the machines'. Full algorithmic constitutions will be part of post-human constitutionalism.

Algorithmic constitutionalism is a phenomenon where the rationality is broad to its extreme form and radically prevails over humanism. This demonstrates that humanism and rationalism are indispensable and inseparable pillars of constitutionalism. Even if algorithmic constitutions provide for humanist teleology and axiology, the non-involvement of human beings in constitutional ontology questions whether we can even talk of constitutionalism. This is because constitutionalism is a phenomenon that aims at safeguarding human liberty, including the free will and free choice of the constitutional framework for political and social coexistence.

Of course, the adoption of an algorithmic constitution seems rather unlikely at the moment, even though it is already possible from a technological point of view. However, a situation where there is a preference for external neutrality and for technocratic constitutional governance is almost unthinkable. The current

COVID-19 crisis and its side effect – 'COVID constitutionalism' – demonstrate that the *demos* may even prefer to be governed non-democratically, not only by authoritarian-populist leaders, but also by experts. Hence, in case of an anti-democratic constitutional moment,[39] when the people show disenchantment with democracy and dare for technocracy, such algorithmic decision-making, including the adoption of an algorithmic constitution, may be put on the table as an option.

The emancipatory power of humanism is hidden exactly in the internal autonomy of the society and the people to forge their own constitutional destiny. Thus, it is not impossible to create a constitutional order simultaneously based on post-humanism (and implicitly and necessarily on anti-anthropocentrism) and on the external moral, political and hyperconstitutional authority of transhuman species (human beings augmented via the achievements of new technologies) or AI. Thus, the introduction on the constitutional scene of a constitutional *deus ex machina* will mark the end of the humanist and emancipatory project of constitutionalism which was triggered by the Enlightenment.

In parallel, we may witness the emergence of new privileged classes – a 'technocratic bourgeoisie', comprising the members of all professions involved in the IT revolution and the algorithmic society, and a 'technocratic elite', legitimating and deriving its authority from the new metaphysics of post-humanism, transhumanism and technocentrism as quasi-secular versions of religion. Thus, transhumanism and technological superiority will inevitably produce new moral codes, new institutional infrastructure, new hierarchies and radically new constitutional ontology, axiology and teleology. This will mark not only the end of constitutional modernity and humanism, but maybe also the end of Homo sapiens as the centre of the constitutional order.

At the moment, it seems that anthropocentrism will not be entirely replaced by technocentrism. It will coexist with other challenging and competing paradigms, such as technocentrism, animalism, transhumanism and 'augmented reality'. However, the eternal question of when quantity turns into quality will inevitably exist.

In the current context of the IT revolution, the secular logic of humanism and the anthropocentric ontology and structure of the constitutional order may be transformed, reconsidered and even endangered by other constitutional ideologies opposing humanism. Animalism and especially transhumanism are but two of them. Antihumanism and post-humanism comprise another group of challenging and competing ideologies deconstructing and critically reassessing humanism. With regard to constitutional ontology, as discussed here, it is necessary to point to some particularly important threats to humanist constitutional ontology. One can outline two main challenges.

[39] For the concept of constitutional moment, see B Ackerman, *We the People: Foundations* (Harvard University Press, 1991) 266.

The first challenge can be summarised as follows. What if constitution is produced in an algorithmic way entirely by post-human forms of AI? Or, much more modestly, what if AI is used just as an aid to technocratic elites to produce a perfect constitution, based on mixed human and post-human rationality, perfecting the technocratic choice of the institutional design? This challenge has already been discussed.

The second challenge consists in the risk that new, postmodern and posthuman technocratic elites may use post-human strategies for legitimation of their special, privileged place as demiurges of constitutionalism based on privileged access to technocratic knowledge. If one of the main goals of constitution-making is to produce the perfect constitution, then it may be instrumentally misinterpreted in order to justify technocratic constituent power based on excessive instrumental knowledge using the achievements of the IT revolution and AI in particular.

If we refrain from using 'thick and demanding versions' of humanism, which are embedded in anthropocentrism and the humanist moral tradition, then we may define the perfect constitution not as the one best serving humanism and humanist versions of justice, but as the best ordered, most well-written and using the most efficient institutional design from the viewpoint of technocratic authority. Thus, technics may be used by technocratic elites as justification of their predominance and, more precisely, of their grip on constituent power the same way as God was used not only in the Christian tradition, but in all religious-based constitutional orders as justification of the power monopoly of the aristocracy, the old elites, the religious power centres, etc.

Consequently, the emergence of new technocratic elites may be paralleled by a new, post-human and even anti-human technocratic ontology of the constitution based on new versions of hyperrational technocratic and algorithmic legitimacy of the constitutional order. Algorithmic legitimacy may be derived from the admiration of a pure and distilled technological way of constitution- and decision-making, and from the belief that technology equals progress. However, hyperrationalism is also paralleled by the instrumental use of human beings if the algorithmic logic so requires. Thus, hyperrationalism might mean the negation not only of humanism (conceived as weakened, biased, outdated ideology), but also of traditional versions of rationalism as Enlightenment ideology. In that regard, a post-human constitutional ontology contains a new legitimacy code that presupposes the deconstruction of humanist normative ideologies and is based on the creation of new constitutional codes of the emerging transhumanist, post-humanist and post-anthropocentric constitutionalism.

Hence, the post-human and post-anthropocentric constitutional ontology is intrinsically related to the problem of the borders and boundaries outlined above. Algorithmic constitutionalism causes deconstruction of the old separation between constituent and constituted powers, as well as their replacement with efficiency-based flaw of algorithmic constitution-making. Such a technocratic approach to constitutionalism-as-algorithmic-constitution-making indeed emancipates constitutional law from the post-religious metaphysics of concepts like national community, common good, common will and constituent power. In this regard, it may contribute to the further emancipation of man as human being from the boundaries of the normative mythology and from the chains of illiberty, and may be perceived as a path towards the further rationalisation of constitutional law.

However, it may also be an indicator of a trend in the opposite direction. Denying humanist and anthropocentric constitutional ontology may be a road to the enslavement of the people justified via extreme, deconstructive and technocratic post-human constitutionalism. Rejection of the human mind and the human will as ultimate masters of the destiny of the constitutionally framed socio-legal community may mean the justification of post-human algorithmic means of purely technocratic, quasi-objective construction of the constitutional reality serving the aims of the new post-human technocratic elite. The people must be allowed to be wrong. The need for a permanent distinction between right and wrong is entrenched in the free will concept that is at the core of humanism and of Western liberal constitutional civilisation. With postmodernism, we also started to understand that 'right' and 'truth' are not permanent phenomena, but only discursive, negotiated ones. And they cannot be negotiated via AI. Thus, algorithmic constitutionalism is intrinsically inhuman and even anti-human (and not just anti-humanist).

In that regard, humanism is also a matter of authority. The establishment of humanism as the strategic normative ideology of constitution, its deconstruction, problematising and eventual replacement, eg by post-humanism, is also a question of the establishment and justification of authority. The anthropocentric authority of humanist constitutionalism may be opposed to the technocratic and technocentric authority of post-humanist, transhumanist or algorithmic constitutionalism.

Humanism defines constitution in terms of the axiology of anthropocentrism. It uses Homo sapiens and its different institutionalisations as human being, citizen, foreigner, refugee and human being at risk (pregnant women, aged person, child, etc) as pillars for organising the constitution. Indeed, there are different ethical or religious systems which may underline the specific type of constitutional organisation of human nature. Nevertheless, all constitutions are anthropocentric, and most of them – especially the Western ones – are also preconditioned upon humanism.

In the algorithmic society, it is not inconceivable that another type of constitutional ideal may emerge. This may be the constitutional prototype of the evolving, problem-solving constitution adjusted via algorithmic procedures according to the logic of efficiency and context adequacy. Indeed, it is important that the constitution is efficient and adjusted to the demands of the context. However, if we elevate these characteristics of the constitution into ultimate constitutional aims detached from humanist values and from the permanent fulfilment of the preservation of human dignity, human freedom and human happiness, then we risk promoting post-human constitutionalism deprived of value anchors. But, there is no such thing as a value-free model.[40] Such algorithmic constitutionalism will be democratically uncontrollable because an algorithm is democratically detached. It will be deprived of the emancipatory potential of human constitutionalism. Moreover, due to its formality, it will be prone to technocratic and authoritarian regimes. Thus, the formality will be formal while being filled with values typical of post-human authoritarian-technocratic quasi-constitutionalism.

Hence, humanist constitutional axiology and teleology are indispensable elements of modern constitutionalism. Their deconstruction will destroy the concepts of constitution, constitutional law and constitutionalism as we have known them since the emergence of Western modernity and in the form in which we have inherited them from the tradition of the Enlightenment. Of course, we may redefine them, centring them on other explanatory and ordering schemes related to the well-being of all living creatures or of all intelligent entities. Thus, we may escape the boundaries of anthropocentrism, speciesism, human supremacism and traditional humanism as suggested by many authors.

However, this is another phenomenon that will go far beyond the conceptual framework of what we traditionally conceive as constitutionalism. We may define it as animalist constitutionalism, post-speciesist constitutionalism or inclusive intelligence constitutionalism, but constitutionalism here will be just formal denomination drained of its humanist content and detached from its intellectual and conceptual pillars rooted in the Enlightenment. Animalist or post-speciesist constitutionalism may provide for equal or similar treatment of all living creatures – humans and animals, but also why not trees? Inclusive intelligence constitutionalism will offer a common constitutional framework for all entities possessing intelligence (although there we will experience huge definitional and conceptual problems). But this will never be real constitutionalism because constitutionalism has been a project for the emancipation and empowerment of the human being and for the improvement of human society.

That is why one can define as genuine constitution, constitutional law and constitutionalism only those phenomena that are produced by the human mind (usually in its collective and public use) aimed at the fulfilment of a specific humanist ideal organised around a constitutional model of the human being and human society and based on humanist values with an anthropological design.

[40] See S Camporesi, 'It Didn't Have to Be This Way', https://aeon.co/essays/a-bioethicist-on-the-hidden-costs-of-lockdown-in-italy?fbclid=IwAR1EhPc_xIRqZ7eE6wacfDEeRNwC4cZ5Q8178cyTc5mkh-yCdfrFVXP9Yqk.

## VI. Humanism as a Matter of Socio-political Choice or as an Objective and Unsurmountable Determinant of Constitutionalism

The necessary anthropocentrism of constitutionalism does not exclude the usefulness of engaging in debates about post-human constitutionalism and algorithmic constitutionalism, especially in the context of the IT revolution and the emerging algorithmic society. Reconsidering traditional concepts, deconstructing secure identities and boundaries, and reflecting on the constitutional future are always not only intellectually challenging, but also socially and scientifically necessary. They should also be critical and timely. And I believe that the time to face the threat of a post-humanist future and the perils of algorithmic constitutionalism has already come.

I do not share the belief in the recent emergence of AI or in the immediate fulfilment of post-humanitarian or transhumanist ideals, dreams and plans. But I am certain that the current information and technology revolution will profoundly change our social and political reality, thus requiring adequate and timely changes to constitutions and constitutional law. The IT revolution is already shaping constitutionalism as theory and practice. However, it is less clearly reflected in institutional constitutionalism and more precisely in the constitutions. Such reflection is more than necessary. It may be confirmative, thus reshaping constitutional design, or prohibitive, leading to the abolition or restriction of technological developments. But it must be reasonable and timely.

I believe that the time for a scientific discourse focused especially on algorithmic constitutionalism has already come. Evidence is the mushrooming of literature on digital constitutionalism.[41] However, most of it lacks an analysis of the impact of the IT revolution on normative constitutional ideologies in general and on humanism in particular. I hope that the current chapter is a modest contribution to the opening phase of this debate.

Finally, humanism is ideology produced by political, moral and social philosophers. It has then been institutionally proclaimed, enshrined, safeguarded and in some cases even entrenched in constitutions, constitutional law and constitutionalism, and subsequently in international and EU law. Thus, humanism is historically a matter of socio-political choice. Without this choice, which has been made for us by generations of constitutional scholars, politicians and philosophers, the institutional design of our socio-political world could have been much different, as it was, for example, in the Middle Ages in Europe and still is in many parts of the world. It was great achievements, but also big catastrophes, such as revolutions and wars, which fostered, triggered and facilitated the socio-political choice for humanism and thus for constitutionalism.

[41] See, eg the literature on digital constitutionalism cited above.

We are living in an age of radical and massive challenges for constitutionalism in the form we have inherited from our forerunners. 'COVID-19 constitutionalism', based on 'health authoritarianism',[42] and paternalism, algorithmic constitutionalism, transhumanism and post-humanism are just some of the challenges to humanist constitutionalism. They are also a matter of socio-political choice. They can be activated, of course, when the circumstances allow it. Among the key determinants here one can mention the degree of technological development, the real or presumed social desire for reform, a degree of social support and, last but not least, the political will for reform expressed by sufficiently influential political elites. Consequently, it should be taken into account that humanism is a matter of socio-political choice and objective determinant of constitutionalism, but not an unsurmountable and eternal pillar of human civilisation. But what is certain is that we should be fully aware of the immense risks of deconstructing and renouncing humanist constitutionalism when the time comes to face its challenges.

[42] See Lachmayer (n 37).

# 2

# Constitutional Dimensions of Information Revolution

DANIEL VALCHEV

## I. *Pro Domo Sua*

When I started working on this chapter, I was uncertain as to what conclusions I would reach at its end. But I promised myself to follow a cautious and careful train of thought, regardless of where it would take me. At the time, I was re-reading a compilation of texts by Umberto Eco (an author who has always impressed me not only with his humbling erudition, but also with the directness on his theses) and there I came across an article of his regarding Norberto Bobbio.[1] In this article, Eco analyses an essay by Bobbio from the 1950s and, more precisely, he focuses on one impressive quote: 'the task of men of culture, today more than ever, is rather to sow doubts than to reap persuasions'.[2] According to Eco, what is impressive is not the idea itself, which nowadays (the article was published in 2004) has an evident truthfulness, but rather the fact that Bobbio conceived it in the 1950s – ie in the years of severe political struggles and acute ideological antagonism in Italy.

In spite of my great reverence for Eco (he is among the 10 or so intellectuals who have most strongly influenced my way of thinking), in this case I will not agree with him. I think that the widespread opinion – 15 years ago as well as today, is different – men of culture ought not to sow doubts. In an environment of increasing chaos, in the ever-growing competition for prominence through profanation or denial, within an inarticulable informational amalgam of facts, opinions and pure publicity, many believe that intellectuals are responsible for the maintenance of the correct collective beliefs.

[1] U Eco, 'Bobbio gli intellettuali e la missione del Grillo parlante', *La Repubblica* (28 September 2004).

[2] 'Il compito degli uomini di cultura è più che mai oggi quello di seminare dei dubbi, non già di raccogliere certezze': N Bobbio, *Politica e Cultura*, ed F Sbarberi (Turin, Einaudi, 2005; first published 1955).

In short, within the current text, I will not induce arguments in favour of liberal democracy, I will not lament its future, nor will I give recipes for its survival and development in the age of information. For, as Bobbio claims in the same essay, 'above the duty for cooperation stands the right to research'. This gives me the self-confidence to be objective in my examination without this necessarily implying that I am neutral in my views.

What I will do is consecutively: (i) present my point of view regarding what happened in the field of access to information and the possibility of spreading information in the last few decades and how it came to be; (ii) induce arguments in favour of the belief that what happened should be defined precisely as information revolution; and (iii) put forward my opinion on how this information revolution affects the contemporary constitutional paradigms, and in particular how it affects the tension between national sovereignty and global constitutionalism, as well as the safeguarding of the representative democracy and the normative ideology of rights.

## II. What Happened in the Field of Information and How did it become Possible?

The scientific discoveries and the technological breakthroughs that we have witnessed in the last couple of decades are so frequent and varying, but also in a way interrelated, that without a certain historical distance, they are hard to rationalise, conceptualise and rate with regard to their significance. That is not to say that we are lacking in such attempts. It suffices to recall Rifkin's *The Third Industrial Revolution*[3] and *The Zero Marginal Cost Society*,[4] or the society of the future drawn by Harari in *Homo Deus: A Brief History of Tomorrow*.[5] Albeit very different, these two attempts are somewhat alike and, to a certain degree, are representative – the authors proceed from the basis of facts, on which they build up expectations mixed with widespread fears and hopes, and finish the whole construct with predictions based on formal logic with a noticeable moral aftertaste.

By no means underestimating the significance of the mentioned authors and the described approach, in this chapter I will make an effort to do something a little different. I will try to stay close to the scientific, respectively technological, facts and to their ascertainable influence on the social environment. On the basis of these findings, I will try to sketch the existing tension in the liberal democratic paradigms. Finally, I will allow myself the liberty of making certain forecasts, which – I would like to strongly stress this point – will be the fruit of my intellectual speculation.

[3] J Rifkin, *The Third Industrial Revolution* (Palgrave Macmillan, 2011).

[4] J Rifkin, *The Zero Marginal Cost Society: The Internet of Things, the Collaborative Commons, and the Eclipse of Capitalism* (Palgrave Macmillan, 2014).

[5] Y Harari, *Homo Deus: A Brief History of Tomorrow* (Harvill Secker, 2016).

An information-focused historical retrospective would reveal that, within human societies, there has been a gradual expansion of the access to information, on the one hand, and of the number (and also the percentage) of people who were able to spread information, as well as the number (percentage) of those among whom information could be spread, on the other.

It is known that within the earliest societies the capability to preserve, reproduce and disseminate information was initially related to human beings – through the properties *of* human memory and with the assistance of language. The chain of memorising and retelling was, for a long period of time, the only manner of intentional preservation, reproduction and dissemination of information (not counting cave paintings). Handwriting profoundly changed this status quo. Thanks to written language, it became possible to permanently store information outside the human memory with the help of a formalised sign system, and with its help, again, to repeatedly reproduce the stored information in a relatively uniform way. Regardless of what the hard drive was – Umberto Eco speaks of vegetal and mineral memory[6] – as a rule, information was restricted to a small intellectual, political or economic elite. The physical bearer of the information was usually unique and hard to copy (usually by rewriting), and often access to it was subject to various considerations and rigid control – Eco himself describes this in a marvellous way in *The Name of the Rose*.[7]

The invention of the printing press dramatically changed this status quo – the access to information rapidly expanded. Even though, during the Renaissance, the manual copying of books had become a lucrative activity, with the introduction of the printing press (the mid-fifteenth century), the number of books in Europe was measured in thousands. In just a few decades after the beginning of book printing, the number of books in Europe had reached between 10 and 20 million.[8] Furthermore, after the end of the Middle Ages, and especially during the Age of Enlightenment, the thirst for books of any nature sharpened, more and more people began writing, and controlling the topics and content became increasingly difficult. There was, of course, control over the writers (from publishers' policy to pure censure), and to a certain extent control over the dissemination (not everyone owned a publishing house, a newspaper or a printing press). However, with the development of printing technology and the simultaneous liberation of writers from their dependence on various ideological frames, as well as with the development of competition, the possibilities of disseminating, as well as receiving, information were further democratised.[9]

[6] U Eco, *Vegetal and Mineral Memory: The Future of Books* (Bibliotheca Alexandrina, 2005).

[7] U Eco, *Il nome della rosa* (Bompiani, 1980).

[8] D Boorstin, *The Discoverers. A History of Man's Search to Know His World and Himself* (Random House, 1983).

[9] Lynn Hunt recognises the printed books of the 18th century, especially novels, as a significant factor in the adoption of the idea of human rights: L Hunt, *Inventing Human Rights: A History* (WW Norton & Company, 2008).

In the mid-twentieth century, probably many believed that the third leap in the access to information (after the written language and the printing press) would involve the electronic dissemination of information with the support of analogue technology (telephone, radio, television). Today, however, we can confidently claim that the huge leap, both in the spreading of information and in the number of people who are able to disseminate it, came thanks to digitalisation, combined with the permanent development of technologies.

Digitalisation is based on the possibility (based on a binary code) to digitise, store, compute and communicate a large volume of information. To put it in simple terms, each thing in the world can be described if we can pose and answer an infinite number of questions whose answer is either yes or no. The concept of digitalisation in and of itself is not new. The Pythagoreans claimed that everything in the world could be expressed by dots and free space as early as in antiquity. It is said that Pythagoreans, again, were the ones who discovered the connection between the length of the string of the lyre and the pitch of the musical tone. Elements of digitalisation can be traced through different eras – it is enough to recall Descartes's coordinate system, which allows for different geometric figures to be expressed (practically designed) through figures,[10] or Leibniz's work on the mechanical calculator.

But what radically increased the significance of the binary code, and digitalisation as a whole, was the development of modern technologies. From today's perspective, we could claim that the two most important technological breakthroughs concerning information are the invention and perfection of the computer – a device for storage, processing and reproduction of information based on a binary code and semiconductors (mainly silicon); and the creation of the Internet, and subsequently the social media based on it.

## III. What is Revolution and Are We Witnessing an Information Revolution?

When I was a student and my views of the world were being formed, the term 'revolution' was a part of the official propaganda rhetoric in Bulgaria and was presumed to denote something positive by default – there is no such thing as a bad revolution; if it is bad, then it is a counter-revolution. In the countries of the Eastern bloc, the revolution had already taken place and further revolutions were not possible (at least, not in our countries). We were told that history had not yet ended because after the stage of socialism would come the stage of communism (and only then it would end), but it was clear that it was coming to its end.

[10] M Livio, *Is God a Mathematician?* (Simon & Schuster, Inc, 2009).

Imagine my surprise when, after the changes of the early 1990s, a similar thesis emerged once more – this time it was Francis Fukuyama who openly declared the end of history.[11] Furthermore, Fukuyama's thesis contains the well-known view that there is no prospect of upcoming revolutions anymore (to Eastern Europeans – ever again). If anyone should urge for an abrupt and profound change in society, this is not a call to revolution, but rather a common urging of revolt. Of course, we could always talk about branch revolutions (in transport, in technology, in education, in family life after the invention of the washing machine or in the life of mothers after the introduction of single-use nappies), but not about a revolution in a general social sense.

Within this chapter, I will use the term 'revolution' to denote any abrupt, profound and complete social change with long-term consequences. By no means denying anyone's right to speak of revolutions in a different context (whether this should be at the expense of the abruptness, the profundity, the completeness of the change or the durability of its consequences) or in a metaphorical sense, I will try to induce arguments in favour of the thesis that the information revolution is indeed a revolution in the adopted sense.

The information revolution is a revolution for several reasons. As previously noted, the word revolution is by default charged with a positive connotation – revolution is something which, despite being capable of causing certain temporary inconveniences due to its abruptness, profundity and completeness, has lasting consequences which will change life for the better. It would be hard to deny that the information revolution, viewed as an abrupt expansion of the access to information and the possibilities of storage, computing and dissemination of information, profoundly and widely affected societies. Within just one generation, the information that is stored and processed by computers and shared via the Internet (including the social media) has managed to transform completely the professional, social and personal lives of the majority of people. This change is not only regarded as something positive by default, but it seems likely to endure.

As a result of the information revolution, today the lack of information is much more seldomly spoken of than certain characteristics of the available information. This can be witnessed easily in the field of education. When I studied at the Faculty of Law, finding textbooks and other literature used to be one of the greatest challenges for students. Sometimes, it would take us days to get our hands on a certain library book. Today, accessing the information a certain book contains is no trouble at all for my students. They have access to a huge volume of information from various sources that exceeds by far each one's capacity to rationalise it. The big question is how today's education could help

[11] F Fukuyama, *The End of History and the Last Man* (Free Press, 1992).

young people cultivate a critical thinking that would allow them to distinguish the relevant from the irrelevant, the true from the false, the significant from the insignificant and the speculation from the facts.

The problem with the huge volume of information is by no means relevant to students alone. Outside the educational institutions we witness an impressive change – the amount of information the average Bulgarian in the nineteenth century would receive in his entire life can now probably be received from one or two Sunday editions of the *New York Times*. This practically unlimited access to information and the unlimited possibilities for storing, computing and disseminating information not only creates huge opportunities for manipulating public opinion, but is also on the verge of becoming its very own antithesis – a lack of information. Present-day people cannot absorb, let alone rationalise, all the information that is being offered to them. They are less and less motivated to seek the original source of information and more and more prone to settle for somebody else's selection, interpretation, opinion or judgement. This leads to the cultivation of public attitudes, which not only did not emerge as the result of a critical contemplation of facts, but are sometimes completely lacking in sense. It suffices to recall that the huge amount of information surrounding the debate about genetically modified foods in the USA resulted in 80 per cent of US citizens endorsing the opinion that the label of every food product containing DNA should indicated that the said product contains DNA.[12] This example, although curious, is not directly related to the current topic. It nevertheless demonstrates that the quantity of information is not in direct proportion to the level of public awareness and, beyond a certain point, it can even lead in practice to a lack of information or the emergence of evidently false or unclear opinions verging on the absurd.

Along with the impossibility of rationalising the huge amount of information, the information revolution entails at least three additional problems for society, which I will only mention: new opportunities for the spreading of untruths; new life forms of myths; and previously unknown opportunities for the creation of an entire parallel reality.

All these questions premise, and will provoke, research interest in various scientific fields, and probably will inspire debate. What we ought to acknowledge nevertheless is that information never was and is not a direct and perfect reflection of reality. It has always been one side, one fraction, one aspect of reality, altered by the intervention of those who gather it and pass it on. Even a photographic image of a natural landscape does not convey reality, but shows only certain sides, fractions and aspects of it, intentionally selected or not by the photographer (in order to confirm this, one need only browse through a couple of tourist advertisements). Thus, every piece of information contains elements of personal attitude, and within information concerning public phenomena and processes, such elements

[12] P Howard, 'Oxford Martin School Inaugural Lecture', www.youtube.com/watch?v=J1kXdA61AQY.

of personal attitude are always considerable and often dominant. The information revolution neither creates, nor eliminates this status quo; it merely enhances it.

It is known that describing a social phenomenon or process is much easier that comprehending it. Comprehension, apart from knowledge of the phenomenon, requires putting it in a certain context. For the current topic, this would mean putting what was referred to as information revolution within a broader view of society, which would include a declared central thesis; necessary, allowed and prohibited mental operations; and a set of defined interrelated notions.

I will proceed from Carl Schmitt's understanding of the development of Western societies in the last few centuries. According to Schmitt, the concepts of the spiritual sphere are contextual insofar as every era has its own domain and, correspondingly, its own idea of culture. While the sixteenth-century Western world was dominated by theology, and during the next couple of centuries it was replaced by the metaphysics of rationalism and related moral paradigms, the central domain of the nineteenth century became economy. As the centre shifts towards a new domain, the domain the centre leaves behind is neutralised.[13] If we follow Schmitt's logic, we could pose at least two questions. The first one is whether the twenty-first century promoted a new domain, through which social phenomena could be contemplated; the second one is whether certain notions and institutions (that embody these notions), which were charged with a certain meaning during the eighteenth and nineteenth centuries, could be contextually maintained in the twenty-first century.

In my opinion, the beginning of the twenty-first century failed to promote a new central domain, different from that of the second half of the nineteenth and the entirety of the twentieth century – economy. Thus, in the Western world, notions such as democracy, constitution, sovereignty and rights (whose meaning was conventionalised during the eighteenth century) still coexist in tension with the aspiration for market growth and the expansion of access to goods – which emerged as early as the nineteenth century – together with the ideology of liberalism, which lies as the basis of their legitimation. The incidentally emerging networks, which contest the hierarchies established within liberal democracy, indeed lead to their partial adjustment. These hierarchies, however (all conditionalities aside), remain within the frame of the same paradigm – hierarchical political models of a liberal democratic type, based on a predominantly network-type economy.

Applied to the current topic, this means considering the state of contemporary liberal democratic constitutional models within the same central domain – economy – and through the prism of information revolution, accentuating (as I have already declared): (i) the tension between sovereignty and global constitutionalism; (ii) the upholding of the representative democracy

[13] C Schmitt, *The Concept of the Political*, expanded edn, trans George Schwab (University of Chicago Press, 2007).

paradigm; and (iii) the preservation of the ideology of rights as a leading normative ideology in the Western world.

## IV. The Influence of Information Revolution on Existing Tensions in Liberal Democratic Constitutional Paradigms

When speaking of law and revolution, many will recall Harold J Berman's two volumes, dedicated to the two (according to him) revolutions that were instrumental to the development of Western legal systems – the Papal revolution and the Protestant revolution.[14] Would it be justified to claim that the information revolution will result in a sort of third revolution in Western-type legal systems and especially in the democratic constitutional models on which they are based?

Whatever definition of democracy we may give, there is no way to avoid the statement that it is governance based on majority support. Every denial of this statement not only leads to a lexical paradox, but also problematises many of the basic parameters of contemporary Western political models (eg universal suffrage with a secret ballot and constitution of the main governing bodies through elections). Furthermore, it is undeniable that today's concept of democracy has a sustainable connection with individual freedom – individual freedom not as a right of participation in the resolution of common matters, as it was perceived in antiquity and also by more recent authors, such as Rousseau (according to Benjamin Constant[15]), but rather as a protected personal perimeter of thought and behaviour, protected from the state and from the moods of the majority that direct the state's policy.

In my opinion, today's concept of democracy can be expressed in the following manner: a governance founded on elections, which is, for the sake of protecting individual freedom, restrained by procedures, bodies of professional elites and a normative ideology.[16] Therefore, contemporary liberal democracy contains a fundamental internal contradiction – it is based on the concept of the people's will (ie the collectivist concept of the dominating role of arithmetical majorities), but also involves a strong individualistic distrust in the decisions of these majorities and thus restrains them with procedures, elite bodies and individualistic normative ideology.

[14] H Berman, *Law and Revolution: The Formation of the Western Legal Tradition* (Harvard University Press, 1983); H Berman, *Law and Revolution II: The Impact of the Protestant Reformations on the Western Legal Tradition* (The Belknap Press of Harvard University Press, 2003).

[15] B Constant, *De la Liberté des Anciens Comparée à Celle des Modernes* (Mille et Une Nuits, 2010).

[16] D Valchev, 'Democracy and Courts beyond the Ideological Banality' in M Belov (ed), *Courts, Politics and Constitutional Law* (Routledge, 2019).

*Procedures* underwent a lengthy process of evolution – from the direct restrictions to suffrage and the vast legislative powers of bodies constituted without elections, to the limitations in the subject and the special procedure for holding of referendums. The second group of restraints consists of bodies with high professional qualifications – governing boards of central banks, constitutional control jurisdictions, etc. Normative ideology is the link between the universally accepted moral views within a society and its legal order. It consists of moral theses that are considered general legal principles and may serve as a standpoint for the courts' interpretation of a legal situation, and in certain (politically sensitive) cases can be used as justification for legal validity.

The tension between global constitutionalism and sovereignty was not caused by the information revolution. It became visible as early as the beginning of the 1990s, when the turn towards a unipolar world gave rise to expectations for the end of the Westphalian model of international relations and even the end of history, in a political sense. An expectation was created of the upcoming end of the national state and, therefore, of its two main legitimising pillars – nation and sovereignty.[17]

The information revolution, indeed, did not give birth to, but rather sharpened, this contradiction and rendered it more vivid. On the one hand, thanks to the information revolution, millions of people came to understand that, in order to achieve a better life sooner, it would be easier to replace their country, rather than their government.[18] On the other hand, the internet-based social networks (Facebook and the like) created a supranational identification based on belonging to a certain group, and gave birth to the feeling of supranational status – nowadays, photography aficionados or vegan cyclists may often find more common ground than, for instance, Belgian citizens among each other. There are probably multiple reasons for this – from geographical emancipation to the imposing of banalised mass culture value concepts, which are beyond the scope of this chapter.

The emergence of cosmopolitan convertible economic and expert elites, in combination with the ever-greater alienation of decision-making from local communities, which led to an increasing degree of uncertainty, nevertheless proved to have the opposite effect – it once again promoted the importance of the concept of sovereignty. One example of this is the Brussels elite, the distrust in whom, despite their meritocratic nature, is not decreasing, but perhaps even increasing. All of this emerged rather boldly amidst the COVID-19 crisis. In spite of the sporadic gestures of international and European support, and of the obvious proofs of how globally interconnected we have all become, the crisis demonstrated that societies are perceived mainly as national state-organised communities. It was no coincidence that one of the first measures for social distancing, even in countries such as the USA, was the closing of national borders.

[17] J Habermas, *The Crisis of the European Union: A Response* (Polity, 2012).
[18] I Krastev, *After Europe* (University of Pennsylvania Press, 2017).

With the decline in expectations for a unipolar world, and with the increasing technological potentials of China, Russia and other countries, the Internet's claim for the status of a global network without an alternative may prove to be unrealistic. The parallel autonomic functioning of two, three or more similar networks could catalyse the formation of several geopolitical unions with a low degree of mutual cultural penetration.

Ultimately, the information revolution does have an influence towards a supranational constitutionalism, albeit one that is perceived as a mutual (not necessarily unidirectional) influence that, at least for now, is not expected to become global. This conclusion is confirmed by the continuing erosion of Western moral, and therefore political, leadership. One cannot ignore the fact that the COVID-19 crisis is the first full-scale crisis since World War II, in which the Western world, and especially the USA, not only does not assume a leadership role, but gives clear signs of confusion and withdrawal.

The second big question concerns the future of representative democracy. It can be formulated thus: almost a century after the rise of the great totalitarian ideologies and regimes, the mistrust in representative democracy in its liberal form is once again increasing. The crisis of liberal democracy and the success of totalitarian ideologies between the two world wars have demonstrated that the combination of a rapidly expanding suffrage and the increasing economic and social anxiety give rise to angry and radical majorities who have very little loyalty to the democratic institutions and the democratic legal order. Indeed, the complicated procedures, the increased weight of the bodies of professional elites, and the passing off of the normative ideology of rights as self-evident and universally valid helped keep this situation under control for almost seven decades. However, today, amidst an expanding information revolution, this seems more and more problematic.

As early as 50 years ago, Marshall McLuhan pointed out that the electronic means of information render the society 'acoustic'.[19] In order to suppress his uncertainty and fears, electronic man, overwhelmed by information, finds refuge in the consumption of goods. It seems that, to him, what is said on television is not as important as the fact that he owns a TV set. The COVID-19 crisis has made evident how these very 'acoustics' are the reason why fear has increased to levels that forced many governments to undertake reluctantly (at least at the very beginning) certain measures that limited important rights, and that will probably prove, in the fullness of time, to have been somewhat different from what was necessary.

It is no secret that the various techniques for recommendation of voters have always gone hand in hand with democracy. But the very logic of liberal democracy increasingly alienates the exercising of power from the paradigms described

[19] M McLuhan, 'Living in an Acoustic World', public lecture (University of South Florida, 1970).

by Foucault (order, numbers, hierarchy, discipline),[20] by replacing making one do something with making them want to do it. For a long time, the printing press was instrumental in exercising such influence. Radio and then television managed to sensibly decrease the influence of, but failed to completely replace, newspapers. However, this is what the internet and social media are about to do. More and more people (at least in the Western hemisphere) receive information through a double intermediary – the person (or computer) that selected and designed the news, and the preferences of the respective Facebook group.

This makes it possible for relatively small political groups relying on expert teams to make successful claims for political power. Political elites are alienated from society, more and more successfully maintaining their relationship with the people through manipulation techniques built on marketing and publicity. At first glance, they adjust themselves to the preferences of the majority in exchange for the majority's recognition that they are authorised to speak on behalf of said majority. In reality, however, relying on the experts, the elites communicate their views to the voters and wait to 'acoustically' hear them echoed. Thus, political elites, in a paradoxical manner, connect the faceless mass of voters to the semi-anonymous expert elites.

Briefly, I do not think the information revolution itself will alter the paradigm of representative democracy, but it will render it less stable. Political elites perforce shorten the horizon of the policies they run; electorates become more and more suggestible and demonstrate a decreasing adherence to long-term goals; and experts become increasingly instrumental, with a narrow specialisation.

Of course, it should be considered that the facilitated communication might entail expectations for direct decision-making by voters. It would stand to reason to ask ourselves – as long as Europeans vote for a Eurovision song every year; TV viewers decide who shall remain in Big Brother on a weekly basis; and Facebook users are daily urged to 'like' or 'dislike' various posts – why should voters only cast a ballot once every four or five years in order to choose representatives, and not participate directly in the decision-making? Would one such call be 'acoustically' increased enough to cause change?

At first glance, whether the information revolution stimulated a transition from representative to direct democracy is a valid question. But in reality, it is hardly likely to precipitate the replacement of representative democracy – at least in the foreseeable future. There are at least two groups of arguments in favour of this conclusion. On the one hand, the average person's willingness to participate in policymaking should not be overestimated. The majority of people expect democracy to allow them to hold decision-makers responsible, rather than to make decisions themselves. Authors such as Rousseau put forward the question of the people's detachment from the common matters as early as the Enlightenment.

[20] M Foucault, *Discipline and Punish: The Birth of the Prison*, 2nd edn (Vintage Books, 1995).

With the informationally overwhelmed person, the step from 'I want my opinion to be asked more' to 'I don't want to be bothered' is even shorter. Furthermore, the general logic of societal development witnesses that the network has a greater capacity to generate change, but the change never leads to a network-based government – it merely crystallises a new hierarchy.[21]

People of my generation are used to considering human rights as unconditional normative ideology. During the decades after World War II, this ideology proved to be rather resilient thanks to its being hierarchically imposed, on the one hand, and developed in judicial practice, on the other hand. Once again, the information revolution, without directly causing the stability of the normative ideology of rights, exerts additional influence on it in such a way that, in a short term, will probably have perceivable results.

It is well known that the ideology of human rights is a product of Western cultural tradition. Like any ideology, it is a system of consistent assertions grounded on value-related reasoning. Although value-related reasoning is by default irrational,[22] it is usually claimed to be provable.[23] Samuel Moyn is correct in pointing out that rights were nationally perceived at least until World War II.[24] The ideology of rights promoted the national idea, and also, in the eighteenth century, served as a means for the creation of the nation and perception of the national idea. It was not until after the war that this ideology started being presented as a means for the creation and perception of a global constitutional order. The problematisation of this global constitutional order is, to some extent, a problematisation of the normative ideology or rights, as well.

The concept of individual freedom, which is the basis of human rights, was put to the test by the rise of terrorism, through the tension between freedom and security. After the 9/11 attacks, the question of limiting freedoms (therefore rights) for the sake of security was persistently put forward. As of now, the ideology of rights stands the test, but this may easily change in the face of new challenges. Once again, I refer to the COVID-19 crisis, which confirms that these concerns are not groundless.

Furthermore, it should be pointed out that the technological revolution does not appear to be slowing down or becoming more predictable. The constant changes in the labour market (new professions and need for frequent retraining) and the rapid changes in the physical environment, in everyday communication and in leisure activities all create a favourable environment for new anxious

[21] N Ferguson, *The Square and the Tower: Networks, Hierarchies and the Struggle for Global Power* (Penguin Books, 2017).

[22] I Kant, *Groundwork of the Metaphysics of Morals* (Cambridge University Press, 2012).

[23] According to Lynn Hunt, ever since human rights assumed a place among the concepts legitimising legal order, they have been considered self-evident. She illustrates this with the American Declaration of Independence and the UN Universal Declaration of Human Rights: Hunt (n 9).

[24] S Moyn, *The Last Utopia: Human Rights in History* (The Belknap Press of Harvard University Press, 2010).

majorities. The situation is quite similar to man's anxiety at the end of the Middle Ages, described by Fromm – men gain economic and spiritual freedom, but lose the security formerly provided by belonging to a certain economic and spiritual constellation.[25] Similarly, individuals today have more freedom in terms of day-to-day life and information but are much lonelier in a world of shaken value hierarchies, of informational oversaturation and of growing economic uncertainty.

The migration crisis in Europe and the debates about migration in the USA revalidated Hannah Arendt's critique of rights.[26] It turned out that democracy can serve not only as an effective means for political inclusion, but also as an effective means for political exclusion. The increasingly popular concept of human dignity, which may look like a source or a continuation of the ideology of rights,[27] might paradoxically prove to be a denial of rights' claim to universal validity. Whether it would be possible to reach a situation where rights remain national and legally instrumentalised, whereas the concept of human dignity replaces them on a global scale as a philosophical postulate, is a question that seems less and less absurd.

## V. Closing Remarks

Claiming that the information revolution has a direct influence on constitutional paradigms would be an exaggeration and, in the end, untrue. But it did exert a strong influence on the social environment, which on the other hand puts traditional liberal democratic models to the test. The information revolution increases the fear of rapid change, which people are unable to comprehend and which arouses in them ever-growing doubts that they will be able to fulfil their life plans. Much like what was described by Fromm, the information revolution intensifies the fear of loneliness and insecurity, as well as creating an additional worry of the incapability to comprehend what is happening.

Of course, the information revolution promotes the idea of humanity seen as a global community. It could be instrumental to the uniting around common values, as long as the proclaimed values are not in a significant contradiction with the conduct based on these values and thus emanate hypocrisy. The visibility of such a contradiction between proclaimed values and reality is enhanced manifold in an open information environment. The late nineteenth and early twentieth centuries provide a sinister but instructive example. The tension between the values declared

[25] E Fromm, *Escape from Freedom* (Farrar & Rinehart, 1941).

[26] H Arendt, 'The Rights of Man: What Are They?' (1949) Summer *Modern Review* 24; later part of *The Origins of Totalitarianism* (Schocken Books, 1951).

[27] J Habermas, 'The Concept of Human Dignity and the Realistic Utopia of Human Rights' (2010) 41 *Metaphilosophy* 464.

during the Age of Enlightenment and the social reality of the late nineteenth and early twentieth centuries gave rise to the two main totalitarian ideologies – communism and fascism. Communism offered a solution to this antagonism by denying reality and promising to replace it with a new one, based on the declared values. Fascism did the opposite – it attempted to replace the values in order to justify reality. We all know what these two experiments caused and how they ended.

Whether it is true that the only thing we learn from history is that people never learn from history, we are about to find out.

# 3

# The Impacts of Technological Revolution on the Role of the State

ATTILA MENYHÁRD

## I. Introduction

Technological revolution is primarily driven by the possibility of collecting, processing and analysing primary and derived data, as well as by online communication. This development creates challenges that reshape the role of the state in society and results in contradictory tendencies. While the social demand for state intervention is higher than ever before, when it comes to controlling Facebook, Google or cyberspace in general the state is forced to rely on such companies and to use them, inter alia, as agents of law enforcement. Ex ante protection requires these companies to be involved not only in the process of enforcement of judgments of courts, but also to decide case by case if certain contents are to be taken down or forbidden. This involves judgements concerning their compatibility with social values. That is, they are to decide if contents generated by users interfere with values like freedom of speech, human dignity, privacy and public interests under the given circumstances and if such values collide, which one to give priority over the other. All of this normally is not to be decided by private actors but by courts and legislators. This tendency threatens the risk of the privatisation of justice. Another consequence is that the state withdraws from its function of controlling transactions via registration systems, and the expanding formalism in civil procedures, supported by applied technology, makes the law and the judiciary redundant, increases the gap between the state and the citizen, and undermines the trust in the law and in the state.

## II. The State as Regulator and Provider of Public Services

The state is not a homogeneous organisation or entity, but a rather complex phenomenon. It is not the aim of this chapter to describe the state or to conceptualise it, but to critically assess the functions of the state in the context of the challenges created by the technological revolution. The state can appear in society and in the economy basically as a regulator and as the power that enforces the law, as a provider of public services or as a market player. Whether the state provides public services as a regulator vested with the public power or as a market player is the state's decision. How far it shares its responsibility with other market players in order to increase social welfare also depends on the choices made by the state. These decisions are driven by policy. The scope of privatisation is to be decided on the grounds of policy as well. Insofar as the state is a market player, it should just be seen as an ordinary owner from the point of view of society and the economy. Insofar as social resources are allocated to market players or they become a public good (*res extra commercium* or *domaine public*), the state functions as a regulator. The regulation of the Internet is an issue precisely because it was privatised by the state that originally developed it.[1] Otherwise it could have been a public service, falling under the scope of right of disposal of the state.

The role of the state in society is traditionally linked to establishing and enforcing the law. As Oliver Wendell Holmes defines the *differentia specifica* of law, 'in societies like ours the command of the public force is intrusted to the judges in certain cases, and the whole power of the state will be put forth, if necessary, to carry out their judgments and decrees'.[2] The state basically has two tasks if it comes to influencing the behaviour of the members of society. First, it has to determine which behaviour is right and wrong. Secondly, it has to define the consequences of the wrongful behaviour, in order to prevent wrongdoings in society. That is how the state influences the behaviour of the individuals and creates incentives to act in the right way. Thus, it is the function of the state to decide what is right and what is wrong in society and to sanction wrongful conducts. This function cannot be allocated to the private sphere or outsourced to private subjects.

The public services provided by the state show a great variety in their direct aims and in their nature as well. Their role is to increase the welfare in society, either by providing professional services or by controlling the legality of transactions, individual behaviour, market activity etc performed by individuals and market players. There is a wide playground for the state to decide if such services are to be provided by private actors or by state administration.

The information and technology revolution may certainly be one of the main factors that influence the development of law and of the legal order. In the context of the information and technology revolution, the legal environment has to face two basically contradictory challenges. First, the legal environment must be open to new solutions, to promoting experimentation and implementing the results of

[1] MD Birnhack and N Elkin-Koren, 'The Invisible Handshake: The Reemergence of the State in the Digital Environment' (2003) 6 *Virginia Journal of Law and Technology* 2, 2.

[2] OW Holmes, 'The Path of the Law' (1897) 8 *Harvard Law Review* 457, 457.

practical research while also attempting to minimise social risks. Secondly, the monopolies provided by the law (via protected rights and intellectual property) make the implementation of innovative steps dependent upon the beneficiaries of such monopolies permitting them. The legal environment needs to seek compromises in protecting such positions insofar as they are supported by public interests but do not go beyond the limit of actual public interests. Finding and maintaining the balance between efficiency and certainty is the key to competitive advantage in the economic sphere and the success of the legal system.

An important part of the underlying legal environment is the allocation of the risks of research and development. The cornerstones for such risk allocation are liability and insurance. It would already seem obvious that risk allocation, with the liability of research institutes, producers and service providers for the development and implementation of artificial intelligence and biotechnology, will soon reach its limits. The healthcare sector, the food industry and transportation (including motor vehicle production) are the most vulnerable branches of industry. Life, health and bodily integrity are the values protected at the highest level of society, and the products and services made and distributed by those sectors create specific risks of personal injury. For this reason, the allocation of such risks is of utmost importance and it is a rather sensitive issue in tort law. The problem is, however, that the proper assessment of fault (compliance with the required standard of conduct) and causal link is almost impossible, due to the complexity of the technology and the network of cooperation behind producing such products and providing such services.

The problems of assessing liability will push the role of insurance to the foreground. Over the last couple of decades, one of the most important structural issues in tort law has been the relationship between liability and insurance, especially the debate on whether no-fault compensation systems based on compulsory insurance could replace tort law and liability. In spite of the wide discussions of the topic in legal scholarship[3] and the introduction of such a system in New Zealand, no further steps of note were taken in this direction. The issue re-emerged, however, a couple of years ago, and it seems that, especially as far as compensation for personal injury is concerned, a general no-fault regime with insurance could bring significant social benefits.[4]

Insurance does not simply allocate the risks, but also spreads them among the members of the community, and that is the feature of insurance that provides its social advantage. A system of compulsory insurance based on a no-fault liability regime seems to be the best tool for allocating and spreading the risks of innovation. Such a system could be implemented either as a statutory scheme or as a

[3] L Sólyom, *The Decline of Civil Law Liability* (Alphen aan den Rign, Sijthoff & Noordhoff, 1980) I.2.

[4] H Koziol, 'Social Security Systems, Risk-Spreading and the Compensation of Damages in the Case of Personal Injury' in H Koziol (ed), *Comparative Stimulations for Developing Tort Law* (Vienna, Jan Sramek Verlag, 2015) 7.

result of product liability. Product liability internalises the costs of compensating the victims, then spreads them among the buyers of the product as the costs are incorporated in the price of the product. Due to the complex nature of artificial intelligence (AI)-driven products and services or those derived from biotechnology, it is rather difficult to allocate the costs of compensation via product liability among the producers as primary risk bearers. The administration of a statutory scheme, on the other hand, may generate higher social costs. The social costs of maintaining such a system can be reduced by constant monitoring and analysing individual risks using smart tools. Exploiting the potentials of the Internet of Things may help to reduce the costs of moral hazard and adverse selection in the context of insurance, which should result in an overall social insurance regime at lower cost.

## III. The State as Regulator

The main driver of technological development is mass production and mass distribution of goods and services. The key factors seem to be the new forms of communication, the collection and transference of information (the data economy), and the growing risks of their interference with public and private interests. This development obviously affects the role of the state in society and the legal order, both as the legislator and a provider of administrative services. These challenges to the state result, however, in contradictory tendencies.

There is a growing demand in society for greater state intervention in regulating social media platforms and the operators of Internet browsers, protecting personal data and allocating rights regarding data and information (eg in the context of the Internet of Things). Regulating Facebook, Google and similar online service providers seems to be a clear demand from society, and is justified simply by the need for public oversight of the flow of information and the content of transferred information per se.

The basic paradigm of a democratic society and market economy is consent. Consent implies freedom and vice versa: we are free to shape our social interactions, undertake obligations, enter transactions and elect the decision-makers of society. Consent is free if the decision is voluntary and informed. Consent represents the most fundamental value of our society, as it is the means of exercising autonomy and maximising self-interest.[5] Information is the precondition for valid consent, and this justifies the importance of information and underlies the public interest in its content and access to it. The freedom to produce, transmit and access information is of public interest. In the paradigm of law, the obligation to

[5] NS Kim, *Consentability – Consent and Its Limits* (Cambridge, Cambridge University Press, 2019) 218.

guarantee this freedom, in vertical as well as horizontal relationships, is imposed on the state. This guarantee is basically provided by the freedom of speech and measures that aim to prevent the transmission of incorrect or false information (media regulation).[6]

The debates over whether cyberspace, including the activity of companies providing public services via the Internet, such as Facebook and Google, can be regulated seem to be over now. The legislators seem to agree that the Internet, especially social media, can and should be regulated, and the first steps in this direction have already been taken.

Without going into the details of the specific features of cyberspace, it can be established that interference with private and public interests can be as wrongful in cyberspace as in the physical world, although such interference is not physical but performed via algorithms. That is, the tool of regulation, as well as the target of the regulation, is the algorithm, the 'code'.[7] Control over conduct in cyberspace is control over the algorithms that determine its content.

Statutory intervention can basically be implemented in two ways: either by using the information model or by prescribing mandatory conduct. The information model is based on the duty of disclosure; if the protection of interests can be guaranteed by a duty to transfer the relevant information to others in order to make informed consent possible, then there is no need for mandatory substantive solutions. Although the information model certainly has its limits, its big advantages include that it complies with the market paradigm and that no restrictions upon freedom of conduct are needed in order to protect the relevant interests. It can be particularly useful in transactions or, in general, in contractual relationships. For example, it can be formulated that users have the right to disclosure of the algorithms that influence their conduct and the information provided to them, as well as how the personal data acquired from them are used and utilised.

The information model can be a proper tool for addressing problems that can be modelled after consumer protection. It is, however, unable to influence the conduct of other users or online service providers; in particular, it is unable to prevent wrongful conduct. That is, for addressing most of the problems, there is a need for prescriptive norms, prohibitions and mandatory requirements. When it comes to the regulation of cyberspace, especially Facebook and Google, a big challenge is that harmful content is produced and shared by users; their behaviour has to be addressed as well. Another problem is that we are speaking about a globalised environment in which there are regional (national) specificities that may require different focuses and different steps by the regulator. The challenges

[6] Ferenc Deák, the famous Hungarian statesman, allegedly commented on the disputes over the first act on the press in Hungary in 1867 with the following words: 'if it were up to me, the act upon the press should consist of only one sentence: it is forbidden to lie'.

[7] L Lessig, *Code – version 2.0* (New York, Basic Books, 2006) 31.

require innovative solutions that involve the users and are able to address the problems at a national level within an international, globalised environment.

## IV. Policy, Rules, Standards

Legal norms exist to implement values.[8] They are rules or standards, depending on how wide a playing field they provide for judicial adjudication. Standards are formulated at a very high level of abstraction and are to be assessed on a case-by-case basis, while rules are as concrete as possible. We assume that legal norms, whether they are standards or rules, have the purpose of influencing the behaviour of individuals by creating incentives for them and they are underpinned by a certain rationale. That is, legal norms, whether as rules provided by the legislator or as judgments by courts that concretise standards, are to implement policy. In other words, it is policy that is to be decided first on the grounds of the values to be implemented in society; then comes the definition of the content of the norm by the legislator (establishing rules) or by the judgments of courts (concretising standards).

The implementation of policy can also appear as court judgments giving priority to one of the competing (or colliding) protected rights. Typically, this is the case if the courts have to decide if the plaintiff's privacy should be protected against the defendant's freedom of speech or which of the colliding rights should be protected in a certain case. In cases regarding the application of standards or deciding the priority of colliding rights, it is the court that has to establish the policy (value) to be enforced. The judgment concerns the implementation of policy. In other words, in the conceptual framework established by Hohfeld,[9] it has to be decided to which party immunity shall be provided in order to protect their right or position against the other party, or to which party the privilege shall be provided in order to establish the other party's duty not to interfere with the privilege. That is the logic of protecting the inherent rights of persons (*Persönlichkeitsrechte*). In this area of law, the judgments of the courts are always policy judgements.

When it comes to influencing the behaviour of players in a market economy, the primary issue for the legal system is liability. Judgments of courts in liability cases transmit messages to the members of society (including legal entities) with the allocation of the risks of losses and the allocation of the consequences of acts and omissions. These messages are to create incentives to behave in a way that it is held to be appropriate by the courts in order to minimise social costs. Judgments of courts in liability cases are the result of weighing different factors of evaluation,[10]

[8] J Habermas, *Between Facts and Norms*, trans W Rehg (Cambridge, Polity Press, 1997) 255.

[9] WN Hohfeld, 'Fundamental Legal Conceptions as Applied in Judicial Reasoning' (1917) 26 *Yale Law Journal* 710, 710.

[10] H Koziol, 'Das bewegliche System, Die goldene Mitte für Gesetzgebung und Dogmatik' (2017) 3 *Austrian Law Journal*, 160, 165.

establishing the content of the required standard of conduct under the given facts of the case. The concept of causation makes it possible to identify the risk-bearer, while the concept of unlawfulness may draw the boundaries of the protection of interests. This flexibility is one of the advantages of tort law and liability. The other advantage is that it provides compensation to the victim for the suffered loss and helps to promote corrective justice in social relationships. The regime of liability, however, certainly has strong limits.

Liability is an ex post reaction of the law in order to create incentives and influence the behaviour of the members of society in order to implement the ideas and principles of a good society. It is, however, also capable of repairing the wrong that occurred, but only within certain limits, and can have an impact only insofar as the obligation to pay damages has a preventive effect. This effect is rather limited if the company found liable is unable to transfer the cost of damages to consumers or other contracting parties, spreading the loss among them. In this way, damages become merely a component of the costs of doing business. The same holds for imposing administrative fines on such market players. If the company is unable to transfer such damages (costs) to others, a high level of damages or fines may result in bankruptcy. This is counterproductive and is not a goal of the law. Hence, a possible solution would be to allocate the risk of unlawful conduct to online service providers and Internet service providers. They can then spread the cost of damages among commercial users.

An efficient regulatory framework must include ex ante measures. Such measures create a complex system of duty of disclosure (information model), with positive obligations to prevent, filter and remove harmful content and responsibility for non-compliance with such obligations. The problem with such measures is that their enforcement requires ex post steps as well. Wrongdoing can only be prevented if such steps are taken before the wrongdoing is completed, eg before the harmful content is published. Such preventive measures, however, seem to be incompatible with the public interest of access to information, freedom of speech and freedom of the press. Their implementation, however, would require an administrative burden that seems impossible to structure and organise in a feasible way. As has been already established by the European Court of Human Rights, the right to privacy does not imply a positive obligation imposed on the legislator to maintain such preventive mechanisms.[11]

As such, the problem remains basically unresolved. If prevention cannot be provided effectively, the reaction of the law and the administration of justice remains an ex post reaction. The time gap between the wrongdoing and the reparation of the wrong can be minimised in the system of the service providers by using, for example, different versions of 'notice and take down' systems. The wrong, however, can no longer be undone and the consequences cannot be remedied. In such a situation, those potentially offended can only rely on the algorithms

[11] ECHR in *Mosley v United Kingdom* [2011] 53 EHRR 30.

applied by the service provider or human intervention in order to get protection or minimise the injury they have to suffer.

## V. The Online Service Provider as Agent of the State

It is evident that it is not possible to guarantee ex ante protection or efficient remedy without involving the service provider providing the platform of communication, ie the operator of the medium for the wrongdoing. Online service providers (OSPs) transmit content to the users; the transmitted content is produced either by the OSP or by other users. It follows from this that harmful content can only be avoided by involving the OSP in the process. Efficient protection requires the active control of the content by the OSP. Thus, the OSP becomes an important element in the regime of legal enforcement.

This changes the role of the state as well, and qualifies the relationship between the state and the OSP as a kind of public–private partnership, also called an 'invisible handshake' in the legal literature.[12] In this partnership, the OSP acts as the agent of the state (and of the community) in the course of legal enforcement. This partnership makes the state dependent on the OSP's conduct and exposes the state to the risks of the 'principal–agent' problem. The principal–agent relationship is described in economics as a situation where the welfare of one of the parties (the principal) depends on the acts of the other party (the agent). In the context of this 'invisible handshake', this means that, through the enforcement of the law, the state functions properly if the OSP performs its task well, but it cannot do so if the OSP fails to perform. At the heart of the principal–agent problem lies the assumption that although the agent is required to act according to the principal's interests, in the event of a conflict of interests, the agent will pursue its own interests instead of those of the principal. As such, the agent is inclined to behave opportunistically, simply because that is rational. The agent is normally also better informed than the principal, and it is rather costly for the principal to monitor and control the agent. In 'principal–agent' scenarios, it is the task of the law to make it rational for the agent to follow the principal's interests if there are conflicts of interests, to reduce information asymmetry and to maintain the level of the agent's performance.

In general, there are two basic types of regulatory strategies that can be implemented by the legislator and the courts in order to reduce the risks of the principal–agent scenario. One is to define the terms of affiliation; the other is to impose constraints upon the agent.[13] In the context of the principal–agent relationship between the state and the OSP, the terms of affiliation would actually mean defining the terms of entry (ex ante) and exit (ex post), while constraints

[12] Birnhack and Elkin-Koren (n 1) 57.

[13] R Kraakman et al, *The Anatomy of Corporate Law*, 2nd edn (Oxford, Oxford University Press, 2009) 39.

can appear as rules (ex ante) or standards (ex post). In this context, terms of affiliation would mean that the state may permit or prohibit the activity of the OSP, making its operation dependent on compliance with statutory requirements. Although the implementation of this type of strategy is not excluded per se, it does not seem to be realistic in the globalised environment in which OSPs normally operate. Providing rules and standards (liability) seem to be more reasonably applicable in this context. Rules and standards are to prevent wrongdoing or to optimise the allocation of the risks of wrongdoing. Rules as well as standards create incentives in order to comply with the requirements of law. If they are too soft, they will not have a preventive effect. If they are too strict, they create incentives for risk avoidance.

Cases such as *Bollea v Gawker*[14] show that a relatively small mistake in controlling the content produced by users and transmitted to the public by the OSP can result in high amounts of damages that can drive the OSP to bankruptcy, which is not only a problem for the OSP, but is a socially inefficient consequence as well. For this reason, OSPs try to remain on the safe side, which is more than understandable as a strategy and is in line with the basic rationality of risk avoidance. That is, in cases where the outcome is the result of weighing colliding interests, the OSP will choose the solution that imposes the lowest risk on it when it comes to testing the outcome against the law. The amount of damages awarded against OSPs such as Facebook or Google and the fines imposed on them by authorities make minimising such risks their key to survival.

While OSPs play a role in creating and transmitting content to users, Internet Service Providers (ISPs) are not involved in creating and transmitting content. Establishing their liability, however, can be reasonable on the ground that they are in the position to internalise the damages they are to pay as part of the cost of the service they provide. This way, they can spread the loss among users, just like an insurance. The peculiarity of the OSPs' and ISPs' liability is that they are not the actual wrongdoers. OSPs only provide and maintain the channels of communication and organise platforms. ISPs are telecommunication companies that simply provide and maintain the technical environment for users to connect with other computers via the Internet. A significant difference between OSPs and ISPs from this point of view is that OSPs are able to control the transmitted content or the availability of the online infrastructure, while ISPs are not normally in a position to oversee the content, nor can they exclude the wrongdoer from access to the Internet, due to the compulsory contractual regimes normally imposed on them. Establishing the strict liability of OSPs and/or ISPs for wrongdoings in cyberspace as a specific form of vicarious liability seems to be logical and compatible with the structure of tort law. Such strict liability follows the principle that the costs of the activity should be allocated where the benefits are. The problem is, however,

[14] NK Chipi, 'Eat Your Vitamins and Say Your Prayers: *Bollea v Gawker*, Revenge Litigation Funding, and the Fate of the Fourth Estate' [2017] *University of Miami Law Review* 269, 280.

that liability imposed on ISPs can work as a form of insurance, by spreading the costs of liability amongst the users, but it cannot produce any preventive effect because they do not influence the behaviour of companies providing services for connecting to the Internet without producing or transmitting content. OSPs, on the other hand, do have control over the appearance of activities performed in cyberspace. As mentioned above, however, the liability they face creates incentives for risk avoidance.

The problem with risk avoidance is that, if conflicting values have to be prioritised, banning the contentious content is always a safer choice than permitting it. If the OSP deleted content because it found the content to involve a risk of interference with the human dignity of others, the risk of being exposed to liability for damages on the ground of limiting the freedom of expression is much lower than the risk of being exposed to liability if the content was found (ex post) to violate human dignity. Hence, the cost of the risk of interference with human dignity is higher than the cost of deleting content unnecessarily. Giving priority to the freedom of speech over the risk of violating human dignity is not normally in the interests of the OSP.

## VI. Privatisation of Justice

The Internet is a very efficient means of communication, and communication has made the Internet the main source of information for members of society today. Wrongful acts in cyberspace can be described as collisions of protected interests (protected values), which require priorities to be established, just like the regime of protecting the inherent rights of persons in legal systems. Protected interests or protected values appear as rights in the legal system. In many cases, the colliding values appear as rights that are protected at an equal rank in the legal system. Typical collisions are those between the right to privacy and the right to freedom of speech, the right to privacy and the right to freedom of the press, and even both parties' right to privacy.

This phenomenon of prioritising colliding values is often formulated in constitutional discussions as restrictions upon exercising such rights one-sidedly. The pitfall of this approach is that, even though it focuses on the rights of each of the parties, it does not contrast them properly. We see the issue either as making choices between protected rights (interests) or as deciding which rights are to be limited due to the enforcement of certain other protected interests; the outcome is the result of an evaluation wherein relevant values are to be weighed against each other. As law is to be seen as converting values into rights, with such an evaluation process, rights are established on the grounds of policy. Ex ante protection, or at least minimising the time gap between the wrongdoing and justice, necessarily requires the active contribution of the OSP to establish priorities between colliding rights, that is, to implement policy by deciding on priorities among competing values and interests.

Control of harmful content with filtering is implemented with algorithms. Algorithms need to be optimised – from the point of view of the OSP – in order to avoid risks. This makes weighing and considering the circumstances of cases impossible, because the algorithm has to be standardised. This may result in the violation of interests because it would, for example, limit freedom of speech in cases where it was not justified or would not protect rights where it was justified. In the course of balancing contradicting social interests, the OSP, as an agent of the state, could and should never function in the same way as the state does. The OSP is a company without the social legitimacy to establish policy and prioritise values.

Such a solution results in the state waiving direct control over social conduct and transferring it to the OSP; at the same time, the state expects this control to be provided by the OSP. The consequence is that the oversight of data, information and qualifying content is allocated to the OSP instead of the state. This is a kind of privatisation of justice. The state can only control the OSP through indirect ex post measures – again, with liability. That is why the policy judgements implemented by the OSP will driven not be by social evaluation, but by risk avoidance. This will certainly distort the protection of values and interests in the community.

In the course of addressing the regulation of OSPs and ISPs, it has to be considered that access to services provided by them is embedded in contractual relationships governed by the standard contract terms of the service providers. Using standard contract terms is the result of mass production and mass distribution of services. The same holds for providing online services. In a way, the phenomena societies face today as a result of technical development fits to a thread of structural changes in contract law that started with the emergence of standard contract terms from the beginning of the twentieth century. As has been established in modern legal thought, there is a danger that the application of standard contract terms undermines the rule of law, pushing market players for the so-called 'public choice'. In relationships governed by boilerplate clauses, the prerequisites of the rule of law – namely, that the norm is knowable by the governed, users are able to follow it and the governed are equal, insofar as the law is enforced against them impartially and in a fair way – are not guaranteed.[15] This danger is not only increased but also becomes quite realistic due to the consequences of the technological revolution. Companies provide services and give justice in a system of contractual relationships concluded with users on the basis of their standard contract terms.

Recently, Facebook has established an 'Oversight Board' in order to control the policy judgements and the prioritisation of values and interests of activities performed via Facebook. The Oversight Board is an independent entity established by Facebook but operated by an independent trust with the task moderating

[15] MJ Radin, *Boilerplate – The Fine Print, Vanishing Rights, and the Rule of Law* (Princeton, Princeton University Press, 2013) 38.

content appearing on Facebook or on Instagram, specifically about handling appeals for blocked or removed content. The Board chooses cases independently, considering cases referred to it by Facebook and users' appeals. It will hear cases in which Facebook decided to leave up or remove content from the social media platform. This structure seems to be a new form of social media governance with a specific form of dispute resolution. The Board can also recommend changes to the standards applied on the platform. The Facebook should report on such recommendations and explain publicly if they are considered. Indeed, establishing such an expert group is a logical step in order to minimise liability risks. If the group of experts confirm certain value judgements, challenges to compliance with the required standard of conduct by the operator will have a much lower probability of success. However, establishing and operating such a system of 'private judiciary' is an obvious challenge to the sovereignty of states. The high level of expertise of the members of the Oversight Board gives a strong legitimacy to their opinion, which places strong pressure on national courts. If the courts of the states were not to accept the opinion of the Board, it may question its members' professional competence. If the national courts do accept the Board's opinion, it may suggest that the states are giving up their sovereignty. Hence, there is no longer any good option for the national courts. Such an expert system is not new; it is also applied in FIDIC contracts in the building construction industry.[16] The difference is, however, that in a contract concluded under FIDIC standard terms, the task of the expert is limited to deciding upon professional issues; it is not authorised to decide on policy.

## VII. The State as Provider of Public Services

Another important tendency that is driven by the application of highly developed IT systems is that they may make certain public services more efficient, which is certainly a priority in welfare states. Controlling transactions from the point of view of compliance with legal requirements can be automated to a great extent, eliminating the time lag between the submission of a request and the decision upon it. This reshapes the title registration systems and also the systems for registering companies. Registration of conveyances or legal entities may become highly automated, making those transactions very quick, but the price of this would be

[16] In 1996, a Dispute Adjudication Board was introduced to the Red Book of Contract Forms issued by the International Federation of Consulting Engineers (Fédération Internationale Des Ingénieurs-Conseils). The Dispute Adjudication Board has the double function of preventing disagreements between contracting parties and resolving disputes that may arise between them at any stage throughout the project, in connection with the contract or with the execution of the contractual works. NG Bunni, *The FIDIC Forms of Contract*, 3rd edn (Oxford, Blackwell Publishing, 2011) 612.

that the state withdraws from controlling their legality. This was the main goal of reforms to the land registry systems in England, Scotland, Turkey and Hungary in recent decades. As a consequence of this development, the role of the state in controlling the transactions may be limited to building the architecture of algorithms and structuring the process, including the maintenance of the infrastructure.

This development shifts the responsibility for compliance with legal requirements from the state administration to the legal professionals assisting such transactions and increases their liability. As a result, the state, the operator of the system and the provider of legal services shall share liability for the failure of transactions. If the failure was the consequence of a malfunction of the system, it should establish the liability of the state. Note, though, that the system is operated by companies that are the state's contracting parties. The position of these service providers is far from clear in cases of data leaks, losing data or other incidents. If, however, the legal service provider was negligent in assessing the legality of transaction, its liability must be established. This is not necessarily the case in traditional systems, where the authority exercises direct control over the legality of transactions.

Electronic communication reshapes not only the administration, but court procedures as well. Changes in procedural laws and the judicial organisation over the past decades have tended to expand formalism: the priority of the written form of communication, the decreasing role of direct communication between the court and the parties (ie citizens) and the growing role of legal representatives (lawyers) in the procedure downgrade justice to a service provided by the state to the citizen; that is, to a product sold to society.

This trend is certainly supported by technological development (online hearings and online dispute resolution, for example). The advantage seems to be obvious: formalities, written communication, less personal contact with oral hearings and shifting the work to legal representatives make civil procedure less expensive for the state. From this point of view, it seems to be efficient.

Efficiency, however, always depends on the goal to be achieved. At this point, it depends on policy. If the goal is not more than to provide an obligatory service to society at the lowest possible price, efficiency may be increased through lower costs. If the goal is to provide justice, efficiency does not depend on the costs of the procedure but on the justice provided, ie the quality of the judgment in the light of the facts of the case and the social evaluation. More correctly, the more the judgment reflects the social evaluation of the case, the closer it is to the goal of giving justice. Expanding formalism does not help in access to justice for the citizen.

The consequence of modern tendencies is the broadening gap between the exercise of statutory power and the citizen seeking justice. Such developments are detrimental to society, because they alienate the citizens from the state and distance law from social justice. If this occurs, the law becomes the limit of seeking social justice instead of promoting it. Our procedural laws, both civil and criminal, are a kind of mixture of oral and written procedure. Oral procedure is not a value in itself, but it is an important element of convincing the court about material or substantive justice whilst, on the other hand, providing the opportunity and the obligation for the judge to establish his or her personal beliefs regarding the case. In other words, oral procedure connects the judge with the reality, which is the key to enforcing justice in society. This is, after all, the primary goal of court proceedings.

The law is designed by its nature for organising social relationships. Procedural laws are to be assessed as social relationships as well. In order to understand the importance of direct communication between the state and the citizen and the role of oral procedure, it is enough to consider the messages of the well-known novel by Franz Kafka, *The Trial*. Josef K, the citizen, is the subject to a procedure that is, for him, completely unknowable and unpredictable. For him, the trial is a labyrinth, and the distance between him and the power taking action against him and providing justice is extremely big.[17] Why was the procedure against the average citizen, Josef K, so evocative in demonstrating the depressing and devastating feeling of separation? Because Josef K did not get the chance to take part in the procedure. The distance between the state and the citizen is so big that, for him, the authorities appear as a pure manifestation of power, nothing more.

This result may comply with the view of autocratic regimes, but is certainly incompatible with the idea of the modern welfare state or with the view that the state is a form of social consent and exists to serve society. Giving up the quest for substantive justice undermines the public trust vested in the state and the law, which results in social dysfunction, because the law and justice cannot be enforced.

Returning to the example of the case of Josef K in *The Trial*, from the point of view of the citizen, it does not really matter if the procedure was a criminal or a civil one. It also could have been a claim for damages or a case of inheritance, as in Charles Dickens's *Bleak House*. We should not accept that substantive justice is less important in civil law cases than in criminal ones, otherwise we build a distance between the citizen as a human being and society. The results of technological developments would suggest that the modern ways of electronic communication may make the personal interaction between the court and the parties unnecessary. The history of civil procedure presents the tendency of impersonal written communication as always being a shift in the procedure towards formality. Formality never promotes justice and increases the distance between the citizen and the state. This gap between the state and the citizen undermines trust in the judiciary and, in the long run, in the law. This result is socially undesirable.

Artificial intelligence is a tool for increasing transparency while also being a tool for manipulation (eg in the context of analysing court practice), which make the role of state intervention contradictory. It is often stressed as a big advantage of smart contracts (if there is such a thing as a smart contract at all) that they are

[17] R Posner, *Law and Literature* (Cambridge, MA, Harvard University Press, 1998) 135.

self-executory. Self-execution is, however, incompatible with the state monopoly on giving justice and may undermine the rule of law. Alternative dispute resolution seems to be a good way of managing social conflicts and it may gain new impetus from implementing AI, but justice should not go private. There is a huge risk that technical developments support formalities that eliminate the human factors because undifferentiated answers to mass problems would certainly push the individual into the background.

## VIII. Conclusions

The impact of technological development should not be assessed without looking at the other consequences of mass production and mass distribution of services and without examining their impact in a data driven economy and society. The context is shaped by the contractual relationships between OSPs and users concluded on the basis of the OSPs' standard contract terms, by the OSPs' involvement in law enforcement and by the fact that the OSPs collect and monopolise much more information than states do. Information is owned not by the state, but by OSP companies. Control over data, information and qualifying content is allocated to the OSP instead of the state.

If it is right that information, as one of the main resources, is the driving force of the modern economy, then this is a problem, because the main resources are normally allocated to states, which only transfer the rights to utilise such resources (eg mining). The responsibility for protecting the autonomy is being shifted to OSPs, ie private companies.

One of the main elements of the rule of law is that individuals are aware of the rules they have to obey or which influence their behaviour. In cyberspace, these rules are algorithms. The minimum requirement of the rule of law should be that those algorithms are knowable to those individuals whose rights and obligations are influenced by them.

Together, these are a challenge to state sovereignty, but this should not necessarily be seen as a negative phenomenon. Service providers are agents of the state in that they perform the state's social function. The problems of the principal–agent scenario need to be addressed, but otherwise this trend only manifests a new form of public–private partnership. This is where its peculiarity lies and that is why it requires a new approach from law and the enforcement of law. The enforcement of law, ie justice, requires the active contribution of the OSP to establish priorities between colliding rights; that is, to implement policy by determining the priorities between competing values and interests. This actually constitutes a privatisation of justice.

# 4

# Global Information Law: How to Enhance the Legitimacy of the Information Order in and beyond the State?

DAVID ROTH-ISIGKEIT*

## I. Introduction

We live in a time where our social existence is pervaded and shaped by the processing of information. This is a truism. Hardly any task could be fulfilled without the retrieval and exchange of information through the Internet and their processing on large servers at other ends of the world. We can arrange to stay at home, quarantined, facing a global pandemic threat, and accept the fact of our physical isolation. Yet it would be much more difficult to imagine a global shut-down when it comes to our connection to the Internet, our informational isolation. Information has become a central factor in our social lives. Yet, unlike the physical aspect of human existence, the informational existence of individual lives lies beyond the scope of the sovereign power of the Westphalian legal order.[1] The legal force of the sovereign national state to impose laws and, ultimately, to exercise coercion in their enforcement is limited when it comes to global information. The nation state becomes merely one actor of many in the regulation of the information order.

This process of multiplication of legal and political spaces and their actors might be called *pluralisation*.[2] Pluralisation is a process that is occurring not only in the area of information and communication technologies (ICTs), but in

* The author would like to thank Golnaz Abdollahi Jafari and Jason Coombe for valuable comments and helpful assistance in the preparation of this manuscript.

[1] See also L Floridi, *The Fourth Revolution* (Oxford, Oxford University Press, 2014) 170.

[2] D Roth-Isigkeit, *The Plurality Trilemma – A Geometry of Global Legal Thought* (London, Palgrave Macmillan, 2018) 31–32.

more areas of the law facing globalisation as an uncoupling from the frame of the nation state. Trade, sports, global construction and finance are, by their very nature, crossing jurisdictional borders. Regime-specific governance, such as in the global law of merchants, *lex mercatoria*, has largely succeeded in solving the coordination problems related to these fields. These regimes are thus not extralegal in the sense that they would escape legal regulation whatsoever.

Pluralisation merely frees the legal ordering from its constraining frame of the national state. While this might have positive effects through more effective, fast and adequate regulation in the respective fields, it loosens the link between citizens and their national state as a mediator of legitimacy. Yet, it is the historical achievement of democratic governance in the national state to provide for a systematic connection of citizens to their polities. Democratic law is a practice of collective self-government.[3] As in Jean-Jacques Rousseau's sketch of popular sovereignty, legitimate rule requires the consent of those subordinated to the legal order.[4]

But what is the political frame for the global law of information? As the impact of ICTs on individual lives increases further, the quest for a legitimacy model is largely open. As the information sphere assumes more and more aspects of daily life and public order functions, it becomes increasingly clear that today's liberties of citizenship depend on the capriciousness of large digital companies. In order to discuss possible solutions, this chapter puts the information order in the context of other areas of global law which have experienced a similar transformation. While these are not always best-practice examples, we might still be able to learn from their experiences to imagine models of a legitimate digital space.

The chapter proceeds as follows: the second part maps the most important phenomena of what is called global information law, its subject, history and actors. The third part describes the growing legitimacy demands of global information law, with its exponentially growing impact on individual lives and its relationship to public order functions. In the fourth part, the chapter discusses the feasibility of foundational sketches of democratic legitimacy in this transnational space. The next part develops alternative 'second-tier' concepts of legitimacy based on administrative law vocabulary. These might mitigate the legitimation problems of global information law for the moment, as the chapter concludes in part VI, yet require consciousness that their legitimating resources remain fundamentally incomplete without reference to a global *demos*.

[3] See in particular J Habermas, *Between Facts and Norms*, trans W Rehg (Cambridge, MA, MIT Press, 1998) ch 3.

[4] Rousseau discusses these questions in the Social Contract. See J-J Rousseau, *Discourse on Political Economy and the Social Contract*, trans C Betts (Oxford, Oxford University Press, 1994).

# II. What is Global Information Law?

The *global law of information*[5] refers to the study of ways in which existing, emerging and disruptive technological advances in the area of ICTs interact with existing laws, be it national, supranational or international. It entails associated implications of these technological advances in furthering the development of new laws, regulatory revision and the overall rethinking of traditional legal conceptions. Current advances range from digitisation and automation technologies to domains covered by ICTs, automated data processing and artificial intelligence (AI)-enabled developments in general, matters related to privacy, data protection, cybersecurity, telecommunications, fintech (financial technology), data-driven economic models and, in particular, networked technologies.

For questions like the reach of the right to free speech and free information on the Internet in between filter bubbles and hate speech filters, the development of advanced artificial intelligence, the areas, limits and conditions connected to its use, big data collection, processing and ownership inter alia from the Internet of Things, public and private cybersecurity and cyberwar, development of network infrastructures and hardware development, the notion of global information law can provide a common frame of thought which might develop shared principles across the borders of single issue areas.

Navigating through multifaceted relationships between technological advances and law may not always be straightforward, as such requires in-depth analyses of applicable facts, the interpretation of the applicable legal and regulatory infrastructure, in combination with a minimum technical know-how. In order to fully grasp the notion of global information law, we have to understand societal effects of the emergence of ICTs as a transformative process. The depth of the current transformation combines with the traditional picture of the international law of communication as a law of sovereign states to a profoundly global area of study.

## A. The Emergence of Information and Communication Technology as a Transformative Process

Transformation processes are not extraordinary, but rather are a normal state of play of political communities. Society is in a constant flux, determined inter alia by technology. If we are to try to grasp and label certain transformations, we must look for overarching paradigms which represent the underlying change. If we speak, for example, of globalisation as a transformation process in world society,

[5] The concept of a global information law, albeit with a different connotation and background, has been coined by C Tietje, 'Global Information Law', Beiträge zum Transnationalen Wirtschaftsrecht Heft 107, http://telc.jura.uni-halle.de/sites/default/files/BeitraegeTWR/Heft%20107.pdf.

we identify the increasing integration through worldwide trade and the associated decrease of political importance of national states and its borders as a shaping development. This reduction to a specific paradigm allows for a simplification of the description in a complex system such as society.

In this context, by speaking of a digital transformation, we attempt to describe and isolate the influence that the capacity expansion of information technologies has on processes of social change. For example, the industrial revolution in the second half of the eighteenth and over the course of the nineteenth century was not triggered in isolation by the development of the mechanical loom and the steam engine, but rather was integrated into a complex macroclimate of societal preconditions, such as the ideological erosion of agrarian economic production.[6] At the same time, the success of digital companies takes root in the social inequality and international politics weakened by great power thinking. The divergence between political and economic frames that becomes apparent in the absence of a unified frame of taxation and redistribution offers the more flexible private actors unprecedented chances of wealth accumulation.

This incorporation into the general climate of world society should not, of course, distract from the fact that technological development is a decisive factor in the current transformation. ICTs – that is the ability to transfer, store and process data – change essential elements of our social coexistence in various areas. Importantly, the development of machine intelligence, the collection and use of big data, and the global network infrastructure serve as basic technologies, which, much like the steam engine, can be used almost universally by adapting to various social subtasks. In this universality of development of a new technological platform and its explosive adaptation to new tasks, and hence also the generation of added value, lies the depth of social change.

The boom in 'artificial intelligence' can be explained, among other things, by the fact that both raw data collection and the computing capacity required for analysis have experienced exponential growth in recent years. The interaction of these factors also creates important synergy effects. Through global networking and, in particular, the widespread connection of the world's population to the Internet, so much raw data on human behaviour can be collected that its own term has been created – big data. Big data refers to the amounts of data that can no longer be meaningfully analysed and systematised by manual work but can only be processed automatically.

The computing capacity required for algorithmic processing is provided, among other things, by the exponentially increasing computer power. The decisive factor here is not that the computing speed of integrated circuits doubles every one to two years in accordance with Moore's law;[7] rather, the real

[6] F Braudel, *Sozialgeschichte des 15–18 Jahrhunderts – Aufbruch zur Weltwirtschaft*, vol 3 (Hamburg, Kindler, 1986) 630.

[7] GE Moore, 'Cramming More Components onto Integrated Circuits' (1965) 38(8) *Electronics* 114.

transformative effect goes hand in hand with the associated falling prices for the general availability of computing capacity. The performance that was built into supercomputers for millions of dollars a few years ago can now be found in common smartphones.

The associated changes possess a transformative – and, for the national state, eroding – profundity as they cover the entire breadth of global society, across territorial borders. Access to the Internet (and hence also via the cloud to large computing capacity) is possible almost everywhere because of the global spread of the mobile Internet. In 2019, for the first time, more than 4 billion people (more than half the world's population) used the Internet.[8] In terms of social impact, this encompassing connection of people to the stream of digitalisation seems even more important than the development of advanced artificial intelligence.

Digital transformation, in the sense of the approach proposed here, describes the type of social change that is triggered by the increasing interaction of human existence with ICTs. This development triggers not only a transformative, but also a modifying effect for the very notion of society, by penetrating and changing the lines of conflict that define it. The individual, whose integrity was protected by his involvement in participatory systems and by the guarantee of privacy under fundamental rights, turns from a political actor into a mere user of the digital infrastructure. Conflicts over natural resources are now conflicts over data. Classic warfare is being replaced by cyberwarfare. Territorial sovereignty becomes conflict over bandwidth and infrastructure. No longer are states the most powerful players in these conflicts; rather, it is those with the best access and control in the global data network that prevail.

## B. The International Legal History of a Law of Information

It is important to acknowledge the fundamental change that has occurred in the scope of information law. Most of its history is a classic showcase of international law.[9] From the year 1865, following the invention of the Morse code, the International Telegraph Union, as an international organization, was responsible for the administration of the first transatlantic cable. In 1932, it merged into the International Telecommunication Union, which is still today an important actor in global communication standard setting and coordination. In 1874, the Universal Postal Union was founded. It regulates the international cooperation of postal services and their cross-border interaction. The law of global communication is thus deeply embedded in traditional international law.

[8] Global Digital Report 2019, https://wearesocial.com/blog/2019/01/digital-2019-global-Internet-use-accelerates.

[9] See, in detail, Tietje (n 5) 6–7.

Obviously, the problem and issue areas of this early information law are entirely different from today's concerns. In particular, the rise of the World Wide Web as a main communication channel has essentially changed the configuration of the information order. Yet, it explains how the first exploratory descriptions of 'international Internet law' have been trying to situate the Internet as a subject matter for national states.[10] Notions like 'cyberterritory' were used to bridge the apparent gap between the spatiality of the international legal order and the universality of the Internet space.[11] While it seemed clear that the decisive novelty, the 'right to freedom of information', needed to be preserved, the main orientation of the legal order remained in the Westphalian frame.[12]

## C. The Emergence of Global Information Law

At least in theoretical representations of global information law, the public governance of the Internet plays the most dominant part. With increasing complexity of the transnational societal structure underlying the Internet, the classic international legal approach has given way to a more plural conception. As the Tunis Agenda for the Information Society concluded at the ITU World Summit in 2005: 'Internet governance is the development and application by governments, the private sector and civil society, in their respective roles, of shared principles, norms, rules, decision-making procedures, and programmes that shape the evolution and use of the Internet.'[13] The global information law is an example of dynamic and accelerating transnational law.

The governance of the different areas of the global communication infrastructure is quite diverse. What is called 'the Internet' is neither a holistic nor a centrally determined entity. It involves many thousands of interconnected networks that are ultimately operated by different providers (corporate, public, governmental, etc). What binds these entities together are common and open standards that ensure the interoperability of these networks. ICANN (the Internet Corporation for Assigned Names and Numbers) is but one self-regulatory mechanism to account for these standards.

The diverse set of actors and types of norms in itself is not a unique feature of a law of information. As in other areas of law beyond the state, transnationalisation leads to the emergence of a multitude of normative systems that are not exclusively dependent on the sovereignty of the national state. Attempts

[10] R Uerpmann-Wittzack, 'Principles of International Internet Law' (2010) 11 *German Law Journal* 1245.

[11] ibid 1254.

[12] See, eg Tietje (n 5) 14.

[13] World Summit on the Information Society, 'Tunis Agenda for the Information Society', WSIS-05/TUNIS/DOC/6(Rev 1)-E (2005), www.itu.int/net/wsis/docs2/tunis/off/6rev1.html.

to define transnational law usually include several factors.[14] Philip Jessup used the term 'transnational law'[15] for law regulating actions transcending national frontiers and meant to integrate public and private law rules.[16] Newer approaches favour a definition that involves the hybrid character of transnational law.[17] For Harold Koh, who identified 'transnational legal process' as a distinctive field of study,[18] it is precisely the hybrid, decentralised norm creation between the international and the domestic that characterises the phenomenon.[19] Ralf Michaels remarked that 'in a transnational paradigm, national and international are no longer strictly separated. Private actors appear in the global sphere; states become in some respects more like private actors.'[20] There seems to be relatively wide agreement that transnational law involves, to varying degrees, a weakening of both the public–private and the national–international distinction.

The paradigm case for transnational law is the emergence of a global *lex mercatoria*.[21] The *lex mercatoria*, the customs of globally active merchants, is nothing new in itself. Commercial law beyond national states has existed ever since there has been trade. Its history dates back much further than the history of sovereignty.[22] The codification of national trade law in the course of the eighteenth century and the regulation of trade through sovereign states had temporarily replaced the more direct and unmediated law imposed by merchants themselves. But, as in the course of the 1950s the importance of the transnational interconnectedness of the global economy grew again, the pressing need to account for an

[14] A helpful discussion on the different meanings of the term in the example of the law of the Internet can be found in L Viellechner, *Transnationalisierung des Rechts* (Weilerswist, Velbrück, 2013) 165–66.

[15] P Jessup, *Transnational Law* (New Haven, Yale University Press, 1956) 2: 'all law which regulates actions or events that transcend national frontiers'.

[16] P Jessup, 'The Concept of Transnational Law: An Introduction' (1963–64) 3 *Columbia Journal of Transnational Law* 1.

[17] Nye and Keohane defined transnational interactions as 'movement of tangible and intangible items across state boundaries when at least one actor is not an agent of a government or an intergovernmental organization' and opposed these to transgovernmental interactions, an interaction between the sub-units of different governments. See JS Nye and RO Keohane, 'Transnational Relations and World Politics: An Introduction' (1971) 25 *International Organization* 332.

[18] See H Koh, 'Transnational Legal Process' (1996) 75(1) *Nebraska Law Review* 181.

[19] H Koh, 'Bringing International Law Home' (1998) 35 *Houston Law Review* 641.

[20] R Michaels, 'Three Paradigms of Legal Unification – National, International, Transnational' (2002) 96 *Proceedings of the Annual Meeting of the American Society of International Law* 335.

[21] The literature is huge. See, eg AC Cutler, *Private Power and Global Authority: Transnational Merchant Law in the Global Political Economy* (Cambridge, Cambridge University Press, 2003); N Jansen, *The Making of Legal Authority: Non-legislative Codifications in Historical and Comparative Perspective* (Oxford, Oxford University Press, 2010); G-P Calliess and P Zumbansen, *Rough Consensus and Running Code: A Theory of Transnational Private Law* (Oxford, Hart Publishing, 2010); T Schultz, *Transnational Legality: Stateless Law and International Arbitration* (Oxford, Oxford University Press, 2014). See initially G Teubner, 'Breaking Frames: Economic Globalisation and the Emergence of Lex Mercatoria' (2002) 5 *European Journal of Social Theory* 199.

[22] See S Ogilvie, *Institutions and European Trade* (Cambridge, Cambridge University Press, 2011) 264–66. For a critical discussion on the use of history in the debate, see R Michaels, 'The True Lex Mercatoria: Law beyond the State' (2007) 14 *Indiana Journal of Global Legal Studies* 447.

unmediated merchant's law paved the way to transcending the regulatory frame of the sovereign state. Some concepts of global information law take reference from this use and have suggested the use of the term *lex digitalis*.[23]

The concept of *global* information law conveys no more information than transnationalism. Yet, I believe the term 'global law' is a useful analytical tool, because it expresses something fundamentally new. According to Neil Walker, it indicates a legal model that increasingly goes beyond the scope of traditional concepts of law.[24] Going global allows for recognition of a specific new momentum of the globalisation of a specific issue area in the concept of law.

It has become increasingly clear that the framework of global governance develops area-specifically as a response to concrete regulatory problems. In some cases, this topical governance might develop into so-called self-contained regimes. As Bruno Simma and Dirk Pulkowski define, self-contained regimes are 'subsystems … that embrace a full, exhaustive and definitive set of secondary rules,'[25] thus preventing the application of general international law to wrongful acts.[26] Quite similar to private transnational bodies, self-contained regimes emerge when a legal decision-making body secures the capacity to develop its own law, thus uncoupling from the general framework of international law.[27] As exemplified by the case of World Trade Organization law, this means a continuous development of the law by the appellate bodies, relatively independent of concerns of general international law.

Currently, global information law is in a crucial phase of development. It has condensed into a normative order,[28] yet its processes are still in the phase of chaos. It has not reached the relatively steady state of a self-contained regime that secures the capacity for its own development of the law. Even though some sub-areas of global information law, such as the ICANN system, are showing the first signs of decoupling from the national space,[29] most of the issue areas (eg data protection, regulation of speech rights) remain interlinked to national jurisdictions. Such development is understandable, given that regimes tend to decouple from national politics first when it comes to purely coordinative questions. In issue areas where fundamental rights are at stake, domestic courts are more hesitant to externalise review and norm-setting procedures.

The next decades will be important milestones for a global information law beyond the state. Here, it will become clear whether there are any chances of a

[23] See, eg S Sassen, *Territory, Authority, Rights – From Medieval to Global Assemblages* (Princeton, Princeton University Press, 2008) 230.

[24] N Walker, *Intimations of Global Law* (Cambridge, Cambridge University Press, 2014) 8.

[25] B Simma and D Pulkowski, 'Of Planets and the Universe: Self-Contained Regimes in International Law' (2006) 17 *European Journal of International Law* 493.

[26] ibid 493.

[27] ibid 485.

[28] M Kettemann, *The Normative Order of the Internet – A Theory of Rule and Regulation Online* (Oxford: Oxford University Press, 2020).

[29] Notably, ICANN had a close relationship to the US Chamber of Commerce, which is currently developing towards more independence.

genuinely harmonised global information order. Crucial for this development are the attempts to stand the law on a broader basis of legitimacy. The next section explains why (unlike traditional international information law) the dynamic legal environment of global information law requires a new basis.

## III. Legitimacy Demands of Global Information Law

The sudden expanse of the importance of global information law has affected, inter alia, the human rights of individuals, most obviously their right to privacy. Further, it has systemic effects that replace and erode the traditional legitimacy model of the nation state based on the idea of collective self-determination. Ultimately, the explosive rise of private power puts the public–private distinction out of balance. The information order as it stands thus produces a legitimacy deficit: it breaks old frames, yet remains unable to construct new ones for their replacement.

The rising importance of a legitimate global law of information involves three interrelated aspects. First, technological advances in the area of ICT further accelerate and continuously open new possibilities for their employment. Secondly, much of what we experience as technological advance is ultimately directed to the economic usability of the advance as a product. Thirdly, this economisation leads to the increasing privatisation of the use of ICTs and the multidimensionality of the resulting legal space.

### A. Impact on Individual Lives

The state has been an important mediator for the global protection of human rights, which undoubtedly constitutes a successful model.[30] In areas beyond the control of the national state, such as the Internet, a particular problem is who stands guard for human rights in the same way. Consequently, an intense scholarly debate about the relationship of human rights with all aspects of information technology, such as network design or hard- and software applications, has evolved.[31]

The privacy and integrity of individual lives are particularly at risk of falling prey to the global information order. Big data involves the accumulation of

[30] See N Bhuta, 'The Frontiers of Extraterritoriality: Human Rights as Global Law' in N Bhuta (ed), *The Frontiers of Human Rights*, (Oxford, Oxford University Press, 2016) 1. For a discussion, see A Peters, *Beyond Human Rights: The Legal Status of the Individual in International Law* (Oxford, Oxford University Press, 2016) 408–09.

[31] For an overview, see G Sartor, 'Human Rights and Information Technologies' in R Brownsword, E Scotford and K Yeung (eds), *The Oxford Handbook of Law, Regulation and Technology* (Oxford, Oxford University Press, 2017) 424–50. For a connection of technical questions of Internet architecture and human rights, see C Cath and L Floridi, 'The Design of the Internet's Architecture by the Internet Engineering Task Force (IETF) and Human Rights' (2017) 23 *Science and Engineering Ethics* 449.

data from very different spheres of individual lives that can be automatically reconstructed and put together to form a digital personal identity as a copy of the physical human existence on the Internet.[32] This data collection is possible as every online activity leaves traces that are submitted either voluntarily or without consent through edge devices as well as plugged-in software in the form of aggregated metadata. Further records are created through the sharing of third-party information, a problem that has become more pressing through the integration of connected devices and the Internet of Things in the private and public spheres. Here, again, individual consent hardly provides a threshold to data collection as spyware transfers individual data to third parties.[33] What is more, the opacity of the data processing leaves individuals clueless about the extent of how and for what purpose their data has been used.[34]

The public sector does not have a satisfactory track record in dealing with this problem to date. Governments seem to downplay the problem, given the improvements in economic efficiency data collection could bring about. For example, the EU General Data Protection Regulation hardly gives sufficient guidance in how to deal with new mechanisms of data processing accelerated by artificial intelligence. While, in the short term, this neglect raises concerns for the protection of individual rights, it also offers opportunities. It makes clear that the attempts to regulate information technology territorially have failed. Here, a new understanding of the form, content and addressees of human rights equally offers opportunities, such as the possibility to bind private actors to human rights standards across national borders.

## B. Systemic Imbalance

The legal discourse has largely neglected the systemic imbalance that results from the dynamics of the information order. While it is important to note how the practices impact on individuals' rights, what is connected to these practices is the imbalance that causes the political system to tremble. Democratic governance relying on collective self-determination is increasingly at risk of falling prey to the manipulation of choices. Such influence on public elections has become prominent in the debate, especially since it has been argued that the American presidential election 2016 was influenced from abroad. Further rumours of foreign influence on democratic elections have arisen since.

Technically, targeted advertisements, targeted news and so-called social media trolls – persons that intentionally spur emotional debate through the spreading

[32] B James, 'Ethics of Identity in the Time of Big Data' (2019) 24(5) *First Monday*, https://journals.uic.edu/ojs/index.php/fm/article/view/9624/7756.

[33] S D Esposti, 'When Big Data Meets Dataveillance: The Hidden Side of Analytics' (2014) 12 *Surveillance & Society* 209.

[34] For a helpful summary of how algorithms impact individual human rights, see L McGregor, D Murray and V Ng, 'International Human Rights Law as a Framework for Algorithmic Accountability' (2019) 68 *ICLQ* 315.

of false information – are able to influence the public perception of a candidate.[35] The Council of Europe suggested in a report that 'Fine grained, sub-conscious and personalised levels of algorithmic persuasion may have significant effects on the cognitive autonomy of individuals and their right to form opinions and take independent decisions'.[36] As Jamieson argues, it is not only the fact that such influence through social media is increasing that should make us worry about the quality of democratic elections, but also that even 'serious' media coverage tends to follow the lines of the influencers. The category of quality media loses its credibility with the devastating effect of a loss in trust in the medium as such.[37]

Closely connected to this failure is the prevalent phenomenon of echo chambers. An echo chamber[38] is normally perceived as a metaphor for the self-reinforcement of specific beliefs in a closed communication system. You only hear, albeit in a slightly changed manner, the sound of your own voice, which in this case might reinforce your belief in the correctness of your claim. Echo chambers might occur as an outcome of targeting algorithms in social media platforms. Yet, as Benkler, Faris and Roberts argue:

> Echo chambers ringing with false news make democracies ungovernable. We can imagine a pluralist democracy in which populations contested elections and won or lost based on their votes, without ever sharing a viewpoint on what is going on in the world.[39]

While some authors warn that the effect of these phenomena has been largely overstated,[40] a meaningful forum for opinion and will formation has yet to be found.

This is the Janus face of digital transformation. 'Techno-social engineering' creates a state where technologies and social forces align and impact how we think, perceive and act.[41] This is also a challenge for the legal discipline. As Shoshana Zuboff notes:

> We rely on categories such as 'monopoly' or 'privacy' to contest surveillance capitalist practices. And although these issues are vital, and surveillance capitalist practices are also monopolistic and a threat to privacy, the existing categories nevertheless fall short in identifying and contesting the most crucial facts of this new regime.[42]

[35] SC Woolley and PN Howard (eds) *Computational Propaganda: Political Parties, Politicians, and Political* (Oxford, Oxford University Press, 2018) 3ff.

[36] Council of Europe Committee of Ministers, 'Declaration on the Manipulative Capabilities of Algorithmic Processes', Decl (13/02/2019)1, 2019.

[37] KH Jamieson, *Cyberwar – How Russian Hackers and Trolls Helped Elect a President: What We Don't, Can't and Do Know* (Oxford, Oxford University Press, 2018) 218.

[38] E Pariser, *Filter Bubble – What The Internet is Hiding from You* (New York, Penguin, 2011).

[39] Y Benkler, R Faris and H Roberts, *Network Propaganda – Manipulation, Disinformation and Radicalization in American Politics* (Oxford, Oxford University Press, 2018) 4.

[40] A Bruns, *Are Filter Bubbles Real?* (Polity, 2019).

[41] B Frischmann, E Selinger, *Re-Engineering Humanity*, (Cambridge: Cambridge University Press, 2018) 4.

[42] S Zuboff, *The Age of Surveillance Capitalism* (New York, Public Affairs, 2019) 14.

## C. Transnational Private Power

Ultimately, the global information order witnesses an unprecedented rise of transnational private power. Academics have continuously tried to exemplify this rise. In 2000, a report argued that of the 100 largest economies in the world, only 49 were countries, while 51 were corporations.[43] The report used a highly debated comparison between the GDP of a country and a company's revenue.[44] Yet what is interesting to illustrate in this respect is that in a revision of the report in 2016, already 71 of the largest economies were corporate.[45] The tendency of large corporations to grow exponentially also finds root in the platform logic of the digital space, which tends to promote winner-takes-all scenarios.

As a side effect, when the state transforms into a digital society, the traditional distinction between public and private as a central aspect of state order disappears. The link between public and private becomes especially visible in transnational concepts of law and politics, which reach beyond the different spheres.[46] What we can observe is that functions that are originally attributed to the public sphere, like communication infrastructures, are increasingly performed by private actors. In addition, norm and standard setting becomes privatised and voluntary. This role change towards the privatisation of public order has not been accompanied by the expansion of public responsibilities of large companies.

While most Western economies saw large waves of privatisation of (communication) infrastructure in the 1970s, the trend has turned since the 2000s and now points towards greater public influence. Yet, this trend has limits: in large parts of the world, private initiative is the only prospect for a connection to the world. We see this, for example, in the growing South-East Asian investments on the African continent and its communication infrastructures.[47] On the other hand, even in industrialised societies, the key infrastructures relevant for the digital transformation are not public. If we consider the reliance on the storage of data on private server clouds, for example, we see a growing dependence of public functions on the provision of private infrastructure.

At the same time, the transnational character of phenomena on the Internet make it difficult to attribute liability to the responsible actors.[48] As a result of its cross-border character, national legislation has difficulty controlling private digital action. Through the clever choice of the legal forum in which they act,

[43] 'Top 200: The Rise of Corporate Global Power', https://ips-dc.org/top_200_the_rise_of_corporate_global_power/.

[44] For discussion, see Floridi (n 1) 174.

[45] M Babic, J Fichtner and EM Heemskerk, 'States versus Corporations: Rethinking the Power of Business in International Politics' (2017) 52(4) *The International Spectator* 20, 27.

[46] HM Watt, 'Private International Law beyond the Schism' (2015) 2 *Transnational Legal Theory* 347.

[47] For a nuanced analysis, see F Lisk, '"Land Grabbing" or Harnessing of Development Potential in Agriculture? East Asia's Land-Based Investments in Africa' (2013) 26 *The Pacific Review* 563.

[48] Roth-Isigkeit (n 2) 39–41.

private companies can effectively determine the conditions for the regulation of technical progress, and the attribution of liabilities and even their taxation.[49] While public communities increasingly raise consciousness of the problem and some measures to combat tax avoidance have been taken,[50] there is still a considerable gap to close.

In order to release the legitimatory pressure of democratic requirements, private companies start to shape the regulatory environment and become norm entrepreneurs.[51] They implement common and voluntary codes of conduct, non-binding ethical guidelines that regulate their behaviour and that of their competitors. While this might sound advantageous, one central aspect is that while they might implement favourable legislative conditions for themselves, such corporate norm-setting is at odds with the principle of democratic self-determination.

Most importantly, increasingly it is corporate actors who determine what is private and what is public. What we consider as private is in fact easily decipherable by data analytics. In turn, what we consider as a public statement might remain unread on a social network, as the sorting and display algorithms see fit.

## IV. Foundational Concepts of Legitimacy

Global information law thus opens a gap between the legitimation resources that are conserved in national states and the legitimacy requirements of actual decision-making. Simply closing the gap through renationalisation of the subject matter is an option that is unavailable as a result of the interdependencies of the network structure of the Internet. For example, national jurisdictions might offer laws against hate speech on the Internet. Yet, unlike in the case of housebreaking, which is an act that can be attributed to a specific physical territory and thus a sovereign jurisdiction, it will not be possible to ultimately contain the whole phenomenon of hate speech within a national legal framework. The search for a foundational concept of legitimacy thus tries to imagine a transfer of the concept of democratic legitimacy to the level beyond the state.

### A. Self-determination as the Gold Standard of Legitimacy

The central concern of a transfer of democratic legitimacy to the level beyond the state is the concept of self-determination. The exercise of political authority in

[49] A Bell, *Forum Shopping and Venue in Transnational Litigation* (Oxford, Oxford University Press, 2003).

[50] See, eg the Anti-Tax Avoidance package of the European Commission of January 2016, www.ec.europa.eu/taxation_customs/business/company-tax/anti-tax-avoidance-package_en.

[51] G Teubner, 'The Corporate Codes of Multinationals: Company Constitutions beyond Corporate Governance and Co-Determination' in R Nickels (ed), *Conflict of Laws and Laws of Conflict in Europe and Beyond: Patterns of Supranational and Transnational Juridification* (Oxford, Hart Publishing, 2009).

any form can only be justified with reference to those who are ultimately subjected to it. In line with the enlightenment model, legitimation requires the identity of the ruler and the ruled. A legitimate global information law thus needs to rely on a reconstruction of democratic authority in the global sphere.

This connection of popular sovereignty to the constitution of the national state appears most clearly in Habermas' understanding of law as a practice of collective self-government. Habermas' discourse theory of law and democracy locates the nodal point of legitimacy in the legal procedures that create the law, given that they fulfil two conditions. First, these procedures must ensure the inclusion of everyone concerned, and secondly, the laws must be created in a deliberative process of collective will formation.[52] The (conservative) hope is that, through the interpenetration of popular sovereignty and legal form, the legitimacy model of constitutional democracy reassembles on the global level.

The decisive aspect of self-determination as the 'gold standard' of democratic governance is a reunion of the active role of those subordinated to the law with legal formality. Klaus Günther has argued that this requirement has already condensed to a universal code,

> which guarantee[s] the minimum requirements of democratic self-determination: the right to change the role between author and addressee of a legal norms, transparency of procedures of opinion and will formation, imputability of decision and responsibility for consequences, equal access to procedures and equal rights of participation for third parties.[53]

## B. Democracy and Institutional Reform

In principle, the democratic governance of the global information order would require far-reaching institutional reform. This reform is often associated with the concept of global constitutionalism. Constitutionalism appeared in the 1990s primarily as mitigation for the legitimation gap as a consequence of the exercise of non-state authority.[54] It is through the assumption of political unity beyond the state, often suggested in the vocabulary of a cosmopolitan community, that constitutionalism can suggest a frame of reference for the exercise of non-state authority.[55]

[52] Habermas (n 3) 121–23.

[53] K Günther, 'Legal Pluralism or Uniform Concept of Law – Globalisation as a Problem of Legal Theory' (2008) 5 *No Foundations – Journal of Extreme Legal Positivism* 18.

[54] S Kadelbach, 'Konstitutionalisierung und Rechtspluralismus – Über die Konkurrenz zweier Ordnungsentwürfe' (2017) 153 *Archiv für Rechts- und Sozialphilosophie* 97.

[55] See, eg M Kumm, 'The Cosmopolitan Turn in Constitutionalism: On the Relationship in Constitutionalism in and beyond the State' in JL Dunoff and J Trachtman (eds), *Ruling the World? – Constitutionalism, International Law and Global Governance* (Cambridge, Cambridge University Press, 2009) 258; M Avbelj and J Komarek, 'Four Visions of Constitutional Pluralism' (2008) 2 *European Journal of Legal Studies* 325. For criticism, see N Krisch, *Beyond Constitutionalism: The Pluralist Structure of Postnational Law* (Oxford, Oxford University Press, 2010) 67: 'It embodies a peculiarly modern trust in the ability of mankind to rationally govern itself.'

The concept of digital constitutionalism[56] is thus directed at the development of an institutional frame that secures minimum conditions of democratic governance. Therefore, it suggests a construction of unity of political order. The unity of legal order, in contrast, comes rather as a by-product for the functioning transfer of the legitimacy of the political order to the practical exercise of authority.

At its heart, digital constitutionalism is concerned with the civilisation of political authority. Arguably, democracy in its current understanding is ill-prepared to create a level playing field between the public and private spheres. There are no visible tendencies of a development of a shared political culture that would be a precondition for a process of bottom-up constitutionalisation of the digital space.[57]

## C. New Institutional Frames

Is there any chance for the foundational model of democratic legitimacy to prevail in the digital realm? From the outset, it seems to have better chances than in other areas of globalised law. Gunther Teubner has argued that constituent power is 'a communicative potential, a type of *social energy*'.[58] Through its origin in communication between physical subjects, global information law arises in the presence of this potential. While intermediaries weaken the connections between individual participants as subjects of the network, the social energy would require 'the consciousness and corporeality of actual people'[59] in order to unfold.

Thus, digital constitutionalisation as the emergence of a constituted order would first require a transnational public sphere[60] where actual people see themselves as subjects of the information order. One central impediment to this individual consciousness is the mediation of individual contributions through corporate platforms. Emerging technologies allow for an alternative organisational integration. For example, peer-to-peer network infrastructures, such as platforms based on distributed ledger technology, would in principle allow for multi-stakeholder relationships whereby it is made possible to reduce dependency

[56] For a first use of the concept, see L Gill, D Redeker and U Gasser, 'Towards Digital Constitutionalism? Mapping Attempts to Craft an Internet Bill of Rights', Berkman Center Research Publication No 2015-15 (2015), https://ssrn.com/abstract=2687120. See also B Fitzgerald, 'Software as Discourse? A Constitutionalism for Information Society' (1999) 24 *Alternative Law Journal* 144. For a helpful discussion on the matter, see E Celeste, 'Digital Constitutionalism: a new systematic theorisation', 33 International Review of Law, Computers & Technology, 76.

[57] Again, in Habermas' words, 'world citizens do not form a collective that would be held together by a political interest in the self-assertion of a way of life that shapes their identity': J Habermas, *The Crisis of the European Union: A Response*, trans C Cronin (Cambridge, Polity, 2014) 64–65.

[58] G Teubner, *Constitutional Fragments: Societal Constitutionalism and Globalization* (Oxford, Oxford University Press, 2012) 63 (emphasis added).

[59] ibid 63.

[60] For an elaboration of this argument in global governance, see P Nanz and J Steffek, 'Global Governance, Participation and the Public Sphere' (2004) 39 *Government and Opposition* 314.

on third parties with centralised governance. Changes in the communication infrastructure might thus substantially improve the ability of a transnational public sphere to emerge.

So far, the concrete formation of a global public sphere has been largely topical on the event of global crisis. Greta Thunberg, for example, has succeeded in raising awareness for the climate catastrophe and provided focal points for a common discourse. Teubner argues that constitutional moments are crucially connected with the experience of crisis. 'Ultimately, then, it is a system's pathological tendencies that bring forth the constitutional moment, the moment of catastrophe, in which the decision is made between the energy's complete destruction and its self-restraint.'[61] Yet, these catastrophes in single areas tend to produce tunnel visions of the public interest of a polity.[62] A global pandemic might raise awareness of problems in the global health system, yet it does not improve the principles of governance of the digital world. Even worse, spill-over effects might lead to distortion within the digital system and introduce a 'state of exception' logic. A recent case is the introduction of surveillance measures in China to enforce contact limitations in the coronavirus crisis.[63] As at the time of writing, the use of mobile phone service provider data to combat the spread of the disease is increasingly discussed in continental Europe.[64] In regime-specific governance, there is competition over which issue receives the most attention from the global public.

Yet, if there is an area to transcend this tendency of regime-specific public interest, it will probably be the area of global information law. Since, in a globalised world, communication provides the backbone of any meaningful political human interaction, it might become the necessary precondition for any topical engagement. There is reason to be mildly optimistic. As Günther contends:

> In the last step, we have to trust the historical experience of the democratic constitutional nation state to ground our hopes that people will re-activate the idea of a constitutionalised democratic self-legislation against the networks of legal experts who only administer the universal code of legality.[65]

## V. Administrative Concepts as Second-Tier Providers of Legitimacy

Foundational concepts are utopian insofar as they need considerable political action to be realised. Looking at the current state of global information law, such

[61] Teubner (n 58) 82.
[62] ibid 156.
[63] *New York Times* (1 March 2020), www.nytimes.com/2020/03/01/business/china-coronavirus-surveillance.html.
[64] *Tagesschau* (27 March 2020), www.tagesschau.de/inland/corona-handydaten-103.html.
[65] Günther (n 53) 20.

institutional reform seems distant. This section illustrates what might be called 'second-tier' providers of legitimacy. 'Second-tier' means that while they do not live up to the demands of democratic constitutionalism, they still introduce some basic legitimacy requirements in global information law.

## A. A Shift in Vocabulary

One of the central legitimation problems of global information law stems from the lack in accountability, transparency and participation. Administrative law principles could provide for criteria for a review of this normative output without necessarily having to relate back to the legitimacy chain that starts with a constituted *demos*. These lower demands make the design and control of review procedures easier to achieve. Referring to administrative law vocabulary, similar to constitutional discourse, entails the hope to be able to connect to conceptual debates in domestic law to understand phenomena of technology law beyond the state.

In this perspective, legitimacy is gradual. Some institutional set-ups are more legitimate than others. Importantly, this gradual concept of legitimacy involves a shift of perspective. It departs from the formal-procedural frame of democratic legitimacy to a Dworkinian line of argument. Dworkin argues that 'any theory about the correct analysis of an interpretive political concept must be a normative theory: a theory of political morality about the circumstances in which something ought or ought not to happen.'[66] Such approaches thus replace the collective will as a formal-procedural point of reference with the 'relatively mundane demand to ensure that appropriate forms of transparency, participation, representativeness, and accountability become an integral part of governance practice'.[67] Currently, however, such modest representations might be the only plausible answer to the challenges of global information law.

## B. Administrative Principles

In practice, this would mean the application of a diverse set of administrative principles to global information law. As a general theoretical approach, the research strand of global administrative law is one of the most influential schools of global legal thought dealing with plurality and the legitimacy of global governance. In this perspective, law beyond the state transforms from a contractual basis into a 'global administrative space'.[68] In this space, a variety of public and private actors produce

[66] R Dworkin, 'A New Philosophy for International Law' (2013) 41 *Philosophy and Public Affairs* 11.
[67] Kumm (n 55) 273.
[68] B Kingsbury and N Krisch, 'Global Governance and Global Administrative Law in the International Legal Order' (2006) 17 *European Journal of International Law* 1.

legal acts with external effects on states and individuals through rule generation, interpretation and application that are not subject to judicial review.[69] Remedy for this lack of review can be found by drawing analogies to rights in administrative procedures. General principles of public law such as legality, rationality, proportionality, rule of law and human rights potentially provide for a legitimating frame.[70]

Other voices have equally suggested that transnational decision-making lacks a frame of reference to ground its authority.[71] Von Bogdandy and Venzke find inspiration for a recalibration of democracy in Articles 9–12 of the Treaty of the European Union, which are supposed to provide a vision of an international democracy.[72] The principles contain basic procedural rules, such as democratic elections of judges, publicness of decisions and due process guarantees.[73] They guarantee a global citizenship on the basis of 'equality, representation, transparency, participation, deliberation, and responsiveness'.[74] The exercise of authority is legitimate when it observes these principles.

Indeed, these general approaches might provide for an increased legitimacy of global information law in the sense that they could begin a process of bottom-up constitutionalisation. If the surrounding institutional frame becomes increasingly dense, leeway for the arbitrary exercise of transnational corporate power shrinks. When, for example, algorithms in social networks are put under obligations of justification, this might at least improve the human rights protection of concerned individuals while at the same time limiting the impediment on collective will formation.

## C. Risks and Benefits of 'Second-Tier' Options

'Second-tier' providers thus formulate non-constitutional concepts to evaluate the legitimacy of global governance. Their central concern is how to preserve the

[69] The concept of global administrative law distinguishes between two general types of administrative action: constititutive and substantive. Sometimes the category of procedural law is added. See B Kingsbury, 'The Concept of "Law" in Global Administrative Law' (2009) 20 *European Journal of International Law* 34. The first type, constitutive administrative law, concerns the delegation of power to administrative bodies and their internal structure. Kingsbury counts these constitutive rules, which in most jurisdictions would belong to the body of constitutional law in the narrow sense to a body of emerging administrative law. The primary advantage of the concept is the capacity to address the second type of global administrative action, which Kingsbury defines as substantive. This type refers to the output of global administration, which can be understood in general terms as producing norms and decisions. Both types have external effects on other global administrative entities, states or individuals, which have to be legitimated through the administrative process.

[70] ibid 32–33.

[71] A von Bogdandy and I Venzke, *In Whose Name? – A Public Law Theory of International Adjudication* (Oxford, Oxford University Press, 2014) 9–10.

[72] ibid 135–6.

[73] ibid 157–8.

[74] Ibid 147.

legitimacy of public arrangements and private norm creation at the same time. Such squaring of the circle might imply considerable risks. If the constitutional type of legitimacy demands is taken out of the picture, these approaches might end up legitimating administrative action that is in fact illegitimate.[75] As Koskenniemi argues, 'legitimacy is not about substance. Its point is to *avoid* such substance but nonetheless to uphold a *semblance* of substance … to ensure a warm feeling in the audience'.[76]

At the same time, 'second-tier' options might be better than nothing. If a global political frame is missing, these fairly general principles could provide for patches for the most pressing problems in the information society. International legal discourse, so the famous argument goes, oscillates between apology and utopia, between concreteness and normativity, always tragically required to give preference to one over the other.[77] Foundational legitimacy requirements seem to be unavoidably utopian, with no possibility of being realised. 'Second-tier' options might reinforce the asymmetries and injustices already present in today's global information law and be apologetic to current power dynamics.

For the moment, the most convincing solution to deal with these dilemmas is a certain consciousness and reflexivity. Most likely, the introduction of basic accountability and justification procedures will be celebrated as a revolutionary achievement of information governance. Facing these celebrations, we should take note of the fact that such minimum requirements of the rule of law are self-evident, in particular when corporations increasingly assume public order functions. Rather, we should continue to insist on a political solution for the information order that keeps its perspective on the truly revolutionary achievement of collective self-determination.

## VI. Conclusion

This chapter has argued that the traditional understanding and scope of global information law has fundamentally changed, given the disruptive effect of technological advances. While traditional dogmatic resources of the international legal order of information retain importance in the interpretation and reading of the law, the pluralisation of the global communication infrastructure has effectuated a shift in actors and institutions. While international law can access the legitimating resources of the sovereign national state, the case is different with processes that

[75] N Krisch, 'Global Administrative Law and the Constitutional Ambition' in P Dobner and M Loughlin (eds), *The Twilight of Constitutionalism* (Oxford, Oxford University Press, 2010) 245.

[76] M Koskenniemi, 'Miserable Comforters: International Relations as New Natural Law' (2009) 15 *European Journal of International Relations* 395, 409.

[77] M Koskenniemi, *From Apology to Utopia – The Structure of International Legal Argument* (Cambridge, Cambridge University Press, 2009).

take place completely outside the traditional frame. Global information law thus has a crucial legitimacy deficit.

In order to overcome this deficit, this chapter has first examined suggestions that link the processes of the global information order back to a foundational concept of democratic legitimacy. While foundational concepts provide an important utopian perspective, they currently have no chance of being realised. 'Second-tier' options, in contrast, are more likely to provide pragmatic mitigation for global information law's legitimacy demands, yet cannot replace the holistic view of a human polity. When the legitimacy debate on global information law picks up pace, it is necessary to be conscious that 'second-tier' options might provide short-term patches yet cannot replace the fundamentally necessary political perspective on the global information infrastructure.

# PART II

# Information and Technology Revolution and Its Impact on Democracy and the Public Sphere

# 5

# The Disruptive Effects of Social Media Platforms on Democratic Will-Formation Processes

HOAI-THU NGUYEN [1]

## I. Introduction

Technological developments in the information age are having an incisive impact on democratic processes in the twenty-first century. On the one hand, facilitated access to information can promote citizens' participation in democratic processes. On the other hand, voters can, through the manipulation and individual targeting of information, be influenced in a much more unregulated, and possibly illegitimate, manner than was possible before, by both political and commercial actors. The disinformation campaigns during the Covid-19 pandemic are just some of the most recent examples, in which much false information has been spread via social networks. Much of the focus of the scholarly debate and research in this area has been on the intentional interference in democratic elections through the purposeful distribution of misleading information over social media networks, and the tension that this poses with the freedom of expression and, albeit to a lesser extent, the right to privacy. In this chapter, I argue that such a focus is too narrow and that the problem goes further than just intentional disinformation campaigns.

Western democratic systems rest on the idea of direct, free, equal and secret elections. This implies voters must be able to make their electoral choices freely, without fear or coercion, but also without any form of manipulation while they form their decision. Such manipulation can occur in different ways in the online sphere and on social media platforms. In addition to (i) the intentional spreading of disinformation with a political motive as mentioned above, manipulation can also be in the form of: (ii) inadvertent sharing of false information

[1] Parts of this chapter are based on the author's previous work in: HT Nguyen, 'Populism in Times of Social Media' in S Hardt, AW Heringa and HT Nguyen Hardt (eds), *Protecting the Liberal Constitution in a Populist Age* (Eleven International Publishing, 2020).

(misinformation); (iii) intentional pushing of (non-problematic) information with a political motive (propaganda); and (iv) inadvertent pushing of (any kind of) information without a political motive through algorithmic decisions. Social media platforms are designed with the objective of attracting users to, and keeping the users on, the platform, as well as making the platform more attractive to advertisers. For that reason, and with a view to achieving this objective, algorithms prioritise certain content over other content on platforms such as Facebook and Twitter. Such prioritisation in pushing information – based on what in essence are economic reasons – can, in turn, influence democratic discourses. It is argued in this chapter that social media platforms are thus not only a tool through which political and commercial actors may exert influence on the will formation of voters. Rather, they are, albeit perhaps unintentionally, themselves actors that disrupt and interfere with the free will-formation process of voters.

This chapter aims to analyse these disruptive effects of social media platforms on the free will formation of voters and to show that the rise and use of such platforms have changed how we communicate not only in private, but, most importantly, also in public. In doing so, it first describes the relationship between mass media and the democratic will-formation process in liberal democracies. The second section analyses the impact of the technological revolution on such processes in general, before the third section takes a look at the different ways in which the democratic will-formation process can be disrupted through social media platforms. The fourth section deals with the various types of such disruptions and explains why the issue goes further than just intentional disinformation. The fifth section then briefly summarises the advantages and disadvantages of the technological revolution for democratic processes, before the sixth and final section concludes with an outlook on how to best mitigate the disruptive effects of social media on democratic will-formation processes.

## II. Mass Media Institutions and Democratic Will Formation

Western democratic systems rest on the idea of direct, free, equal and secret elections. Elections lie at the heart of systems of representative democracy, which rest on the basic principle that those who govern are, at regular intervals, elected by those who are governed, thus setting them apart from systems of direct democracy.[2] It is through regular elections that the represented are able to express their wishes and it is through regular elections that the representatives will, in general, be held accountable for (not) responding thereto. That democratic elections must be fair and free is necessarily implied in the concept of liberal democracy, also being

[2] B Manin, *The Principles of Representative Government* (Cambridge University Press, 1997) 6.

expressed, for example, in terms such as *freiheitlich demokratische Grundordnung* in Germany.

Free elections do not, however, mean only that both voters and those to be voted should have equal participation rights and that voters must be able to cast their votes without coercion. It necessarily also implies that voters can form their opinion and make their electoral choice in an open and free process, without pressure or other undue influences. This requires the opportunity of unimpeded collective and personal political will formation, which, in turn, translates into the right to freely receive (politically relevant) information, a right inextricably linked to freedom of free speech in the political context and a right also protected by it. The Bundesverfassungsgericht has, for example, stated in this regard that the freedom of speech and the freedom of the press under Article 5 of the German Basic Law also guarantees the free formation of public opinion.[3] This is because a democratic state necessarily requires a free, open and unregulated will-formation process by the people, which, in turn, accumulates in the election of parliament itself.[4] This, in turn, requires a well-functioning public sphere, in which public opinions can be formed on the basis of freely available information. Only in a polity in which the public has free access to information can they exercise proper democratic control.[5] The task of providing such information falls in the first instance to institutions of mass media, such as television, radio and newspapers,[6] who serve to inform and educate the public by putting information into context and providing a place for societal debates, thereby influencing the formation of public opinion.[7]

Traditionally, the kinds of issues that became public discussion points were influenced by the media. The media's strategic use of triggering and framing certain topics could have a decisive influence on whether those topics became part of the political public sphere.[8] According to Habermas, journalists, together with lobbyists, advocates, experts, moral entrepreneurs and intellectuals, carry the political communication in society.[9] Politicians, located in the centre of the political system, both take part in the formation of and need to respond to public opinion.[10]

[3] BVerfG, Judgment of the Second Senate of 19 July 1966, 2 BvF 1/65, para 136.

[4] 2 BvF 1/65, para 136.

[5] J Habermas, S Lennox and F Lennox, 'The Public Sphere: An Encyclopedia Article' [1974] *New German Critique* 49, 49.

[6] J Habermas, *Strukturwandel der Öffentlichkeit* (Luchterhand, 1962).

[7] BP Lange, 'Media and Elections: Some Reflections and Recommendations' in BP Lange and D Ward (eds), *The Media and Elections: A Handbook and Comparative Study* (Lawrence Erlbaum Associates, 2004) 208.

[8] J Habermas, 'Political Communication in Media Society: Does Democracy Still Enjoy an Epistemic Dimension? The Impact of Normative Theory on Empirical Research' (2006) 16 *Communication Theory* 411, 415.

[9] ibid 416.

[10] ibid 416.

Public opinion is important for representative democracy and responsive governments insofar as they indicate a frame of reference for what citizens would accept as legitimate decisions by the government.[11] The act of casting a vote is then nothing but the end result of the opinion-formation process of each individual voter.[12] Achenbach and Müller-Mall argue that an election not only presupposes the individual will-formation of each voter, but at the same time it also constitutes the readable (*lesbar*) expression of collective political will formation of the electorate, through the synchronisation and equalisation of the act of voting itself (same time, same ballot paper, same number of votes).[13] In this way, it builds a link between the will-formation process of the represented before the cast of the ballot with the actions of those representing them afterwards.[14] In this sense, it is only through elections that the subset of individual interests of voters are turned into categorical societal interests,[15] not least through the political parties functioning as the intermediary.

In a liberal democracy, citizens rely on the media to provide them with information, on the basis of which they then form an opinion, whether political and otherwise. The media is expected in this regard to provide the public with orientation in a 'complex and otherwise unmanageable society'.[16] Similarly, those representing the citizens in a political system may equally rely on the media to put information into context prior to taking policy decisions. In fact, there is a certain interdependence between the traditional media, understood here as mass media institutions of press, television and radio, and the politicians, at least when the former was still the dominant media form in the public sphere.[17] While politicians relied on journalists to have their policies and messages transmitted to the wider public, journalists relied on politicians for their stories and information.[18]

The rise of social media has had an effect on this relationship by changing the way we communicate not only in private, but also in public. While it is true that new digital media have not replaced, but rather exist in addition to, the traditional media (ie the press, radio and television), what has changed is that 'online

[11] ibid 418.

[12] J von Achenbach and S Müller-Mall, 'Die Wahl und das Kreuz – Formalisierung und Form des Demokratischen' in A Koschorke (ed), *Komplexität und Einfachheit* (JB Metzler, 2004).

[13] ibid.

[14] ibid.

[15] S Piattoni, 'The European Union: Legitimating Values, Democratic Principles and Institutional Architectures' in S Piattoni (ed), *The European Union – Democratic Principles and Institutional Architectures in Times of Crisis* (Oxford University Press, 2015) 21–22.

[16] F Zimmermann and M Kohring, 'Mistrust, Disinforming News, and Vote Choice: A Panel Survey on the Origins and Consequences of Believing Disinformation in the 2017 German Parliamentary Election' [2020] *Political Communication* 1, 4.

[17] C Fisher, D Marshall and K McCallum, 'Bypassing the Press Gallery: From Howard to Hanson' (2018) 167 *Media International Australia* 57, 58.

[18] Fisher, Marshall and McCallum (ibid) also note that this 'symbiotic' relationship was not without conflicts as journalists were at the same time expected to hold the government accountable, which could be conflicting with their dependence on politicians.

technologies serve communication processes that are no longer one-directional'.[19] Instead, social media platforms in particular have transformed the way in which we communicate in the public sphere from a 'one-to-many' structure between traditional media and the wider public to a 'many-to-many' structure, in which essentially every citizen can distribute information to a wider audience through social media platforms.[20]

The relationship between media and citizens, but also between media and politicians, as described above, is thereby diffused. First, it has become more and more difficult for traditional media institutions to inform the public with a view to influencing the formation of a public opinion, as they have found themselves increasingly in competition with an increasing number of media alternatives, both online and offline. A highly fragmented media system, in which a variety of different media outlets exist, arguably also makes the political system in which it operates more vulnerable towards disinformation and false messages. In turn, a political system in which there is a universal recognition of a limited number of news media of high quality and reputation will have a more unifying effect on its audiences.[21] Secondly, traditional media outlets also find themselves perhaps no longer indispensable as a means for politicians to communicate with their voters. Or, put differently, the rise of social media platforms no longer necessitates journalists as an intermediary between politicians and citizens.

This is at the same time accompanied by a trend of increasing mistrust in the traditional media. In the last decades, the traditional media, such as television, radio and newspapers, have lost their authority and are increasingly viewed as the mouthpiece of the (political) elite.[22] Trust in traditional media sources varies not insignificantly between the different countries in the European Union, with small variations between the type of media outlet, according to a survey conducted on request of the European Commission in February 2020.[23] While, on average, 70 per cent of the respondents of a Eurobarometer report of February 2018 trust or tend to trust the information they receive through the radio,[24] in Hungary it was 50 per cent, in Italy 57 per cent, in Germany 75 per cent, in Spain 74 per cent, in France 76 per cent and in Finland as many as 91 per cent of the respondents.

[19] B Thomass, 'Deficits and Potentials in of the Public Sphere' in J Trappel et al (eds), *Media in Europe Today* (Intellect, 2011) 123.

[20] J Tucker et al, 'From Liberation to Turmoil: Social Media and Democracy' (2017) 28 *Journal of Democracy* 46, 48–49.

[21] E Humprecht, F Esser and P Van Aelst, 'Resilience to Online Disinformation: A Framework for Cross-National Comparative Research' [2020] *International Journal of Press/Politics* 1, 8.

[22] P Gerbaudo, 'Social Media and Populism: An Elective Affinity?' (2018) *Media, Culture & Society* 745, 748–49.

[23] Flash Barometer 464, 'Fake News and Disinformation Online', Survey conducted by TNS Political & Social at the request of the European Commission, Directorate-General for Communications Networks (February 2018), https://ec.europa.eu/commfrontoffice/publicopinion/index.cfm/survey/getsurveydetail/instruments/flash/surveyky/2183.

[24] 15% fully trust and 55% tend to trust the information accessed through the radio.

For information accessed through television in the EU, an average 66 per cent of the respondents indicated that they trust or tend to trust such information,[25] with 47 per cent in Hungary, 56 per cent in Italy, 70 per cent in Germany, 57 per cent in Spain, 63 per cent in France and 90 per cent in Finland doing so. For information accessed through printed newspapers and magazines, in the EU an average 63 per cent of the respondents indicated that they trust or tend to trust such information,[26] with corresponding figures of 33 per cent in Hungary, 60 per cent in Italy, 70 per cent in Germany, 65 per cent in Spain, 71 per cent in France and 90 per cent in Finland.[27]

Users that have become more sceptical and no longer trust that the traditional media are providing them with trustworthy political information are more inclined to rely on alternative media outlets for orientation.[28] This does not necessarily mean that users who have a sceptical view on mainstream media are more inclined to refer to online media outlets, as subsequent studies have shown that 'scepticism or trust in online news were not related to using many of the features of online technology'.[29] Thus, users who trust the mainstream media will still consume mainstream media, both offline and online. Sceptical mainstream media users, however, show a correlation to the consumption of non-mainstream websites.[30] This, in turn, provides a good opportunity for any actor looking to spread disinformation to step in and reach their audience via non-mainstream media outlets, including but not necessarily limited to social media. Social media can thus constitute an ideal place for distrustful citizens to look for and exchange information, alternative to that found in established media, which they might be more inclined to believe, if not for the simple reason that they diverge from the mainstream media coverage.[31] So, while social media can serve as an alternative media source for citizens who distrust the mainstream media, this can pose a significant problem in that the lack of a filtering exercise normally done by journalists makes, for example, the creation and sharing of disinformation much easier.

## III. The Impact of Technological Revolution

The IT revolution has brought with it a rise of alternative media platforms, most notably social media platforms such as Facebook, Twitter, TikTok and Instagram.

[25] 12% fully trust and 54% tend to trust the information accessed through television.

[26] 10% fully trust and 53% tend to trust the information accessed through printed newspapers and magazines.

[27] Flash Barometer 464 (n 23).

[28] Y Tsfati and Y Peri, 'Mainstream Media Skepticism and Exposure to Sectorial and Extranational News Media: The Case of Israel' [2006] *Mass Communication & Society* 165.

[29] Y Tsfati, 'Online News Exposure and Trust in the Mainstream Media: Exploring Possible Associations' [2010] *American Behavioral Scientist* 22, 39.

[30] ibid.

[31] Zimmermann and Kohring (n 16) 4.

What distinguishes social media platforms from traditional media such as TV, radio or press is that it offers users – in this case politicians, voters and interest groups – the possibility to directly engage with and communicate with citizens and to circumvent journalistic interventions.[32] Information, whether political or not, can be transmitted on social media directly to voters without having journalists filtering, editing or framing the content, as would be common in press, television or radio. Doing so requires neither special technical knowledge nor unlimited financial means.[33] At the same time, social media platforms, through their algorithmic architecture, can influence what information is being transmitted to their users, what is prioritised and what is silenced. It is thus not entirely true that social media platforms give politicians direct access to voters without any kind of filters. It is more that the type of filter has changed, from journalistic editing to algorithmic ranking.

On the one hand, this means that voices can be enabled to be heard on social media that, for example, might normally be excluded from the public debate because they are not represented in the traditional mass media. This can include both citizens and political outsiders that, for one reason other another, are not part of the public debate in the mainstream media, which can play a gatekeeping role in this regard. Social media thus makes it possible for citizens to find like-minded people as well as to find politicians and political parties which they would like to support. This was also witnessed, for example, during protest movements such as the Arab Spring, the Gezi Protests in Turkey and the Stuttgart 21 protests in Germany.[34]

On the other hand, it can also mean that it becomes succinctly easier to spread false information, whether intentionally or unintentionally. By bypassing journalistic filters, any politician, but also any other user, can influence public discussions without having to have their information necessarily fact checked. Indeed, this has been a contentious problem throughout the Covid-19 crisis, and most recently with regard to statements by US President Trump, which resulted in Twitter starting to flag his tweets. Whereas, in the past, populist politicians mostly had to rely on coverage in tabloid media to become visible, social media platforms have now made it much easier for them to gain 'direct, unmediated access to the people's grievances'.[35] In addition to bypassing the gatekeepers in the traditional media that might be reluctant to print or broadcast certain messages in their coverage, politicians, and in particular populist politicians, can bypass the risk of having their messages edited or altered before they appear in print or TV by posting on social

[32] N Ernst et al, 'Populists Prefer Social Media over Talk Shows: An Analysis of Populist Messages and Stylistic Elements across Six Countries' (2019) 1 *Social Media + Society* 5.

[33] K Jacobs and N Spierings, 'A Populist Paradise? Examining Populists' Twitter Adoption and Use' (2019) 22 *Information, Communication & Society* 1681, 1683–84.

[34] A Haller and K Holt, 'Paradoxical Populism: How PEGIDA Relates to Mainstream and Alternative Media' (2019) 22 *Information, Communication & Society* 1665, 1667.

[35] H Kriesi, 'The Populist Challenge' (2014) 37 *West European Politics* 361, 363.

media. This is because in the mainstream media, journalists can – and do – edit information by deleting or adding certain aspects, as well as put it into context based on their own negative or positive evaluation of the content.[36] Such edits can be avoided by directly posting the message on social media.

By doing so, there is also no longer a need for politicians to adapt their language, or political message, to the requirements of the mainstream media journalists in order to be able to transmit their messages.[37] Concretely, this means that employing more offensive language is easier, as it is no longer edited before publication by the traditional media.[38] In fact, the use of particularly offensive language might even be beneficial on social media as provocative messages can go viral within minutes, potentially even spilling over into the traditional media without any further edits.[39] Alternatively, politicians can employ very simple, if not oversimplified, language on social media, without having to risk that it will be subsequently edited by journalists, to reach their audience. This is particularly the case for Twitter, a platform designed for short and straightforward communication,[40] and for populists, who, through social media, can become a relevant political actor in the political system and shape political opinion.[41] As a consequence, established media institutions find themselves increasingly less able to control the political discourse. Whereas, before social media, they could significantly structure the discourse because they were indispensable for any political actor seeking to reach their voters,[42] this is no longer necessary the case. The political discourse has thus 'lost the guard rails which have kept political competitors from the extremes where they would normally remain ostracised and without access to resources'.[43]

Social media not only offers the direct, unmediated access to the wider public described above, it also enables a high degree of personalisation of messages and the easy targeting of specific audiences. Microtargeting practices, for example, make it possible for campaigns to be highly personalised and adjusted to the individual preferences and political affiliations of each voter. In addition, political parties can use the filtering effects of social media platforms[44] and behavioural targeting techniques to ensure that only messages that are aligned with voters' political beliefs are advertised and shown on their social media feed, often to the

[36] Jacobs and Spierings (n 33) 1684.

[37] A Jungherr, R Schroeder and S Stier, 'Digital Media and the Surge of Political Outsiders: Explaining the Success of Political Challengers in the United States, Germany, and China' (2019) 1 *Social Media + Society* 4.

[38] S Engesser et al, 'Populism and Social Media: How Politicians Spread a Fragmented Ideology' (2017) 20 *Information, Communication & Society* 1109, 1123.

[39] Jacobs and Spierings (n 33) 1683–84.

[40] ibid 1685.

[41] Jungherr et al (n 37) 2.

[42] ibid 4.

[43] ibid 4.

[44] P Lee et al, 'Social Media and Political Partisanship – A Subaltern Public Sphere's Role in Democracy' (2018) 35 *Telematics and Informatics* 1949, 1950.

exclusion of other information.[45] Such reinforcement of messages in the users' newsfeed is often referred to as a so-called 'filter bubble', which can emerge when users on a platform (choose to) communicate exclusively with like-minded users to the exclusion of other users.[46]

Filter bubbles can arise both through the intention of the users involved (self-selected personalisation) and through the way social media platforms prioritise content in their newsfeed (preselected personalisation).[47] While self-selected personalisation relates to the platform users' deliberate choices regarding what kind of information they would like to see and engage with – and what kind of information they are avoiding, such as information which would challenge their political opinion – preselected personalisation concerns the way in which social media platforms choose to personalise the content displayed in the users' newsfeeds through algorithmic decisions without the users' explicit knowledge or consent about the latter.[48] By exposing users exclusively to positions that are compatible with their views and by fortifying such views, there is the danger that such filter bubbles reinforce existing attitudes without providing the users with alternatives views. In particular, where this concerns controversial topics, social media filter bubbles can make users feel that their views or beliefs are acceptable even if they are not approved of by society at large.[49] At the same time, research has shown that the more often a statement is repeated to a person, the more that person will believe in the truthfulness of the statement.[50] This means that continuous exposure to the same or similar views on social media can also have an effect on what users believe to be valid messages. As a consequence, repeated exposure to content on social media which correspond to users' belief systems might not only result in them believing that their views, which are rejected by the wider public, are acceptable; it might also lead to a consolidation of such beliefs by increasing the perceived validity of the content.

Such filter bubbles can have an effect on the formation of public opinion in a political system. For example, they can have a mobilising effect by bringing together people that share the same political views, even where there was no prior links between them.[51] Because social media platforms offer a place for like-minded people to come together, to influence each other and to validate each other's viewpoints in a very selective manner, they can ultimately end up socialising

[45] Committee of experts on Media Pluralism and Transparency of Media Ownership, 'Study on the Use of Internet in Electoral Campaigns: The Rules of the Game: the Internet, Social Media and Election Communication', MSI-MED (2016)10rev4, 14–15.

[46] A Bruns, 'Filter Bubble' (2019) 8 *Internet Policy Review* 1, 4.

[47] F Zuiderveen Borgesius et al, 'Should We Worry about Filter Bubbles?' (2016) 5 *Internet Policy Review* 3.

[48] ibid 3.

[49] Lee et al (n 44) 1951.

[50] L Hasher and D Goldstein, 'Frequency and the Conference of Referential Validity' (1977) 16 *Journal of Verbal Learning and Verbal Behaviour* 107.

[51] Gerbaudo (n 22) 748–49.

themselves into a certain worldview.[52] This becomes even more exacerbated where the consequence drawn from this by users would be the avoidance of the mainstream media altogether.[53] In addition, the relationship between political parties, citizens and social movements become much more intertwined and their distinction becomes much more fluid on social media than in a media environment where the traditional media have a clear gatekeeping function,[54] thus creating a feeling of closeness between the politicians and citizens. The sharing of (political) information can nowadays be done basically instantly on platforms such as Twitter and Facebook, as well as across borders and internationally. Twitter's retweet function in particular can create a snowball effect,[55] with messages capable of going viral within a matter of minutes.

These general effects of social media platforms on the way politicians can communicate with voters and exert influence on the public will formation can be used to manipulate voters in different ways, not only by intentionally spreading disinformation. Most notably, voters can, through the use of social media and in light of the lack of any journalistic filters, be manipulated through: (i) the intentional spreading of false information with a political motive (disinformation); (ii) inadvertent sharing of false information (misinformation); (iii) intentional pushing of (non-problematic) information with a political motive (propaganda); and (iv) inadvertent pushing of (any kind of) information without a political motive through algorithmic decisions.

## IV. Different Forms of Disruption

> The power to influence opinions lies with those who can most widely and effectively disseminate a message. If you control … the algorithms that decide dissemination, you control the messages people see. And if you control the messages, you control the people reading them.[56]

While this quote speaks about messages in general, different types of messages can be distinguished when we talk about ways in which the pluralistic information landscape, which operates with a view to forming the public opinion, is disrupted through the rise and functioning of social media.

[52] B Krämer, 'Populist Online Practices: The Function of the Internet in Right-Wing Populism' (2017) 20 *Information, Communication & Society* 1293, 1302.

[53] ibid 1302.

[54] S Stier et al, 'When Populists Become Popular: Comparing Facebook Use by the Right-Wing Movement Pegida and German Political Parties' (2017) 20 *Information, Communication & Society* 1368.

[55] Jacobs and Spierings (n 33) 1686.

[56] R Diresta, 'Computational Propaganda: If You Make It Trend, You Make It True' [2018] *The Yale Review* 12, 26.

Much of the research in this field is concerned with intentional disinformation, ie the spread of false information, often also labelled 'fake news', in an attempt to influence democratic will formation and thereby electoral outcomes. Fake news in this context is understood as information that is verifiably false and intentionally spread in order to mislead the audience.[57] While the existence of 'fake news' is neither a new phenomenon nor restricted to social media platforms, its spread, 'fuelled by the technologies of social media, is happening at an astonishing pace'.[58] There are several reasons why social media platforms seem particularly conducive to the spread of false information. As has been explained above, the rise of social media platforms has had as an effect on the falling away of journalistic filters. This means that the barriers to entry in the media have significantly dropped, and 'Because reputational concerns discourage mass media outlets from knowingly reporting false stories, higher entry barriers limit false reporting'.[59] In addition, the way social media feeds are viewed and consumed, often on small phone screens, makes it more cumbersome and difficult for the users to assess the truthfulness of information.[60] Also, the filter bubbles, as described above, make it easier for disinformation to be spread: the way the filter bubbles work suggests that users who get false news on Facebook or other social media are less likely to receive news or evidence that would counter 'an ideologically aligned but false story'.[61]

The sources from which disinformation spreads can vary. Actors trying to produce and amplify false information via social media range from independent trolls, bots and conspiracy theorists to highly partisan media outlets, foreign governments and even the mainstream media.[62] Two prominent instances in which outside parties tried to interfere with the political will-formation processes in democratic elections by using 'algorithms, automation, and human curation to purposefully distribute misleading information over social media networks'[63] are the use of bots – created by actors outside of the UK and the USA – in the 2016 Brexit campaign and the 2016 US presidential election.[64]

[57] H Alcott and M Gentzkow, 'Social Media and Fake News in the 2016 Election' (2017) 31 *Journal of Economic Perspectives* 211, 213.

[58] L Anderson, 'Getting Acquainted with Social Networks and Apps: Combating Fake News on Social Media' (2018) 35 *Library Hi Tech News* 1, 1.

[59] Alcott and Gentzkow (n 57) 214.

[60] ibid 220.

[61] ibid 220.

[62] J Tucker et al, 'Social Media, Political Polarization, and Political Disinformation: A Review of the Scientific Literature' (Hewlett Foundation, 2018) 22.

[63] S Wolley and P Howard, 'Computational Propaganda Worldwide: Executive Summary', Computational Propaganda Research Project Working Paper No 2017.11 (2017) 1.

[64] For the use of bots in these instances, see P Howard, S Woolley and R Calo, 'Algorithms, Bots, and Political Communication in the US 2016 Election: The Challenge of Automated Political Communication for Election Law and Administration' (2018) 15 *Journal of Information Technology & Politics* 81; M Bastos and D Merca, 'The Brexit Botnet and User-Generated Hyperpartisan News' [2017] *Social Science Computer Review* 1.

This is all the more problematic in light of the fact that studies have shown that a growing number of people are forming their preferences on the basis of inaccurate factual beliefs.[65] This is different from people who are simply misinformed. The former people may not know certain things, but they are also more susceptible to a change in preference as a response to cues they receive from the political argument; for them, 'the way that competitive political elites frame an issue determines which set of reasons for or against comes to mind and thus what [they] decide'.[66] This is, however, not necessarily the case for misinformed people, who are much more unlikely to change their beliefs and preferences.[67]

However, the problem is not only that fake news can be more easily spread, but also that it is more difficult to rebut on social media. This is because false information does not need to be spread with a political motive in order for it to be able to adversely influence the political discourse. In fact, the message does not even have to be a political message in order for it to have a political effect. For example, think of the message that vaccination is harmful to children. This is not a political message as such, and it is often shared with no political motive in mind but simply for information purposes. Voters that share this message may even genuinely believe it is true, thus categorising this as misinformation rather than disinformation, which is the *intentional* spreading of false information. Nonetheless, such a message can have an impact on the way voters form their political will and commit to certain policy preferences. As already mentioned, research has shown that the more often a statement is repeated to a person, the more that person will believe in the truthfulness of the statement.[68] If, therefore, a user on social media sees the same message being repeatedly shared on their newsfeed by friends and family, and on the basis of that starts to believe in the truthfulness of the message, it can have an impact on the way they form their political choices. In times of social media, anyone can produce and share content that reaches a wide audience. Messages on social media can even have an impact on political will formation even where no political intentions are involved.

In a similar vein, a message need not be false in order to have adverse effects on democratic processes. A third form of manipulation can also occur where the message is not false but is nevertheless pushed with a political agenda. For the purpose of this chapter, this phenomenon will be called propaganda. Similarly to fake news, propaganda is of course not a new phenomenon, or one that is exclusive to social media. In fact, many political leaders, particularly those in authoritarian regimes, may rely on TV or the press to spread their messages in an attempt to be re-elected. The difference now, however, is the ease with which politicians and other actors can do so via social media, as well as the difficulty which users

[65] Humprecht et al (n 21) 2.
[66] JH Kuklinski et al, 'Misinformation and the Currency of Democratic Citizenship' (2000) 62 *Journal of Politics* 790, 809.
[67] ibid 809.
[68] Hasher and Goldstein (n 50) 107.

may have in identifying propaganda as such. If a voter in a liberal democracy consumes a newspaper or a TV show, in normal circumstances the voter will know where this newspaper or TV host stands on the political spectrum. The opinion or news segment shared therein can not only be put more into context, but also those consuming the news have a choice as to whether or not to be exposed to that particular point of view by tuning in to a certain show or opening a specific newspaper. To put it differently: a voter reading a conservative newspaper will know that the opinions expressed in the paper are conservative. This is not necessarily the case on social media, where messages are not flagged for users as regards the political stance of the person sharing it. A politically conservative message may not necessarily be immediately recognised as such, making it more difficult to place it within a political context and therefore to provide the public with the orientation it needs to form an informed political opinion.

All three forms of manipulations are exacerbated by the way social media platforms themselves function. Social media platforms are designed with the objective of attracting users to, and keeping users on, the platform, as well as making the platform more attractive to advertisers. For that reason, and with a view to achieving this objective, algorithms prioritise certain content over other content on platforms such as Facebook and Twitter. For example, offensive and emotional content that in traditional media outlets would be edited before publication might even be beneficial on social media as provocative messages on social media can go viral within minutes, potentially even spilling over into traditional media without any further edits.[69] In 2018, Facebook announced that it would

> prioritise posts that spark conversations and meaningful interactions between people. To do this, we will predict which posts you might want to interact with your friends about, and show these posts higher in feed. These are posts that inspire back-and-forth discussion in the comments and posts that you might want to share and react to.[70]

A study found that during the following year (2019), the English-language publisher with the most engagement by users on Facebook was the Republican-biased US news channel Fox News, followed by NBC and the BBC. While political content was dominant and made up more than a third of the most engaged posts, the study found that other most commented-on articles on Facebook often concerned the most divisive topics, most notably relating to religion and abortion.[71] If content is thus ranked and shown to users according to the extent of interaction with a certain post, and if posts on the most divisive topics receive the most interaction, it would seem plausible for Facebook to prioritise exactly such content.

[69] Jacobs and Spierings (n 33) 1683–84.

[70] Facebook, 'Bringing People Closer Together' (11 January 2018), https://about.fb.com/news/2018/01/news-feed-fyi-bringing-people-closer-together/.

[71] Newswhip, '2019 Guide to Publishing on Facebook', http://go.newswhip.com/rs/647-QQK-704/images/Facebook%20Publishing%202019_Final.pdf.

Such prioritisation in pushing information based on what in essence are economic reasons can, in turn, influence democratic discourses. Social media, as a newly emerged platform of political communication, is not geared towards the harmonisation between and reconciliation of different viewpoints, which is indispensable in a well-functioning democracy. In the fast pace of the Internet, there is little time to engage in deep reflection and discussion with opposing political opinions. Instead, messages on social media tend to augment and fortify specific positions and agendas,[72] perhaps not least because moderate, balanced statements are less likely to go viral on platforms such as Twitter and Facebook than sensationalist and emotionalised content. In other words: 'With the rise of social media, the balanced press statement is replaced by the provocative tweet.'[73]

It can therefore be argued that social media platforms are not just a tool through which political and commercial actors may exert influence on the will formation of voters. Rather, they are, albeit perhaps unintentionally, themselves actors that disrupt and interfere with the free will-formation process of voters.

## V. Advantages and Disadvantages of Technological Revolution

The technological revolution and the rise of social media platforms have both advantages and disadvantages for democracy. On the one hand, social media platforms facilitate the provision of information and also enable voices to be heard that might otherwise be excluded from the public debate. They also facilitate the creation of social and democratic movements, including cross-border movements, by making it possible for like-minded people to find each other and to find politicians whom they would like to support. Some of the many examples are protest movements such as the Arab Spring, the Gezi Protests in Turkey and the Stuttgart 21 protests in Germany, but more recently also the Friday for Future movements.

On the other hand, and as described in this chapter, the rise of social media can also pose a risk to (liberal) democracy to the extent that it takes away the capability of journalists in the traditional media, ie television, radio and the press, to structure the political discourse by filtering information and putting that information into a larger context. In the time of Twitter and Facebook, anyone can post any kind of information online, which does not only go unchecked, but, in some instances, can also go viral in a matter of minutes, without any journalistic verifications as to its truthfulness. This has two consequences: first, it has become

[72] T Wischmeyer, 'Making Social Media an Instrument of Democracy' (2018) 25 *European Law Journal* 169, 173.
[73] Ibid 173.

decidedly easier for anyone, with or without mal-intent, to share false, or at least partially false, information. Secondly, social media platforms also enable the augmentation and amplification of certain positions without any accompanying moderating comments, as would be the case in the traditional media through journalists. Both consequences result in a danger for liberal democracy because they work against the existence of a balanced media landscape, in which citizens can inform themselves freely in order to form a public opinion that will be expressed through the act of voting.

## VI. Outlook

A liberal democracy that is based on free election necessitates a well-functioning public sphere in which a balanced media landscape informs citizens with a view to forming a public opinion. This has arguably been rendered more difficult through the technological revolution and the rise of social media platforms. The main causes for the disruption of this relationship between democratic processes, the public sphere and democratic will formation are the changes in which we communicate not only in private, but also in public. The falling away of journalistic filters, which allows for the unmediated exposure of citizens to any kind information, in conjunction with the way social media platform algorithms are designed are argued to have an adverse effect on the democratic will formation in a polity. Such effects, however, go further than just intentional spreading of disinformation over social media networks. Instead, the disruptive effects of social media can also occur through inadvertent sharing of false information, intentional pushing of (non-fake news) information with a political motive and inadvertent pushing of (any kind of) information without a political motive through algorithmic decisions. So far, regulators on both the national and European level have struggled to regulate the platforms in a way that mitigates such adverse effects.

Different jurisdictions have attempted to regulate the problem of online disinformation in different ways. For example, the German Network Enforcement Act (NetzDG), which came into effect on 1 January 2018, combats hate speech on the Internet by requiring social media platforms to set up a complaint mechanism and to delete obviously illegal content (eg breach of public order, incitement to hatred, insult or defamation) within 24 hours of receiving the complaint, where possible.[74] In a similar fashion, we have seen the adoption of an EU code

[74] For discussion of the German NetzDG Law, see M Hong, 'Hate Speech im Internet – Grundrechtliche Rahmenbedingungen ihrer Regulierung' in M Albers and I Katsivelas (eds), *Recht & Netz* (Nomos 2018); H Tworek and P Leerssen, 'An Analysis of Germany's NetzDG Law', Working Paper of the Transatlantic High Level Working Group on Content Moderation Online and Freedom of Expression (2019); W Schulz, 'Regulating Intermediaries to Protect Privacy Online – the Case of the German NetzDG', HIIG Discussion Paper Series (2018).

of conduct on hate speech, a French co-regulation approach with social media platforms and a UK online harms paper.[75] The question that poses itself in light of these measures is, however, how well they are suited to counter the adverse effects of the ways that social media platforms operate on democratic processes insofar as messages posted and shared do not constitute hate speech or other illegal content.

If the objective is to ensure a pluralistic information landscape on social media, in which the people can access and exchange information in a comprehensive manner with a view to forming public opinion, any regulation of social media platforms should have as an aim making more transparent not only the source and truthfulness of messages, but also the reason why they are shown to users in the first place. As was explained in section III, social media platforms choose to personalise the content displayed in the users' newsfeeds through algorithmic decisions, often without the users' explicit knowledge or consent about the latter. By requiring social media platforms to make transparent to users why certain content appears in their newsfeed as well as to provide users with easy access to information that is not appearing in their immediate newsfeed based on algorithmic decisions, the users' own abilities to assess and put into context the information they see could be supported.

The argument here is that if journalists fall away as the intermediary that filters information for the citizens and puts that information into a larger political context, then such a task necessarily falls to each individual citizen themselves. And if the argument is accepted that social media platforms are not just a tool through which political and commercial actors may exert influence on the will formation of voters but, rather, are, albeit perhaps unintentionally, themselves actors that disrupt and interfere with the free will-formation process of voters, then the public must also recognise the platforms' roles as such and act accordingly. The expectation is not for the ordinary citizen to take over the tasks of a full-time journalist, but it is imperative that the formation of the political will in a polity does not hinge on the design of social media platforms. Rather, citizens themselves must be able to seek out a pluralistic information landscape even where it is not offered to them on a silver plate, as well as be able to recognise where such a pluralistic information landscape might be lacking.

[75] For an overview of attempts to regulate online platforms, see M Vermeulen, 'Online Content: To Regulate or Not to Regulate – Is That the Question?', APC Issue Paper 2 (2019).

# 6

# Data Revolution and Public Will Formation: Regulating Democratic Processes in the Digital Age

SASCHA HARDT

## I. Introduction

In a polity constituted as a representative democracy, the assumption that all political power emanates from 'the people' is axiomatic. It is deeply entrenched both in the letter of the law and in any common rendering of the narrative that gives shape and colour to the term 'democracy' in our minds. In a democracy, we are taught, it is the role of the public to choose the aim and direction of the state.[1] The will of the public expresses itself through the citizens' vote. Through elections and plebiscites, it both informs and legitimises policy decisions, legislation, government formation and the exercise of executive power. And because this is so, it is fundamental to our understanding of democracy that the exercise of the democratic vote must be free, equal and secret in order to produce a true, undistorted image of the public will.

Equally necessary for the democratic pedigree, however, is that the formation of the political opinion of all individual citizens – the stuff that, ultimately, the public will is made of or which, even if one were to postulate a difference between it and the sum of its parts, informs it – takes place based on information freely obtained from independent and diverse sources. Consequently, in addition to statutory and constitutional safeguards aimed at protecting democratic processes as such, many liberal democracies have a battery of legislation in place which guarantees freedom of the press and seeks to prevent media monopolies and other information-related distortions of personal and public will formation. However, the freedom of such will-formation processes is increasingly under threat.

[1] T Christiano, *The Rule of the Many: Fundamental Issues in Democratic Theory* (Westview Press, 1996) ch 5.

Over the past decade, three parallel and interrelated developments have begun to accelerate into a process of profound and lasting impact on democratic processes. These developments are: (i) an exponential increase in the possibility to obtain and analyse large amounts of personal and other data ('big data'), resulting in highly accurate and personalised information on citizens' political views and prospective voting behaviour; (ii) the increasing ubiquity of social media in public discourse in general and in political communication in particular, as a means of both personalised microtargeted advertising and, in due course, the single most important medium of public debate; and (iii) the commercial exploitation of the latter two developments for the purpose of exerting political influence.

The technological developments that are revolutionising political communication will, as such, not be rolled back or contained; neither will the ensuing social changes. Attempts to do so, be it by sections of the political classes or by parts of society, are futile. Instead, it is the responsibility of legislators, policy-makers and scholars to react to new technological and social realities in a way that recognises their presence and embraces the opportunities they bring, but also protects liberal democracy from the dangers they hold. With a view to the latter point, this chapter argues that the three developments outlined above, taken in conjunction, bear the potential to undermine the freedom of public will formation, thereby not merely changing the results of elections and referenda, but also compromising the legitimacy of their results. In this fashion, the digital revolution has the potential to provoke a legitimacy crisis of liberal democracy itself.

Based on a critical review of existing theoretical descriptions of public will formation, this chapter therefore makes the case not for a containment strategy for social media and digital communication in politics, but for (greater) positive legal regulation of the connected phenomenon of 'big data'-driven microtargeted campaigning and offers first perspectives for a more coherent public law response.

## II. Mass Data Analysis, Microtargeting and Social Media

One of the most impactful technological developments with regard to democratic life in recent years lies in the combination of 'big data' – the computational analysis of very large datasets to reveal patterns, trends and associations relating to human behaviour and interactions – with personalised campaigning, also referred to as microtargeting. The International Institute for Democracy and Electoral Assistance (IDEA) offers a helpful description:

> By analysing specific datasets, political parties can achieve a highly detailed understanding of the behaviour, opinions and feelings of voters, allowing parties to cluster voters in complex groups. Such clusters can subsequently be targeted with online political

> advertisements that speak to their concerns and that are in line with their opinions. These online messages can only be seen by those voters in the targeted clusters. This is called digital microtargeting.[2]

The desire to understand with ever more precision the individual (psychological) and group (sociological) processes shaping personal and collective political opinions and decisions, and to subsequently use that understanding to manipulate or influence citizen's views and actions, is far from new: 'From Science comes Prevision; from Prevision comes Action',[3] goes Auguste Comte's famous dictum, which political actors in democracies have always taken to heart. As such, the practice of analysing publicly available data (on voters' names, addresses, gender, jobs, income levels, family circumstances, ethnicity, religious affiliation, consumer behaviour, etc), and subsequently tailoring political messages and political advertising to specific groups of citizens thus identified, has also been commonplace in democratic polities for a long time.

Electoral campaigns operate with limited financial resources and limited staff and time capacities; hence, they choose to focus their efforts on those geographical areas and groups of potential voters that are most crucial to their electoral success, or most likely to be swayed by campaign efforts. Accordingly, targeted campaigning – and even efforts to microtarget or personalise campaign efforts down to the individual voter – are by no means a novel phenomenon. Moreover, political actors have always been eager (and forced by competition) to incorporate and exploit the possibilities offered by newly developed media in their campaign strategies.

In this regard, the shifts that currently follow the advent of political campaigning via the Internet differ little from those in the wake of politicians' discovery of the opportunities of television in the mid-twentieth century.[4] Moreover, as Tom Dobber et al correctly note, 'It would be an oversimplification to point to "the Internet" as a game-changer in political communication, because of the rapidly changing nature of the Internet itself'.[5] The revolutionary capacity of digital microtargeting supported by computational mass data analysis with regard to democratic processes does not lie in the novelty of either, but in the exponentially increased scale and precision of both. For a better understanding of the (present and, in particular, future) impact of this development, it is useful to briefly outline how digital microtargeting works in combination with computational mass data analysis, and how this differs from traditional targeting approaches.

[2] IDEA, *Digital Microtargeting* (Political Party Innovation Primers, 2018) 6.

[3] A Comte, *The Positive Philosophy of Auguste Comte* (Batoche Books 2000) vol 1, 43, as cited in WA Gorton, 'Manipulating Citizens: How Political Campaigns' Use of Behavioral Social Science Harms Democracy' (2016) 38 *New Political Science* 61, 63.

[4] *cf* P Norris, *A Virtuous Circle: Political Communications in Postindustrial Societies* (Cambrige University Press, 2000).

[5] T Dobber et al, 'Two Crates of Beer and 40 Pizzas: The Adoption of Innovative Political Behavioural Targeting Techniques' (2017) 6 *Internet Policy Review*.

## A. Data Collection

Political contestants have always collected voter data to help inform and design their campaign efforts. For this purpose, they made use of publicly available data, such as existing voter registers with publicly listed names and addresses,[6] general demographic and statistical data, as well as other data specifically collected by or on behalf of the political contestants themselves, for instance through opinion polling and canvassing.

The processes and sources of data collection, as well as the storage and usability of datasets, have become exponentially more efficient through technology in recent years. The above-mentioned data, now harvested faster, more efficiently and at much lower cost by political parties, state agencies and commercial firms, is now augmented by extremely large sets of consumer data (eg from online payments, social media activity and browsing behaviour) collected and traded as a commodity by commercial actors. In addition, very large quantities of data can be stored more easily and at lower cost than even a few years ago in larger servers.

## B. Processing of Collected Data

Political candidates have an interest in collecting as much data as possible about potential voters, since such data allows for voter segmentation, ie breaking down the electorate into smaller divisions based on identified special interests, previous voting behaviour, income level. Subsequently, campaign advertising is specifically designed to respond to the points of interest of a specific segment, and communication methods chosen based on which type of political advertising a segment is supposedly most receptive to.

While voter segmentation and campaigning to different segments of the electorate with different content and communication methods was common practice long before the advent of the Internet, recent technological developments have revolutionised this practice insofar as sophisticated algorithms allow electoral candidates to make much more accurate, narrow and detailed predictions about the opinions and voting behaviour of citizens. Very large datasets, in which publicly available or canvassed data is combined with commercialised consumer data, allows electoral candidates to understand and predict the behaviour their electorate 'with laser-like precision',[7] and down to the individual person.

Importantly, segmentation can be informed by structural factors. In parliamentary elections, for instance, one such factor is the applicable election system: in proportional representation systems, where the aim of an electoral campaign is

[6] The amount and extent of publicly available voter data differs greatly between jurisdictions. While in the USA a voter's name and address are usually publicly available and other data (eg a person's vote in previous elections or information on donations made to political causes) can also be accessed, such data is protected in countries with stricter data protection legislation, such as Germany. *cf* IDEA (n 2).

[7] Gorton (n 3) 70.

simply to generate as many votes for the campaigning party as possible, segmentation will mainly be used to identify groups or individuals that are potentially receptive to campaigning on different issues, for instance in order to prepare specific advertising messages, each focusing on the issues deemed most effective among a certain group of voters, while ignoring or downplaying positions of the campaigning party that this group is likely to find less relevant or reject. Another important segment to identify are non-voters who are potentially sympathetic to the campaigning party and susceptible to messages that will trigger them to vote.

In majoritarian election systems, on the other hand, the analysis is likely to focus on identifying geographical areas and electoral districts in which the race between electoral candidates is open. Within these districts, potential swing voters can be segmented out to concentrate targeted campaign efforts specifically on them, for instance by issuing political messages of special relevance to local communities or even individuals.[8] Conversely, voters residing in districts deemed already decided or voters deemed unreceptive to messages from a particular electoral candidate are likely to be ignored and may therefore be 'deprived of an entire spectrum of political stances which the parties do not communicate to the entire public, which, in turn, creates inequalities in terms of the available information on which the voters base their political choices'.[9] In jurisdictions and election systems where this is legally possible, voter segmentation will not only inform election campaigns, but also – once a party has attained a position of power – the manipulation of district boundaries (gerrymandering), thereby contributing to an entrenchment of the political status quo.

Instantaneous and cheap online communication also allows campaigners not just to rely on algorithm-assisted estimations and hunches as to what type of message will resonate with which voter profile, but to 'test' slightly different online messages on very large numbers of Internet users and to fine-tune them according to the recipients' responses (by monitoring how long they stay on the site, how quickly/frequently they click, etc), thereby further enhancing the effectivity of their campaign while collecting even more data.[10]

## C. Personalised Communication through Social Media

Once equipped with highly detailed voter profiles, electoral contenders are able to issue personalised campaign advertising. In principle, this too is not a novel

[8] IDEA (n 2) 13.

[9] Committee of Experts on Media Pluralism and Transparency of Media Ownership (MSI-MED), 'Study on the Use of Internet in Electoral Campaigns: The Rules of the Game: The Internet, Social Media and Election Communications', DGI(2017)11, 15. In this respect, see also J Bayer, 'Double Harm to Voters: Data-Driven Microtargeting and Democratic Public Discourse' (2020) 9 *Internet Policy Review*. Bayer emphasises the point that microtargeting causes double harm, since it not only selects specific individuals as receivers of relevant information but necessarily also *de-selects* the remainder of the population, thereby amplifying informational inequality among voters.

[10] IDEA (n 2) 11.

device – addressing voters personally through mail, telephone or email messaging has been a common practice for a long time. The advent of social media, however, has broadened the possibilities of communication.

For campaigners, two types of social media access to their electorate can be distinguished: owned/earned and paid.[11] In an owned/earned social media setting, users communicate in a closed environment; information displayed to them, for instance in a Facebook newsfeed, is selected by the social media platform's own algorithm based on the user's earlier activity on the platform (or otherwise online). This leads to the creation of filter bubbles, in which social media users will only be exposed to content which is likely to match their interests, opinions and habits, while content that is likely to conflict with the latter will rarely be brought to their attention.

That has important consequences for microtargeted campaigning. In an owned/earned social media setting, electoral candidates are unable to present content to voters who have not already been identified (by the algorithms of the social media site) as likely to sympathise with their cause. Nevertheless, campaigners can launch carefully designed messages into existing filter bubbles, thereby helping to further fortify and entrench the beliefs held by their supporters and preventing them from being swayed by campaign messages of competing contestants. An Internet user who receives significant portions of her political information from within a social media filter bubble and forms her political opinion on the basis of such information is thus likely to develop a stable and increasingly entrenched political stance.

In a paid social media setting, on the other hand, social media platforms offer campaigners (and commercial advertisers) access to their users for payment, thereby enabling electoral candidates to transcend filter bubbles and issue campaign messages to users who are otherwise less likely to be exposed to content that does not correspond to their political preference.[12] Since the operational model of social media platforms is entirely based on user profiling, these platforms are able to offer paid access to users with a very high degree of specificity and personalisation.

In conclusion, the development of highly precise mass data analysis techniques and the precision of the resulting knowledge about voter characteristics (interests, preferences, etc) in combination with microtargeted communication through both social media and traditional channels allows electoral candidates to campaign with an exponentially higher degree of precision and efficiency, at costs considerably lower than for traditional mass advertising or targeted campaigning through traditional media. Political parties and candidates on the campaign trail, as well as campaigners (organised and private) for causes subject

[11] ibid 15.
[12] ibid.

to plebiscites, have made use of these techniques at a rapidly increasing rate. The Council of Europe's Committee of Experts on Media Pluralism and Transparency of Media Ownership (MSI-MED) found that, between 2006 and 2017, the share of spending on political advertising spent on digital channels rose from 6 per cent to 36 per cent, thereby slightly surpassing television advertising. In individual countries, most notably the UK, spending on digital campaigning rose above 50 per cent.[13]

As with any impactful technological development, many commentators, journalistic and scholarly alike, have found the rise of digital microtargeting in political campaigning alarming.[14] However, especially after the revelations about the involvement of data analytics firm Cambridge Analytica (and related entities) in Donald Trump's presidential election campaign, the Brexit campaign and many other campaign efforts around the globe, the body of scholarly literature analysing digital microtargeting has grown both in volume and refinement, adding some important caveats to the often somewhat sensationalist and fear-inducing journalistic coverage of the matter. For instance, Baldwin-Philippi found that the increase in effectiveness of political campaigns resulting from the introduction of microtargeting based on big data analysis has been overstated, and that digital microtargeting is more labour-intensive (and therefore more costly) than often assumed, so that 'campaigns often do not execute analytic-based campaigning tactics as fully or rigorously as possible'.[15] Also, claims of the ubiquity of digital microtargeting may (as yet) be overstated; according to one study, such practices are much more common in the USA than in Europe, except for the UK, where parties 'have been quick to emulate online microtargeting campaigns'.[16]

There is thus little consent among scholarly observers as to how dangerous the nexus of big data and microtargeting is, but this is largely owing to disagreement about the current extent of the phenomenon, that is, how far this trend has progressed so far. At the same time, there is little reasonable doubt about its dangerous potential. After all, it is all but certain that relevant technology will develop further, making tools and services relative to data analysis and microtargeting both more effective and cheaper, thus increasing the likelihood of its use in political campaigning. In other words, even if the problem is now smaller than some believe, it is almost certainly getting worse.

[13] MSI-MED (n 9) 12–13.

[14] One very popular account of the matter is given in C O'Neil, *Weapons of Math Destruction: How Big Data Increases Inequality and Threatens Democracy*, 1st paperback edn (Broadway Books, 2017).

[15] J Baldwin-Philippi, 'The Myths of Data-Driven Campaigning' (2017) 34 *Political Communication* 627, 631.

[16] FJ Zuiderveen Borgesius et al, 'Online Political Microtargeting: Promises and Threats for Democracy' (2018) 14 *Utrecht Law Review* 82, 84.

# III. Will Formation and Legal Regulation

## A. Personal Will Formation as an Essential Component of Democracy

It is common to think of elections, referenda and similar democratic processes as moments in which the public will is formed or, if we assume its existence prior to the vote, manifests itself. On election night, the will of 'the people' becomes sufficiently tangible to be translated into legitimate political leadership and actual policy decisions. At the same time, however, voting in elections and referenda can also be described as a mere act of utterance, albeit simultaneously by all voters, of the results of prior processes of individual will formation in all citizens individually.[17] According to von Achenbach and Müller-Mall, the understanding of the electoral process as the expression of a collective will actually existing prior to the election is 'as complex as it is naïve', but it serves to 'legitimise unknown political acts in an unknown political future through a generalisation of the political will of the individual that is numerically fixed in the election result and thereby ultimately fictitious'.[18]

Democratic legitimacy is thus produced by a dual reading of democratic voting as both the expression of the priorly formed will of every individual voter and the manifestation of the (to some degree fictitious) collective will; it arises only out of the combination of both aspects. This is easily illustrated by comparing two scenarios. In the first scenario, each voter is able to form her political opinion freely on the basis of a wide range of information and to express her individual political will through her vote, but the electoral process as a collective act is distorted – for instance, as the result of fraudulent miscounting or an election formula that attaches greater weight to particular segments of voters. In a modern liberal democracy, such an election would lead to an outcome likely considered unrepresentative of the public will by most. It would therefore not be deemed to produce democratic legitimacy for the decisions taken or political personnel appointed as its result.

In the second scenario, the electoral process and formula is flawlessly fair, the electoral outcome perfectly mirroring the public will supposedly expressed in the popular vote. However, the earlier process of individual will formation informing that vote was heavily distorted, for instance by severely limiting voters' exposure to information by influencing the information displayed to them on their preferred social media platform, or by targeting them with personalised information specifically geared towards exercising the greatest possible influence on the individual voter's opinion and voting behaviour. Arguably, also in this scenario,

[17] J von Achenbach and S Müller-Mall, *Die Wahl und das Kreuz – Formalisierung und Form des Demokratischen* (Metzler, 2015).

[18] ibid (my translation).

the democratic process as a whole would be compromised and would, in the eyes of most, produce little to no legitimacy for its results in terms of policy and personnel choices.

It is in the interest of democratic legitimacy to shield both the formation and expression of the public will and the prior, individual process of personal will formation from distortions. Even if the distinction between the two is artificial and to a certain degree fictitious, it enables us to assess legal arrangements for the purpose of protecting democratic processes from distortion with a clearer view.

Before we can turn to an assessment of the adequacy of existing legal arrangements and recommend possible alterations or additions, we must assess whether the recent developments in political campaigning brought about by combining mass data analysis with microtargeted advertising through social media (and other channels) constitutes – or has the potential to constitute – a veritable distortion of will formation processes. After all, as we have seen, the finding that voter data analysis and means of political communication are subject to development and refinement alone does not merit this conclusion. An additional complication is presented by the fact that big data and microtargeted campaigning do not take away an individual's freedom to access other information of her own choosing or limit the availability of such information in principle. Instead, microtargeting merely exploits existing and observable choice patterns.

A powerful argument in favour of nevertheless viewing big data analysis and microtargeted campaigning as distortive of free will-formation processes in a democratic society has been put forward by Cass Sunstein, based on a proposition that merits quoting in full. Sunstein writes:

> [A] well-functioning system of free expression must meet two distinctive requirements:
>
> First, people should be exposed to materials that they would not have chosen in advance. Unplanned, unanticipated encounters are central to democracy itself. Such encounters often involve topics and points of view that people have not sought out and perhaps find quite irritating. They are important partly to ensure against fragmentation and extremism, which are predictable outcomes of any situation in which like-minded people speak only with themselves. I do not suggest that government should force people to see things that they wish to avoid. But I do contend that in a democracy deserving the name, people often come across views and topics that they have not specifically selected.
>
> Secondly, many or most citizens should have a range of common experiences. Without shared experiences, a heterogeneous society will have a much more difficult time in addressing social problems. People may even find it hard to understand one another. Common experiences, emphatically including the common experiences made possible by the media, provide a form of social glue. A system of communications that radically diminishes the number of such experiences will create a number of problems, not least because of the increase in social fragmentation.[19]

[19] CR Sunstein, *Republic.com* (Princeton University Press, 2002); reproduced in CR Sunstein, *Republic 2.0* (Princeton University Press, 2007) 5–6.

The first of Sunstein's requirements addresses the core of any will-formation process: if we, as citizens, are to develop a political will or opinion beyond pre-existing convictions, teachings or beliefs – which is a central feature of both personal development and societal discourse by necessity – this cannot be done without exposure to extraneous input. While none of the developments outlined above impede our capacity to actively seek such exposure, filter bubbles and closed-group communication among sections of society, both on social media platforms and generally, significantly reduce surprising, unanticipated encounters with new or foreign ideas. In an electoral context, highly personalised political communication based on voter segmentation also diminishes the electorate's chance of meeting the second requirement. Read in the light of recent developments of hyper-partisanship and the rise of political and social extremism in many polities around the globe, the resulting loss of societies' capacity to engage in fruitful democratic discourse seems to be becoming a tangible reality. Importantly, the harm to democratic processes that emanates from the lack of exposure to new or alternative information, as well as the increasingly separated spheres of experience of different segments of society, is first and foremost caused at the level of personal will formation. More importantly still, it is well hidden, since what is impeded is not the individual voter's freedom to expose herself to a variety of different views, nor that of different segments of the electorate to share a common experience of societal issues, but their opportunity to do so. We do not feel the loss.

## B. Existing Legal Instruments to Protect Personal Will Formation

One of the structural reasons why law and legal scholarship has so far been slow to react to technological developments that have been so impactful on the operation of democracy is that neither electoral laws themselves, nor laws governing political parties, campaign advertising or other legally regulated aspects of democratic processes have been violated on a large scale as a consequence of these developments.[20]

Legal regulation of electoral processes (including referenda) in liberal democracies traditionally focuses on safeguarding the freedom and fairness of the vote itself, but also of political will formation.

On the one hand, liberal democracies grant citizens the fundamental rights to freedom of assembly, freedom of expression and the right to receive information. The latter right is sometimes codified specifically, such as in Article 19 of the Universal Declaration of Human Rights, which refers to the right to 'seek, receive and impart information and ideas', or Article 5 of the German Basic Law, which

[20] A notable exception may be violations of (national) privacy and data protection rules, whose enforcement across national borders and in the digital space of the Internet is notoriously difficult.

guarantees the right 'to inform [oneself] without hindrance from generally accessible sources'. Elsewhere, the right to receive information is taken to be necessarily implied in freedom of expression; this is, among others, the view taken by the US Supreme Court.[21]

On the other hand, the laws of many polities erect legal barriers against information monopolies and the abuse of financial or media power in democratic processes. As the MSI-MED noted in its 2017 study on the use of Internet in electoral campaigns, political speech is not just the form of speech that enjoys the most extensive legal protection, thus safeguarding the right of citizens to impart, receive and exchange political information; it is also highly regulated when it comes to the communication between electoral candidates and the public during election periods. Such communication is often subject to legal regulation, which may include limits on paid political advertising and campaign spending, on airtime for campaigning or on financial contributions from various types of actors (individuals, corporations, foreign entities). Other forms of regulation involve free advertising space or airtime in equal measure for all electoral candidates, aiming at a degree of fairness and equality of arms between contestants unequally equipped with financial and other resources.[22]

It is therefore by no means correct to speak of the domain of personal will formation as a *rechtsfreier Raum*, a legal vacuum. It is equally clear, however, that even without outward violation of the legal goods protected by existing legal rules – freedom of expression, freedom to receive information, equality of arms in electoral campaigns, as well as freedom, secrecy and equality of the democratic vote itself – harmful distortions of the will-formation processes necessary in a democratic society do take place. A rethinking of the legal regime surrounding these processes is therefore in order.

## IV. Towards Legal Rules to Mitigate Adverse Effects of Mass Data Analysis and Microtargeting in Political Campaigning

Big data enables ever more precise predictions of voter preference and behaviour; the technological development of new means of influencing personal will formation cannot be halted, much less taken back. This should be the point of departure for any discussion of possible legal responses to the phenomenon: even if one believes that the harm done to democratic processes and their legitimacy output

[21] See SN Mart, 'The Right to Receive Information' (2003) 95 *Law Library Journal* 175; for a further discussion of the extent of the right to receive information in US law, see J Kennedy, 'The Right to Receive Information: The Current State of the Doctrine and the Best Application for the Future' (2005) 35 *Seton Hall Law Review* 789.

[22] MSI-MED (n 9) 3.

is currently overstated, the fact that technology will be developed further, will become cheaper and easier to commercialise, and will be employed where relevant actors see the possibility and use of doing so means that the freedom of personal will formation is facing a serious threat with the potential of undermining the legitimacy of the results of democratic processes.

There is also little reason to believe that some – in particular, European – jurisdictions are somehow immune to the negative effects of data-driven campaigning and microtargeting. It has been noted that at least some EU countries are legally and socially better equipped to face the more dangerous aspects of big data and microtargeting and that 'Cultural, legal, institutional, financial, and other constraints will continue to block the more intrusive campaigning practices now seen in the USA'.[23] However, these constraints are likely to be a temporary defence at best, not least because the current weakening of traditional patterns of stable party affiliation in many Western democracies[24] creates pressure on political actors and parties to devise new forms of engagement with a more volatile electorate.[25]

Yet, designing an adequate legal response is not easy. There is little plausibility to the idea of approaching the problem caused by microtargeting through a blanket legal ban on the use of certain technological tools or services per se. Even without considering the technical difficulties of enforcing such a ban – such as the possibility to move online activities to other jurisdictions – it would be at odds with the principle of freedom of expression of electoral candidates, as well as, potentially, the freedom to receive information on the part of the targeted voters. Instead, legislation should be adopted that helps keep the adverse effects of microtargeted digital campaigning within bounds and, crucially, makes electoral candidates' efforts in this field as transparent as possible. Regulatory efforts in three key areas appear realistic in this regard: (i) data protection; (ii) campaign funding/spending; and (iii) the regulation of voter targeting via social media platforms.

Arguably, the most useful regulatory tool to mitigate the adverse effect of microtargeted campaigning short of banning it outright is data protection. Effective data protection keeps the 'raw material' for microtargeting – massive quantities of relevant voter data – in short supply. Jurisdictions differ very widely in the extent to which their citizens' personal data may be collected and used for analysis and targeting purposes. In all EU Member States, the European Union's General Data Protection Regulation (GDPR) tightly limits the use of personal data by political parties to members, former members and persons in 'regular contact' with the parties, and requires that 'appropriate safeguards' are observed when using such data.[26]

[23] CJ Bennett, 'Voter Databases, Microtargeting, and Data Protection Law: Can Political Parties Campaign in Europe as They Do in North America?' (2016) 6 *International Data Privacy Law* 261, 274.

[24] For an analysis of the interrelation between digitalisation and the perceived decline in party affiliation, see A Chadwick and J Stromer-Galley, *Digital Media, Power, and Democracy in Parties and Election Campaigns: Party Decline or Party Renewal?* (SAGE Publications, 2016).

[25] Bennett (n 23) 274.

[26] IDEA (n 2) 18.

While the GDPR has only been in force since 2018, it has been noted that it is likely to make microtargeting more difficult in the EU than in other jurisdictions with weaker data protection rules, such as the USA.[27]

However, the GDPR is a highly complex piece of legislation; its requirements, which apply to many different uses of personal date as well as political campaigning, are sometimes 'vague and abstract', and compliance has been less than ideal.[28] More importantly, however, even clear rules can potentially be bypassed by outsourcing data processing to service providers and social media platforms that can potentially escape national and regional regulation, for instance through legal manoeuvres like moving legal responsibility for user data outside of the European Union (Facebook). Despite numerous enforcement difficulties, stepping up data protection rules, also with regard to the initial collection of data to be analysed, is bound to remain one of the most important regulatory tools with regard to mass data analysis and microtargeted campaigning. Arguably, the effectiveness of legal data protection mechanisms depends to a very large extent on the sensitisation of the population and the acceptance and active participation of voters in data protection efforts. Therefore, public debate and awareness campaigns should continue to accompany legislative efforts in the area of date protection.

Strong data protection legislation is clearly important in tackling the threat to liberal democracy posed by political microtargeting at its root, yet it is hardly sufficient. As we have seen, the emergence and strategic use of social media plays a very significant part in the effectiveness of microtargeted political campaigning. The nature of communication through social media makes for an alignment of interests between campaigners, platform operators and users: algorithms select content to be displayed to users based on identified user preference combined with the interest of the platform in users spending as much time on the platform as possible; campaigners can use the ensuing patterns both to extract preference data and to launch targeted messages; users frequently experience a stream of information that reinforces and consolidates views and opinions previously held. This alignment of interests and its result, the much-discussed filter bubble, can develop into a threat to liberal democracy where social media is or becomes the primary source of political information.

However, regulatory intervention to avert this dangerous dynamic faces many problems. On the one hand, a 'fundamental conflict' has been diagnosed 'between the need to regulate content on social media as a means to ensure an open and balanced public discourse and the need to protect the right to free speech in a democracy'.[29] On the other hand, filter bubbles and personalisation of provided information are only partly the result of the actions of information providers and

[27] T Dobber, R Ó Fathaigh and FJ Zuiderveen Borgesius, 'The Regulation of Online Political Microtargeting in Europe' (2019) 8 *Internet Policy Review* 7.

[28] ibid.

[29] H-T Nguyen, 'Populism in Times of Social Media' in S Hardt, AW Heringa and H-T Nguyen (eds), *Populism and Democracy* (Eleven International Publishing, 2020) 83.

social media platforms; for an important part, they are the result of user choice, and it is not for regulators to decide whom users 'befriend' or 'follow' on social media.[30] Nevertheless, a possible and arguably necessary regulatory response consists of transparency requirements for social media platforms. While the technical details of the algorithmic steering of news streams may be legitimate corporate secrets, social media platforms should be required to disclose in an understandable and accessible manner why users see certain content and, as the case may be, who paid for it.[31]

With regard to funding/spending, it has been observed that especially the more intricate microtargeting services are very costly – prohibitively so for some campaigns.[32] At the same time, parties and campaigns may easily be able to bypass existing campaign expenditure caps (where these apply), since the relevant services are not territorially bound and can easily take place in foreign jurisdictions.[33] While funding is by necessity a crucial factor in the competition between election campaigns, a degree of fairness and equality (or at least similarity) of arms could be brought about by introducing spending caps where they do not yet exist and by bolstering enforcement of such caps by limiting foreign spending by campaigns independently of the purpose of such spending (advertising, digital services or otherwise). For some jurisdictions, such as the UK, 'a surprising lacuna' has been noted with regard to the regulation of foreign campaign spending.[34] Additionally, digital service providers and social media platforms should be required to publish information about the extent and source of money spent on political advertising (including both data analysis services and paid political messaging) relevant to or visible in the jurisdiction in which the election or referendum in question takes place, in order to reveal funding sources that are nominally unaffiliated to official campaigns (private contributors and privately funded campaign efforts).

## V. Conclusion

In recent years, three parallel technological and social developments have revolutionised political communication: first, mass data collection and analysis ('big data') offers predictive knowledge of voter preference and behaviour, and potential ways of influencing the latter. As a result of this increase in predictive

[30] ibid.

[31] The additional and equally necessary discussion on fact-checking and the flagging of obvious falsehoods or disinformation posted by political actors on social media would exceed the scope of this chapter. It should be noted, however, that the prevention of disinformation and its strategic dissemination through social media channels is a significant component of the threat constituted by data-driven campaigning and makes regulation all the more necessary.

[32] Zuiderveen Borgesius et al (n 16) 88.

[33] IDEA (n 2) 18.

[34] M Harker, 'Political Advertising Revisited: Digital Campaigning and Protecting Democratic Discourse' (2020) 40 *Legal Studies* 151.

knowledge, it is now possible to design microtargeted and even personalised communication. Mass data analysis and personalised campaigning are facilitated and reinforced by the growing importance of social media in political communication (and communication in general), whereby the inherent dynamics of social media amplify the tendency of many individuals to form 'filter bubbles' of like-minded persons.

While none of these three developments is in itself new – technological changes have occurred before, personalised campaigning has often been attempted, albeit on the basis of much less, and less sophisticated, data, and political filter bubbles are no invention of the digital age – the conjunction of all three developments, their commercial exploitation and their sheer scale merits the term 'revolutionary'. Arguably, they constitute a threat to the freedom of political will formation. The latter is often deemed guaranteed if adequate safeguards for freedom of speech are in place.

However, it has been shown that a functioning democracy requires at least a degree of exposure to and engagement with different political ideas, motives and opinions. Changing habits in media consumption and communication (in particular, the growing importance of social media, whose content is highly personalised), in conjunction with data-driven and microtargeted campaigning, severely limit chance exposure to the political 'other', and thereby structurally affect personal and public will formation. A long-term result of these developments may be a decrease in legitimacy of outcomes of democratic processes, and a decline in legitimacy of liberal democracy as such.

Preventing these adverse effects on liberal democracy through regulatory legislation is difficult: first, many of the effects outlined here are the result of choices made by individuals (eg with regard to their communication and media consumption habits), and limiting these choices would mean limiting the freedom of expression and the freedom to receive information. Secondly, big data analysis, the design and dissemination of campaign messages through the Internet, and social media platforms and their commercial activities all potentially escape the reach of most (national or regional) regulatory authorities and can be moved to other jurisdictions without much trouble.

Nevertheless, I argue that a number of regulatory interventions are helpful and necessary to mitigate the threat to liberal democracy posed by mass data analysis and microtargeted campaigning through social media. First, strong data protection rules and their stringent enforcement are useful in limiting the collection of personal data for analysis. Secondly, while personalisation of social media news streams is partly user- and platform-driven, commercial personalisation in particular should be regulated through transparency obligations for social media platform operators. Thirdly, legal rules on political campaigning and campaign spending should be designed in such a way as to create transparency regarding the use of mass data analysis and microtargeted campaigning.

# PART III

# Monetary Sovereignty and Taxation in the Information Technology Era

# 7

# Monetary Sovereignty in Conditions of Technological Revolution

MARKO DIMITRIJEVIĆ

## I. Introduction

The subject of analysis in this chapter is the concept of monetary sovereignty in terms of technological revolutions, which in the field of contemporary monetary law, as a hybrid branch of law, has a significant effect in providing monetary stability as a pure public good. In this context, the chapter points to the genesis and classical structure of monetary sovereignty as a crucial integral component of political sovereignty (besides fiscal and financial sovereignty) and basic principles of monetary law that determine its scope in practice, such as *lex monetae* and *lex contractus*, with particular attention to the external effect of the *lex monetae* principle that occurs outside the border of national monetary jurisdiction.

Contemporary monetary law increasingly finds its sources in some of the new legal and economic facts which are caused by international monetary agents when concluding certain interstate agreements in the domain of secondary legislation. In the conditions of the global economic and financial crisis, they perform the function of fulfilling the legal gaps in the primary sources of monetary law. These facts can also be found in some new technological developments which have fundamentally changed the traditional pattern of monetary norm implementation and invoke the real and logical need for further development of monetary law *nomotechnics*.[1]

The most significant changes in the way of monetary sovereignty implementation are no longer attached to the circumstances of monetary integration when states approach monetary unions because the much greater challenge for its measurement is the impact of information technology on the development of currency. When a monetary system finds itself faced with new circumstances, such as technological innovation, it will be de facto modified to a greater or lesser extent to reclaim financial legitimacy, accountability and credibility.

[1] Nomotechnics implies the practical activity (methods) of law making.

The emergence of digital money as the product of technological revolution (at first glance) does not modify substantially the monetary prerogatives resulting from the monetary sovereignty of the state. Nevertheless, it needs to adjust to the newly emerging economic conditions. The author believes that the establishment of full monetary sovereignty in the process of creating digital money is necessary because postulates of a social theory of money indicate that in certain epochs of human civilisation the character and property of money was determined by the public opinion about what money is and not what the state has declared as a legal instrument of payment.

In considering monetary sovereignty, we must take into account the fact that monetary systems were initially developed beyond states and that modern forms of money, such as banknotes, were created and designed in the payment system. The state began to regulate banknotes by monetary law regulation much later in their improved form. This fact can be used as an analogy for the scenarios with digital currency, especially cryptocurrency as the most popular and dominant form. It is managed without any central bank control, which means that, at the same time, there are no monetary prerogatives behind the process of its issuance. The aim of this chapter is reflected in the identification of the essential characteristics and manifestations of the constituent components of monetary sovereignty in the conditions of technological revolution, which indicate the tendency of its evolution and adaptation to new monetary circumstances.

## II. Historical Review and the Main Features of Monetary Sovereignty in Contemporary Monetary Law

According to some authors, monetary sovereignty can be regarded as a constitutional part of political sovereignty. Another group points out that the concept of monetary sovereignty is older than political sovereignty because it originated in the Roman period (and, according to some, even earlier, in India and the Babylonian Empire). In contrast, the concept of political sovereignty was created much later, during the Renaissance (1567), by Jean Bodin.[2] It is interesting that, historically, the concept of monetary sovereignty has not enjoyed recognition by the international community for very long. However, it is a key institution of international monetary law that has not explicitly found justification and protection in any of the articles of the Agreement on the Founding of the International Monetary Fund (IMF). The first official recognition of the concept does not have its source in jurisprudence, but in the judiciary of the former Permanent

[2] RA Mundell, 'Money and the Sovereignty of the States' in A Leijonhufvud (ed), *Monetary Theory and Policy Experience* (Palgrave, 2001) 299–337.

Court of International Justice. The right of the state to wholly and independently regulate all issues relating to the definition and use of local currency is explicitly recognised in a judgment concerning the legitimacy of a public loan in the case of *France v Serbi*.[3]

Contemporary restrictions (both legal and economic) that determine the scope of sovereign monetary authorisations of the state have been the subject of comprehensive analysis and interpretations in diverse legal, financial and political publications. In today's circumstances, the majority of authors consider that the concept of monetary sovereignty could not be regarded as static, which could then simply be reduced to a set of catalogue authorisations, ie the rights of the state and other public legal collectives in the monetary flow. On the other hand, on the conditions of existence of monetary unions, a significant number of authors advocate the thesis of an intense 'erosion' of monetary sovereignty, which, according to their perceptions, exists only in the figurative sense. Of course, in the globalised economic and financial relations, there has been a transformation in the concept of monetary sovereignty. Nevertheless, we can only speak of the tendency of the monetary sovereignty evolution of the same, not of its absolute or relative weakening instead adapting to modern economic occasions and international circumstances.

Thus, we can observe that monetary law increasingly finds its sources in new legal and economic facts which were formed by international monetary agents when concluding certain interstate agreements in the domain of secondary legislation. In the conditions of the global economic and financial crisis, they perform the function of filling in legal gaps in the primary sources of international monetary law.[4] The *ratio* of its origin should be sought in the pursuit for an ex post justification of state powers in monetary flows during a period when the central government is weakened in almost all countries.[5] Legal constraints on the manifestation of monetary sovereignty come out of customary international law and concluded international agreements, the most influential of which is the IMF Agreement. In contrast, the most considerable economic constraints are embodied in the consequences of globalisation and the deepening integration of the financial market.

In the analysis of the concept of monetary sovereignty, a direct or an indirect method can be applied.[6] The first, direct, method starts from the notion of monetary sovereignty as an element of general sovereignty, which must be inviolable

[3] *Case Concerning the Payment of Various Serbian Loans Issued in France (France v Serbia)*, Judgment of 12 July 1929, PJC Rep Series A Nos 20–21. The main question referred to the conditions under which the holders of Serbian bonds were entitled to obtain the payment of the nominal amount of their coupons.

[4] M Dimitrijević, 'The Evolving Concept of Lex Monete in European and International Monetary Law' (2019) 63(4) *Foreign Legal Life* 81, 92.

[5] CD Zimmermann, 'The Concept of Monetary Sovereignty Revisited' [2013] *European Journal of International Law* 797, 818.

[6] S Besson, 'Sovereignty in Conflict' [2004] *European Integration Online Papers* 1, 3.

and complete, while the other, indirect, method proceeds from the fact that all sovereign authorisations (and so monetary sovereignty) are derived from the same source, that is, the capacity of the state for independence. In the literature, the concept of monetary sovereignty is said to be 'essentially competitive in nature', in the sense that it does not merely express normative standards, which makes its perception different for different individuals. It leads to the emergence of misunderstanding about the optimal way for its effective implementation in practice, the meaning of the concept per se.[7]

The concept of monetary sovereignty in practice has a dual character: in addition to positive components, it includes normative components. The concept of monetary sovereignty is much more than a 'mere' framework of the state powers and duties in the field of national and international monetary and legal relations. In the context of globalised economic and financial flows, this concept carries out the functions of a legal benchmark for evaluating modern ways of implementing the sovereign authorisations of the state in the field of monetary obligations. It helps us to perceive the essence of complex and heterogeneous factors that form the norms of international monetary law. The contemporary concept of monetary sovereignty undoubtedly follows the conceptual continuity of the doctrinal and historical origins of classical monetary sovereignty. Still, today it is fundamentally very dynamic, as its positive and normative components continuously evolve in the conditions of the international economic environment. The characteristics of modern monetary sovereignty are essential complexity (it must have different dimensions to its meaning), a criterion character (but with the absence of a universal criterion of consistent application) and normativity, since it expresses and includes mutually different values.[8]

The main issue in connection with the manifestation of monetary sovereignty concerns the determination of the *locus*, ie the holder of sovereignty. Thus, in monetary literature, one can observe the perceptions that sovereignty belongs to national governments that enjoy discretionary powers over its precise implementation or imply the original authority of citizens delegating to governments or international organisations through a specific functional model. For this reason, representatives of the state and socio-psychological theory on the legal definition of the concept of money have different views on the structure and scope of monetary authorisations.

In the analysis of monetary sovereignty, the current issues are related to the problem of its normative value, the scope of its application (geographic and material) and the method of its implementation. In addition, the analysis should include the very fragile issue of the rights of states that have limited their monetary sovereignty by joining monetary unions.[9] Practice shows that the benefits of

[7] ibid.
[8] ibid 4.
[9] A Hertogen, 'An Unusual Suspect? Monetary Sovereignty and Financial Stability' (2010) 1 *Goettingen Journal of International Law2* 243, 266.

full monetary sovereignty are particularly valuable to countries with more rigid economic systems because it is easier to mitigate and prevent economic shocks. In such circumstances, the central bank monitors the monetary policy, while the government seeks to exceed all barriers to the free flow of foreign trade.[10] The influence of legal norms on choosing the optimal monetary policy is crucial in circumstances where the state wants to restore shaky credibility in monetary flows because it makes clear the precise legal commitment of the government to a 'balanced behavioural trajectory' which it will not be so easy to turn into a monetary game.[11]

## A. *Lex Monetae* in Traditional Monetary Law

The basic principle of monetary law is the principle of *lex monetae*, which implies that entities that conclude a public loan contract are generally free to choose the currency in which the loan will be denominated (but once they make this choice, no later decisions of the state issuance can affect its validity). This means that replacing the existing currency with a new one (which can be observed in some countries during periods of hyperinflation to avoid a complete collapse of the monetary system) does not affect the nature and duration of the contractual monetary obligation.[12] The monetary literature states that this principle not only applies to the definition of a currency unit, but also determines its subunits, as well as specific items that have the status of legal tender. Widely viewed, it is clear that the principle of *lex monetae* is in the function of protecting the legal security and interests of bona fides contracting parties. The principle finds its place in the Charter of the United Nations (Article 2, page 7) in the form of state nominalism, ie state theories on the legal definition of money. This principle can also be defined negatively as an inability of states to influence the determination of monetary units in other countries.

The application of the principle follows the perception of civil law that monetary obligations are durable, even in the case of currency termination, in which the contract is concluded. Various theoretical approaches to the content of the principles can be found in the monetary law literature. It is common to make a distinction between the principles of the *lex monetae* in the narrow and broader sense.[13] The narrow definition includes the right to define the currency (in particular when of the old currency exchange with a new one), while the broader meaning includes all primary and secondary legislation protecting the domestic currency. A narrow definition was formulated by the Association for International Monetary

[10] ibid.

[11] BA Simmons, 'International Law and State Behavior: Commitment and Compliance in International Monetary Affairs' (2000) 94 *American Political Science Review* 819, 835.

[12] M Giovanoli (ed), *International Monetary Law: Issues for the New Millenium* (Oxford, Oxford University Press, 2001).

[13] ibid.

Law at its Taipei Conference in February 1998, where the *lex monetae* was defined as 'the right of a state or group of countries that have a common currency to define or redefine a currency unit and to determine the exchange rate between the new and the old currency unit' (that is, the unit they want to substitute), which includes the definition of the so-called recurrent link.

## B. The Monetary Dimension of *Lex Contractus*

The principle of *lex monetae* should not be confused with the principle of legal continuity (*lex contractus* or *lex cause*), which implies the freedom of contracting parties to conclude a particular contract.[14] The freedom to conclude a contract and to determine all of its essential elements (*essentialia negotii*) and sporadic elements are the universal principles of civil law. Its contents include the legal protection of the contracting parties' interest in the event of a change in the particular circumstances under which the contract was concluded, or the issue of its validity. In the field of monetary obligations, *lex contractus* has unique consequences in case of conversion of the currency in which the contract on a public loan was concluded.

Under the conditions of monetary integration, this principle was especially relevant in the formation of the European Economic and Monetary Union (EMU), through the liberalisation of economic and financial flows, the creation of a European monetary system and the introduction of a single currency.[15] For this reason, EC Regulation 1103/97 confirmed the continuity of previously concluded contracts on monetary flows and transfers to protect the interests of the legal order, and in particular the principles of already acquired rights (the principle of retention).

In the case of the EU, the majority of authors state that the unilateral transfer of monetary sovereignty is realised without the contextual transfer of legislative and regulatory powers. This is best illustrated by the centralisation of monetary policy at the communitarian level and the financial supervision that is still carried out by the national central banks. The controversy arising from the plan is because the *lex monetae* has been transferred to the EU. The great challenge in determining the monetary sovereignty in the EMU is to measure the level of remaining national monetary sovereignty and set the boundaries between the Member states. It is hard to decide on where the sovereignty of one Member State ends and where the monetary sovereignty of another Member State begins.

At this point, I must emphasise the importance of *monetary disputes* as a special kind of administrative disputes, which involve a central bank (active or passive procedural legitimacy) as the keeper of the *lex monetae*. Due to the specific

[14] RM Lastra, *International Monetary and Financial Law* (Oxford, Oxford University Press, 2015).

[15] C Hermann and K Dornacher, *European and International Monetary Law – An Introduction* (Munich, Springer, 2017).

nature of relationships and outcomes, monetary disputes cannot be guided by the interests of the politically influential members of the EU and justified by reasons of pragmatism. They must be primarily motivated by the protection of supreme monetary institutions that perform their tasks in the interests of society and economy, which was confirmed in the case of OMT (outright monetary transaction).[16] The European Court of Justice confirmed legitimacy and legalities to the proposed measures of the European Central Bank (ECB), explaining it by the fact that the OMT programme falls under the programme of a unified monetary policy which the ECB conducted following the monetary strategy to preserve monetary stability (ie price stability as the primary goal, which is more consistently realised by the application of these measures). Note that in monetary disputes, the requirements for the assessment of constitutionality and legality are subject to certain limitations. Although, for some theorists, this decision represents another confirmation of the expansion competence trend of the communitarian institutions by the provisions of secondary legislation, I consider that in this case the conduct of the ECB was not contrary to the provisions of primary law, but rather represents a new way of manifesting the competence in conditions of crisis.

## III. Monetary Sovereignty and Technological Progress: A Case of Electronic Money

Adequate monetary legislation must be set in the function of pursuing the general social interest of a particular community. Unlike other forms of purely civilian legislation, it cannot be a trivial matter for artful nomotechnics (which, for the competent monetary legislator, does not have to be a problem). The concept of money is multilayered, and legal science cannot ignore its economic functions and the psychological effects that its application brings with it in the form of various distortive effects. It refers to changes in the behaviour of citizens concerning money, its functions, purpose and importance in everyday life. At the same time, an essential circumstance of current cash flows is the fact that cash transfers are increasingly implying cash payments in terms of the use of banknotes or coins. It is slowly becoming a relic of the past, because some monetary jurisdictions prohibit such payments, which must be replaced by cheques or wire transfers in orders to combat tax evasion.

The development of monetary law over the past two decades has highlighted the need to adapt the postulates of state (institutional) and social theory of money to the demands of a knowledge society and the development of new technologies. In this sense, there is a fundamental change in the approach to the legal

[16] This programme contains sophisticated monetary measures for buying bonds in secondary financial markets.

definition of money and the currency unit, which was especially noticeable with the adoption of the first amendments to the IMF Agreement and the final abandonment of the gold standard (1978), thus virtually abolishing the link between the currency units and the value of the real economic assets of which it is made. The advent of electronic money marked the beginning of the so-called 'quiet revolutions' in monetary legislation around the world and the gradual transition from the traditional (banknote) system to the electronic payment system. The reason why citizens have accepted electronic money lies in the fact that the mentioned changes were implemented in a carefully and purposefully managed manner without the need for citizens to change their economic behaviour in their role of monetary users, ie there is a subjective attitude towards traditional money that still enjoys a high degree of trust.

Monetary law theorists often use an analogy to explain the new tendencies regarding the legal regulation of monetary relations and speak about 'the radical transition from the Copernican era (in which everything revolved around the sun – gold) to Einstein's era of universal relativity'.[17] Monetarists often use this analogy to understand new trends in the development of international monetary law, bearing in mind that the astronomer mentioned above is also the creator of the pioneering work in the field of monetary matter, *De Moneta Cudenata Ratione*, dating back to the fifteenth century. It is interesting to note that in his 1888 utopian novel, *Looking Forward*, Edward Bellami also predicted the formation of a cash-strapped society and anticipated the abandonment of the fixed exchange rate. Although the mentioned work *Looking Forward* is quite radical, in some issues it also foresees the complete abolition of commercial and central banks. Undoubtedly, the author's sense of a comprehensive understanding of how monetary relations are regulated by law has been more than impressive. What is not emphasised in both of the above-mentioned works is the process of globalisation of economic flows and the emergence of financial conglomerates, which, in cooperation with the development of telecommunications technologies, enabled the circulation of large amounts of money in commercial traffic without significant restrictions for a relatively short time. Overall, it led to the emergence of virtuous money in a globally integrated financial market.

Assigning *lex monetae* to the central bank as the supreme monetary institution of national monetary law seems like a logical solution. Nevertheless, we must ask ourselves whether such a solution is normatively effective, given that central banks are today expected to perform a large number of tasks, both in the field of monetary stability and in the area of general financial security. Specifically, central banks are increasingly expected to perform the role of the bank of last resort, as well as other tasks in the sphere of macroprudential policy. Therefore, some monetary legislation in the world has also granted the right to issue electronic money to

[17] M Giovanoli, 'Virtual Money and Global Financial Market: Challenges for Lawyers' [1996] *Yearbook of International Financial and Economic Law* 3, 24.

commercial banks or the government (which may be associated with certain difficulties, as monetary agents need to address these tasks). Thus, the central bank can also devote itself to achieving the desired economic growth for a nominal gross domestic product that is consistent with inflation targets and real economic growth.[18] The IMF, as the primary arbiter of international monetary law, must exercise global control over monetary policy, which increasingly receives those above 'electronic term'. It implies that all such entities must participate to some degree in the creation of electronic money for the process itself to achieve legality and legitimacy. The emergence of electronic money, in my view, does not substantially modify the monetary prerogatives arising from the monetary sovereignty of the state, but merely adapts them to new economic circumstances.

Just as in law there is no universal definition of money in the traditional sense, so there is also a noticeable absence of legal definitions of electronic money (although there are different economic and technical definitions of it). However, the presence of electronic money as a legal means of payment requires the search for an adequate legal definition, which must begin with a consideration of the conditions under which electronic money is used in legal transactions and a comparative analysis of its characteristics with traditional money.[19] Electronic money is viewed as a kind of electronic surrogate for physical money in new economic circumstances.[20] Electronic money first appeared in Japan in the mid-1980s in the form of prepaid cards accepted by individual telephone companies, railroads and carriers. In contrast, electronic money appeared in Europe and the USA in the early 1990s to replace the use of cash for low-value transactions. Electronic money is a digitised monetary obligation, and therefore a complete definition of electronic money in the modern monetary literature is one where it is viewed as 'a set of information transmitted by issuing an electromagnetic amount based on a contractual obligation with an electronic currency issuer to fulfil a monetary obligation specified by a specific contract'.[21]

A large number of laws determine the legal basis for issuing and using electronic money where the law on the central bank and the law, which regulate the work and operation of commercial banks, can be recognised as fundamental. At the same time, precise solutions appear in the commercial code, the law on the general administrative procedure (electronic signature), foreign exchange law and the criminal code. We can see that such a broad legal basis is in the function of protecting legal certainty and consumer rights, since the use of electronic money can bring uncertainties that must be eliminated. For the monetary legislators of countries that do not have extensive practice in the use of electronic currency,

[18] J Jordan, 'The New Monetary Framework' [2016] *Cato Journal* 367, 384.

[19] N Sugiura (trans JJ Luyat), 'Electronic Money and the Law: Legal Realities and Future Challenges' [2009] *Pacific Rim Law & Policy Journal Association* 110, 120.

[20] M Sıddık-Yurtçiçek, 'The Legal Nature of Electronic Money and the Effects of the EU Regulations Concerning the Electronic Money Market' [2013] *Law & Justice Review* 276, 321.

[21] ibid.

setting a broad regulatory framework for regulating its use is crucial to providing business security.

The implementation of the traditional monetary law principles in the field of electronic money remains unsuccessful, which is why it is necessary to update the settings on which it is based. Electronic money is most often seen in the monetary literature as a form of transfer value contained in a digital file on a computer or a microprocessor that is part of a smart card.[22] To achieve wider acceptance of electronic money in legal transactions, it is necessary to fulfil specific requirements, which can be classified into both broad and narrow monetary law requirements. The first one implies that electronic money as a means of payment is accepted within the boundaries of a monetary jurisdiction; to represent the final means of payment exempt from credit and other conditions; to circulate freely in legal transactions; and that it is self-sustaining–meaning that it does not require new money emission, clearing or settlement.

In addition to the conditions above, there is a requirement in the narrow sense for its judicial recognition in monetary disputes and treatment as a standard currency, since the emergence of electronic money in foreign trade per se in monetary law remains merely a fact and nothing more than that. Certainly, for this condition to be implemented in a legally correct manner, the court must have specialised knowledge for resolving monetary disputes in which the IMF (often) participates as an intervener. Adequate regulation of electronic money requires institutional changes that encompass both the adoption of consumer protection laws and the inclusion of various industries in the automated payment system.

## IV. Monetary Sovereignty and Cryptocurrencies

Here, I must emphasise that the term 'electronic currency' should not be equated with the so-called cryptocurrencies, which are a form of digital money. The cryptocurrencies, which have been intensively developing for the last 20 years, do not enjoy legal protection because there is no monetary legislation that regulates them. At the same time, the use of these 'hidden currencies' is associated with several uncertainties, reflected in the absence of banking controls, as banks do not act as financial intermediaries in their use; the absence of the issuer (public or private entity); the impeded protection of the personal rights and privacy of its users; and all other uncertainties that involve loss of value due to the destruction of the software which creates it. It is important to emphasise that electronic (not digital) money issued by private entities (which is judicially recognised as money) can be accepted as legal tender, which, of course, does not mean that the central bank loses crucial position in money creation because it holds supervisory functions in cases with private entities.

[22] Giovanoli, *International Monetary Law* (n 10) 371.

Legal regulation of monetary relations in times of intense and rapid technological revolutions is a *conditio sine qua non* for maintaining monetary stability, both at the national and the international level. In the context of globalised capital flows and electronic payment systems, the effects of monetary instability, characterised by the undermining of the authority of monetary jurisdiction, the collapse of the monetary system and the relativisation of monetary (state) management functions, are not territorially limited only to space within the operation of concrete monetary legislation, but also to other countries that are connected with the affected one in geographical terms or represent their foreign trade partners. The reason for this (negative) spill over of monetary instability lies in the fact that all monetary jurisdictions inevitably participate (either directly or indirectly, with varying degrees of intensity) in the creation of an international monetary order, the fundamental principle of which is to preserve the monetary balance as the primary component and the precondition of general economic stability. Monetary law is the prime answer of the legal science to changes that follow the law of values when the scope of legal rules in the monetary sphere is sustainable.[23] Monetary law, without any discussion, in circumstances where the law of values appears to be somewhat unstable in all world economies, must be treated as a branch of modern jurisprudence. The monetary law is embedded in the very foundations of the overall legal architecture.[24] Even in circumstances where the law of values remains unchanged in space and time, it would not at the same time mean the need to abolish monetary law. It would still point to its undeniable theoretical significance, but with the practical relevance reduced.

The technological revolution has redefined the established notion of monetary law about the role of the central bank as the sole issuer of money. Namely, the use of technology in the creation of new money that is accepted by monetary users violates the first rule of banking law that there should be no natural persons in the role of the issuer. Making money is, therefore, a material project: it proceeds by intervening in the way people relate to resources, and it distributes profits and costs as it does. Money should serve both public and private purposes equally, irregardless of how it is designed (in ways that are democratic or dictatorial, stable or fragile).

Although it is indisputable that in the conditions of technological revolution, the central bank must redefine its functions and tasks in the sense that they should not be at the expense of monetary security, which is its primary task. The role and the increased number of individuals involved in the creation of cryptocurrency should not be ignored, because it would be at the same time ignoring the postulates of the social theory of money (according to which the attitude of citizens

[23] The law of value as the crucial regulative economic principle expresses the essential connections between social work, the value and the price of goods. Its *ratio* lies in the fact that the source of a commodity value is an abstract labour.

[24] E Hirschberg, 'Modern Problems of Monetary Law' (1973) 6 *Comparative & International Law Journal of Social Affairs* 272.

about what money is, is essential). The process of further developing the use of cryptocurrency should be pursued outside the jurisdiction of the central bank. Therefore, despite ECB and IMF press releases indicating that the percentage use of cryptocurrency is still low relative to the use of conventional money, the future development and polarity of cryptocurrency cannot be predicted with a high degree of certainty. The sensitivity of money and changing consumer preferences are best reflected in the aftermath of the global financial crisis, which requires timely and careful preparation of legal regulations for issuing cryptocurrency, which must take place under the watchful eye of a central bank. While monetary sovereignty as the primordial category of traditional monetary law seems incompatible with the digital technologies used in its creation, the fact is that monetary sovereignty, as a constituent element of political sovereignty, is inseparable from the existence of the state, unlike the various forms of money that have changed throughout monetary history.

Legally regulating the issuance and use of cryptocurrency would bring the necessary legal certainty in this segment of monetary flow. Even if the use of cryptocurrency were to diminish over time (because so far its use has been based on the trust that citizens indicate), it must still be regulated by law. If eventually citizens do not trust it anymore, I believe that outdated (depreciated) legal rule is better than the primary absence of any legal regulation (legal gaps). I believe that the central bank is an institution *sui generis* that cannot be replaced by any other institution in the field of monetary policy, far fewer individuals or guilds authorised to issue a cryptocurrency. The classical postulates of economic analysis of law do not support the existence of legal rules that do not apply, because they are then economically inefficient. Still, these postulates should not be implemented for cryptocurrency given their sensitive nature.

The problem of cryptocurrency use is not only a severe legal, economic and political issue, but a psychological and cultural issue too. The role of the central bank in legal tenders for the creation of money cannot be played by individuals. That is not ethical and represents an insult to all the effort and specialised skill that the central bank spearheads and advocates to maintain a stable value of the currency. Central banks are at a turning point in that they are required to take account of fiscal policy (in addition to the goals of general monetary and economic policy), as well as the new role of bank of last resort, ie they must knowingly violate the prohibition on public debt monetisation. In today's circumstances, their competences are continually evolving as a result of complex changes in the financial market that are becoming increasingly technocratic. Central banks today no longer only take into account monetary sovereignty, but also fiscal sovereignty, and contribute to the fight against organised crime and the prevention of financial terrorism, and even the protection of the environment. Not all these 'new' competences are related to the original jurisdiction of the issuance of money. If the legislator already thinks that the monetary legislation should also determine them, there is no reason not to place the control of the use of cryptocurrency under its jurisdiction. It de facto remains in the sphere of monetary policy of the new millennium. Of course, the process of legal regulation of cryptocurrency by the central bank also requires specific technical and technological prerequisites and full attention to the protection of the monetary rights of monetary users in cyberspace, which is a very complicated task. Nevertheless, in cooperation with competent agencies, it can be implemented.

I believe that monetary sovereignty in the conditions of technological revolution is not weakened, nor will it cease to exist. It must undoubtedly be conceptually and fundamentally adapted to the demands of a post-information knowledge society based on accelerated technological progress and innovation in all aspects of life. There are numerous examples of central banks at the national level that started with the initial regulation of digital money. However, it is noticeable that there is still no global initiative that would be implemented by the IMF or the ECB as significant arbiters of international monetary law. Nevertheless, a growing number of reports by the institutions above are beginning intensive discussions and advocating studies on the careful monitoring of the development and implementation of cryptocurrencies. There are also some new developments, as cryptocurrencies become an accompanying element of so-called smart contracts that redefine the outstanding obligations law.

Although cryptocurrencies are currently viewed as alternative money, it should be noted that monetary history has been very rich in such examples. Conventional money, as we know it today, has come a long way from the exchange of goods, gold and silver, through the emergence of paper money, to the use of electronic money, PayPal and cryptocurrency. Alternative money, unlike traditional money, does not have all four well-known economic functions (unit of account, store of value, medium of exchange and standard of value). These functions cannot, however, be ignored, as, over time, they could develop and make up for their shortcomings.[25]

The introduction of information technology has also significantly altered established perceptions of how monetary finance is separated in practice. It is especially evident with the widespread use of digital currency and electronic money that takes place outside the existing monetary legislation, without the central bank's supervision and the financial backing of commercial banks. At the end of 2016,the IMF pointed out for the first time the challenges that central banks would face in the gradual digitalisation of the digital currency; so, too, did the ECB, which, in its reports, is warning increasingly of the benefits and less of its use, stabilisation and control. The role of monetary law is becoming crucial in this field. The monetary legislator will face numerous challenges in legalising such a payment method and providing security and legal protection. Various economic studies emphasise that its expanding use will increase the degree of systemic risk within the financial system (viewed in a global context) because of the international character of electronic money.[26]

[25] S Harald, *The Future of Money* (FinanzBuch Verlag, 2017).

[26] M Dimitrijević, *The International Monetary Law Institutions* (Nis, Center for Publication of Law Faculty, 2018).

I also agree with the so-called Friedman dilemma that, even in circumstances where electronic (digital) money would become dominant in the financial market, the central bank cannot lose its regulatory role. It can only talk about adapting the techniques it uses to target inflation in the face of institutional changes in the money market. The cryptocurrency, as currently the most common form of digital currency, has certain usage inconsistencies that open the door to numerous abuses. It may be left without adequate judicial protection, given the absence of sound monetary law. Still, citizen participation in such transactions is based on voluntary risk-conscious deliberation and space not under the watchful eye of the central bank. The frequency of such operations in the commercial sector, the acceptance of cryptocurrency as a legitimate means of payment by large multinational companies and the trust that a large number of monetary users bring them only emphasise the need for some form of legal regulation to preserve monetary stability and protect consumer rights.

It is undoubtedly clear that cryptocurrencies are a form of monetary innovation that can be seen in the broadest context as new instruments, tools and procedures by which monetary preferences are realised. It is evident that the history of monetary and financial innovations is still far from being (finally) written and that it is influenced by many factors besides the mentioned technical and technological process, such as inelastic demand for existing money, financial problems of the governments, interdisciplinary competition in the field of monetary and fiscal policy, and legal loopholes in existing legal solutions that are used against the general intention of legislators.[27] Monetary innovations can achieve the full purpose if they are recognised and justified as such by domestic monetary law. The law serves as a guarantee for the preservation of already acquired rights and continuity and predictability in the application of monetary norms that inform citizens on time about all consequences of their financial choices.

Taking into account the dangers posed by so-called cybercrime, which is inherently related to digital money, the role of the central bank is crucial in preventing, enforcing and fulfilling the purpose of criminal law in the area of monetary system misuse and the prevention of money laundering and terrorism.[28] Although the role of the central bank in this area is indirect, it does not diminish its importance or contribution in preventing such socially dangerous phenomena that occur beyond the boundaries of legal and legitimate economic activities. It simultaneously protects and strengthens the existing transmission mechanisms of monetary finances and preserves the reputation of the banking system. The new initiatives of the ECB to set up a particular office to prevent money laundering and other economic crime may have a positive impact on the national central banks of Member States that causes them to initiate similar initiatives at the level of domestic law.

[27] P Bernholz and R Vaubel, *Explaining Monetary and Financial Innovation: A Historical Analysis* (Munich, Springer, 2014).

[28] DA Leslie, *Legal Principles for Combatting Cyber Laundering* (Munich, Springer, 2014).

Adding new competencies to the central bank can be a complicated legislative process, given the fact that the number of its delivery tasks has increased since the global financial crisis. Today, in many monetary jurisdictions, central banks perform complex tasks in the area of monetary policy. The crisis has dispelled the illusions that central banking could be a scientific endeavour, firmly grounded in rigorous models, supported by communicative strategies whose ultimate goal was to train financial markets to interpret the central bank's interest rate signals adequately. Their institutional and political position has been challenged.[29] The goals for which the central bank is now responsible often conflict with one another, which implies priorities when choosing a specific purpose as dominant at a particular point in monetary history, but also raises the question of central bank responsibility. Should a significant increase in the share of cryptocurrency against cash become reality, the absence of legal regulation by the central bank could be very dangerous to the social order and protection of the rights of monetary users. Indeed, regular monitoring of events that involve the use of cryptocurrency may promptly indicate the adoption of the necessary regulation. It also requires excellent coordination with the competent authorities of the central bank. Resolving potential conflicts between these goals will require technocratic, and, for some, deeply political, judgements that throw into question the dominant paradigm of central bank independence.

## V. Conclusion

In considering the relationship between monetary sovereignty and the repercussion of technological revolution, we must take into account the fact that, in a sense, it is about the collision between the traditional way and the modern way of regulating ongoing monetary flows. Namely, monetary sovereignty, as a key institute of monetary law, is primordial and has directed the full development of this hybrid branch of law, in which the public law element is still predominant above private law. We must not forget that monetary sovereignty is older than even the very concept of political sovereignty.

On the other hand, cryptocurrencies are a product of postmodern consumer society in which the way to satisfy preferences is qualitatively different from the historical factors that caused the emergence of monetary sovereignty. The cryptocurrencies are a direct reflection of modern times, when consumers want to reduce not only their financial cost, but also the time and psychological costs they incur in classically satisfying the sales reps. However, unlike electronic money, which falls under the *lex monetae* as the country's first and most significant monetary prerogative, cryptocurrencies are not uniquely regulated in monetary law.

[29] C Goodhart, D Gabor, J Vestergaard and I Ertürk, *Central Banking at a Crossroads: Europe and Beyond* (London, Anthem Press, 2014).

The reason for this is that they are the result of technological innovations of an individual over which the central bank, as the custodian of monetary sovereignty, has no power, nor is the process of creating them in any way related to the legal tender for money. Rather, it is based on the economy of sharing and the use of mathematical algorithms, which are not currently found in monetary policy or legislation designed to protect and strengthen the impact of monetary sovereignty.

That does not in any way mean that the current monetary law solutions are outdated and do not follow the flow of time and all that the technological revolutions carry. Rather, it indicates the real and logical need for further efforts from lawyers and economists to regulate this phenomenon optimally. Monetary sovereignty in its more or less traditional form has survived all monetary and financial innovations in the market over a long period of monetary history. That undoubtedly indicates its importance for the survival of the social community, and its denial means the negation of the genuine social need for the legal regulation of money by independent state agencies. Indeed, the central bank as the supreme monetary institution is not infallible, and its work cannot be seen as a panacea for all the problems that arise in a single economy. Nevertheless, it remains necessary and irreplaceable in the financial market.

Monetary sovereignty (like the central banks that guard it) adjusts to the new needs of society. However, these changes must be carefully managed, because if they are too swift and based on vague relative forecasts of the impact of the technological revolution on monetary flows, there will be no new monetary legislation credible enough from the general democratic and financial legitimacy viewpoint. The central bank, as the guardian of monetary sovereignty in the context of uncontrolled technological advances, must persevere in its primary task of stating precisely the sovereignty of the delegated state against the hegemony of private interests, though not, of course, in a way that hinders technological progress in monetary transmission. Nevertheless, anyone can count on secure cash flows, personal data protection and compensation for damages in case of breach of smart contracts using cryptocurrencies.

In the conditions of technological revolution, monetary law can use its hybrid character as an advantage. At the same time, its sources, in which the norms of secondary legislation prevail, are much better adapted to the emerging social and economic needs than the classical branches of law, because they are significantly more flexible than the norms of primary legislation. The flexibility of the secondary sources of monetary law also ensures the flexibility of the structure of monetary sovereignty, which can always find sufficient room for a sophisticated monetary legislator to derogate, abolish or create a new postulate that must not contradict existing principles. The adoption of further central bank responsibilities in times of crisis demonstrates this best, which means that there is potentially room for the optimal legal regulation of the use of cryptocurrency if the need arises. The individuals who created the sub-currencies do not indicate a dilution of monetary sovereignty.

I believe that this speaks only in support of the fact that monetary sovereignty is prone to the tendency to adjust and is somehow generated from the 'personal monetary sovereignty' that each person carries within. It only confirms the vitality of monetary sovereignty, which represents much more than a certain ideological concept, because it has its grain in every man, which is the meaning of the social theory of money (man creates money and grants it such status).

Also, I would like to emphasise that the tendency for monetary sovereignty to evolve in a time of technological revolution (and become more 'digital') must be accompanied by a simultaneous process of evolution of central bank competencies. That requires a comprehensive study about the level of development that has been achieved in central bank law, which is an independent legal discipline that exists outside the scope of general monetary law but undoubtedly must be complementary to it. This issue becomes especially relevant and gains importance in the context of increasing monetary disputes as a special kind of administrative disputes, in which we can see the full implementation of the active and passive procedural legitimacy of the central banks, who act as guardians of monetary sovereignty. The existence of legal gaps related to the under-explored link between monetary sovereignty and technological revolution (and the untimely derogation of primary sources of monetary law that would undoubtedly confirm its credible presence in the issue related with digital currencies) can have severe consequences for overall legal, economic, political stability and consumer protections.

I believe that the existing monetary laws governing the work of central banks must contain provisions that regulate the supervision and control of issuers and users of cryptocurrency. However, some studies indicate that the current number of transactions made in digital currencies is still modest, so it cannot endanger the use of official money in circulation. The reason for the proposed provisions lies in the fact that it is always better to have a legal rule that will allow the implementation of monetary sovereignty in the process of issuing digital currency, even though it may not be applied in many cases (since it may not be necessary), than to have a legal gap in the segment of the central bank's control mechanism in that area. It is difficult to imagine that in a dynamic technological context, such a provision would remain without implementation. The implementation of such provisions would not have been economically costly from the point of an economic analysis of law if it had incorporated in positive monetary legislation as a security benchmark. However, the recent initiatives taken by major EU institutions and IMF reports argue for the need to establish control on the use of such currency to prevent its abuse in financing terrorism, money laundering and international tax evasion.

# 8

# Conceptual and Legal Challenges to the Public Order of States Stemming from Cybercurrencies

BENJAMIN MORON-PUECH, JÉRÉMY CORNAIRE
AND HARRISON COLINS

## I. Introduction

The development of new information and communication technologies have changed the way that agents hold and exchange currencies. Intrinsically linked to the economic development of our societies, the evolution of the currencies has progressed through the centuries with the increase in globalisation. This progressive dematerialisation, backed up by the birth of the Internet, brings new opportunities. In the early twenty-first century, many other numerical active assets, or 'cybercurrency', were created, assets which contain several names, such as 'crypto assets', 'e-money' and 'cryptocurrency'. In this chapter, the prefix 'cyber' will be used as recommended by the French Language Enrichment Commission (Commission d'enrichissement de la langue française),[1] although it is quite uncommon in the common law world, where the prefix 'crypto' is preferred. According to the Commission, the word equivalent to the prefix 'crypto' should not be used since it can give the impression that such currencies are well protected, which is not always the case. Also, coins and bills both use a cryptographic process. The prefix 'cyber' instead relates to the idea that this currency is linked to the Internet and can circulate on its network, which is an essential feature of cybercurrency. As for the second part of the word, 'currency' will here be used instead of 'asset' because it will be shown that cybercurrencies are indeed currencies.

Cybercurrencies, which have existed for more than 30 years, cannot be ignored anymore by the sciences, including legal science, and scientists should now work

[1] Commission d'enrichissement de la langue française, 'Vocabulaire de l'informatique (liste de termes, expressions et définitions adoptés)', *JORF* (23 May 2017) www.legifrance.gouv.fr/affichTexte.do?cidTexte=JORFTEXT000034795042. We are grateful to Étienne Quillot for giving us easy access to the valuable documentation of this Commission.

seriously on its conceptualisation. Indeed, in the future, it is likely that cybercurrencies will become more and more prominent, and may even replace traditional currencies. At least, this seems to be the ambition of Mark Zuckerberg, the CEO of Facebook, and of his 28 initial partners (Booking, eBay, Paypal, Spotify, etc), who revealed their project for a cybercurrency on 18 June 2019. Baptised 'Globalcoins' by some of the observers of the project, it was finally called Libra.

The 'White Paper'[2] that followed the announcement enlightens us on the name chosen for it. Libra refers both to a mass unit used under the Roman Empire and also the Latin for balance. Libra, however, is not the only cybercurrency. The website 'coinmarketcap.com' identified 2104 cybercurrencies in January 2019, the pioneers being 'Digicash', created in 1989, and then 'Cybercash' and 'E-gold'. One year later, in 2020, 5066 cybercurrencies could be counted on the website, most of them born from money-raising ventures involving initial coin offerings. Returning to Libra, the project entails two functions: first, the transfer of money between individuals; and secondly, online payment. These two functions are executed instantly through a wallet that will be developed by the companies using Libra. From this wallet, the user will be able to buy, sell and store coins from the autonomous application or directly from the platforms of Facebook: Whatsapp and Messenger. To manage Libra, Facebook opted for an association, the Libra Association, based in Geneva – where there is almost no taxation. By choosing an association, Facebook is trying to prove that it is not the only company controlling Libra, which could be a way to gain the trust of their users following the Cambridge Analytica scandal.[3] Indeed, within the Libra Association, every member has a seat.

The Libra project divided the social debate as soon as it was announced. Some believed in its economic advantage (low transaction costs) and its potential to democratise the access to financial services, while others – especially politicians from Europe[4] and the USA – worried for their sovereignty and about the risks of money laundering, terrorist financing, data monetisation, abuse of dominant position and threats to financial stabilisation. These criticisms – some of which were directly expressed in front of Mark Zuckerberg by the US Congress[5] – had a real effect on the Libra project. Due to this political-media pressure, some initial partners decided to quit the project (Mastercard, Visa, Vodafone, eBay), while other stayed but pushed for a rethink of the project. The project was finally amended. First, changes were made in the cybercurrency protocol. Secondly, the name of the wallet Facebook was developing on its own for the Libra protocol was

[2] Libra Association, 'Libra White Paper' (April 2020, modifying the original version of June 2019), https://libra.org/en-US/white-paper/?noredirect=en-US.

[3] 'Libra, données personnelles, désinformation … Mark Zuckerberg passe un sale moment face au Congrès américain', *20minutes.fr* (24 October 2019), www.20minutes.fr/high-tech/2635243–20191024-libra-donnees-personnelles-desinformation-mark-zuckerberg-passe-sale-moment-face-congres-americain.

[4] France24, 'Paris, Rome et Berlin cherchent à interdire la Libra, la cryptomonnaie de Facebook', www.france24.com/fr/20191018-france-italie-allemagne-interdire-libra-cryptomonnaie-facebook-banques.

[5] ibid.

changed from Calibra to Novi,[6] in order to avoid any confusion between the Libra association and the Facebook wallet.

However, it is very unlikely that these changes will lead to fewer critics of the Libra project, which is fundamentally a challenge to state sovereignty due to its transnational nature. But Libra does not just cause problems for states; it also challenges lawyers, who, at least in France, are struggling to fit Libra into one of their legal categories in order to regulate it properly. Are Libra and its fellow cybercurrencies money? To answer this question, it is necessary to clarify the new conceptual universe surrounding Libra and cybercurrencies more generally (section II). The chapter will then show why cybercurrencies can be seen as a revolution that is both monetary (section III) and legal (section IV).

## II. What are Cybercurrencies?

To understand cybercurrencies, it is necessary to integrate them into the broader concepts of digital assets and cyberassets. According to the French Language Enrichment Commission, a digital asset is made of 'numerical datas, which the property or the right of use is an element of a physical or legal person's estate'.[7] Even though French law can sometime be confusing,[8] digital assets are not limited to cyberassets which circulate on the Internet. This notion also encompasses multimedia content, software and licences. As for cyberassets – and this time the French Legislator has it quite right[9] – they include cybertokens and cybercurrencies made up of many cybercoins.

The distinction between cybercoins and cybertokens is often misconstrued in practice: the name 'cybercoin' is sometimes used to designate a cybertoken, and vice versa. Also, the words 'cybertoken' and 'cybercurrency' are used to refer to cyberassets in general. However, there is a big difference between them. Indeed, a cybercoin is an asset that belongs to its own blockchain. Bitcoin, Litecoin and Ethereum are cybercurrencies composed of cybercoins whose transactions are registered on the same blockchain, creating proof of the transaction. These cybercoins are totally autonomous, in contrast to cybertokens, even though cybertokens may be registered on the same blockchain. To illustrate the utility of cybertokens, let us take the example of a smart contract running with Ethereum whereby an ether (a coin of Ethereum) is transferred from A to B, then a cybertoken is given to B enabling him to access A's music. In this way, intermediates such

[6] J Raynal, 'Où en est Libra, le projet de cryptomonnaie de Facebook?' *La Tribune* (27 May 2020), www.latribune.fr/entreprises-finance/banques-finance/ou-en-est-libra-le-projet-de-cryptomonnaie-de-facebook-848778.html.

[7] French Language Enrichment Commission, 'Advisory Opinion' (forthcoming).

[8] See Art L.54-10-1 of the Monetary and Financiary Code (CMF), which seems to limit digital assets to cybertokens and cybercurrencies.

[9] ibid. However, this article does not use the expression 'cybercurrency', and expressly denies the qualification of currency, as explained below.

as Google Play or Apple Store are avoided, and this permits individual creators to sell their work directly to consumers and to receive the whole price of the transaction. Indeed, a transaction passed through this medium usually does not cost anything to the user.[10] The project Tron has been developed on this model.

There are many and various cybertokens, even though French law does not really reflect this diversity. According to Article L.552-2 of the Monetary and Financial Code, which was introduced by a Bill ('the Pacte Act') adopted on 22 May 2019,[11] cybertokens are 'any intangible asset representing, in digital form, one or more rights that can be issued, registered, preserved or transferred by means of a shared electronic recording device allowing the owner, directly or indirectly, to be identified of the good'. This definition is interesting, but it fails to illustrate the diversity of tokens. To understand this diversity, one can look at the reports made on cyberassets by the Swiss Federal Authority of Financial Market Surveillance (Finma)[12] and the MP Pierre Person.[13] Three categories of tokens can be identified. First, 'security assets', also called 'investment tokens', are a group of tokens representing an economical value, corresponding either to the right to perceive the interests of a debt, in the sense of the law of obligation, or the right to participate to company and to be entitled to its benefits according to corporate law. These tokens can represent obligations, actions or derivative products, but also some physical goods negotiable on the blockchain, like buildings. Secondly, 'utility tokens' provide access to a digital use or service, based on the use of a blockchain infrastructure, as in the case of the Tron system mentioned above. Finally, there are 'currency tokens', which are accepted as a means of payment for the purchase of goods or services.

Returning to cybercurrencies, it is common to distinguish three generations.[14] The first generation is marked by the advent of Bitcoin in 2008.[15] It is based on blockchaining technology, which relies on a peer-to-peer network that allows assets to be stored and transferred seamlessly and securely. However, this first generation has shortcomings[16] in terms of its lack of scalability, that is, its ability to

[10] Minors in charge of validating the transactions may sometimes collect a commission, but quite often – as is the case for Bitcoin – they are remunerated for their work through the issuance of coin by the protocol governing the cybercurrency. On this subject, see S Mignot, 'Le Bitcoin: nature et fonctionnement' (2015) 149 *Banque & Droit* 10.

[11] French Parliament, Loi relative à la croissance et la transformation des entreprises, no 2019-486 www.legifrance.gouv.fr/affichTexte.do?cidTexte=JORFTEXT000038496102.

[12] Finma, 'Guide pratique pour les questions d'assujettissement concernant les *initial coin offering* (ICO)' (16 March 2018), www.finma.ch/fr/~/media/finma/dokumente/dokumentencenter/myfinma/1bewilligung/fintech/wegleitung-ico.pdf?la=fr.

[13] P Person, Rapport d'information relatif aux monnaies virtuelles, no 1624, www.assemblee-nationale.fr/dyn/15/rapports/cion_fin/l15b1624_rapport-information.

[14] M Grabowski, *Cryptocurrencies, A Primer on Digital Money*, Routledge (2019).

[15] S Nakamoto, 'Bitcoin: A Peer-to-Peer Electronic Cash System' (2008), https://bitcoin.org/bitcoin.pdf.

[16] C Dark, D Emery, J Ma and C Noone, 'Cryptocurrency: Ten Years On' [June 2019] *Bulletin of the Reserve Bank of Australia* 195, www.rba.gov.au/publications/bulletin/2019/jun/pdf/cryptocurrency-ten-years-on.pdf.

adapt to a change in the magnitude of demand, in particular its ability to maintain its functionalities and performance in the event of high demand. In addition, there are governance issues. For example, to be modified, the blockchain of an electronic money (e-money) requires a consensus from the 'minors' certifying the transactions, a consensus that is very difficult to obtain. Volatility is another issue. This then leads to the development of new projects.

The second generation appeared around 2014. The best-known cybercurrency of this generation is Ethereum. This new generation is capable of processing several operations in parallel. In theory, the system is therefore faster and better supports scaling (the evolution of demand). Beyond the technical improvement, this generation – more precisely, Ethereum since the ERC-20[17] – introduces another innovation via the integration of smart contracts. This allows an operation to be carried out automatically as soon as a condition is fulfilled, such as the delivery of a good or a service. However, the good scalability of the network is at the expense of security – the risk of piracy is greater[18] – but also of persistent governance and volatility issues. This led to the development of a third generation of cybercurrency.

Cybercurrency projects of the third generation were developed in response to the problems encountered by the previous generations. The aim was therefore to build networks based on better governance systems and better scalability solutions. Also, with the multiplication of cybercurrencies, a need for interoperability between blockchains started to emerge, and this was another issue that cybercurrencies of the third generation started to address. Finally, some cybercurrencies of this generation also address the volatility issue and have therefore been given the enviable label of 'stablecoin'.

Two projects in this generation are worth mentioning. The first is the IOTA (Internet of Things Application) project, which replaces the blockchain protocol with the Tangle one.[19] This new protocol still works peer-to-peer, but without any blocks or chains. Instead, every transaction refers to only two past transactions. The second is the Libra project mentioned above, which retains the blockchain but in a closed mode, whereby only certain people can validate transactions, which allows for greater speed. Libra also seeks to solve problems linked to volatility, high conversion fees and taxation through the use of underlying assets whose prices are not so volatile.

Most of these cybercurrencies are therefore backed by state currencies such as the euro, the dollar or the yen. Others are based on raw materials (oil, gold, natural gas, etc) or on the value of other cybercurrencies. The Libra, for example, is backed by a basket of currencies: the US dollar (50 per cent), the euro (18 per cent), the

[17] S Polrot, 'Qu'est-ce qu'un token ERC20?', www.ethereum-france.com/qu-est-ce-qu-un-token-erc20/.

[18] E Braun, 'Des pirates dérobent près de 40 millions de dollars de crypto monnaie', *Le figaro* (21 July 2017).

[19] European Parliament, TAX3 committee, 'Cryptocurrencies and Blockchain' (2018) 42, www.europarl.europa.eu/cmsdata/150761/TAX3%20Study%20on%20cryptocurrencies%20and%20blockchain.pdf.

Japanese yen (14 per cent), the pound sterling (11 per cent) and the Singapore dollar (7 per cent).

## III. Cybercurrencies, a Monetary Revolution

The aim of this section is to demonstrate that cybercurrencies such as the Libra are indeed carrying out a monetary revolution. The technological innovations that have made it possible to create cybermoney are in fact bringing about such significant changes in the medium used to conduct economic exchanges that they cannot simply be described as developments. It is a revolution that involves the creation of a new type of money. In order to prove this, it is necessary to recall two great revolutions: the appearance of commodity currencies and then fiat currencies (section IIIA). It will then be possible to demonstrate that cybercurrencies, including Libra, are also leading to such changes that it is possible to speak of an economic revolution in their regard (section IIIB).

### A. Past Monetary Revolutions

The appearance of money was in itself a revolution. It should be remembered that 10,000 years ago, at a time when human beings lived mainly on the fruits of their hunting, fishing and gathering, trade was limited. Barter and gift were then more than enough for them, just as they still are today for some Aboriginal cultures. However, these instruments began to show their limits in the transition from an economy of predation to an economy of production, where human beings settled down to become farmers and breeders. This Neolithic revolution, as described by the Australian archaeologist Vere Gordon Childe,[20] took place at different times in various parts of the world: from 8500 BC in the 'Fertile Crescent' region (Middle East), to 7500 BC in China and 3500 BC in America. However, this production and sedentarisation increased the density of populations and thus the possibilities of exchanges among them. Under these circumstances, the two existing instruments of exchange show their limitations, as supply does not always meet demand. Consequently, the social conditions for the emergence of an instrument of exchange other than barter and gift were met. This is the invention of commodity money.

As its name indicates, this money is based on a commodity commonly accepted by all because all consume it.[21] Initially, these are goods that satisfy an essential need for the whole community, whether it be a commodity from agriculture (tea,

[20] N Journet, 'Vere Gordon Childe (1892–1957) La révolution néolithique', *Sciences humaines* (2016) HS 20 Les grands penseurs des Sciences Humaines, 63–66.

[21] M Delaplace, *Monnaie et financement de l'économie* (Malakoff, Dunod, 2017) 20–32.

barley, wheat) or from livestock farming and fishing (cattle, cod, etc). It is quite possible to speak of money here, insofar as the commodity is no longer sought after for its own sake, but for its function as an instrument of exchange. It is also a revolution, since for the first time an instrument has appeared that makes it possible to mediate exchanges: an unwanted good is exchanged for a universal instrument that is then exchanged for a desired good. Since there are many goods that can be used as money, rules of exchange are put in place (a sack of wheat equals a sack of apple) to achieve more universality and interoperability.

Nevertheless, this form of money has a number of drawbacks. From a logistical point of view, it is difficult to transport (because of its weight or its moving nature when it is an animal), to store for long period due to its perishability and to divide (at least for livestock), which makes it inconvenient for remote transactions or transactions of small amounts. These difficulties are initially solved by means of commodity substitution. Instead of using goods that satisfy an essential need for the whole community, one turns to rarer goods, such as certain shells (cowries) or precious stones and metals. While the problems of divisibility and perishability are thus solved, the problem of transport is not completely solved for operations involving large monetary quantities. Similarly, new problems are emerging, such as falsifiability (cowries were later reproduced in Europe using glass paste) or the need to weigh the precious goods accurately. All this leads to their replacement by another type of currency: fiat coins and, in particular, metal coins.

Although metallic coins, which appeared in Asia Minor, India and China in the seventh century BC, were not created to facilitate trade, but rather to perform religious, fiscal and then military functions,[22] they ended up playing a considerable role in trade, replacing commodity coins. For private individuals, their advantages in terms of forgery, transport, divisibility and perishability should be kept in mind. But it is above all by comparing them with commodities based on the same metals that they are made of that one can understand the truly revolutionary character of fiat money both for private individuals and the sovereigns who coined them. As its name suggests, this money is decreed – fiat meaning in Latin 'let it be' – with the state providing its guarantee.

First of all, the state guarantees that the coin has the value inscribed on its reverse side, regardless of its weight or exact composition. This makes it unnecessary to examine each coin separately to verify its properties. It is also a guarantee of acceptance, since kings will gradually require their subjects to accept coins bearing their seal on the obverse. But fiat money is also particularly interesting for sovereigns, who gradually understood that it can enable them to finance their economy. Indeed, sovereigns can attribute to these metal coins a face value lower than their intrinsic value based on the price of its metallic components. This is what is called a divisional money, a process that will later be amplified with the development of

[22] J-M Thiveaud and S Piron, 'De la monnaie électronique à l'invention de la monnaie d'électron: en Lydie au VIIe siècle avant Jésus-Christ' (2015) 32 *Revue d'économie financière* 271.

another type of fiat money (paper money), or transposed to non-state currencies created by banks and guaranteed by stocks of goods (fiat money).

Other innovations will occur in the following centuries. One example is the invention of paper money, another form of fiat money alongside metallic money. Paper money appeared in China during the Song Dynasty (960–1279) and was used in Europe from the seventeenth century onwards to limit the risk of theft and to solve the problems of metal scarcity. The discovery of scriptural money should also be mentioned, bringing to a climax the dissociation between the sign (the entry into an account) and the signified (the value associated with it) and also enabling banks, closely controlled by the state, to create new and considerable volumes of money that would allow the financing of future industrial revolutions.

Not all of these later innovations, however, constitute revolutions. Only fiat money introduces a real break both in the secondary functions that it fulfils alongside its function as an instrument of exchange (as a instrument of guarantee for individuals and as an instrument of economic control for the state) and in its unprecedented centralised governance. None of the three above-mentioned innovations (divisional money, paper money and scriptural money) call these elements into question. To see another monetary revolution emerge, we must wait for the emergence of cybercurrency.

## B. The Current Monetary Revolution

Inherent to technical progress and social evolutions, money has slowly evolved in order to adapt itself to a continuously increasing digitalised society, seeking safety, simplicity and speed. It would be tempting to date that third revolution back to the advent of e-money, which brings the dematerialisation of money to its extreme.[23] According to Article L.315-1 of the Monetary and Financial Code, e-money is a monetary value stored in an electronic form, in a cell phone or a gift card for instance. Backed by legal currencies such as the euro, it is, however, only an electronic extension of a fiat currency. Its etymology reminds us of this. The first coins made in Lydia during the Iron Age were made of a material found in the River Pactole and called *electrum*![24]

Therefore, it is not the invention of electronic money that constitutes a revolution. The revolution will come a few years later, with the integration of the Internet into the design of currencies itself. The revolution introduced by cybercurrency is not so much the result of the immaterial nature of cybercurrency, insofar as e-money or scriptural money is as immaterial as the Libra is: at the very least, the only existing material is the inscription of a series of characters on a hard drive or on a book of account. Nor does the revolution result from its alleged unfalsifiability

[23] A Laurent and V Monvoisin,. Les nouvelles monnaies numériques: au-delà de la dématérialisation de la monnaie et de la contestation des banques. (2015) 18 *Revue de la régulation* 1.

[24] Thiveaud and Piron (n 23).

linked to the irreversible recording of passed transactions. Indeed, this has already been seen with the stone money used on the island of Yap, where exchanges were recorded on enormous millstones, making the transactions unforgeable given the means available to its inhabitants.[25] Nor is the revolution the result of the absence of a state governing it or its circulation outside a territory controlled by a state. For example, Maria Theresa Thalers, which were demonetised in 1858, continued to circulate and be used outside Austria until the 1960s.[26]

The revolution stems from the fact that cybercurrency, while being regulated by computer protocols, is the first currency whose governance can be decentralised. For the historians of money, its verticality is the characteristic feature of fiat money.[27] As soon as this feature disappears, it would seem relevant to talk about revolution. But could we not then argue that it is less a revolution than a mere return to the commodity money used in the past? Not at all, because cybercurrencies are regulated by a protocol and can be managed by the consensus of their users, unlike convenience currencies. Indeed, in some respects, this monetary revolution is leading to the creation of a hybrid money, borrowing the possible absence of verticality from commodity money and the existence of governance from fiat currencies.

Having thus shown the revolutionary character of cybermoney from the point of view of economical science, let us now turn to legal science.

## IV. Cybercurrencies, a Legal Revolution

Many authors or institutions nowadays refuse to recognise cybercurrency as a form of money. In doing so, they refuse to draw the consequences of the monetary revolution entailing cybercurrencies in the field of law (section IVA). Despite this refusal, it is possible to identify the revolution that cybercurrencies caused to the legal concept of money, a revolution that is appropriate for our societies and to which some states seem to have already committed themselves (section IVB).

### A. A Legal Revolution Denied

In France and elsewhere, many lawyers refuse to classify cybercurrency as money, an opinion that has been written into the law after the Pacte Act of 22 May 2019, where cybercurrency was qualified as 'non-monetary'.[28] There seem to be various reasons for this refusal. On the technical side, there is the fact that the definition

[25] S Bourgeois-Gironde, 'Le Bitcoin, entre représentation naïve et innovation théorique' (2015) 159 *Banque & Droit* 23.
[26] ibid.
[27] Thiveaud and Piron (n 23).
[28] L.54-10-1 MFC.

of money in the current legal systems is based, among other things, on the existence of state control. For example, the US Uniform Commercial Code defines money as 'a medium of exchange currently authorised or adopted by a domestic or foreign government'. So, considering the place given to the state by this definition, cybercurrencies cannot, until they have been authorised or adopted by states, be qualified as money.[29] The same opinion can be found in France among authors who consider that cybercurrencies will not be money as long as they are not recognised and accepted by the state.[30] Other authors underline the difference between cybercurrencies and traditional currencies in order to conclude that they are not money.[31]

However, all the arguments put forward in this context refer to a conception of money centred on fiat money and ignoring commodity currencies. This is the case with the argument that cybercurrencies would not be legal tender, which, if followed through, would lead to commodity money being refused the qualification of money! This also applies to the argument related to the absence of a bank account, which is intrinsically linked to the development of scriptural money as a form of government-controlled fiat money. Similarly, arguments based on the fact that cybercurrency would not be linked to a debt from the bank where a deposit had been made or that it would not have a counterpart in the form of a physical asset are only relevant if the concept of money is limited to that of fiat money. As for the argument that cybercurrencies could not be a store of value,[32] this is misleading since the latest generation of cybercurrencies can be stable;[33] moreover, stability is not an inherent property of fiat currencies, as revealed by economic history.

The French National Bank is running a very similar argument. In a 'focus' published in 2018, this institution takes up these economic arguments by articulating them around the three functions that money would have according to the dominant economic theory[34] and by showing that cybercurrencies 'do not fulfil, or only very partially' fulfil, these functions.[35] As the arguments return to those

[29] MD Rayburn, 'Bitcoin When the Bank Breaks: Uncertainty in the Treatment of Bitcoin & Other Cryptocurrencies in the Face of Bankruptcy' (2019) 16 *New York University Journal of Law & Business* 257.

[30] Romain Zanolli, 'Essai d'une théorie juridique de la monnaie à partir de la notion de cours' (PhD thesis, Paris University, 2019).

[31] D Legais, *Fasc 535: actifs numériques et prestataires sur actifs numériques*, JurisClasseur commercial no 74 (LexisNexis, 2019). This author argues he is summarising the opinion expressed in a report presented to the French Government (J-P Landau and A Genais, 'Les crypto-monnaies', report to the Minister of Economy and Finances, July 2018). However, if this report indeed underlines these difficulties, the qualification of money is not excluded in it. This is only the opinion of this scholar.

[32] G Lemme, 'Virtual and Crypto-currencies: Is This Money?' (2019) 4 *Revue de droit bancaire et financier* 38.

[33] See above section II.

[34] AH Meltzer and M Friedman, 'V° Money' in *Encyclopædia Britannica*, www.britannica.com/topic/money.

[35] French National Bank, 'L'émergence du bitcoin et autres crypto-actifs: enjeux, risques et perspectives', focus no 16 (5 March 2018), https://publications.banque-france.fr/sites/default/files/medias/documents/focus-16_2018_03_05_fr.pdf. See also European Central Bank, 'Virtual Currency Schemes – A Further Analysis' (2015), www.ecb.europa.eu/pub/pdf/other/virtualcurrencyschemesen.pdf.

outlined above, it is not necessary to demonstrate their flaws again. On the other hand, it is necessary to discuss another kind of argument, no longer related to economics but to law.

The French National Bank denies the quality of money to cybercurrencies on the basis of two legal arguments: first, 'cybercurrencies are not recognised as legal tender'; and secondly, they are not recognised as a 'means of payment' either. However, these two arguments are not convincing. With regard to the first argument, the French National Bank begins by quoting Article L.111-1 of the Monetary and Financial Code, which states that 'the currency of France is the euro'. This text does not rule out the possibility that other instruments may be classified as money; it simply states that the official currency, the legal tender, is the euro. In other words, we come back to the legal tender argument criticised above. The second argument is particularly ill-founded and refers to the concept of means of payment. This is defined by Article L.311-3 of the Monetary and Financial Code as an 'instrument that enables any person to transfer funds, regardless of the medium or technical process used'. Although this definition is particularly broad and none of its words contains the idea of legal tender, the French National Bank maintains that cybercurrency cannot be a means of payment.

Although highly debatable, this last argument is nevertheless interesting in two respects. First, it highlights the fact that the French National Bank itself is aware that legally defining money in relation to legal tender is limited, since it also seeks to demonstrate that it would not be a means of payment. However, it is precisely around a similar notion – a commonly accepted payment instrument – that eminent economists focus in order to define money.[36] This argument of the French National Bank thus seems to reinforce the analysis of the monetary classification supported here. Secondly, the absence of any serious explanation for rejecting the classification as a means of payment suggests that the cause of the rejection of the monetary classification lies elsewhere, in political rather than technical reasons.

It is reasonable to think that if a number of scholars or institutions refuse to classify cybercurrency as money, it is also perhaps because cybermoney challenges the power of states over currencies and the benefits they derive from it. As one French legal scholar writes: 'States cannot admit competing currencies to their own. It is a matter of sovereignty.' The same scholar concludes that 'one cannot consider Bitcoin from a legal point of view without first considering it from a political point of view'. Fiat money is indeed a central instrument in the functioning of states. Being the guardians of money, states have the power to decide how much money they issue directly or through the banking institutions they control.[37] They can thus decide to issue more of their own currency to refinance their economy, to the detriment of other holders of currency, whose monetary wealth is weakened by such issuance. It is this advantage of fiat money for states that has led some liberal

[36] Meltzer and Friedman (n 35) defines it as 'a commodity accepted by general consent as a medium of economic exchange'.

[37] Lemme (n 33).

economists, in particular the winner of a 'Nobel Prize' for Economic Science Friedrich Hayek,[38] to advocate for the end of the state monopoly on currencies. It should be noted, however, that Hayek only proposes the multiplication of fiat currencies, which, unlike decentralised cybercurrencies, does not directly challenge the custodian's power to issue money to the detriment of other holders. This monetary issuing power is then only indirectly limited by the play of competition: if the state issues too many currencies in its own interest, holders will turn to other currencies, which will then cause the value of the state currency to fall, to the particular detriment of the state. In any case, it is this advantage that states derive from fiat money that is being jeopardised by cybercurrencies.

Surprisingly, however, this reason is almost never clearly stated in state reports, which, on the other hand, do not fail to put forward other political considerations (in the form of a scarecrow?) for rejecting cybercurrencies: the risks of strengthening terrorism and corruption or the risk of undermining an international policy because of the open possibility of evading exchange control policies or economic sanctions decided against certain countries. While these political risks exist, it seems that it has not yet been proven that they would be considerably reinforced by cybercurrency. The French anti-money laundering authority, Tracfin, even acknowledges in its 2018 annual report that, to date, 'cases of money laundering using crypto-currencies remain poorly documented and reported cases of terrorist financing through these instruments remain relatively anecdotal'.[39] Moreover, all these practices, although rightly feared, did not wait for the existence of cybercurrencies, and there is nothing to suggest that a framework that respects the specificity of cybercurrencies would not make it possible to curb this risk. Moreover, to take the example of money laundering, it must be noted that Tracfin is receiving an increasing number of reports of suspicions of money laundering linked to cyberassets and has set up a specialised investigation unit, which clearly shows that these fraudulent operations can be detected and thwarted.[40] It is difficult to see how the mere existence of these risks would be a relevant reason to block the development of cybercurrencies, particularly by denying them the status of currency in official speeches, especially since their recognition would be advantageous for states.

## B. A Legal Revolution to be Carried Out

The thesis defended here is that states must lead a revolution in the legal concept of money and fully recognise that cybercurrencies are a form of money parallel to fiat money. In other words, it is a matter of admitting that a money can exist

[38] A Hayek, *Denationalisation of Money* (London, The Institute for Economic Affairs, 1976).

[39] Tracfin, 'Rapport annuel d'activités, 2018', www.economie.gouv.fr/files/web_RAA_tracfin-2018.pdf.

[40] ibid.

even though it is not endowed with a specific guarantee by the state concerning its acceptability (legal tender), its authenticity or the risks of default by the depositary bodies. In our opinion, a distinction must be made within the rules currently governing money in order to separate, on the one hand, the rules concerning monetary means of payment in general, which should be extended to cybercurrencies, and on the other, those which have to do with the state (exchange policy, state guarantees, etc) and which should continue to benefit only fiat money. Basically, it is a question of specifying the concept of money in order to create a common regime and special regimes.

Such a revolution in the legal concept of money would, in our view, have a number of advantages. First, it would make it possible to better regulate cybercurrencies instead of leaving them in a form of lawlessness where precisely those risks mentioned above can be realised. Recognising them as money in no way implies that states should renounce regulating them. On the contrary, it is by recognising their quality that we can best apply the existing regulatory mechanisms to them and thus justify the competence of the regulatory authorities.

The position of the French National Bank mentioned above thus seems to us to be counterproductive: by refusing to make cybercurrencies into real currencies, it is depriving itself of the possibility of regulating cybercurrencies effectively and can only issue warnings by means of alarmist statements to its users.[41] Similarly, by refusing to consider that cybercurrencies can be money or means of payment, the Monetary and Financial Code exempts organisations offering cybercurrency transfer services from reporting obligations in the context of the fight against money laundering and terrorism. Making these entities subject to these obligations requires the intervention of the parliament, which may take several years. Thus, in France, while money transfer organisations have been subject to these reporting obligations since 2009,[42] the restrictive interpretation adopted has hindered the application of these obligations in the context of cybermoney laundering.[43] It took more than seven years to introduce a provision which, without denying the monetary disqualification of cybercurrency, made bodies acting as intermediaries in cybercurrency transactions subject to these reporting obligations.[44] The dogmatic refusal to classify currency as such resulted in the French government being prevented from using the suspicious transaction reporting obligation as an instrument to combat money laundering and terrorist financing for seven years.

On the other hand, the acceptance of cybercurrency as money and the regulation it would imply would be likely to promote the development of cybercurrency by reassuring its users. From the point of view of the European Union, this

[41] G Goffinet, 'La régulation du *Bitcoin*' (2015) 159 *Banque & Droit* 142.

[42] Arts L.561-2, 1° *bis*, L.522-1 and L.314-1, 6° MFC as modified by ordonnance no 2009-866 of 15 July 2009.

[43] Tracfin, 'Tendances et analyse des risques de blanchiment de capitaux et de financement du terrorisme en 2015', www.vie-publique.fr/sites/default/files/rapport/pdf/164000777.pdf, p 71.

[44] Art L.561=2, 7° *bis*, introduced by ordonnance no 2016-1635 of 1 December 2016.

would contribute to the policy of diversification of payment services it has been promoting for years.[45] It would also allow states to apply to their own currencies the technological innovations resulting from the technological innovations already made or to be made for cybercurrencies. It is thus striking that there is an increasing number of announcements by states and international organisations that they are considering the development of their own cybercurrencies. For example, the European Central Bank (ECB) announced that it is possible to create an EU cybercurrency managed by the ECB,[46] and the Venezuelan government made an announcement regarding the issuance of Petro, a state cybercurrency backed by oil.[47]

The legal revolution in the concept of currency that we are calling for – that is, the dissociation between a common law and special laws – already seems to us to be perceptible in certain legal orders, where it can be noticed that some rules governing traditionally fiat money are being extended to cybercurrencies, while others are reserved to fiat money or even to cybercurrencies. This is partly the case in the USA and in France.

In the USA, on the one hand, the federal or state authorities have taken the position that, with regard to tax legislation[48] or legislation on currency exchanges,[49] cybercurrencies should not be considered as money. This is understandable insofar as the tax treatment of the currency or the rules on currency exchange imply the idea of sovereignty, which is not found in the case of cybercurrencies. On the other hand, several court decisions have held that cybercurrencies should be treated as money under the rules on money laundering or the fight against fraudulent financial arrangements. The courts have thus rejected the arguments of individuals who, in order to escape prosecution, had invoked the lack of competence of a prosecuting authority that could only intervene in relation to money, which their cybercurrency would not have been.[50] Even in states with a narrow definition of money, centred on fiat money, such as Florida, courts have held that if cybercurrencies could not be characterised as money under the narrow definition, they could at least be characterised as payment instruments and thus be subject to anti-money-laundering legislation.[51]

[45] Directive on payment services in the internal market, 2007/64/CE, 13 November 2007; Directive on payment services in the internal market, 2015/2366, 25 November 2015.

[46] European Central Bank, 'Exploring Anonymity in Central Bank Digital Currencies' (4 December 2019), www.ecb.europa.eu/paym/intro/publications/pdf/ecb.mipinfocus191217.en.pdf.

[47] 'Le Vénézuela émet son Petro, l'anti-Bitcon', *Le Parisien* (21 February 2018).

[48] Internal Revenue Service, 'Notice 2014'21' (2014), www.irs.gov/pub/irs-drop/n-14-21.pdf.

[49] Texas Department of Banking, 'Regulatory Treatment of Virtual Currencies under the Texas Money Services Act', Supervisory Memorandum no 1037 (April 2019), www.dob.texas.gov/public/uploads/files/consumer-information/sm1037.pdf.

[50] *SEC v Shavers*, No 4:13-CV-416, 6 August 2013, FD Tex' *US Dist and United States v Ulbricht*, 31 F Supp 3d 540, United States District Court, SD New York, https://casetext.com/case/united-states-v-ulbricht-11.

[51] *State of Florida v Espinoza*, 30 January 2019, 264 So 3d 1055 (Fla Dist Ct App 2019), https://casetext.com/case/state-v-espinoza-53.

This conclusion has not, however, led to cybercurrency losing the status of digital asset. This qualification has been used in other cases to justify the competence of US authorities to intervene in relation to commodities but not money. For example, a federal court in Massachusetts was able to justify the jurisdiction of the Commodity Futures Exchange Commission by rejecting the applicant's argument that cybermoney is not a commodity but money. The Court did not allow itself to be confined to the applicant's binary reasoning ('it is a currency, therefore it cannot be a commodity') and, without excluding the classification of money at any time, simply held that the cybercurrency in question was indeed a commodity over which the Commodity Futures Exchange Commission had jurisdiction.[52] One can only agree with this analysis, which is consistent with the idea that cybercurrency is a digital asset. In short, one can see in the USA the emergence of a common law of the currency, as well as a special law specific to fiat money. However, the emergence of a special law for cyberassets is not yet well characterised in the USA.

The situation in France, on the other hand, is different and instructive. Although, as we have pointed out, cybercurrency is still not qualified as money in the law, which uses long periphrasis to refer to it and nevertheless apply the rules on the fight against money laundering and terrorist financing, a special law on cybercurrency has nonetheless emerged. Indeed, the legislator intervened, on the basis of the aforementioned Pacte Act of 20 May 2019, to establish a special licensing regime – mandatory or optional – for providers of digital asset services, France thereby becoming the second state, after Malta, to adopt a legislation specific to cybercurrencies.[53] This regulatory regime thus imposes mandatory registration of cybercurrency providers involved in the most dangerous transactions (deposit service or service of exchange for fiat money) and allows optional registration for other transactions, which then opens up certain advantages, such as the possibility of canvassing customers more actively than through simple advertising.

This legal framework seems to be a step in the right direction, in that it preserves the freedom of the actors involved in cybercurrencies and the specific nature of it. Similar legislation could be enacted, but drawing more inspiration from US law for the recognition of the quality of money in cybercurrencies.

[52] *CFTC v My Big Coin Pay, Inc*, 334 F Supp 3d 492, 494 (D Mass 2018), www.cftc.gov/sites/default/files/2018-10/enfmybigcoinpayincmemorandum092618_0.pdf.

[53] W O'Rorke and A Lourimi, 'L'encadrement à la française des prestataires sur actifs numériques' (2019) 5 *Revue de droit bancaire et financier* 13.

# 9

# The 'Algorithmic Revolution': Fair Taxation, Social Pact and Global Governance

STEFANO DORIGO

## I. The Algorithmic Revolution: Its Essential Characters

In a world that is changing at a dizzying pace, both at the economic and the social level (much less, as we will see, at the legal one), we often hear talking about 'digital revolution'[1] or 'industry 4.0'.[2] These expressions – journalistic, of course, not technical – refer to the most relevant aspects of the new global set up: the digitalisation of the economy, with the preponderance of dematerialised services; and the robotisation of the production processes of material goods. For the purposes of this chapter, I prefer to use the formula 'algorithmic revolution': it seems to be able to better represent with a single expression the multiple aspects of the new course of the globalised economy and society.[3]

On closer inspection, the algorithm is the element that distinguishes the digital economy, which is characterised by its dematerialisation, but also the traditional economy, made of material goods built inside factories, but through less human labour and more automated robots. At the same time, it is still the algorithm that increasingly influences individual and social life: to give an example, access to social media takes place through digitised applications based on algorithms, and

[1] One of the first studies to use the term 'revolution' referring to the digital economy was that of Tapscott, *Blueprint to the Digital Economy: Creating Wealth in the Era of e-Business* (New York, 1998).

[2] The name 'Industry 4.0' is generally attributed to Henning Kagermann, Wolf-Dieter Lukas and Wolfgang Wahlster, who used it in a report presented at the 2011 Hanover Fair, entitled 'Industrie 4.0: Mit dem Internet der Dinge auf dem Weg für4.industriellen Revolution'. In 2016, the English version, Industry 4.0, was taken as one of the keywords of the World Economic Forum meeting in Davos (Switzerland).

[3] Some authors prefer the term 'cybernetic revolution', making reference to the possibility of control (both of humans and machines) that the new paradigm is able to realise: see Simoncini, 'Diritto costituzionale e decisioni algoritmiche' in Dorigo (ed), *Il ragionamento giuridico nell'era dell'intelligenza artificiale* (Pisa, 2020) 37ff.

it is the latter that, profiling the user's choices, can allow advertising to be adapted to the users.

It is, therefore, the algorithm that allows digital platforms to work, permitting users to make use of goods and services without moving from their homes and, at the same time, enabling multinational companies to acquire data essential for the production of their profits; and it is always the algorithm that drives intelligent machines, equipped with artificial intelligence, allowing the robotisation of the production of goods and services. There is, in short, an inextricable interweaving between the digital economy, based on the supply of intangible goods, the traditional robotic economy and consumer habits, and the role of the productive workforce: the unifying element is precisely the algorithm,[4] capable of creating digital platforms and allowing machines to carry out more numerous and complex activities in a much faster time.

I think it is right, in this regard, to talk about a real revolution, which is relevant to the economy, society and the law.

The revolution of the economy, driven by the algorithm, is in some ways facing everyone. The digital economy is characterised by the advent of dematerialised goods and services and by the shifting of the core business of companies from the sale of these goods to the apparently free provision of virtual spaces (digital platforms), in which it is the collection of user data that represents the real economically (and profitably) relevant asset.[5] These data, after their collection and profiling, are then sold to commercial operators, who use them to create personalised offers through the digital media. Moreover, the algorithmic revolution in the economic field does not stop with this aspect, however relevant. As has been mentioned, the algorithm in fact influences industrial production, since the robotisation of production processes, made possible by the use of artificial intelligence, gives an evident competitive advantage to those companies that can afford the huge investments involved therein.[6]

Closely linked to the deep changes in the economy and industry induced by the algorithm is the social aspect of the revolution. Once again, there are two profiles that must be taken into account in this regard. The sovereignty of the algorithm profoundly influences individual and social habits, with the almost constant presence of people on the network, the growing virtuality of relationships and the substantial transfer, through personal data, to third parties of the control over one's own life and spending habits.[7] At the same time, as mentioned above, the

[4] One can speak about the existence, in practice, of a special authority of the algorithm. See the point of view expressed by Shirky, 'A Speculative Post on the Idea of Algorithmic Authority', www.shirky.com/weblog/2009/11/a-speculative-post-on-the-idea-of-algorithmic-authority/.

[5] A deep analysis of the main characters of the digital economy can be found in the document issued by the OECD, 'Tax Challenges Arising from Digitalisation' (2018).

[6] Some in-depth analysis on that topic can be found in Dorigo, 'Robot and Taxes: Turning an Apparent Threat into an Opportunity' [2018] *Tax Notes International* 1079.

[7] For a critical view, see O'Neil, *Weapons of Math Destruction. How Big Data Increases Inequality and Threatens Democracy* (New York, 2017). The deep impact of the use of data in contemporary economies

diffusion, in the field of manufacturing, of systems based on artificial intelligence entails the elimination of human relevance for activities with less added value, with the consequence that it becomes necessary for human workers to acquire highly specialised niche skills, in order to be able to operate in areas (currently) precluded to intelligent machines and therefore avoid being excluded from the world of work.[8]

Finally, and this is the subject that will be dealt with in the following paragraphs, there is the impact of the algorithmic revolution on the world of law: an inevitable impact, due to the multiple legal implications that the new phenomena just outlined generate, but also problematic, at least for the moment. In the face of rapid and sometimes tumultuous phenomena, the law often reveals a slowness which makes it very difficult to regulate them in time and to foresee the effects they are going to cause. It is not just a question, however, of the different speed of the algorithmic world compared to the legal world. Upstream, there is a much more important and insidious phenomenon: the substantial unknowability of the algorithm.[9] This is, in fact, the result of research that is carried out by private actors. It is thus covered by strict privacy laws, and is therefore unknowable in its content and mode of operation. In fact, the core of the algorithmic revolution remains, with the exception of the few 'initiates' who are its inventors and owners, completely unknown to consumers, users and legal operators, thus making any actions aimed at understanding and legally regulating the phenomena that belong to the algorithm even more complicated.

## II. Algorithmic Revolution and Tax Law: General Considerations

Most of the features summarised above can also be found in the context of tax law. The dematerialisation of the typical activities of digital multinationals, made possible by the algorithm, brings with it the consequence that it is difficult to know in which territory these multinationals act and obtain their income. Consequently, the two fundamental concepts of international taxation – residence and source – become increasingly difficult to be located.[10]

has been highlighted by Mayer-Schönberger and Range, *Reinventing Capitalism in the Age of Big Data* (New York, 2018). See also Mayer-Schönberger and Cukier, *Big Data. A Revolution That Will Transform How We Live, Work and Think* (London, 2013).

[8] In that sense, see Roubini, 'Where Will All the Workers Go?' *Project Syndicate* (31 December 2014), https://www.project-syndicate.org/commentary/technology-labor-automation-robotics-by-nouriel-roubini-2014-12?barrier=accesspaylog.

[9] The algorithm has been defined as a 'black box' precisely because of its substantial opacity: Pasquale, *The Black Box Society: The Secret Algorithms that Control Money and Information* (Harvard University Press, 2015).

[10] Pistone, 'La pianificazione fiscale aggressiva e le categorie concettuali del diritto tributario globale' [2016] *Rivista Trimestrale di Diritto Tributario* 395.

The fact that business in the digital world is based on dematerialised goods and services makes physical presence through material structures, such as offices, factories and warehouses, superfluous. Therefore, digital business is free to move across states without any particular difficulty, since it is not linked to any territory by forms of stable and tangible presence, which by their nature are not easily moveable.[11] At the same time, even the source of income becomes malleable, since transactions are dematerialised, they can occur in a non-place (such as the cloud) and, since they are not linked to the production and delivery of a good that can be placed in a certain physical space, they depend on the location of the user with his device, an element that by its nature is changeable and uncertain. The identification of the state that has the right to tax the relevant income therefore becomes completely questionable.[12] Moreover, in the context of the digital economy, determination of the taxable income is also uncertain, since, as has been said, most of the time the user does not pay a sum of money, but accesses the service free of charge by providing his/her personal data; it is therefore difficult to determine what the economic value of that transaction is for the company.[13]

The fiscal problems of the use of algorithms can also be seen in the field of intelligent machines used in industrial production. Here, with physical goods being sold against payment on traditional markets, there are no problems related to the residence of the company or to the identification of the source of its income. However, there are situations in which some companies can gain a competitive advantage over others by investing in automation and thus achieving higher production levels at lower cost. This entails the replacement of human labour (but also, to a certain extent, the intellectual labour force), with a consequent loss of revenue for the state, since workers who lose their jobs to robots no longer have a salary and are therefore no longer subject to income tax. There is an additional cause of suffering for the public coffers that is linked to the increased pressure on them to finance social support measures for those (categories of) workers thus expelled from the production system.[14]

[11] Brauner, 'Taxing the Digital Economy Post-BEPS, Seriously' [2018] *Intertax* 462; Cipollina, 'I redditi "nomadi" delle società multinazionali nell'economia globalizzata' [2014] Part I *Rivista di diritto finanziario e scienza delle finanze* 21.

[12] De Wilde, 'Tax Jurisdiction in a Digitalizing Economy; Why "Online Profits" Are So Hard to Pin Down' [2015] *Intertax* 796.

[13] One of the main characters of the digital economy, as often emphasised by the OECD, is that it is based on the economic exploitation of 'hard-to-value' intangibles. Brauner, 'What the BEPS' [2014] *Florida Tax Review* 98 stresses that 'hard-to-value intangibles … means intangibles that the current arm's length-based transfer pricing regime is unable to regulate'. See also OECD, 'Guidance for Tax Administrations on the Application of the Approach to Hard-to-Value Intangibles' (June 2018).

[14] It should be noted that some commentators share the idea of public intervention to protect the weaker categories. They propose, among other things, a 'national dividend', made by requiring each technological enterprise to confer part of its actions to a public trust, so that every member of the community becomes de facto a shareholder. Therefore, rather than disincentivising the development of robotics by introducing a tax, the 'national dividend' would allow the well-being of all members of a given society even if all human workers were to be replaced by robots. See the position of Varoufakis, 'Taxing Robots Won't Work, Says Yanis Varoufakis' www.weforum.org (2 March 2017).

As in all revolutions therefore, new, unexpected situations occur rapidly (and with violence – not in a physical sense, but with reference to the incisiveness of the change that is imposed on the pre-existing situations), and as such are not covered by the legal regulations in force, designed and implemented for very different situations. At the same time, a category of subjects emerges (be they digital multinationals or manufacturing companies capable of automating their production processes) who are able to take advantage of such situations, drawing a (albeit lawful, since it is carried out in strict compliance with the rules in force) fiscal advantage to the detriment of both competitors and the community, and ultimately subjecting the social pact to a very strong tension. Finally, and as a consequence of the operation of the two elements just mentioned, there are clear breaks in the economic and social order, with the drainage of public resources and the simultaneous emergence of social tensions fuelled both by small local businesses, pressed by digitisation, and by the mass of workers for whom social protection by the state is becoming increasingly problematic due to the loss of revenue mentioned above.

In short, the fiscal component of the algorithmic revolution first impacts on the economy, but then – once again, according to the typical features of all revolutions – it spills over to society and the public systems designed to ensure its well-being.

One has to wonder, then, whether tax law, with its current principles and rules, is able to cope with this emergency, mitigating social risks by means of a fair redistribution of wealth among the members of the community or whether, on the contrary, it proves to be inadequate for this purpose, as many of its basic concepts and institutions need to be rethought, taking into account lessons from other branches of law (international and EU law as well as constitutional law), since what is at stake (starting from tax revenues) is the entire system of individual and collective rights, as well as the rules of the economy based on a level playing field and the social function of the enterprises.

In order to answer to that question, it is necessary to start from a critical analysis of two cases, one relating to the digital economy, the other to the robotisation of production processes, which can allow the verification – albeit in objective differences – of the common problems and challenges that both raise.

## III. The Tax Issues of the Digital Economy: The Case of Digital Multinationals

Digital multinationals, according to both the documents released by the European Commission[15] and the findings of courageous journalistic investigations, have

[15] During the last years, the EU Commission started several investigations against many multinational enterprises, mostly based in the USA, contesting that their group schemes violated the EU state aid rules. Some of the main cases involved digital enterprises such as Google, Apple and Amazon. The Commission then released the documents concerning those schemes, thus revealing the complex

made extensive use of the unique characteristics of their business (relevance of intangibles, non-existence of material structures such as factories, limited need for labour), misalignments between the tax systems of individual jurisdictions and the age of international tax law rules to implement aggressive forms of international tax planning, with the consequence of shifting the tax base outside the states where the market is located (which are often those with the highest tax rates) and placing it in systems without income taxation, whether as a result of a generalised regulatory choice or as a consequence of the stipulation of agreements with local tax administrations.[16]

A significant example of these policies is the case of Google – a case that has not so far aroused direct reactions from the international community or the EU Commission, but which has been the subject of some media clamour.[17] It seems that the US parent company – instead of organising the Internet sites with search engines in the various states of the world directly from the USA, thus subjecting the income flow to taxation at the high rates provided for there – has in fact created an articulated transnational structure, involving, a first Irish company, with its head office in Bermuda (and therefore resident there for tax purposes under Irish law), to which the rights of exploitation of Google's intangible assets were licensed; a Dutch company, a sublicensee of the same rights; which, in turn, sublicensed to another Irish company, this time resident in that country. The latter organised and operated websites in various states, but without a physical presence in those states such as to constitute a permanent establishment (and to thereby attract income for tax purposes in those states); the revenues were then channelled (through the payment of royalties to remunerate the granting of the right of use) from Ireland, where they would be subject to very limited taxation, via the Netherlands, back to Ireland: here, however, the income itself was not subject to taxation since, as mentioned above, this holding company was considered to be resident for tax purposes in Bermuda, where, as is well known, there is no taxation on corporate income. At the same time, the USA had no reason to tax the (untaxed) income of the Irish subsidiary for transparency (that is, regardless of the dividend perception), since under US rules residence depends on the place of incorporation and therefore that company was deemed to be resident in Ireland and not in a tax haven like Bermuda.

group structures put in place in some countries to deepen the tax burden. For an interesting review of the EU findings and the defences of the main multinationals involved, see 'Google, Facebook Defend "Double Irish" before EU Parliament Tax Committee' (17 November 2015) https://mnetax.com/google-facebook-defend-double-irish-tax-planning-eu-parliament-committee-11993.

[16] Of the many authors who have written about the fiscal issues of the digital economy, one can recall Kofler, Mayr and Schlager, 'Taxation of the Digital Economy: A Pragmatic Approach to Short-Term Measures' [2018] *European Taxation* 123; Schön, 'Ten Questions about Why and How to Tax the Digitalized Economy' [2018] *Bulletin for International Taxation* 278; Greggi, 'Il caso Apple: vecchi e nuovi limiti europei alla potestà impositiva statale nei tax rulings' [2016] *Quaderni costituzionali* 817.

[17] In absence of formal investigations by, for example, the EU Commission, some authors have nonetheless highlighted the tax avoidance schemes set up by some digital multinationals, including Google. See Rixen and Dietsch, *Global Tax Governance. What's Wrong with it and How to Fix it* (Colchester, 2015), https://ssrn.com/abstract=2734829.

In sum, the complex mechanism summarily described allowed Google to transfer the huge revenues generated in states with ordinary tax regimes to a non-taxing jurisdiction, due to a number of circumstances, both in fact and in law:

1. the object of the business is an algorithm, therefore the economic flow resulting from its exploitation can be moved from one state to another through the game of licences and sublicences;
2. the digital presence, which through the Internet site makes it possible to approach the market of a certain state, does not, at present, configure a permanent establishment and therefore does not allow the latter to attract revenues from users placed in that market for tax purposes; and
3. the tax residence of a company can be located in a low-tax state, taking advantage of the peculiarities of internal rules and the circumstance that the digital business, being dematerialised, does not require any stable physical structure, as such difficult to move.

The Google case shows how digital multinationals, without violating any domestic or international standards, and even scrupulously observing them, are able to avoid the taxation of the outlet markets on the huge income produced all over the world.

In other cases, as mentioned above, this result has been achieved not so much by exploiting loopholes in the network of international conventions and internal regulations as by taking advantage of the willingness of local tax authorities to conclude agreements granting particularly advantageous tax treatment in exchange for investments made by the taxpaying company in the territory.[18] This happened, for example, in the Apple case, where the US multinational company channelled all revenues from sales in Europe and the Middle East to its subsidiary in Ireland.[19] However, the latter had entered into a series of rulings with the Irish tax administration – agreements provided for in domestic law – by which it had obtained a completely derisory taxation of its income, according to the EU Commission's proceedings against Ireland for breach of the EU state aid rules.[20]

These examples highlight the main problematic features of the taxation of the algorithmic revolution, with reference to the digital economy. First of all, international tax rules are overtaken by events: thus, from the Google case, it emerges that the notion of a permanent establishment, until now linked to the physical, material presence of a company in a state other than the state of residence, is not

[18] See, inter alia, Traversa and Sabbadini, 'State-Aid Policy and the Fight against Harmful Tax Competition in the Internal Market: Tax Policy in Disguise?' in Haslenher, Kofler and Rust (eds), *EU Tax Law and Policy in the 21st Century* (Alphen aan den Rijn, 2017) 107ff.

[19] Bal, 'Tax Rulings and State Aid Investigations: The Apple Case' IBDF White Paper (1 October 2016).

[20] EU Commission press release, 'State Aid: Ireland Gave Illegal Tax Benefits to Apple Worth up to €13 Billion' (30 August 2016), https://ec.europa.eu/commission/presscorner/detail/en/IP_16_2923. On the wide implications of the case concerning Apple, see Bal, 'Tax Rulings, State Aids and the Rule of Law' in Van Brederode (ed), *Ethics and Taxation* (Singapore, 2019); Lang, 'Tax Rulings and State Aid Law' [2015] *British Tax Review* 391.

able to apply to dematerialised phenomena, the presence of which is not physical, but nevertheless is such as to allow the multinational to obtain large revenues in each state without paying any tax on it.[21] At the same time, the new players in the digital economy, being multinational groups and because of the absence of material constraints in their business model and the ease with which they can quickly move the intangible object of their activity, can modify their organisational chain so as to place the tax base in a jurisdiction with a low or no tax burden.[22]

The speed of new business models, the dematerialisation of their object, the slow adaptation to new situations of international and internal rules on taxation and, finally, the lack of coordination between the tax disciplines of the various states involved, including in the context of the European Union, allow digital multinationals to erode the tax base in the states with ordinary tax rates and to move profits into accommodating legal systems, both in terms of rates and the possibility of concluding advantageous rulings.[23] The countries in which users are located, whether they are companies that buy advertising space on Google or consumers that buy Apple products (just to remain within the context of the two examples given above), thus lose revenue, despite the fact that digital companies exploit the local infrastructure and the market: with the consequence that, in the presence of fewer resources available, the state must restrict welfare mechanisms of protection, while creating enormous inequalities both between commercial operators (disadvantaging those who do not have the same ability to move between states as the digital multinationals do) and between members of the community (with the risk that the less well-off classes, deprived of adequate levels of welfare, further worsen their condition and thus endanger social peace).[24]

## IV. The Robotisation of Production Processes

The other aspect, albeit apparently different and distant, of the algorithmic revolution that has been evoked is that of the robotisation of production processes. Here, we are faced with a situation that is certainly not impalpable, such as that linked to digital business, but is equally disruptive in terms of economic, social and fiscal relations. In some states, and in certain sectors within them, the development of

[21] One author held that the structure based on the interaction between Art 5 and Art 7 of the OECD Model has entered into crisis with the advent of the digital economy: Sapirie, 'Permanent Establishment and the Digital Economy' [2018] *Bulletin for International Taxation*. See also Gutmann, 'Globalisation et justice fiscale' [2002] *L'année Fiscale* 109.

[22] The elusive nature of the notion of the place where value is created in the digital economy is highlighted by Schön, 'Ten Questions about Why and How to Tax the Digitalized Economy' [2018] *Bulletin for International Taxation* 280.

[23] Pistone, 'La pianificazione fiscale aggressiva e le categorie concettuali del diritto tributario globale' [2016] *Rivista trimestrale di diritto tributario* 395.

[24] The consequences of tax avoidance by digital MNEs over the welfare systems of the states involved is critically highlighted by Yang, Cahill and Hood, 'Corporate Profits' Tax Avoidance: How the "Double Irish" Impedes Global Social Progress and Removes the Prosperity Base Needed for Future Generations' in Thomakos and Nikolopoulos (eds), *Taxation in Crisis* (Cham, 2017) 103ff.

artificial intelligence is allowing companies not only to replace workers in purely material tasks – as has been the case since the last decades of the last century – but also to do without human presence at all, through learning processes (machine learning) that allow the machine to detach itself from its purely executive function (which still requires a human being to direct it) and to become autonomous.

We are aware of many cases of successful replacement of human workers by robots. In Hamburg, for example, the innovative Altenwerder port terminal is one of the most advanced in the world: opened in 2001, it offers a futuristic scenario, with gigantic cranes that move without man's supervision, unloading containers from ships, while self-driving trucks, running on virtual tracks, take the containers and move them from one side of the port to the other. Only a part of the port is dedicated to more complex operations, ie those of unloading from the terminal to the port, which require human drivers. Productivity as a whole is 40 per cent higher than that of a traditional terminal: for that reason, a number of experiments are still underway to implement investments in the complete automation of cranes.

Another case is that of a hospital in Silicon Valley, which invested in 19 robots to reduce operative expenses. These smart carts can haul supplies around the hospital, making deliveries and pickups at a fraction of the costs of human workers. According to further reports, the hospital is considering firing up to 140 workers since setting up the robots, thus obtaining a 65 per cent reduction in labour costs.[25]

Again, Amazon is equipping its warehouses with tens of robots, capable of rolling out automated packing, moving packages from one site to another and even placing the correct package onto moving machines. This is an interesting example of robotisation of a truly digital multinational enterprise, which hence realises a significant overlap of the two scenarios we are talking about.

The algorithm, therefore, revolutionises production, detaching it from the human contribution and ensuring considerable advantages to companies that have the necessary capital to make this type of investment. The consequences do not seem to be any less disruptive than those that accompany the rise of digital multinationals. On the one hand, the improved production capacity of robotic companies and the lower cost incidence allow them to gain increasing market shares, to the detriment of competition from smaller companies unable to make the required technological investments. On the other hand, a very large proportion of low-skilled workers are destined to lose their jobs,[26] so that the social gap widens (and, with it, social peace is endangered as a result of inevitable proletarisation);[27]

[25] The case is reported by Qureshi and Syed, 'The Impact of Robotics on Employment and Motivation of Employees in the Service Sector, with Special Reference to Health Care' [2014] *Safety and Health at Work* 198.

[26] It is, however, interesting to note that most of the enterprises involved in the process of robotisation, like Amazon, have declared that they will invest money in the 'upskilling' of their employees, in order to avoid disruptive consequences for their social situation.

[27] According to a recent study conducted by PwC, jobs at risk as a result of robotisation of production processes will amount to about 30% by 2030 and even reach 44% halfway through that decade: 'Will Robot Really Steal Our Jobs?', www.pwc.co.uk (February 2018). A survey by McKinsey & Company

at the same time, the state loses revenue from disappearing income taxes (as a result of redundancies) but faces increasing costs in the corresponding social security payments, so that the financial capacity to cope with the increase in demand for public intervention becomes critical.

Robotic enterprises are taxed on their income produced in their state of residence in the same way as any other enterprise; from this point of view, there would not seem to be any favourable situation compared to other operators. However, equal treatment is only apparent, since these firms enjoy a strong organisational and productive advantage, due precisely to the replacement of the human labour force by the machines equipped with artificial intelligence, and thus show a greater capacity to contribute to public expenditures.[28]

Here, too, the inadequacy of the tax rules, designed for a completely different context, proves to be very relevant, if not decisive. There do not seem to exist, at the present time, forms of levy that have a greater impact on companies that invest more intensely in automated and intelligent machines; on the contrary, in many states, we have recently witnessed the introduction of tax benefits aimed precisely at encouraging the replacement of traditional production methods with cybernetic systems.[29] Therefore, not only is the organisational advantage not compensated with greater withdrawals, but the system even reserves tax advantages for companies that find themselves in this privileged condition.

## V. The Common Problematic Context of the Two Branches of the Ongoing Algorithmic Revolution

The algorithmic revolution, therefore, manifests two only apparently different profiles: there is the branch of the digital economy, which is typically dematerialised, and that of the robotic industry, which is linked to material production but is also largely dehumanised. Both of these branches share the fundamental role

in November 2017 estimated that by 2030 around 800 million workers could be expelled from work if they do not acquire new skills, as a result of the spread of automation. The OECD, though with a lower degree of alarmism, has recently confirmed the risks of a substantial loss of jobs in the robotic era: Nedelkoska and Quintini, 'Automation, Skills Use and Training', OECD Social, Employment and Migration Working Papers No 202 (14 March 2018), www.oecd-ilibrary.org.

[28] This seems to be the position held by Englisch, 'Digitalisation and the Future of National Tax Systems: Taxing Robots?' (5 September 2018), https://ssrn.com/abstract=3244670.

[29] Indeed, the choices of the Italian legislator (as well as that of many other Western States, particularly within the EU) do not appear to reserve any space for using a fiscal leverage aiming at regulating this phenomenon. In fact, for several years, the number of tax reliefs measures for companies investing in technological innovation has multiplied. It is sufficient to consider the example of the credit for investments in research and development, the patent box regime or the discipline on innovative start-ups up to the super and hyperdepreciation. The underlying idea is that the technological development should, in the medium term, resolve the problems it initially helps to generate. This seems to be the position of the International Labour Organization (ILO), which showed that the job-loss rate has decreased in correspondence with the advent of digitalization: ILO, 'The Impact of Technology on the Quality and Quantity of Jobs', Issue Brief no 6 (March 2018).

of the algorithm: in the first case, the algorithm is the very object of economic activity; in the second, it is the medium. In any case, it is around the algorithm that the new economic model of the revolution we are concerned with is built and this makes the substantial homogeneity between the two situations evident.

From a fiscal point of view, the links between the situations are multiplying. First of all, there is the misalignment between the tax rules and the new cases. The former apply to situations that are in fact now outdated by the speed of the algorithmic world. The protagonists of the latter therefore find themselves free to operate in an open context, without precise limits of positive law. Thus, digital multinationals can operate in a market without a physical presence and therefore legitimately claim the seeming impossibility that the resulting income be taxed accordingly. In the same way, 4.0 industries can make extra profits – thanks to the machines and therefore in some way to the detriment of the social system – without them being subject to higher taxation than ordinary companies, even though they show a stronger ability to pay. There is, in short, an advantage that certain operators, but not others, can acquire on the market as a direct consequence of the delays of the tax system compared to the speed impressed by the algorithm.

However, the acquisition of a competitive advantage does not only impact on the rules of the market. The markets are, of course, strongly altered in favour of some players – those who, thanks to the algorithm, can save taxes compared to the average of competing companies and therefore can either offer goods and services at a lower price or channel fresh money flows into further investments all over the world. The breaking of the market equilibrium also implies a breaking of the social pact – that is, the pact that binds the affiliates together and involves the obligation to finance public expenditures in relation to the wealth possessed and regardless of the expected return (in terms of public services that can be personally used).

The digital multinationals – it is worth repeating again in order to avoid misunderstandings – without violating any rules but taking advantage of national and international regulatory gaps, exploit the digital infrastructures and the market of the various states in which they operate without, however, contributing in any way to the expenses necessary to improve those infrastructures and to feed that market. At the same time, robotic companies can make extra profits without any additional tax burden compared to ordinary situations, even if they put a heavy pressure on the social system of the states, unloading the costs (both economic and social) of their technological innovation choices on public structures and, therefore, on the rest of the taxpayers. These situations do not depend on the opportunistic choice of one or the other operator, but arise from a series of structural deficencies of the international tax system, as such very dangerous in the present day and even more so in perspective.

It seems to me that this is the most alarming consequence of the algorithmic revolution as seen under the prism of tax law. It is not so much that some operators can generate unimaginable profits, such as would put them in competition even with sovereign states; rather, it is that these profits are not, in the majority of cases, submitted to a fair level of taxation in the state (or states) where they are generated and therefore where the need for a more intense participation in public expenditure is greater. We are therefore faced with a situation in which the enjoyment of a more favourable tax position is at odds both with the indefectible solidaristic aspect of tax duty[30] and with the social connotation of enterprises which is now emerging strongly in doctrinal reflection and practice. This means that the market advantage, with the connected increase in available profits, is not – as it should be – the presupposition for the assumption of a duty of solidarity to share a part with the territorial and social communities where that result has been made possible; on the contrary, in a paradoxical reversal of situations, it is the result and consequence of the failure to fulfil the duty to contribute to the public expenditures of the state in which the value was created and, distinct but related, to direct the selfish aims of the enterprise towards objectives of social utility, or at least such as not to harm the local community.

One understands, then, how the fiscal consequences of the algorithmic revolution, if not governed, risk calling into question the very foundation of the social pact to which the fiscal duty is connected as a manifestation of solidarity within an organised community, not only within the borders of the individual state, but also in a wider sphere (as the experience of the European Union teaches).[31]

## VI. The Possible Reactions of the Tax System: Interventionism or Laissez Faire?

We have seen that tax law is at the heart of the revolution and its effects. It seems that some of the unintended consequences of the emerging structure stem precisely

[30] For a thorough analysis of the link between taxation and solidarity both in a national and a supranational dimension, see Sacchetto and Pezzini (eds), *Il dovere di solidarietà* (Milan, 2005). The extent of the doctrinal debate on the function of the tax and its link, through the ability to pay, with the principles of substantial equality and solidarity prevent us from giving an adequate account here. We can, however, limit ourselves to observing that, in the analyses of scholars on the subject, we can constantly see the rapprochement between the contribution to public expenditures and the need to take into account the role of the taxpayer within the social organization: see, eg Gallo, 'Ratio e struttura dell'IRAP' [1998] *Rassegna tributaria* 636. It follows that tax is the instrument through which the individual participates in such an organization, both as a person who benefits from the goods and services made available by the state and as a contributor to the relevant expenses. Thus, if there is a tax, it means that there is a social structure within which the taxpayer moves.

[31] A number of studies have flourished recently on EU citizenship and solidarity: Donachov (ed), *EU Citizenship and Federalism. The Role of Rights* (Cambridge University Press, 2017); Biondi et al, *Solidarity in EU Law. Legal Principle in the Making* (Cheltenham, 2018); D Thym (ed), *Questioning EU Citizenship. Judges and the Limits to Free Movement and Solidarity in the EU* (Oxford, 2017); A Silveira, M Canotilho and P Madeira Froufe (eds), *Citizenship and Solidarity in the European Union. From the Charter of Fundamental Rights to the Crisis to the State of the Art* (Brussels, New York, 2013); J van de Walt and J Ellsworth (eds), *Constitutional Sovereignty and Social Solidarity in Europe* (Baden-Baden, 2015). Concerning taxation, see K Pantazatou, 'Promoting Solidarity in Crisis Times: Building on the EU Budget and the EU Funds' [2015] *Perspectives on Federalism*.

from the inability of tax rules to renew themselves, adapting to phenomena that occurred after their formulation. It is a question, however, of investigating whether tax law can recover a positive role in the management and regulation of the situations described.[32] In this respect, there is no unanimity of opinion. On the one hand, there are the advocates of an incisive role for tax law, in the sense that new forms of taxation should be imposed on new activities, allowing states with ordinary tax regimes to recover revenue for their own welfare needs.

In this sense, the Organisation for Economic Co-operation and Development (OECD) is considering initiatives to modernise the concept of nexus, that is, to reshape the link that the non-resident company should have with the market country in order for the latter to tax the income generated therein. The aim is to set aside a purely material link, which is inadequate with the digital presence made possible by the algorithmic revolution, and to move towards some form of economic and/or immaterial presence.

Hence, it is advocated that the non-resident company should have a permanent establishment in a state on the basis of a 'significant digital presence'[33] – a situation that would allow the state where the website or social platform visitors are located to tax the sums that the digital multinational company obtains through this presence.[34] In the same direction are the proposals of those who, with reference to the robotisation of industry, advocate the introduction of more intensive forms of taxation for those companies that use intelligent machines on a massive scale without the human labour force and thereby create an economically assessable productive and organisational advantage.[35] These trends are based, albeit with no minor differences in detail, on the recognition of the need for the state to take back the role of manager of innovative phenomena through taxation which, although in the short term may slow down technological and digital evolution,

[32] The role of tax law in the management of situations of crisis has been emphasised by Lesage and Vermeiren, 'Neo-liberalism at a Time of Crisis: the Case of Taxation' [2011] *European Review* 43.

[33] Requena and González, 'Adapting the Concept of Permanent Establishment to the Context of Digital Commerce: From Fixity to Significant Digital Economic Presence' [2017] *Intertax* 3. A seminal proposal for a new PE nexus based on digital presence has been advocated by Hongler and Pistone, 'Blueprints for a New PE Nexus to Tax Business Income in the Era of the Digital Economy', WU International Taxation Research Paper Series No 2015–15 (20 January 2015), https://ssrn.com/abstract=2591829.

[34] In her conclusions delivered to the Court in Case C-482/18, AG Kokott held that a website has a genuine link with a state for tax purposes if it offers its services using the national language of that state. For a comment, see Dorigo, 'Il superamento dei criteri di collegamento "tradizionali" nell'epoca dell'economia digitale: le conclusioni dell'AG Kokott nella causa Google e la problematica localizzazione del reddito d'impresa' *Rivista di diritto tributario online* (6 December 2019).

[35] In a famous interview in February 2017, the entrepreneur Bill Gates foreshadowed the introduction of a 'robot tax'. This tax was designed to guarantee to the state a revenue for compensating the equivalent loss of revenues due to automation. Gates, '"The Robot That Takes Your Job Should Pay Taxes" Says Bill Gates' (17 February 2017), https://qz.com/911968/bill-gates-the-robot-that-takes-your-job-should-pay-taxes. The reasoning behind his view is quite straightforward: if machines replace human beings in carrying out certain work activities, then tax authorities can no longer impose a tax on the income that was previously perceived for those same activities by the latter. Hence the idea to introduce a form of taxation that has an equalising impact.

makes it possible to guarantee the social and economic balance between the various members of the community.

Moving in the opposite direction are those who value the role of the market and believe it capable of autonomously finding the balance between the opposite conditions.[36] Indeed, the introduction of a levy with a balancing function could have the opposite effect, inducing the most advanced operators to abandon the state that imposes it, thus depriving it of the advantages (in terms of investments and infrastructures) that its presence alone can guarantee. This solution is widely supported in the debate on how to regulate the effects of productive robotisation,[37] but there is also a trace of it with reference to the digitalisation of the economy: one can recall the relevant example of the USA, which has always been reluctant to introduce ad hoc tax rules and is even prepared to threaten commercial retaliation against systems that try to introduce unilateral tax measures.[38]

The first direction, which we could define as 'sovereign', is based on the strong role of states and the redistributive effect that a tax can generate; the second, on the other hand, is 'liberalist' or 'marketer', in the sense that it opposes any regulation on the basis of trust in progress and the ability of the market to find the antidote to the inequalities that new phenomena initially produce. Both appear weak, as they are based on controversial assumptions. The sovereigntist approach in fact fails to resolve the problem of capital flight that is linked to the new economy as a result of the unilateral, and therefore uncoordinated, introduction of restrictive fiscal measures; liberalist theories, in the same way, seem to value an abstract philosophical vision that increasingly appears to be denied at a practical level, with the observation of the persistent inequalities that favour only certain large operators to the detriment of most of the others.

A third way can, however, be proposed. This seeks to combine economic freedom and the protection of the tax revenues of states by enhancing, as a balancing element, individual and social rights in a supranational perspective. If we look at the two opposite solutions just mentioned from this point of view, they both appear unsatisfactory. Leaving the achievement of balance to the free play of the market clearly leads to the risk that the element of profit is overestimated and the protection of workers' and consumers' rights is exposed to risk. This may mean that the *lex mercatorum* achieved by practice can balance the opposing needs of technological development of companies and the interest in maintaining acceptable levels of revenue for the states; however, the subjects most directly exposed to consequences of the algorithmic revolution may not have any advantage, if the

[36] See Falcão, 'Should My Dishwasher Pay a Robot Tax' [2018] *Tax Notes International* 1273, who argues that it cannot be said with certainty that automation and AI are necessarily synonymous with technological unemployment and therefore negative effects: technological change could also create new types of work.

[37] See, inter alia, Abbott and Bogenschneider, 'Should Robot Pay Taxes? Tax Policy in the Age of Automation' [2017] *Harward Law and Policy Review* 145.

[38] Kaye, 'US Tax Sovereignty and the BEPS Project' in Rocha and Christians (eds), *Tax Sovereignty in the BEPS Era* (Alphen aan den Rijn, 2017) 279ff.

market remains the prerogative of a few operators and the national systems do not have a truly effective power of control and direction towards them.

In the same way, the opposite solution achieves an excessively centralised arrangement and thus risks causing unintended effects, once again to the detriment of the weaker subjects. The unilateral introduction of a heavier tax regime for the enterprises of the algorithmic revolution could slow down the technological development of the state, with repercussions precisely on the social categories most deserving of protection; at the same time, the lack of coordination between states would induce the enterprises to move their digital or industrial business to other, more generous countries from the point of view of tax benefits.

A multilateral approach is therefore needed to make it possible to regulate the activities of algorithmic companies while avoiding the negative consequences of unilateral measures.[39] Multilateralism means synthesis, in order to ensure that national systems do not remain capable – by failing to comply with supranational guidelines – of exerting unfair competition while at the same time reducing the gap with traditional companies. One could, therefore, think of the negotiation of multilateral international instruments aiming at driving states to introduce uniform taxation systems for high-tech corporate income:[40] the guarantee of a minimum level of taxation would protect the revenue of the most advanced states (and therefore the stability of national welfare systems); the uniformity of rules, at least those essential for the functioning of the tax, would make it extremely difficult for multinationals to move their business elsewhere in search of better conditions.

This is, without doubt, not a new proposal for tax law. A 'global tax governance' has been discussed for some time now[41] and, with reference to the profiles of international cooperation, has largely been achieved.[42] However, in this case, it should be a 'substantial' multilateral intervention, ie it should deal with the fundamental

[39] Many authors have addressed the issue of the rise in multilateralism in tax law. One can make reference to Garcia Antòn, 'The 21st Century Multilateralism in International Taxation: The Emperor's New Clothes?' [2016] *World Tax Journal* 148; Pistone, 'Coordinating the Action of Regional and Global Players during the Shift from Bilateralism to Multilateralism in International Tax Law' [2014] *World Tax Journal* 3.

[40] The idea of a 'single tax' to be applied through an international coordination between states has been developed by Avi-Yonah, 'A Perspective of Supra-nationality in Tax Law' in Brauner and Pistone (eds), *BRICS and the Emergence of International Tax Coordination* (Amsterdam, 2015) 33.

[41] The idea of an international organisation dedicated exclusively to taxation issues was developed by Rosembloom, Noked and Helal, 'The Unruly World of Tax: A Proposal for an International Tax Cooperation Forum' [2014] *Rivista di diritto tributario* 183. Along the same lines, another author emphasised the need for closer cooperation between the tax administrations of the various states: M Stewart, 'Transnational Tax Information Exchange Networks: Steps towards a Globalized, Legitimate Tax Administration' [2012] *World Tax Journal* 152.

[42] Some authors have observed that the traditional 'defensive' model, which is the very concept of unilateral taxation, is giving way to a supranational approach, based on international cooperation between states, even though it is a path full of difficulties: Cipollina, 'Profili evolutivi della CFC Legislation: dalle origini all'economia digitale' [2015] Part I *Rivista di diritto finanziario e scienza delle finanze* 356.

elements of a tax linked to the profits of the algorithmic economy. In short, the aim should be to reach a global agreement for the introduction of a global system of taxation, based on the recognition of a minimum level of taxation for income deriving from activities related to that economy and applicable in any system. There are two considerations that need to be made in this respect.

First of all, the OECD has been working for some time now on a common proposal to introduce a form of 'minimum tax' in the digital economy:[43] according to this project, the source state, in the event that the state of residence of the company for some reason does not levy taxes on the income it produces, would be entitled to intervene, levying a tax to the extent that it reaches the minimum level provided for. The work of 'pillar II'[44] is proceeding slowly, but the approach seems to be acceptable and could therefore be extended to the case of the robotisation of industry: it could be argued, for example, that exceeding a certain level of automated production (measurable by the degree of replacement of human workers with robots) should in any case produce a consequent greater imposition, in the first instance in the state where this phenomenon occurs but, failing that, in the states of the outlet markets for the finished products.

The proposal for a minimum level of taxation, to be applied alternatively in the states involved that show the political will to apply the new rule, would have the effect of underlining the solidarity function of the tax, as an instrument of participation in public expenditures for the benefit of all affiliates, including the less well-off. It would not, in short, be a sanction against entrepreneurial phenomena that are and remain lawful and positive. The tax would, instead, serve to redistribute wealth not only within a single system (what is the function of the tax in state systems), but also in a supranational context. Here, the now irreversible interrelation between states, regional authorities and the international community requires the pursuit of a broader redistributive justice, which fills the gaps not only between classes, but also between different states.[45]

This perspective could have very broad implications and can only be hinted at here. However, the current emergency caused by the coronavirus demonstrates the interdependence, for better or for worse, of the states that are part of the globalised world; the decisive importance of technological evolution; and, lastly and consequently, the need for fiscal justice involving those economic operators most advantaged by progress, in order to provide states and international bodies

[43] Englisch and Becker, 'International Effective Minimum Taxation – The GLOBE Proposal' (11 April 2019), https://ssrn.com/abstract=3370532.

[44] 'Pillar II' of the Base Erosion and Profit Shifting (BEPS) Project (also known as GLOBE: 'global anti-base erosion' proposal) aims at introducing a minimum level of taxation on the profits of multinational enterprises. See Pistone, Nogueira, Andrade and Turina, 'The OECD Public Consultation Document "Global Anti-Base Erosion (GloBE) Proposal – Pillar Two": An Assessment' [2020] *Bulletin for International Taxation* 62.

[45] This is the topic of tax justice, which is explored by Hongler, *Justice in International Tax Law* (Amsterdam, 2019); Essers, 'International Tax Justice between Machiavelli and Habermas' [2014] *Bulletin for International Taxation* 54.

(I am thinking in particular of the EU) with the resources to intervene as a matter of urgency and protect the most vulnerable parts of the population.

There are many difficulties in achieving an arrangement like the one suggested. As shown by the ambiguities that characterise multilateral projects on transnational taxation, the weight of states and their will to hold fiscal power are still strong.[46] Moreover, it is the tax choices that often decide national elections and it is therefore natural that states do not want to limit their margin of discretion in this regard. Thus, the multilateral convention concluding the BEPS project is largely undermined in its practical scope by the freedom granted to states to limit its effects through options and reservations.[47] The international debate on fair taxation of digital multinationals is still stalled – and the pandemic emergency will not allow the OECD to meet the self-imposed deadline of the end of 2020 to make a proposal in relation to minimum tax. The EU has also failed to approve the Commission's March 2018 proposals for directives on the taxation of the digital economy,[48] or to include a single mention of the importance of the tax variable in the final document of the European Parliament's work on civil law rules on robotics.[49]

The decision-making power therefore remains – and is the greatest source of concern – with the states, which are driven to take unilateral and therefore uncoordinated measures. As a result, not only are they at risk of not being effective, they also represent the trigger for conflicts of a wider scope, as demonstrated by the reaction of the USA to the introduction of a digital tax by the French Parliament.[50] I do not believe, however, that this rigidity should weaken efforts. The doctrine must propose solutions beyond the immediate prospects of realisation because

[46] This is strongly remarked on by Greggi, 'Rise and Decline of the Westphalian Principle in Taxation: The Web Tax Case' [2020] *EC Tax Review* 6.

[47] Dorigo, 'L'impatto della Convenzione multilaterale BEPS sul sistema dei trattati contro le doppie imposizioni: verso un diritto tributario internazionale dell'incertezza?' [2019] *Rivista trimestrale di diritto tributario* 375.

[48] Becker and Englisch, 'EU Digital Service Tax: A Populist and Flawed Proposal', *Kluwer International Tax Blog* (16 March 2018).

[49] In an interim report published in May 2016, the Committee on Legal Affairs of the European Parliament underlined the possible negative effects in relation to the development of artificial intelligence and robotics on the level of employment and, consequently, on the social security systems of the Member States. In particular, in the report in question, the Committee encouraged all the Member States to consider the introduction of 'corporate reporting requirements on the extent and proportion of the contribution of robotics and AI to the economic results of a company for the purpose of taxation and social security contributions': European Parliament, Committee on Legal Affairs, 'Draft Report with Recommendations to the Commission on Civil Law Rules on Robotics', doc 2015/2103 (INL) (31 May 2016) para 23. A position that assumed the possibility of subjecting to a higher tax level those companies whose income was likely to be influenced by the use of robotic procedures instead of human labour was thus envisaged. However, as a result of numerous criticisms from scholars, the European Parliament, approved a Resolution on 'civil law rules on robotics'. Within the Resolution, any reference to a robot-related tax disappeared in favour of a vague formula without prescriptive effects which merely commits the EU Commission to 'analyse the different possible scenarios and their consequences on the sustainability of the social security systems of the Member States': ibid para 44.

[50] 'Donald Trump Threatens France over Digital Transaction Tax', *Financial Times* (26 July 2019).

of historical and political contingencies. In this sense, and also referring to the wide debate that has developed in recent years on a philosophical rather than a juridical level,[51] the re-evaluation of the solidaristic function of tax, even beyond the borders of the individual legal system, appears to be a fundamental key to interpreting the new phenomena:[52] thanks to it, in fact, both the greater burden imposed on companies operating in high-tech sectors and the need for the results of this imposition to be shared in a supranational perspective can be easily justified.

## VII. Conclusions: New Algorithmic Revolution and Ancient Principles of Taxation

The implications of the algorithmic revolution are multiple. Tax law is at the centre of that revolution, but around it, and in particular around the duty of solidarity to pay tax for the benefit of the weaker members of the community, further problematic areas arise. While it is true that, in the abstract, the digitisation and robotisation of the economy, each in its own area, bring progress and increases opportunities, it has been seen that they are linked to the pursuit of undue tax advantages, made possible by the application of inappropriate tax rules to the new context. This situation, in turn, impacts on the ability of states to maintain their revenue and ultimately harms the weakest actors in the chain: workers, small local entrepreneurs, consumers.

The myth of progress capable of self-regulating well-being for the benefit of all seems to have waned. However, as we have seen, it seems unlikely that states will soon find an agreement to introduce a uniform and fair tax system at the global level.

However, things may change quickly in the near future. The coronavirus pandemic, which has suddenly appeared to disrupt the lives of each of us, could just as quickly impose a generalised change in economic and fiscal perspective. The health, existential and economic crisis induced by the virus could, in fact, contribute to the emergence of a different concept, genuinely supportive and centred on strong principles of international collaboration. The pandemic has dramatically demonstrated the imbalances, inequalities and (I am thinking especially of the European Union) the selfishness that still characterises the globalised world. In short, it has laid bare the inability of the algorithmic revolution to create a better world.

It seems, then, perhaps easier to affirm a different vision, based neither on the egoistic prevalence of state sovereignty nor on the unbridled freedom of

[51] See Dietsch and Rixen, 'Redistribution, Globalisation, and Multi-Level Governance' (28 September 2014) https://ssrn.com/abstract=2502523.

[52] Koche, 'Fiscalità e globalizzazione: pensare il diritto tributario in un quadro filosofico-giuridico transnazionale?' [2019] *L'altro diritto. Rivista* 41.

companies to pursue their profits at all costs; a vision that places the needs of the weakest at the centre and calls on the states to cooperate with each other so that the traditional principles of just taxation can be realised. There is no equality without solidarity, but solidarity is born from the awareness that in the hands of every person who participates in a community there are rights but also duties. Fiscal duty should therefore once again acquire its importance, while projecting itself beyond the borders of the individual state into a global dimension.[53]

Without global tax justice, there will always be legal systems willing to welcome the shrewdest taxpayers, allowing them to save taxes and thus deprive the states where they operate of the resources to finance social spending. In sum, we can say that the new requirements triggered by the algorithmic revolution should find a satisfactory answer in the old basic concepts of tax law, even if they are revised in the light of a multidisciplinary approach that emphasises their international, European and constitutional connotations.

As always happens after every danger, the return to normal life will bring with it new aspirations and plans. It is to be hoped that the lesson of the pandemic will influence the ongoing projects at international level and push states and multinationals to embrace solutions of equity and fiscal responsibility.

[53] An author suggested that 'an internationalist conception of justice concerned with securing the tax sovereignty of independent polities may need to prescribe the creation of globally redistributive institutions': Van Apeldoorn, 'BEPS, Tax Sovereignty and Global Justice' [2018] *Critical Review of International Social and Political Philosophy* 478.

# PART IV

# The Impact of Information and Technology Revolution on Courts and Administration

# 10

# The Impact of Information and Communication Revolution on Constitutional Courts

ANGIOLETTA SPERTI

## I. Introduction

Information is vital to democracy in many different ways: in the processes in which citizens' opinions are formed and aggregated in 'public opinion', in the procedures of representation and in the mechanisms of accountability that 'freshen democracy and sustain its legitimacy'.[1] Looking at some of the technological innovations that have abruptly changed the properties of information and communication, altering political, institutional and social contexts, scholars have distinguished in the USA (but, with some delay, the same steps can be identified in European countries) four major information revolutions since the nineteenth century.

The first one emerged in the 1830s, and was due to the establishment of the national postal service and the rise of the newspaper industry. Those innovations contributed to the creation of the first national-scale system for communicating political information. The first revolution made political information widely available for the first time.

The second revolution occurred at the end of the nineteenth century as a consequence of the second industrial revolution. In that stage, information became enormously complex and highly differentiated due to the large number of private and public actors engaged in the exchange of information, including organised interest groups.

The third revolution was brought about by the widespread diffusion of broadcasting from the 1950s to the 1970s, and entered a second stage with the diffusion of cable television. The television made it possible for political actors to communicate directly with a larger audience. In Italy, for instance, the widespread

[1] B Bimber, 'How Information Shapes Political Institutions' in DA Graber (ed), *Media Power in Politics* (Washington, CQ Press, 2007) 8ff.

diffusion of TV led to the adoption of law no 103 of 1975, which made possible the direct broadcasting of messages to citizens from the most prominent institutional figures (the President of the Republic, the Speakers of the two Houses of Parliament and the President of the Constitutional Court).

Since the 1990s, we have entered a new stage of communication and information revolution, related to the rise of Internet and associated technologies. This revolution has deeply affected the communication of political actors and branches of government, and scholars have addressed the potential applications of new information and communication technology to the political process. As the new media 'emerged as some of the leading ways in which parliaments can become more open, transparent, and accountable public institutions, as well as foste[r] greater engagement with citizens',[2] some scholarly works described them as significant means for strengthening the representative process and democratic citizenship.[3] In contrast, other contributions addressed the dangers of 'electronic democracy', focusing on populism, electronic surveillance and the atomisation of social life.[4]

After the political branches of government, constitutional and supreme courts have been the latest institutions to enter the public arena and make use of new communication technologies. This chapter aims to analyse how the recent changes in the world of communication are affecting constitutional and supreme courts which in the past have traditionally refrained from engaging into direct communication with the public.

In the first part of the chapter, I will describe how constitutional and supreme courts have been transforming their communication strategies in the last few years. I will focus my analysis on European courts (in particular, on the constitutional/supreme courts of Italy, France, Spain, England and Germany). Although many courts have adopted new methods and strategies to reach a larger audience, I will focus on those courts that are most illustrative of the trend. I will devote special attention to the Italian Constitutional Court, whose recent media and communication strategies have been significantly modified in order to foster greater engagement with citizens. As has been emphasised, although the organisation of the judiciary largely differs from country to country, when it comes to the relationship between courts and the media, there are many similarities among the different jurisdictions.

In the following sections, I will address the consequences of the communication revolution on courts' relationship with public opinion. I argue that such

[2] J Griffith and C Leston Bandera, 'How Are Parliaments Using New Media to Engage with Citizens?' (2012) 18 *Journal of Legislative Studies* 496.

[3] S Coleman, 'Cutting Out the Middleman: From Virtual Representation to Direct Deliberation' in B Hague and B Loader, *Digital Democracy* (London, Routledge, 1999).

[4] C Bellamy and J Taylor, *Governing in the Information Age* (Milton Keynes, Open University Press, 1998); S Coleman, JA Taylor and W Van De Donk, 'Parliament in the Age of the Internet' (1999) 52 *Parliamentary Affairs* 366.

transformation can be described using two adjectives: *direct* – because courts are now transmitting their own message to the public proactively and without the support of the press or other media – and *dialogic* – because courts are at the same time entering into dialogue with public opinion or with specific groups of society.

In the second part of this chapter, I will discuss the objections that have been moved against the communication revolution of constitutional courts. Courts are perceived as jeopardising their impartiality and, in the long run, their legitimacy by inserting themselves into public discourse. At the same time, it has been argued that courts are looking for popular support and are therefore acting like institutions belonging to the political branches. I aim to clarify that many of the objections against the communication revolution of constitutional courts are because constitutional courts have been the last institutions to enter a revolution of communication and that criticism often moves from a 'traditional' and preconceived notion of public opinion referred to political institutions.

## II. The Recent Trend in Constitutional Courts' Communication Strategies: From Indirect to Direct Communication

As constitutional courts speak through their rulings, they have traditionally been cautious towards the media and the press. Nonetheless, in the last few years, courts have expressed a common concern about the difficulty in providing a proper understanding of their judgments. They fear, in the first place, that the large number of cases and the technicalities of legal jargon could prevent an adequate understanding of constitutional rulings and their impact on citizens' lives.

The Presidents of the Italian Constitutional Court, for instance, have repeatedly emphasised that the large number of constitutional cases makes it difficult for citizens to fully understand 'the entirety of the Constitutional Court's role'[5] and 'to grasp the real message of the Court behind legal rules and procedures'.[6] In other words, as the former President Paolo Grossi stated in 2017, the Court has the feeling that 'so far, public opinion has not been able to gain a clear perception of its role in citizens' life':[7] with the exception of a few landmark cases of general

[5] U De Siervo, 'Incontro con la stampa in occasione della presentazione della Relazione sulla giurisprudenza costituzionale nel 2010', Rome, 10 February 2011, www.cortecostituzionale.it/documenti/relazioni_annuali/Incontro_con_la_stampa_25022010.pdf.

[6] P Grossi, 'Relazione sulla giurisprudenza costituzionale del 2017', www.cortecostituzionale.it/documenti/relazioni_annuali/grossi2018/grossi_relazione2018.pdf.

[7] The booklet is available online. See P Grossi, 'Cos'è la Corte costituzionale' 5, www.cortecostituzionale.it/documenti/download/pdf/cosa_corte.pdf (arguing that the purpose of the booklet is to strengthen the role of the Court as 'guardian of the Constitution'). But see the interview with justice G Amato, 'In piedi. Esce la Corte' *La Repubblica* (29 March 2019) 38ff.

interest, a recent survey (2017) has revealed that only 15 per cent of Italians know the Constitutional Court and are aware of its role and powers.[8]

Therefore, in order to provide better information about the Court's activities, in 2012 the Italian constitutional court published online a booklet entitled 'Cos'è la Corte costituzionale' ('What Is the Constitutional Court'). The publication describes in plain words the role of the Court in the Italian system of government, its composition and main powers, and the procedures for the selection of justices. Also, the Court's website was fully revised in 2016 and 2019. The current online version is easily accessible by both the general public and legal experts, with different sections aimed at each. In the section for the general public, a webpage entitled 'The One Hundred Cases that Changed the Life of Italians' is also available;[9] it gives users the opportunity to watch short videos of the justices explaining some of the Court's historical rulings.

The German Constitutional Tribunal has analogously improved its communication. On the Court's website, a number of informative videos provide easy information on the organisation and daily work of the Tribunal and on its landmark decisions.[10]

The French Conseil constitutionnel has also gone through a similar communication revolution: in 2018, it established a professional Communication Service under the supervision of the Secretary General and has since fully revised its website in order to make information about its activities more accessible.[11] At the same time, in order 'to modernise the way in which decisions are written',[12] the Conseil has recently broken with the tradition of structuring its rulings into a list of *considérants* and adopted a more common style of writing its judgments, consisting of numbered paragraphs.

In the UK, the Supreme Court has been specifically exempted from the statutory prohibitions on broadcasting and photography which apply in England and Wales and Northern Ireland. At the same time, the Supreme Court has been

[8] G Lattanzi, 'Relazione sul tema della 'Comunicazione istituzionale' all'ordine del giorno del bilaterale con il Tribunale federale costituzionale della Germania' (26–28 June 2019) 1, www.cortecostituzionale.it/documenti/news/CC_NW_20190902.pdf; for a similar remark about the United States Supreme Court, see R Davis, *Justices and Journalists: the US Supreme Court and the Media* (Cambridge, Cambridge University Press, 2011) 20. However, it should also be noted that the attention span of citizens is influenced by many different factors, both collective and individual. Although much attention is usually paid to constitutional courts, knowledge of courts' work and cases depends on personal factors, such as store of knowledge and political engagement.

[9] See www.cortecostituzionale.it/jsp/consulta/rapporti_cittadini/vita2.do.

[10] See www.bundesverfassungsgericht.de/EN/Service/Infothek/Filme/filme_node.html.

[11] 'Un nouveau site pour le Conseil Constitutionnel. Repenser l'interface pour ouvrir le Conseil au public citoyen' *Medium* (14 February 2018), www.medium.com: 'Nous voulions rompre avec le sentiment d'arriver sur un site réservé à une élite. L'action du Conseil Constitutionnel touche au contraire chacune d'entre nous et c'est une nécessité citoyenne de la rendre compréhensible. C'est pourquoi, il a été notamment décidé d'ajouter un chapô introductif pour chaque type de décision dans les affaires en instance, permettant de saisir en quelques mots les enjeux du sujet'.

[12] See the press release of the President of the Conseil constitutionnel of 10 May 2016, www.conseil-constitutionnel.fr/conseil-constitutionnel/francais/actualites/2016/communique-du-president-du-10-mai-2016.147341.html.

undertaking a wide programme of media relation activity, consisting of highlights briefings and press summaries of the Court's judgments, and assuming a more proactive approach to briefing journalists when more complex cases are released. Further, the Supreme Court releases extrajudicial lectures delivered by the justices and interviews, and has a larger online presence (through its website, a YouTube channel and, since 2012, a Twitter profile).

In the second place, courts worry that journalists will report only the sensational elements of their rulings or select cases on controversial issues that have a greater chance of capturing the attention of public opinion. Scholarly works about the relationship between the media and constitutional courts are still scarce, but a significant scholarship has addressed institutional communication of lower courts of general jurisdiction (in particular criminal courts) and how they interact with public opinion. It is beyond the purpose of this chapter to address representations of courts and judicial activity in the media and the press, but it is worth remembering that journalists usually tend to transform judgments into 'news' and have a preference for drama, scandal, personalisation and simplification.[13]

In a recent edited book on the relationship between justices and the media, Taras has emphasised that

> High Court judges in most countries seem to share many of the same fears in dealing with journalists. They worry that their judgments, which are often the product of weeks and sometimes months of writing and rewriting and are based on a complex series of precedents and highly refined legal arguments, will be misunderstood and/or sensationalised by reporters who have little or no legal training. They look on aghast as journalists sometimes get the facts wrong, pick winners and losers without understanding the judgment, and criticise judges who are unable and/or unwilling to respond to attacks. Of particular concern is when the reasons for their judgments are not included in stories, thus leaving the impression that decisions are not based on legal reasoning but on political prejudices or personal biases.[14]

Although public attention towards constitutional and supreme courts is usually high, there is the risk that the meaning of long and complex decisions could be twisted. As Taras emphasises, journalists tend to simplify the outcome of the cases and to 'humanise' parties, describing them as winners or losers. For instance, a recent landmark case of the Italian Constitutional Court on the right to die (case no 242 of 2019) has been widely described by the press as a victory for the counsel of the terminally ill patient, although the Italian Constitutional Court is

[13] See L Moran, 'Mass-Mediated "Open Justice": Court and Judicial Reports in the Press in England and Wales' (2014) 34(1) *Legal Studies* 143, quoting S Chibnall, *Law and Order News: An Analysis of Crime Reporting in the British Press* (London, Tavistock, 1997); Y Jewkes, *Media and Crime* (London, Sage, 2011). In the USA, see FD Gillian and S Iyengar, 'News Coverage Effects on Public Opinion about Crime' in DA Graber (ed), *Media Power in Politics* (Washington, CQ Press, 2007) 127. In Italy, see G Giostra, 'La giustizia penale nello specchio deformante della cronaca giudiziaria' [2018] *Rivista di diritto dei media* 3, 3, astrid-online.it; E Amodio, *Estetica della giustizia penale. Prassi, media, fiction* (Milan, Giuffrè, 2016).

[14] D Taras, 'Judges and Journalists and the Spaces in Between' in R Davis and D Taras (eds), *Justices and Journalists. The Global Perspective* (Cambridge, Cambridge University Press, 2017) 9.

not a court of last resort and the decision on the merits of the case is delivered by the judge who submitted the issue of constitutionality to the Constitutional Court.

The difficulty is amplified by the fact that, today, news circulates with extreme speed: 'media communication is instant, it occurs in real-time and renounces thinking and argument'.[15] A recent contribution on the relationship between the UK Supreme Court and the press emphasised that as journalists have priority access to cases and press summaries, it is possible to identify reports on the Nexis database just one minute after the case has been released.[16]

Therefore, constitutional courts have realised the importance not to lose control of their message: as the former President of the Italian Constitutional Court Giorgio Lattanzi has recently stated, 'the Court has become fully aware that in order to communicate with public opinion it is not sufficient anymore to release press summaries, to publish cases in ordinary ways or to submit them to scholarly analysis'. He added that the Court 'has realised that it needs other ways of communication in order to reach all the people and let them easily understand the rulings that can change their life'.[17] In other words, 'the Court has become fully aware of its duty to go out of her building, to know and be known, because to know and to be known mean to understand and explain the Constitution'.[18]

In the UK, the 2010–11 annual report of the UK Supreme Court featured a section entitled 'Telling Our Story through the Media', where the Court detailed all 'traditional and non-traditional [media] that help communicate the work of the Court to the widest possible range of audiences'.[19]

It should be noted that although courts have always fulfilled their duty to explain and 'to foster the values of the Constitution',[20] the new awareness of their role has thrown up some novelties.

First, it is a duty that courts want to fulfil directly, without the intervention of the press and the media. In the past, courts engaged with the public mostly during their regular meetings with representatives of the press. Thompson describes public audience participation as a form of 'mediated quasi-interaction'[21] because the press usually mediates between the Court and public opinion.

[15] D Stasio, 'Il ruolo sociale del giurista impone una comunicazione più inclusiva' (2018) *Questione Giustizia* 23 March 2018, www.questionegiustizia.it/articolo/il-ruolo-sociale-del-giurista-impone-una-comunicazione-piu-inclusiva_21-03-2018.php.

[16] LJ Moran, 'Judicial Institutional Change and Court Communication Innovations. The Case of the UK Supreme Court' in Davis and Taras (n 14) 261–62.

[17] ibid.

[18] See the interview to the former President of the Constitutional Court G Lattanzi, 'La nostra Costituzione è uno scudo per i più deboli che siano italiani o stranieri' *La Repubblica* (31 January 2019) 5.

[19] See *The Supreme Court Annual Report and Accounts 2010–11*, www.supremecourt.uk/docs/ar_2010_11.pdf.

[20] ibid. See also WJ Brennan Jr, 'Why Protect the Press?' (1980) 18 *Columbia Journalism Review* 59, 59; F Sauvageau, D Schneiderman and D Taras, *The Last Word: Media Coverage of the Supreme Court of Canada* (Vancouver, UBC Press, 2006) 21 (arguing that the Supreme Court of Canada also has the power 'to construct and impose a real and symbolic universe on Canadian society').

[21] JB Thompson, *Political Scandal: Power and Visibility in the Media Age* (Cambridge, Polity Press, 2000).

For instance, the Italian Constitutional Court engaged with the public only on the occasion of its annual press conference, when the President of the Court explained all the Court's main activities and judgments of the past year. Other courts share a similar perspective on the courts' new role in communication. Radmila Dragičević Dičić, a Judge of the Supreme Court of Cassation of the Republic of Serbia, emphasised at the opening of the judicial year of the European Court of Human Rights in 2018[22] that 'the mission of judges and court representatives is to convey the messages of the court and show citizens that the judiciary, as the third branch of government, plays an extremely important role in their everyday lives'. Therefore, she argued, 'Courts need to adapt to the stronger influences of the media revolution and a new communication practice'.[23]

> The main rule of the good communication strategy should be that communication of courts with public should always be proactive. If courts don't tell their story, someone else will. First story out shapes message, second story is always reactive. We should either work with the press or they will work without us … If courts and judges do not actively participate in communicating their own story about what they do and how they do it, they risk that the message public is receiving may not be true, positive, or affirmative and very often it will violate the basic human rights. Courts should be constant relevant source of information, or they will have to deal with half information, arbitrary interpretation of the different authors and media scandals.[24]

Secondly, courts feel that ordinary ways to engage with the public are no longer satisfactory. Courts are aware they need to develop new communication strategies in order to get in touch with the people. For instance, the Italian Constitutional Court has opened its building to the public, hosting an exhibition entitled 'The Face of the Court'. The exhibition featured more than 60 photographs of the justices and the men and women that work 'behind the stage'. As stated by the President of the Court, Marta Cartabia, the initiative aims to show 'the human face' of the Court and its 'proximity to the people', and to transmit the message that 'the Constitution is the house of the Italians, a house where they can feel safe'.[25]

The Italian Constitutional Court has also adopted new strategies to foster communication with the people: as the former President of the Court, Giorgio Lattanzi, stated in 2019, the Court must 'get out of its Palace' and 'reach all the people'.[26] Therefore, the Court has recently launched an 'absolutely uncommon

[22] R Dragičević Dičić, 'The Authority of the Judiciary'. *Communication Strategies. Opening of the Judicial Year of the European Court of Human Rights*', Friday 26 January 2018', www.echr.coe.int/Documents/Speech_20180126_Dragicevic-Dicic_JY_ENG.pdf.

[23] ibid.

[24] ibid.

[25] See the interview to the President of the Constitutional Court M Cartabia, 'Porte aperte alla Consulta' *Corriere della Sera* (27 March 2019).

[26] See the report of the President of the Constitutional Court G Lattanzi, 'Relazione del Presidente Giorgio Lattanzi nella riunione straordinaria del 21 marzo 2019', www.cortecostituzionale.it/documenti/relazioni_annuali/lattanzi2019/Relazione_del_Presidente_Giorgio_Lattanzi_sull_attivita_svolta_nell_anno_2018.pdf at 2.

initiative, unprecedented in the history of the Italian Republic and probably in the world':[27] the 'Journey in Italy', a tour of the Court along two different 'routes', the 'journey in the schools' and the 'journey in the prisons'. The initiative – highly criticised by some Italian constitutional scholars, who read a political purpose behind it – has so far led the Court's justices to visit more than 30 schools (often in poor and crime-stricken districts) and approximately 10 prisons across the country. Each step of the initiative has been brought to the attention of the public through videos available on the You Tube channel of the Court, photo galleries on the Court's website, interviews with major and local newspapers and magazines and, finally, a documentary film[28] (which premiered at the Biennale del Cinema in Venice and was broadcast on national TV).

In Europe, the French Conseil constitutionnel has pursued a similar strategy to connect with the country: since 2016, it has launched an initiative called 'Découvrons notre Constitution',[29] whose purpose is to raise young generations' awareness about constitutional values. Also, since February 2019, the Conseil has expressed its purpose 'to get closer to the citizens' and 'has carried out a "petite revolution de Palais", launching an initiative called "audiences hors le murs"'.[30] In order to convey the message of 'a living Constitution', for the first time justices left the Conseil historical building and held oral arguments in other locations across the country (Metz, Nantes).

Finally, it is worth remembering that, analogously, the Supreme Court of Canada – often at the forefront in terms of openness towards the media[31] – sat outside of Ottawa for the first time in its history and held hearings in Winnipeg. The President of the Court described the initiative as 'an event open to anyone' and an opportunity for the people to get 'a front-row seat to history'.[32]

## III. From Monologue to Dialogue with the Public

The transition of constitutional courts from an indirect to a direct communication brings about a second change, the passage from monologue to dialogue with public opinion. The opportunity to have access to a great deal of information does not only imply a radical change in communication strategies of the courts; it also offers new possibilities of dialogue and interaction with the public.

[27] See the presentation of the docufilm and the speech of the President of the Constitutional Court G Lattanzi at www.cortecostituzionale.it/jsp/consulta/vic/vic-auditorium.do.

[28] The film, entitled *Viaggio in Italia: la Corte costituzionale nelle carceri*, was directed by Fabio Cavalli.

[29] www.conseil-constitutionnel.fr/evenements/concours-decouvrons-notre-constitution.

[30] www.conseil-constitutionnel.fr/rapport-activite-2019-numerique/audiences-hors-les-murs.php.

[31] S Harada, '"The Uncomfortable Embrace" The Supreme Court and the Media in Canada' in Davis and Taras (n 14) 81.

[32] See www.cbc.ca/news/canada/manitoba/supreme-court-historic-hearing-winnipeg-1.5296489.

This transformation is the natural consequence of the courts' decision to assume a direct role in the interaction with public opinion. As public opinion – by its definition – implies a separation between the public and the state, and the former is placed in a critical and rational position before issues of general interest,[33] 'there should be a two-way stream of communication allowing them to communicate, to transmit to the State and its branches the will of citizens and, conversely, to inform citizens about the activities and the decisions of the State'.[34]

In the present landscape, constitutional courts need the media and public opinion, just as the media and public opinion need the courts. Whereas, a few years ago, constitutional courts were mostly interested in providing transparency through adequate information about their activities by the means of the press, today courts attach great importance to communication. The two dimensions (input and output, transparency and communication) are closely intertwined.

Therefore, the journeys of the Italian Constitutional Court and the French Conseil constitutionnel across their countries also resulted in 'an opportunity for mutual dialogue'. A former President of the Italian Constitutional Court argued that

> in the beginning the Court felt the need to get out its Palace, to meet civil society and inform citizens of its activities and decisions. Along the way the journey turned out to be more than a means of communication but an opportunity for mutual enrichment.[35]

In the same vein, the President of the Canadian Supreme Court described the initiative of the audience outside of the Supreme Court's building as an opportunity of mutual advantage for the Court and the public. He argued:

> The initiative is justified by the importance of ensuring access to justice for all. As the highest court in Canada, the Supreme Court is the ultimate guardian of the Canadian Constitution, and as such enjoys privileged status with respect to the protection of the rule of law. This implies an important responsibility, particularly in terms of access to the court. For several years now, Canadians have been able to watch our audiences on television or on our website, read our decisions online and follow our activities on social media. But Canada is a vast country, and not everyone can travel to Ottawa to the Court at work, in person.
>
> This initiative of the Court aims at bringing the institution closer to the citizens in order to foster public confidence in the judiciary. It also has an educational vocation, so that the judges of the Court will take advantage of their stay in Manitoba to meet with several members of the legal community, Manitoba Aboriginal communities, Francophone communities and, of course, the general public.[36]

[33] G Sartori, 'Opinione pubblica' in *Enciclopedia del Novecento*, vol IV (Istituto dell'Enciclopedia Italiana, Roma, 1979) 937ff, part § 1.

[34] P Mancini, *Manuale di comunicazione pubblica* (Bari, Laterza, 1996) § 1.

[35] See Lattanzi, 'La nostra Costituzione è uno scudo' (n 18) 5.

[36] 'Questions au Très Honorable Richard Wagner, juge en chef du Canada' [2019] *Rapport d'activité du Conseil Constitutionnel* 81.

In the UK, the communications team of the Supreme Court works proactively to support accurate coverage of the Court's decisions and wider work, and to engage in a dialogue with the public. The Supreme Court usually communicates judgments in a timely and accessible manner in the media and online, but, as stated in the Supreme Court annual report, 'it is not unusual for judgments to receive widespread coverage, provoke discussion on twitter or for #UKSupremeCourt to trend on social media'.[37]

## IV. The Reasons Behind the Communication Revolution of Constitutional Courts

The comparison among constitutional courts of their different legal systems suggests that the main reason behind their communication revolution lies in the transformation of communication in recent times. The new developments in media technologies forced the courts to adapt themselves, but at the same time offered new opportunities to foster their message and interact with the public. As Taras argued, despite the differences among judicial systems and the features of judicial reviews of legislation, 'when it comes to the nature and values of the media … the landscape is pretty much the same'.[38] Communication is now instant, global and interactive, and it based not only on the traditional media (TV, radio, newspapers, magazines etc), but also on networks and virtual communities that easily join people who share common interests and purposes.

Courts have become fully aware that they need to profit from the new opportunities and strengths of communication, otherwise – as mentioned above – the media will provide their own perspective on courts' rulings and activities. Beverly McLaughlin, former President of the Supreme Court of Canada, described the new relationship between the Supreme Court and the media as 'a mutual, if sometimes uncomfortable embrace'.[39] Constitutional courts and the media, she clarified, 'need each other' because

> Electronic media, including television and new web-based media, now represent the primary means by which the vast majority of people receive their news. They constitute uniquely powerful means to provide information to the public about the administration of justice and the decisions of judges and juries.[40]

[37] *The Supreme Court Annual Report and Accounts, 2018–19*, https://assets.publishing.service.gov.uk/government/uploads/system/uploads/attachment_data/file/806799/uksc-annual-report-2018–19.pdf.

[38] D Taras, 'Introduction' in Davis and Taras (n 14) 8.

[39] B McLachlin, 'The Relationship between the Courts and the Media', remarks of the Right Honourable Beverley McLachlin, PC, Chief Justice of Canada, Carleton University, Ottawa, Ontario, 31 January 2012, www.scc-csc.gc.ca/court-cour/judges-juges/spe-dis/bm-2012–01–31-eng.aspx.

[40] ibid.

Quoting Justice William Brennan Jr of the United States Supreme Courts, she also emphasised that

> the press needs the Court, if only for the simple reason that the Court is the ultimate guardian of the Constitutional rights that support the press. And the Court has a concomitant need for the press, because through the press the Court receives the tacit and accumulated experience of the nation, and – because the judgments of the Court ought also to instruct and inspire – the Court needs the medium of the press to fulfil this task.[41]

As courts need each other and their interests are inextricably intertwined, Justice Loughlin concluded that

> As the media invent and re-invent themselves, so must judicial understanding evolve of how we relate to the media. Courts 'should promote dialogue with members of the media to the end of ensuring that reporting is accurate, prompt and appropriately complete.[42]

Scholarly works on public opinion have also emphasised that 'media are something more than a simple support to public debate'.[43] They perform an active role as citizens and public actors, because they are also capable of producing opinion[44] and participating in public discourse. Therefore, 'their ability to produce opinion, to foster trends and ideas, to provide interpretations on issues in the public agenda, becomes a structural variable of communication and cognitive intermediation'.[45] As, at the same time, journalists tend to transform judgments into news and the former often suffer 'narrative hijack',[46] it is possible to argue that changes in communication are the main reason behind a proactive role of courts in communication.

This does not imply that specific reasons regarding each jurisdiction should be ignored: as far as the French Conseil constitutionnel is concerned, for instance, the recent changes in communication can also be read in connection with the introduction of the *question prioritaire de constitutionnalité* (QPC) in 2010, which enables ordinary judges to request a priority preliminary ruling from the Conseil on the validity of statutory provisions within a trial pending before them (a posteriori judicial review).[47] The reform has deeply changed the role of the Conseil because in the

[41] ibid.

[42] ibid.

[43] V Price, *Public Opinion* (Newbury Park, Sage Publications, 1992) 82.

[44] Although the origins of public opinion can be traced in modern era, it is worth remembering that, according to Plato, δόξα (that is, belief, opinion, in contrast with ἐπιστήμη, knowledge) is not only opinion, but also the faculty or capacity to produce opinion. See N Bunnin and J Hu, *Dictionary of Western Philosophy* (Malden, Blackwell, 2004) 192.

[45] See G Grossi, *L'opinione pubblica. Teoria del campo demoscopico* (Bari, Laterza, 2004) § 4.2.3.

[46] R Cornes, 'A Constitutional Disaster in the Making? The Communications Challenge Facing the United Kingdom's Supreme Court' [2014] *Public Law* 266.

[47] See M Cappelletti, *Judicial Review in the Contemporary World* (New York, Bobbs-Merrill Co, 1971); M de Visser, *Constitutional Review in Europe. A Comparative Analysis* (Oxford, Hart Publishing, 2014).

past, from its establishment in 1958, it could only hear challenges against the laws prior to their promulgation (a priori abstract judicial review of legislation).

The UK Supreme Court – one of the newest supreme courts, established in 2005 (Constitutional Reform Act 2005) and opened in October 2009 – analogously feels a great need to communicate to the public the judicial institutional change. As Moran emphasised, 'the greater separation of powers created new demands on the judiciary to communicate the nature, value and legitimacy of their work to a variety of audiences and in particular the public'.[48] In the same vein, the former Head of Communication of the UK Supreme Court argued that

> since the parliamentary debates around the creation of a Supreme Court to replace the Appellate Committee of the House of Lords, it has been widely acknowledged that one of the reasons for the creation of such an institution was not only to achieve a fuller visible separation of constitutional powers within the UK, but also to enable the Court to better communicate its work to the public. Leaving the confines of the House of Lords' administration and built estate has enabled the new Court to place some emphasis on public outreach and engagement, and to devote resources to better communication with the media.

As the comparative analysis makes clear, the communication revolution of courts draws attention to the public who are able to take advantage of the new opportunities offered by the new communication channel, but at the same time has a duty to inform or develop expectations. That is the reason why courts describe their new role of communicating with the public as 'a social duty'. In their own words, the dialogue with citizens is conceived as a 'mission',[49] a 'responsibility'[50] or 'a task',[51] coming from the need to foster a constitutional culture and communicate 'the idea of a democratic, plural, open and tolerant society'.[52] In other words, behind the assumption of a proactive role in communication by constitutional courts, there is not only the will to provide accurate information about judgments and courts' work, but also the awareness of the duty 'to educate the constitutional conscience of citizens'.[53]

## V. The Communication Revolution and the Risks of Politicisation of Courts

The courts' transition from monologue to dialogue with public opinion and their assumption of a proactive role in communication provide new reasons for

[48] L Moran, 'Judicial Institutional Change and Court Communication Innovations. The Case of the UK Supreme Court' in Davis and Taras (n 14) 256.

[49] See Dragičević Dičić, 'The Authority of the Judiciary' (n 22) 1.

[50] See Lattanzi, 'La nostra Costituzione è uno scudo' (n 18) 5.

[51] See Cartabia (n 25).

[52] See Lattanzi, 'La nostra Costituzione è uno scudo' (n 18) 5.

[53] ibid 5. See also the contributions mentioned in n 20 above.

questioning constitutional justice. As constitutional courts engage directly with public opinion and public opinion – by definition – wields significant political influence, it has been suggested that th erecent communication revolution puts courts' independence and impartiality at risk. 'Courts are perceived as jeopardising their impartiality by inserting themselves in public discourse which in the long run could be detrimental to their legitimacy.'[54]

Scholars express fear that the courts could be influenced by the prevailing mood of public opinion when solving socially or politically controversial disputes. Furthermore, it has been argued that the courts could turn to public opinion for support and legitimacy, like political branches of government.[55]

Those objections probably prompted the Italian Constitutional Court to clarify that its new dialogue with public opinion is not motivated by a political purpose. After emphasising the need for the Court to get in touch with 'the real country' in prisons and schools, the former President of the Constitutional Court, Giorgio Lattanzi, pointed out that

> the Court should not follow public opinion. The Constitution, with its fundamental principles of democracy, liberty, equality and solidarity is the only guide of the Court. In other words, the Court cannot and must not follow the mood of the Country, if they are not in line with the Constitution.[56]

Issues concerning the legitimacy of judicial review in a representative democracy and how public discourse and societal changes affect constitutional courts' case law or courts forge constitutional change[57] lie at the foundation of the judicial review and it is beyond the scope of this chapter to address them thoroughly.

[54] de Visser (n 47) ch I, § 5.

[55] In Italy, those arguments were expounded by a large number of scholars when the Constitutional Court entered its communication revolution. See, eg A Morrone, 'Suprematismo giudiziario. Su sconfinamenti e legittimazione politica della Corte costituzionale' [2019] *Quaderni Costituzionali* 1, 251. In France, the idea of public opinion as a source of legitimacy of the Conseil has been advanced for a long time due to the a priori judicial review of legislation. See L Favoreu, 'La légitimité du juge constitutionnel' (1994) 2 *RIDC* 581, who argued that 'la véritable sanction de la légitimité de la justice constitutionnelle est donnée ou apportée par l'opinion publique'; B François, 'La perception du Conseil constitutionnel par la classe politique, les médias et l'opinion' (2003) 2 *Pouvoirs* 105, 133ff. See also, after the introduction of the *question prioritaire de légitimité constitutionnelle (QPC)*, A Vlachogiannis, 'Le Conseil constitutionnel face au changement de circonstances de fait: réflexions à la lumière de l'expérience américaine' (2010) 11*Jus Politicum. Revue de Droit Politique* 1, http://juspoliticum.com/article/Le-Conseil-constitutionnel-face-au-changement-de-circonstances-de-fait-reflexions-a-la-lumiere-de-l-experience-americaine-789.html. In Germany, see R Lamprecht, 'Kooperation und Konfrontation. Das Bundesverfassungsgericht und die Medien – Nahe und Distanz' (2012) 5 *Zeitschrift fur Rechtspolitik* 149, 149 (arguing that the relationship between media and the Constitutional Tribunal supports and protects the Tribunal against political attacks when it releases its judgments on controversial issues). In the USA, see D Strauss, 'The Modernizing Mission of Judicial Review' (2009) 76 *University of Chicago Law Review* 860 (arguing that in the last years, a different approach to the Constitution – which he names 'modernization' – has emerged because the Supreme Court tries to anticipate trends in public opinion instead of taking lessons from the past and that, at the same time, 'a modernizing court, instead of facing down popular majorities, yields when it finds out that it has misgauged public opinion').

[56] Lattanzi, 'La nostra Costituzione è uno scudo' (n 18) 5.

[57] For a general introduction, see de Visser (n 47). In the wide literature on the topic, see also A Stone Sweet and M Shapiro, *On Courts, Politics and Judicialization* (Oxford, Oxford University

However, it should be noted that those who express criticism against the communication revolution of courts argue that constitutional courts could become: (i) interpreters; (ii) conversers; or even (iii) representatives of minority groups or of the public community as a whole.[58] In other words, they believe that constitutional courts are acting as institutions that interpret, select partisan interests or represent a (large or small) part of civil society.[59]

As I wrote in another contribution on the relationship between public opinion and the Italian Constitutional Court,[60] in my opinion, criticism against the communication revolution of constitutional court should be addressed moving from the different functions that public opinion performs. Although, as I will clarify below, courts should not underestimate the risks behind the changes in their public communication, it is important not to focus only on the traditional relationship between public opinion and political branches.

In their statements, justices and chief justices often make clear that their purpose is to foster a culture of the Constitution and to raise awareness about the importance of their role in the life of citizens. In performing this task, courts are neither selecting partisan interests nor representing a part of civil society; conversely, their direct dialogue with the public is functional to the transmission of constitutional values. It would be different if justices were defending partisan interests or commenting or justifying their own judgments.

This implies that when courts are fostering a culture of the Constitution, they are favouring only the second function of public opinion, to promote social integration. In particular, courts ensure that there is a sufficient level of consensus on constitutional values. In my opinion, most of the criticism that has been expressed against the transformation of public communication of constitutional courts moves from the traditional function that public opinion has always been performing towards political institutions, that is, its instrumental role in the process of opinion formation and decision-making in a democracy.[61]

Therefore, the ability of constitutional courts to actually achieve their purpose to favour social integration around constitutional values and the possibility that, in turn, public opinion – unified around constitutional principles and values – could exert influence on political decisions are two separate issues which operate

Press, 2002). In the USA, see J Balkin, *Constitutional Redemption: Political Faith in an Unjust World* (Cambridge MA, Harvard University Press, 2011); D Nejaime, 'Constitutional Change, Courts and Social Movements' (2013) 111 *Michigan Law Review* 877; R Siegel and R Post, 'Popular Constitutionalism, Departmentalism and Judicial Supremacy' (2004) 92 *California Law Review* 1027; G Torres, 'Some Observations on the Role of Social Change of Courts' (2006) 54 *Drake Law Review* 895. On the relationship between the German Constitutional Tribunal and public opinion, see G Vanberg, *The Politics of Judicial Review in Germany* (New York, Cambridge University Press, 2005).

[58] Morrone (n 55) 278.

[59] ibid.

[60] See A Sperti, 'La Corte costituzionale e l'opinione pubblica' (2019) 4 *Diritto e Società* 735.

[61] On the two roles of public opinion – public opinion as 'rationality' or public opinion as 'social control' – see H Childs, *Public Opinion: Nature, Formation and Role* (Van Nostrand Reinhold, 1965). But see also TL Glasser and CT Salmon (eds), *Public Opinion and the Communication of Consent* (New York, Guilford Press, 1995).

at different levels and should be analysed separately. In my opinion, when scholars object that constitutional courts are interpreting, selecting or representing partisan interests, they are instead transferring to courts the consequences of the main and manifest function of public opinion: 'to influence or determine the actions … or structure of their government'.[62]

## VI. Conclusion

In my opinion, objections against the transformation of public communication of constitutional courts are due to the fact that constitutional courts have been the last institutions to engage in dialogue with public opinion. Whereas parliaments and political institutions soon discovered the potentialities of public communication to promote and amplify their political message, constitutional courts have been the last institutions to enter the communication revolution.

Although, as mentioned above, the new ways of communication offer the opportunity 'to convey the messages of the court and show citizens that the judiciary, as the third branch of government, plays an extremely important role in their everyday lives'[63] while, at the same time, retaining control of their information, constitutional courts should not disregard the risks of the new approach. As Hamilton argued, the judiciary has 'neither force nor will, but merely judgment'.[64] Therefore, it has been said, 'public deference' is 'the most powerful weapon in justices' arsenal'.[65]

Deference and regard for constitutional and supreme courts basically depend on three factors:

1. The respect for the symbols of the institution, because symbols allude to the authority and prestige of the courts, but at the same time communicate continuity in the respect of the law, and therefore, trust.
2. The prestige of and respect for each justice, because 'the prestige of the courts is also nourished by the quality of those who compose them and by their personal behaviour'.[66]
3. Finally, as mentioned above, respect depends on the prestige and trust that courts enjoy in public opinion and, therefore, by the courts' ability to meet popular needs and better match the public changing expectations.

The communication revolution of courts has deeply affected both the second and the third factors. It has increased media exposure of justices. Many justices, across different jurisdictions, have become public figures who attract more attention

[62] See H Speier's classic definition of 'public opinion' in 'Historical Development of Public Opinion' (1950) 55 *American Journal of Sociology* 376.
[63] Dragičević Dičić, 'The Authority of the Judiciary' (n 21) 1.
[64] Hamilton, *The Federalist*, no 78.
[65] Davis (n 8) 19.
[66] R Bin, 'Sull'imparzialità dei giudici costituzionali' [2009] *Giurisprudenza costituzionale* 4015.

than the courts themselves. In the USA, scholarly works have demonstrated how justices increasingly interact with reporters and how they are adjusting themselves to their newfound celebrity.[67] This marks a great change from the past, when justices maintained that they only had a distant relationship with the press, and public appearances and interviews were rarities.[68]

The German Constitutional Court is analogously facing a change in public exposure of justices. Some scholarly works have emphasised how private interviews with justices attract more attention than articles about the institution as a whole and, at the same time, some public statements from the President of the Tribunal have attracted criticism from academics and politicians, who considered them inappropriate to his institutional role.[69]

In Italy, the justices are releasing a great number of interviews to explain the courts' initiatives, and the press has twisted the meaning of some statements from the President of the Court, Marta Cartabia, forcing her to release a public statement to better clarify her thoughts and 'not to bring discredit on the Court'.[70]

As far as the respect of the courts as institutions is concerned, it is worth remembering how former President of the Constitutional Court, Giorgio Lattanzi, has justified the Court's dialogue with the 'real country', arguing that 'the Court must know the prevailing ideas, the sentiments and moods of the country', but he has also emphasised that 'the Court must not run after them'.[71] However, it is hard to deny that the public exposure of the Court and its direct contact with the public are increasing the risk that the Court could 'yield to the temptation of popular support'.[72]

In conclusion, the communication revolution of constitutional courts calls them to a new responsibility, both at individual and institutional level. At individual level, this is because, as the prestige and respect of the courts also depend on the respect and prestige of their members, justices have a duty to refrain from releasing statements that transmit a personal message and should speak only in the name of the institution to which they belong. At institutional level, courts should not stimulate public approval of their rulings, but should look only for support of their institutional role. This implies that, in order to preserve their own legitimacy, courts should find a new way to mediate between transparency and seclusion, proximity and distance from public opinion.

[67] See VJ Stricker and R Davis, 'Press Coverage of the United States Supreme Court' in MJ Rozell and JD Mayer (eds), *Media Power, Media Politics* (Rowman and Littlefield, Lanham, 2008) at 87. See also Davis (n 8).

[68] See R Davis, 'The US Supreme Court and the Journalists Who Cover It' in Davis and Taras (n 14) 287ff.

[69] C Holtz-Bacha, 'The German Constitutional Court and the Media' in Davis and Taras (n 14) 101ff.

[70] See Corte Costituzionale, 'Comunicato stampa su articolo de *La Verità*, press release of 28 April 2018, www.cortecostituzionale.it/documenti/comunicatistampa/CC_CS_20180430082703.pdf.

[71] Lattanzi, 'La nostra Costituzione è uno scudo' (n 18) 6.

[72] A Pizzorusso, 'La Corte costituzionale tra giurisdizione e legislazione' (1980) V *Il Foro Italiano* 117, 120.

# 11

# The Constitutional Limits of Digital Justice

ARTUR FLAMÍNIO DA SILVA AND DANIELA MIRANTE

## I. Introduction, Scope and Methodological Approach

In the twenty-first century, artificial intelligence has reached several sectors of society. The legal system has not been an exception. Changes in the functioning of the judicial system have been long overdue: old facilities that can no longer answer to the needs of society, outdated information and working systems, paper overload, geographical distances working as barriers to the access to justice are just some of the issues. Thus, if the need for digital justice arises,[1] it is because, for our new model of society, the traditional court system is no longer viable or even satisfactory.[2]

The modifications produced by globalisation of this brave new digital world[3] have caused new frameworks to emerge in the sphere of different legal professions, such as legal academia and legal practitioners. New technologies in general, and digitalisation in particular, have had an increasing impact both on courts and on all the dispute resolution instruments and procedures. This interaction between justice and technology has led to constitutional concerns about the use of intermediate platforms (eg WhatsApp, Zoom, Skype and any other platforms that offer the means to conduct a videoconference and, therefore, to approach people

[1] This need for a new type of access to justice as a direct result of the 'growing discontent with the courts and the desire to enhance access to justice, moving beyond a court-centric approach' is discussed in O Rabinovich-Einy and E Katsh, 'Access to Digital Justice: Fair and Efficient Processes for the Modern Age' (2017) 18 *Cardozo Journal of Conflict Resolution* 637, 639. Therefore, in this sense, digital justice can act as a mechanism to promote a more efficient access to justice, since it would allow courts to 'reduce some of their caseload, channeling appropriate disputes to quicker, less expensive and more flexible processes' (ibid).

[2] Although, it must be stated that digital justice is not 'a panacea for the ills of traditional dispute resolution': see O Rabinovich-Einy and E Katsh, 'Digital Justice: Reshaping Boundaries in an Online Dispute Resolution Environment' (2014) 1 *International Journal of Online Dispute Resolution* 5, 36.

[3] Establishing a parallelism with A Huxley, *Brave New World* (New York, Harper Perennial Modern Classic, 2010).

who are subject to geographical borders), Big Data, algorithms and codes in the application of justice.

The issues surrounding the triangular relation between information, technology and law are not completely unknown or uncharted.[4] In fact, the permanent evolution of society has acted as a catalyst for change.

In this regard, the recent health pandemic caused by COVID-19/SARS-CoV-2 has been giving place – in a rather successful way – to the best environment for the discussion about digital justice and its legitimacy.[5] The establishment of social withdrawal – whether through law or soft law instruments – has been a major factor of disruption in the traditional structures of justice, which rely mainly on social contact.[6] As a result, many countries are currently facing a virtual standstill of their judicial systems, which may cause severe damage to all the interveners.

This scenario of imperative social distancing and confinement shows the novelty of our analysis. Indeed, if there was already a massive need to overcome the metaphorical shackles resulting from the traditional structures of justice centred in a paper–person paradigm, the need for an alternative digital justice[7] is now both undisputable and inexorable.

In this light, the wide-ranging purpose of this chapter is to emphasise the possibility of the advent of a real digital justice. However, considering the broadness of this topic, and in order to circumscribe it to a more concise object, we choose to focus our text on the issues surrounding the constitutional legitimacy of the said digital justice and its use. During this analysis, it is imperative to ascertain the connection between the adoption of a digital justice system and its relationship with the fundamental legal standards[8] common to the majority of democratic states governed by the rule of law.[9] This new framework raises several questions and doubts, namely about what the protection of fundamental rights is concerned, setting digital justice on a collision course with constitutional rules, for example, those that establish procedural fundamental rights.

[4] E Katsch and J Rifkin, *Online Dispute Resolution: Resolving Conflicts in Cyberspace* (San Francisco, Jossey-Bass, 2001); E Katsch and O Rabinovich-Einy, *Digital Justice: Technology and the Internet of Disputes* (Oxford, Oxford University Press, 2017); R Susskind, *Online Courts and the Future of Justice* (Oxford, Oxford University Press, 2019); J Rifkin, 'Online Dispute Resolution: Theory and Practice of the Fourth Party' (2001) 19 *Conflict Resolution Quarterly* 117.

[5] It must be stressed that our discussion is not rooted around the dimension or the nature of the conflict, eg civil disputes of low value. Instead, we aim to discuss some of the problems that result from the use of digital justice regardless of the nature of the conflict that exists between the parties. For another methodological approach, see Susskind (n 4) 11.

[6] One can consider, as an example, the judicial hearings, the diligences for the production of proof or, even, the submission of proceedings in the court administrative services.

[7] By digital justice, we are referring not only to the jurisdictional activity developed through digital methods, but also to cases in which the decision is achieved through the resource to pre-established algorithms and codes, eg decisions made entirely by machines free from or with scarce human interaction. Nonetheless, the concept of digital justice will be fully developed in the subsequent topics.

[8] Or, in other words, legal principles. Among such set of principles, one can find the rights to fair decisions, to a fair process, to an open or transparent justice, and to a distributive, proportionate, enforceable and sustainable justice. See Susskind (n 4) 75.

[9] For instance, the right to a fair trial or to due process.

For that reason, throughout the development of our analysis, we are bound to adopt a critical perspective. Therefore, we will question not only the advantages and the disadvantages resulting from this change of paradigm, but also the compatibility of some of those solutions with the constitutional framework. Concurrently, it is necessary to explore the problems arising from 'the introduction of technology in the court rooms'.[10]

Naturally, our standpoint is not restricted to the traditional legal system – the courts. Indeed, it is crucial to include in our inquiry the alternative dispute resolution methods. They not only offer ways of resolving conflicts – assuming a complementary position to the judicial structures – but also serve as a domain with long-standing experience in what concerns the use of digital means. In some countries, eg Portugal, such mechanisms of arbitration rely, in some specific fields, on a procedure mainly developed through digital or fully digitised resources.[11] Methodologically, we have decided to take into consideration only the European common standards established by the European Court of Human Rights (ECtHR).[12]

## II. The Concept of Digital Justice

The term 'digital justice' has become a commonplace in the legal lexicon; however, it is far from being a consensual notion or from having a common definition among legal scholars. One can present a wide array of justifications for this fuzziness. First, the concept of digital justice does not present itself as clear or obvious to practitioners and academics. It is rather an ambiguous notion, characterised by its uncertainty and mobile features, which is only natural if we consider the diverse realities it encompasses.

Secondly, and to increase the difficulty of such a definition, it is often a given and unquestioned concept, accepted in some non-critical way: it is a common reality that we recognise when we see it, but which we systematically fail to conceptualise.[13]

Thirdly, the process towards the elaboration of definitions or conceptualisations has intricate connections with – or is even non-severable from – the author's perception of reality and the world. Therefore, even when aiming at objectivity,

[10] J Donoghue, 'The Rise of Digital Justice: Courtroom Technology, Public Participation and Access to Justice' (2017) 6 *MLR* 995.

[11] In some cases, a face-to-face arbitral session between the parties and the arbitrator(s) is even non-existent. This also happens with other alternative dispute resolution methods, such as mediation.

[12] For more about the European Convention on Human Rights (ECHR) as a constitution, see S Greer and L Wildhaber, 'Revisiting the Debate about "Constitutionalising" the European Court of Human Rights' (2013) 12 *Human Rights Law Review* 655.

[13] The concept of digital justice must not be confused with data justice. For more about the problem of data justice, see L Taylor, 'What Is Data Justice? The Case for Connecting Digital Rights and Freedoms Globally' (2017) 4(2) *Big Data & Society* 1.

the result will always be related to the author's legal paramount reality. Thus, definitions regarding recent domains will fail to be unanimous.

Nevertheless, for the current purposes, it is essential to try to put forward a notion of digital justice, in order to understand the realities encompassed by it, as well as to anchor our study. Thus, our efforts to determine what should be understood under the guise of digital justice are limited to the scope of our chapter. We are not aiming to conceptualise, in a universal way, what should be understood as digital justice.

In this sense, our concept of digital justice must be defined as both an 'emerging concept'[14] and a polymorphic one. On the one hand, it can refer to the jurisdictional activity that is developed through digital methods, as, for instance, the electronic development of the proceedings or the hearings conducted through videoconference.[15] On the other hand, it may concern the hypothesis in which the decision is achieved through the recourse to pre-established algorithms and codes, eg a decision reached entirely by machines free from or with scarce human interaction. Both realities fit into the geometry of our concept and are, unequivocally, unified by a common characteristic: the recourse to digital mechanisms.

## III. Advantages and Challenges of Digital Justice: A Quest for Equilibrium?

The use of new technologies and the digital revolution in such a profoundly traditional system as the legal one can be approached from two different angles: the advantages resulting from it or the challenges or difficulties – not to use the expression 'disadvantages'[16] – that it brings and so need to be comprehended and transcended.

The next paragraphs aim to present the advantages or the positive results arising from the shifting to a system of digital justice. First, and in a rather self-evident way, one can consider that a digital approach may act as a facilitator of the citizens' access to justice. Several arguments can be offered to sustain such a statement.

In the first place, one must take into consideration that the commonly enshrined right of 'access to justice' is composed of several aspects. To be given access to

[14] See J McLean, *Changing Digital Geographies Technologies, Environments and People* (London, Palgrave Macmillan, 2020) 70ff.

[15] This feature of digital justice is also commonly labelled as e-justice. See J Püls, 'E-Justiz – Perspektiven in Deutschland und Europa' in W Lüke and J Püls (eds), *E-Justiz: Notare als Mittler und Motoren im elektronischen Rechtsverkehr* (Baden-Baden, Nomos, 2011) 76ff.

[16] By departing from the concept of disadvantage, we are trying to change the focus. In effect, the binary system of positive–negative, advantage–disadvantage, good–bad is not always suitable when one is analysing and debating a new reality. Indeed, it would be too much of a temptation to immediately label as a downside something that, despite being unknown, can, in fact, act as a stimulus for change and evolution.

justice means one's right to present one's own conflict to a court and to achieve a solution over a reasonable timescale, to have a fair trial, but it must also mean to have the right to be advised and represented by a lawyer, among others. The simplicity of the formula 'access to justice' can, indeed, be deceiving. An apparently simple concept comprises a profound amplitude of meanings, all of which have a strong connection to the concept and foundation of a democratic state.

The main question is to understand to what extent the adoption of digital justice can contribute to improving the access of the common citizen to justice. The answer can only be obtained through the arrangement of numerous elements. Foremost, and as universally known, judicial systems have been, on a worldwide basis and for centuries, rooted in an almost unquestionable duet: paper-based structures and formalism. These characteristics, along with the development of social relations, which have been heightened by the consolidation of a truly global society, have led to an array of inefficiencies in the judicial system that, in practice, act as a deterrent for citizens to seek justice for their problems.[17]

Adopting a justice system anchored in digital means would allow, first, the abandonment of the paper-based features of justice. The court proceedings would be, therefore, increasingly dematerialised. The information would be used as digital data, thus removing the need for exhaustive paper archives. The impact of such a transformation must be seen within a holistic approach, considering its consequences and manifestations.

Mainly digital proceedings impact on three fundamental areas: the reduction of costs,[18] the increasing of efficiency and a gateway for a fairer treatment of all the parties involved. Under the guise of 'cost reduction', we can identify two main macro-groups: financial costs and time-saving costs.

Regarding financial costs related with non-digital proceedings, and considering the state position, one cannot ignore that there are severe expenses resulting from the acquisition, use and subsequent archiving of such a huge amount of paper, as well as from the human resources that such a volume of information and material action require. In fact, a deficit in human resources can be deemed to be one of the major causes for the backlog of cases. For the parties, on the other hand, the amount of formalities and administrative procedures they are required to follow – such as presenting certified copies and files, sometimes in duplicate or triplicate – can become an even bigger economic burden, aside from the expenses related to court or legal representation expenses. Adopting a different modus operandi would lead to a different approach to judicial proceedings: a greener, more efficient version of judicial proceedings.

[17] For a metaphorical approach to the barriers in the access to justice, based in Franz Kafka's *The Trial*, see Katsh and Rabinovich-Einy (n 4) 39.

[18] For an approach to this issue, see Z Loebl, *Designing Online Courts: The Future of Justice is Open to All* (Alpheen aan den Rijn, Kluwer Law International, 2019) 17ff; see also Rabinovich-Einy and Katsh, 'Digital Justice' (n 2).

On the other hand, and focusing now on the time-saving possibility, the opportunity to develop both hearings and sessions through digital means allows the parties to detach themselves from geographical limitations, blurring the distances between them and the judicial court. Therefore, all the stakeholders in judicial proceedings can participate, in real time, in the proceedings, without having to submit themselves to travelling or put all of their obligations on hold. Such a solution is particularly appealing for witnesses who must present themselves in court and sometimes, due to a rescheduling or an unforeseen event, are prevented from completing their task, despite all the setbacks they may have endured on its account.

This advantage assumes a particular interest in times of imposed social distancing and confinement, since it is not necessary to concentrate all the interveners in a closed space. Adjusting to a remote-work system, which does not depend intrinsically on material grounds, would have prevented the delays and suspensions caused by the COVID-19/SARS-CoV-2 pandemic.

A second advantage can be found in the domain of low-value disputes. In general, when facing a low-value dispute, most citizens choose, in a rather economic rationality approach, not to pursue a judicial answer for their conflicts. Judicial proceedings involve a wide array of costs: they present an economic burden and are time-consuming.[19] Furthermore, the formality and inhospitality of the judicial environment – which is not appeaseable or even user friendly for those who lack legal education – and the growing distance that citizens feel regarding the traditional structures of justice all act as inhibitors of the search for judicial protection. In this context, digital justice may be a suitable option to help narrow the access to justice gap. That is already a reality in the consumer law disputes across the European Union.

The existence of digital justice may act as a way of guaranteeing justice to all those conflicts with low value, especially if it leads to a diminution of the proceedings' costs or to the reunification of citizens with the legal system. An identical approach could be implemented in the judicial system. Nevertheless, it must be emphasised that this option for a form of digital justice must not be seen as a downgraded form of justice. As previously mentioned, the concept of access to justice has a variable configuration, covering different procedures, such as the traditional courts and the alternative dispute resolution methods; what we did not state at the time is that justice must always be available to all, and with the same quality.

Thirdly, the informality that usually accompanies digital justice may be of assistance in reshaping the systematisation and organisation of the procedures related to judicial proceedings. This new approach to the system can, without compromising its quality or any of the parties' fundamental rights, allow the suppression of

[19] See, among others, G Howells, 'Consumer Law Enforcement and Access to Justice' in C Twigg-Flesner (ed), *Research Handbook on EU Consumer and Contract Law* (Cheltenham, Edward Elgar Publishing, 2016) 408.

time-consuming procedures, enhancing the function of justice. Hence, informality may go hand to hand with celerity and the reduction of bureaucratic burden.[20]

Last but not least, digital justice has the advantage that it can potentially increase the publicity of proceedings.[21] If proceedings are held through the use of digital technology, not only can the written awards be made available online, but so can the hearings be made available, for instance, through streaming or online platforms. This would fulfil the aphorism 'justice must not only be done, it must also be seen to be done'.[22]

Despite all the positive effects arising from the adoption of a digital justice paradigm, it is unquestionable that there are also challenges involved in this equation. The transition from traditional to digital technologies is a new path, and one that raises questions and concerns, particularly because it affects structures that are well entrenched in our global society. Therefore, all the concerns about modifications to the geometry of the justice system must be addressed with interest and curiosity, since they have the ability to promote the development of this new reality.

One first apprehension concerns the very essence of the concept of digital justice, ie justice achieved through the use of digital technology. In fact, the use of technology requires the user to have some know-how or familiarity with it. However, and despite the fact that new generations are generally almost proficient in the use of technology, since it is an important part of their daily life from early days, there is still a wide group of people – approaching the topic in the broadest form possible – that are not familiar with the recourse to technology.[23] Diverse categories can be found within that group: there are technology illiterates, technology amateurs and even illiterate people in the purest sense of the word, ie those who cannot read or write. The main challenge is, thus, to avoid the exclusion of someone's access to justice due to their inability in the technological domain or their lack of access to the Internet. In the same sense, the root to digital justice cannot be anchored on technology – be it software and hardware – that is so high-priced and so sophisticated that it becomes a mechanism of exclusion, rather than a path to justice.[24]

[20] See J Zeleznikow, 'Can Artificial Intelligence and Online Dispute Resolution Enhance Efficiency and Effectiveness in Courts' (2017) 8 *International Journal for Court Administration* 30.

[21] Addressing the criticisms directed at the lack of transparency in artificial intelligence, SW Hofmann-Riem, 'Artificial Intelligence as a Challenge for Law and Regulation' in T Wischmeyer and T Rademacher (eds), *Regulating Artificial Intelligence* (Cham, Springer Nature, 2020) 17.

[22] *R v Sussex Justices, ex parte McCarthy* [1924] 1 KB 256, [1923] All ER Rep 233. On the limits of justice transparency, see Susskind (n 4) 197ff. For a general approach to the problem of transparency in artificial intelligence, see T Wischmeyer, 'Artificial Intelligence and Transparency: Opening the Black Box' in Wischmeyer and Rademacher (n 21) 76ff.

[23] According to the European Commission, digital exclusion is still a risk, particularly if one considers that '80 million Europeans never use [the] Internet either because they don't have a computer or it is too expensive': European Commission, 'Digital Inclusion for a Better EU Society', www.ec.europa.eu/digital-single-market/en/digital-inclusion-better-eu-society.

[24] For the analysis of some compensatory mechanisms to elude the problem of digital exclusion, such as the assisted digital, see Susskind (n 4) 218ff.

A second level of concern, and one that may require a close follow up by the responsible authorities, has to do with the lack of generalised technical means suitable to guarantee the security of proceedings promoted through digital justice means, as well as the protection of personal data.[25]

The last challenging point is the lack of immediacy in the context of digital justice. Traditionally, in most European and Western legal orders, judicial proceedings – whether of a civil or criminal nature – are anchored in a particular legal principle: the principle of immediacy.[26] According to this, all evidence must be produced or presented in court in its original form. Consequently, if hearings take place from afar or if witnesses are questioned through a videoconference, the direct result is the absence of physical proximity or immediacy.

## IV. Fundamental Human Rights in a Digital Justice Context: Can Consent Serve as a Cornerstone According to the ECHR?

This topic aims to explore an interesting question, which although not frequent, can be of particular importance for the domain of digital justice, remarkably in the context of legally imposed social distancing and confinement. As a general principle, judicial proceedings are carried out within the premises of a judicial court in the presence of the necessary involved parties and according to a set of defined procedural rules. Therefore, the proceedings follow their terms according to the paper-based structures, as well as in the physical presence and the involvement of all. Nonetheless, in the midst of the recent health pandemic, it has become impossible, in most countries, to continue to provide the access to justice, namely the continuation of judicial proceedings, in the same conditions as before. As a result, these are days when the judicial system has almost stood still, with all the damage that might result from that forced interruption.

In the search for an alternative answer, some countries, among which is Portugal, have enacted extraordinary legislation in order to attempt to minimise

[25] See N Marsch, 'Artificial Intelligence and the Fundamental Right to Data Protection: Opening the Door for Technological Innovation and Innovative Protection' in Wischmeyer and Rademacher (n 21) 33ff. In this regard, the European Ethical Charter on the Use of Artificial Intelligence in Judicial Systems and Their Environment, adopted at the 31st plenary meeting of the CEPEJ (Strasbourg, 3–4 December 2018) establishes that 'the right of data subjects not to be subject to automated decisions significantly affecting them without their point of view being taken into account, the right to obtain information about the reasoning underlying the data processing carried out by algorithms, the right to oppose such processing and the right to a legal remedy'.

[26] On the principle of immediacy in criminal proceedings, see Article 6(3) ECHR: 'Everyone charged with a criminal offence has the following minimum rights: (d) to examine or have examined witnesses against him and to obtain the attendance and examination of witnesses on his behalf under the same conditions as witnesses against him.' See also C Grabenwarter, *European Convention on Human Rights. Commentary* (Munich, CH Beck, 2014) 163–64.

the damage resulting from social distancing and confinement. In Portugal, the general rule in this time of pandemic is the suspension of all judicial deadlines. The legislator has, though introduced an exception: there is a generic permission for the continuation of proceedings through electronic or digital means only when and if all the parties involved express their agreement to do so.[27] So, for proceedings to be developed in digital form, two requirements of distinct yet complementary natures must be verified: one objective and the other subjective.

On the one hand, it calls for an objective analysis of the real and adequate possibility of continuing the procedures through online platforms to be made. Thus, it is imperative to ascertain if such digital procedures – in a broad sense, the law refers to appropriate means of distance communication, namely conference calls, video calls or equivalent – are appropriate to continue to develop the proceeding. On the other hand, it is indispensable to have the agreement of the parties involved in the proceedings on the adoption of this digital form of action. In this specific case, the central question resides in the fact that parties can, through the expression of their consent and on a voluntary basis, choose to carry their judicial proceedings in this form.

Therefore, the parties' consent is of crucial importance and raises a rather complex set of questions. It is questionable whether it is possible to use this consensual approach in other situations: for instance, if it is admissible for the parties to waive their procedural guarantees, namely those of access to a judicial – physical – court, and to submit their dispute to an online court or an artificial intelligence judge. In other words, to what extent can their consent act as a legitimising cause for the waiver of the guarantees established in Article 6(1) of the European Convention on Human Rights (ECHR).[28] A further problem resides in the determination of the nature of those online tribunals or artificial intelligence judges[29] and their compatibility with Article 6 ECHR, namely whether they are qualified as tribunals for the effects of that article.[30]

[27] See Law No 4-A/2020 of 6 April 2020, specifically Art 7(5), al a).

[28] This issue was already mentioned in the European Ethical Charter on the Use of Artificial Intelligence in Judicial Systems and Their Environment. Particular attention should be given to point 8, where it is expressly referred that 'There is also a need to consider whether these solutions are compatible with the individual rights enshrined in the ECHR. These include the right to a fair trial (particularly the right to a natural judge established by law, the right to an independent and impartial tribunal and equality of arms in judicial proceedings) and, where insufficient care has been taken to protect data communicated in open data, the right to respect for private and family life.'

[29] In other words, the hypothesis where there occurs a complete removal of the human judge from the application of the law – the decision being achieved through a set of algorithms. Our concept is closer to the one that assumes that 'judges might be replaced by machines': see Susskind (n 4) 277ff. This notion must not be confused with 'online judging', since this is a different reality that involves 'the determination of cases by judges but the parties do not gather together in a bricks-and-mortar courtroom': Susskind (n 4) 60.

[30] Article 6(1) ECHR establishes that 'In the determination of his civil rights and obligations or of any criminal charge against him, everyone is entitled to a fair and public hearing within a reasonable time by an independent and impartial tribunal established by law. Judgment shall be pronounced publicly but the press and public may be excluded from all or part of the trial in the interests of morals,

The question has already been analysed and answered by the ECtHR, in the domain of alternative dispute resolution methods in general and arbitration in particular. When questioned about the possibility of the waiver of the procedural rights established by the ECHR in its Article 6(1), the ECtHR determined that:

> Neither the letter nor the spirit of Article 6 of the Convention prevents a person from waiving of his own free will, either expressly or tacitly, the entitlement to the guarantees of a fair trial … However, if it is to be effective for Convention purposes, a waiver of the right to take part in the trial must be established in an unequivocal manner and be attended by minimum safeguards commensurate to its importance … Furthermore, it must not run counter to any important public interest.[31]

On another decision, the ECtHR ruled that:

> In the Contracting States' domestic legal systems a waiver of this kind is frequently encountered both in civil matters, notably in the shape of arbitration clauses in contracts, and in criminal matters in the shape, inter alia, of fines paid by way of composition. The waiver, which has undeniable advantages for the individual concerned as well as for the administration of justice, does not in principle offend against the Convention.[32]

According to the jurisprudence of the ECtHR, the parties may partially waive the procedural guarantees established by Article 6 ECHR, as long as their decision is based on a truly voluntary – and thus based on their free will – act. An identical vision is sustained by the European Commission of Human Rights (EComHR). In fact, when examining the possibility of the parties to waive their procedural guarantees in voluntary and mandatory arbitration, it ruled that:

> Commission notes that a distinction must be drawn between voluntary arbitration and compulsory arbitration. Normally Article 6 poses no problem where arbitration is entered into voluntarily … If, on the other hand, arbitration is compulsory in the sense of being required by law, as in the case, the parties have no option but to refer their dispute to an Arbitration Board, and the Board must offer the guarantees set forth in Article 6(1).[33]

The second question resides, as previously said, in the qualification of the nature of online tribunals or artificial intelligence judges, ie if they can, for the purpose of

public order or national security in a democratic society, where the interests of juveniles or the protection of the private life of the parties so require, or to the extent strictly necessary in the opinion of the court in special circumstances where publicity would prejudice the interests of justice.' Even though this is not a central feature of this chapter, we must highlight that the concept of civil rights used in Article 6(1) ECHR must be interpreted in a broader sense than its national congeners. The concept of civil rights in the ECHR is, indeed, an 'autonomous' meaning and 'As a consequence each case is judged on its individual merits and the interpretation given is not always commensurate with the applicant's national law': S Schiavetta 'The Relationship between e-ADR and Article 6 of the European Convention of Human Rights Pursuant to the Case Law of the European Court of Human Rights' (2004) 1 *Journal of Information Law & Technology* 6.

[31] See *Sejdovic v Italy* App no 56581/00 (ECtHR, 1 March 2006) 86.

[32] See *Deweer v Belgium* App no 6903/75 (ECtHR, 27 February 1980) 49.

[33] See *Bramelid v Sweden* (1983) 38 DR 49.

the ECHR, be considered as tribunals.[34] A distinction must be drawn. In situations where the digital justice mechanisms lack a voluntary nature, and are therefore mandatory for the parties, they can only be qualified as a tribunal, under the scope of Article 6 ECHR, if they fulfil all the requirements established by that article.

Hence, their procedural guarantees need to be equivalent to the ones established for other tribunals, otherwise there will be a breach of the ECHR Article 6. Nonetheless, there might be a safeguard for this. Moreover, it is possible to sustain that no breach of the ECRH will occur if those mandatory mechanisms contemplate an appeal procedure that allows for a tribunal to have jurisdiction for a full review of the merits of the decision. In this context, such an appeal mechanism can guarantee the parties' fundamental rights enshrined in Article 6.[35]

In the following paragraphs, we will analyse some hypotheses that may, in this context, present themselves as challenging if confronted with Article 6 ECHR.

## V. A Constitutional Approach to Digital Justice through the Lens of Judicial Discretion

The digital justice universe is, naturally, an almost new world, full of promises and hopes – especially if one acknowledges the insufficiencies of the traditional legal systems.[36] Nevertheless, besides the wonder, there is also the unknown, which is, in turn, full of dismay, questions and legal perplexities. Acknowledging the broadness of this domain, and considering the scope of this chapter, it is necessary to select only one particular question from all the challenges surrounding the triangular relation between artificial intelligence, digital justice and the legal system.

To this end, the following paragraphs aim to develop a critical analysis of one main topic. We will discuss, in the light of the use of robot judges in the traditional legal system, the limits of the use of digital technology and artificial intelligence in judicial procedures, namely regarding the problems related to the cases that involve judicial discretion.

The concept of robot judges must first be clarified. When referring to robot judges, we are not adhering to the idea of an actual robot physically resembling a human being; rather, our concept is anchored on the substance of their activity abilities rather than on their physical shape.

Consequently, with this concept in mind, we aim to encompass all artificial intelligence systems that have the aptitude to produce a decision-like product

[34] On the concept of tribunal under the scope of ECHR, see Grabenwarter (n 26) 114ff.

[35] See Schiavetta (n 30).

[36] On the possibilities that artificial intelligence can provide to the legal system domain, see B Cooper, 'Judges in Jeopardy!: Could IBM's Watson Beat Courts at Their Own Game?' (2011) 121 *Yale Law Journal Online*. With a sceptic approach to the theme, see J Morison and A Harkens, 'Re-engineering Justice? Robot Judges, Computerised Courts and (Semi) Automated Legal Decision-Making' (2019) 39(4) *Legal Studies* 1.

when given both the factual context and the legal parameters. They have some characteristics that may, to some extent, be similar to the cognitive abilities of a human being and, in that sense, their algorithmic capacity allows those mechanisms to produce something that is similar to the activity developed by judges.

The use of robot judges is a complex reality with a variable geometry.[37] At first glance, it is possible to theorise two macro-models of digital justice. The first model reveals a completely automated system functioning uniquely on an algorithmic base and without the intervention of a human judge. It represents a complete replacement of the human figure of the judge, leaving the machine to process the data and render a decision through computational models.

There is also a second possible system, which can be qualified as a hybrid system. In this instance, the artificial intelligence produces a semi-automated decision that will be combined with the final supervision of a human judge. Here the machine learning mechanism acts as a support mechanism for the judge, playing the role of an auxiliary.[38]

The first hypothesis, where there is a complete removal of the human judge from the application of the law – decisions being achieved instead through a set of algorithms – remains only a remote possibility, about which many are sceptical.[39] Regardless, this is the most problematic scenario. Moreover, despite being far fetched, the use of robot judges is already raising concerns in many domains, including in the fields of judicial bias and judicial discretion.

To proceed with the analysis, one must conceive, even if only on a theoretical level, of a judicial system, or a part of said system, that relies, at first instance, only on automated courts. Hence, the application of the law will be exclusively based on algorithms and the entire procedures developed during those cases will be the product of those machines' activity. As a result, all the decisions are freed or purged from human intervention and obtained only through a set of machines, which are fed with an identical amount of data.[40] Consequently, this system will give rise

[37] On the possibilities that artificial intelligence can provide to the legal system domain, see Cooper (ibid).

[38] Morison and Harkens (n 36). The mechanism is a risk assessment software and has been under several criticism. On COMPAS, see D Kehl, P Guo and S Kessler, 'Algorithms in the Criminal Justice System: Assessing the Use of Risk Assessments in Sentencing' [2017] *Responsive Communities*, www.cyber.harvard.edu/ publications/2017/07/Algorithms 2, 18ff; Morison and Harkens (n 36) 8ff.

[39] Morison and Harkens (n 36) 9. Sharing this sceptic view and stating that 'delegating implementation power to intelligent machines makes no more (or less) sense than delegating such power to an exclusive subset of humans – like the priests and knights of yesteryear. Could we do this? Yes, of course we could. But democratic values counsel otherwise', see K Brennan-Marquez and S Henderson, 'Artificial Intelligence and Role-Reversible Judgment' (2019) 109 *Journal of Criminal Law & Criminology* 137, 155–56. Against, defending that its plausible to have such a change, see RM Re and A Solow-Niederman, 'Developing Artificially Intelligent Justice' (2019) 242 *Stanford Technology Law Review* 243, 243.

[40] Although, it must be noted that 'the neutrality of algorithms is a myth, as their creators consciously or unintentionally transfer their own value systems into them': see the European Ethical Charter on the Use of Artificial Intelligence in Judicial Systems and Their Environment, 57.

to 'standardised, systemised, packaged' decisions, far from a 'bespoke activity'.[41] A system with those traits will surely raise problems in the field of judicial discretion.

In fact, cases that require the use of judicial discretion do not seem appropriate to be decided by systems of artificial intelligence. Although an artificial intelligence machine can be 'taught' to develop some type of legal reasoning through the use of 'computational models of legal reasoning',[42] it can never replace the evaluation performed by a human being. Furthermore, this substitution of the human intervention of the judge may lead to some difficulties in the legal system.

First, the parties may fail to accept – and to comply with – the decision issued by such an artificial intelligence system, since this form of adjudication of the law may be seen with suspicion or, concurrently, because they fail to understand its reasoning or solution.[43]

Secondly, the use of artificial intelligence systems of legal reasoning has the disadvantage of crystallising the data used to render a decision. Unlike what happens with human beings, those systems will be unable to achieve a resolution that is in compliance with environmental, social or even emotional stimuli. So, unlike what occurs with a human judge, one cannot expect machines or robot judges to adjust to other standards besides the ones with which they were initially programmed. Their source code will be, at least until more advanced technology is conceived, completely dependent on human intervention to change or update their parameters, ie their algorithms.

Nonetheless, and even if it were possible to surpass the two previous challenges, one cannot ignore that there is an insurmountable limit established by Article 6(1) ECHR, ie those mechanisms without a human judge component can, under no circumstance, be qualified as tribunals for the purpose of the ECHR. Furthermore, this difficulty in not open to a consent-based solution. Consequently, this means that even if the interested parties so desire, they cannot legitimate such a dispute resolution mechanism through an act of will.

This scenario must not be confused, however, with the hypothesis in which technology acts as an assistant either directly to the judge or to the development of dispute resolution proceedings, as is the case of online dispute resolution mechanisms.[44] In these particular cases, the consent given by the parties is sufficient to ensure the compatibility of those procedures with the requirements foreseen

[41] Morison and Harkens (n 36) 11. On bespoke legal works, see R Susskind, *Tomorrow's Lawyers. An Introduction to Your Future*, 2nd edn (Oxford, Oxford University Press, 2017) 25ff.

[42] Morison and Harkens (n 36) 2. For further analysis of this topic, see CR Sunstein, 'Of Artificial Intelligence and Legal Reasoning' (2001) 8 *University of Chicago Law School Roundtable* 29, https://chicagounbound.uchicago.edu/cgi/viewcontent.cgi?article=12376&context=journal_articles.

[43] Re and Solow-Niederman (n 39) 262ff.

[44] On the online dispute resolution, see Loebl (n 18) 3ff.

in Article 6 of the ECHR, even if that requires the waiver of some procedural guarantees. The main point is that the waiver must result from an effective act of free will and that the result is not obtained exclusively through an artificial intelligence system.[45]

## VI. Final Remarks

Originally a futuristic idea rooted in only the most creative imaginations, artificial intelligence is nowadays an effective reality. In fact, the introduction of artificial intelligence in our daily life has been increasing rapidly, embracing almost all sectors, from medicine to teaching or from essential services to the film industry. As a social product, the law sector has not been an exception and has been undergoing several transformations in connection to the digital enhancement of its procedures. However, these modifications have not come in a single wave or with a single degree of intensity, and have therefore been affecting our judicial systems in a rather progressive form.

Initially, technology presented itself as a way of overcoming the judicial systems' material insufficiencies, mainly those related to their paper-based structures. In this sense, technology has allowed the judicial system to start introducing digital procedures that stimulate their performance, leading both to an increase in efficiency and a reduction of the burdens brought on from the overuse of antique procedures.

In a second movement, however, the relation between technology – or artificial intelligence – and the judicial system has ceased to be one of mere technical assistance, evolving to one of cooperation. In this context, those mechanisms have started to play a role in assisting judges in their function of deciding and applying the law.

The future promises to offer further realities which have hitherto been imaginable only in the field of science fiction. Among those possibilities, one can identify the figure of robot judges. It is indeed possible that, in the near future, especially conceived artificial intelligence mechanisms may, to some extent, be able to produce a result similar to legal reasoning, through the use of computational

[45] In this context, the European Ethical Charter on the Use of Artificial Intelligence in Judicial Systems and Their Environment recommends that parties 'be informed in a clear and comprehensible manner whether the processing of their dispute is done in an entirely automated way or with the involvement of a mediator or arbitrator. In addition, the information given to litigants must be honest and must avoid giving them the impression that a court is involved (in this connection, the term 'online court' is often used for this type of platform, whereas technically their purpose is to provide alternative dispute resolution services). These are two essential factors in enabling litigants to make an informed choice, possibly disagreeing with the advice and deciding to go to a real court within the meaning of Article 6 of the ECHR. Furthermore, in view of the requirements of Articles 6 and 13 of the ECHR, forms of review of the online dispute resolution procedure and its outcome by state courts should always be considered, especially where the litigant has consented to fully automated online dispute resolution' (65).

models. In those situations, the artificial intelligence mechanisms, named robot judges, will be given a new position within the legal system: from auxiliaries to main characters, ie a complete substitution of the human judge by artificial intelligence. The equation will have changed from the 'traditional' science fiction idea of human race v robots to robots developing activities that depend on human-like reasoning.

Notwithstanding, this artificial intelligence revolution has a velocity and characteristics of its own, taking place at a different pace from that seen in the field of constitutionalism. Additionally, the humanist idea that serves as a foundation of constitutionalism clashes with this override of human judges by artificial intelligence structures. In other words, our constitutionalist matrix is not compatible with the full replacement of the human judge by the artificial intelligence judge. On this view, not even the consent of the parties could serve as a basis for legitimising this full replacement.

Nevertheless, it may still be possible, under certain conditions, for an artificial intelligence programme to produce a decision through legal reasoning in compliance with Article 6 ECHR. In order for this to be possible, it is, however, imperative that such decision be, at all times, submitted to a full review of its merit by a human judge. Thus, the human judge must always be bestowed with the power to review the machine's decision.[46]

Even so, it is not plausible that, in the near future, the human judge's role will be completely replaced by dispute resolution systems that are strictly based on artificial intelligence. Technology, despite all its advances, is not yet at that stage of evolution. But or when that possibility arises – beyond the ethical and moral issues that it may trigger – it is imperative not to lose sight of its limits, especially those that are a product of our constitutional systems.

[46] With a similar position, see C Prince, 'Digital Justice' (2018) 34 *Computer Law & Security Review* 920, 921: 'A key condition for the effective functioning of the constitutional state is that the courts be capable of fully implementing its task of affording legal protection. Reinterpreting this condition in the modern age implies that courts should remain explicitly vigilant when it comes to digitisation.'

# 12

# The Impact of Artificial Intelligence on Administrative Law

ALESSANDRO PUZZANGHERA

## I. Introduction

Administrative law has undergone a significant transformation over the past few decades, due, in part, to the impact of new forms of technology on administrative activity. The impetuous development of artificial intelligence (AI) in the context of Italian administrative law, both in policy and in the main sectors of its organisational, administrative and jurisdictional activity, marks the end of an era.

The term AI does not encompass a simple concept, as it contains a series of notions, each of which is an expression of complexity: robotics, machine learning, the development of complex algorithms, artificial neural networks, game theory,[1] and so on. The interconnectedness of AI and administrative law is already evident in these historic times, in which we are witnessing the transition from a computer mainly used for archiving purposes to a computer used in a more functional manner in administrative activity.[2] This process generates a plethora of issues that are taken into consideration here, with particular regard to the intermediation of the administrative provision.

In this respect, the so-called administrative relationship that is established between citizen and administration, rendered functional by the issue of a legislative measure, is affected by this process even before a provision is issued, not to mention the effects on the interaction between an administrative decision and its consequent effects on judicial review.[3] The questions that such situation opens up

[1] Game theory is used in computer science, with the objective of understanding and designing algorithms in strategic environments.

[2] In recent times, there have been a number of new approaches in public administration law due to the telematic services. An example is the telematic administrative process, which is of more functional manner in administrative activity.

[3] The partial, or even total, replacement of a judge, particularly in decision-making, constitutes a real issue and raises doubt since, from an objective point of view, it must be ensured that AI is able to accomplish all tasks autonomously, free from human intervention or conditioning.

are manifold: if, in the case of a decision made by an individual, one is willing to 'accept' error, save contesting it in a court of law, is one willing to accept a decision taken by software that should be 'neutral'?

At a time in which the formulation of any national, international or European law appears to be complicated, where very often the administrative judge must attempt an interpretation that is appropriate to a specific and unique case, it is legitimate to ask whether AI would discern how to proceed in such instances. Indeed, a computerised decision must not lessen the safeguards of a citizen but must be open to verification.

We are, therefore, faced with a double challenge, both technological and legal. A wise use of AI systems and programs should increase efficiency and performance in public service, while at the same time complying with constitutional and legal requirements and those norms in general that characterise administrative law. For its part, legal challenge must restrict the use of new forms of technology and determine its application without placing unjustified and unnecessary obstacles in the way of technological development.

The aim of this chapter is, therefore, to investigate, with a critical attitude and a multidisciplinary approach, the impact and the resulting effect that artificial intelligence has had in the sphere of Italian administrative law, also in relation to specific national circumstances within the EU area.

Indeed, AI, given the great results it has already achieved in the ever-evolving medical field, will become, in the not too distant future, an excellent auxiliary tool for administrative law. It will not only help the administrative assistant in the preliminary phases of the administrative process, concerning the admissibility, eligibility, validity and compatibility of applications, but also play a much more important role in the decision-making phases, especially if approved by the EU and the European Court of Human Rights.

## II. The Introduction of AI into the Administrative Network

Research in information technology (IT) and AI is aimed at exploring the fundamentals, approaches and techniques that allow for the design of hardware and software systems capable of providing the electronic processor with performance powers that, for a common observer, would appear to be exclusive only to human intelligence.[4] AI was originally founded as a discipline in 1956, during a seminar held at Dartmouth College in Hanover, New Hampshire. One of the most famous definitions, attributed to Marvin Minsky, an American mathematician and scientist and a pioneer of the sector, is: 'artificial intelligence is the science of making

[4] *cf* F Amigoni and V Schiaffonati and M Somalvico, *Intelligenza artificiale* (Rome, Enciclopedia della scienza e della tecnica, 2008).

machines do things that would require intelligence if done by men'.[5] Through 'artificial neural networks', which transmit the connections of the human brain to a computer, a computer device should be able to understand natural language, to learn and self-perfect, and to interpolate incomplete information.[6]

At this time, there are already numerous concrete and widespread applications of AI, often supported by large public and private investment,[7] such as in vehicles with assisted or fully autonomous driving. The most recent studies and experiments also consider the possibility of coding ethical choices with which to program the devices.

Of particular interest is the social experiment conducted by the Massachusetts Institute of Technology, which, through a portal called 'moral machine', collected data on solutions deemed morally acceptable in potentially ethical issues deriving from traffic flow. This was achieved through a simple online survey in which users were asked to indicate the choices that the self-driving vehicle should make in the presence of dangerous situations (caused by the unforeseen or irrational behaviour of other road users) which would result in the death or injury of passengers or pedestrians.

Unlike in administrative decision-making, processors that make decisions, even at a complex level, are an existing reality. However, it is not easy to imagine any form of judicial safeguard that allows for the recovery of an actual situation prior to the endorsement of an illegitimate (or inappropriate) choice.

On this point, it is interesting to observe the relationship between an automated decision and the processing of personal data. The recent EU Regulation 2016/679 (the so-called General Data Protection Regulation, GDPR) refers to the right of the interested party not to be subjected to a decision, based solely on automated processing, that may include a measure which could assess personal matters and bring legal consequences that could significantly affect him and his person. This is also defined in Article 22, paragraph 1 GDPR: 'the interested party has the right not to be subjected to a decision based solely on automated processing, which may have legal effects on him or his person'.

The right of an interested party to not be subjected to decisions based solely on automated processing can, however, be limited by any legislative measures, necessary and proportionate, aimed at safeguarding public interest, such as national security, defence, prevention and the investigation, detection and prosecution of crimes. It is up to the state to consider the possibility of granting an administration, through suitable legal provisions and in limited circumstances, the power to embrace decisions based solely on automated data processing.[8]

[5] See T Stonier, *The Evolution of Machine Intelligence* (London, Springer, 1992).

[6] See V Buscema, *Discrezionalità amministrativa e reti neurali artificiali* (Il foro amministrativo, 1993) 620ff.

[7] For example, in 2016, the US Department of Transportation announced plans to invest $3.9 billion in subsequent years for research on automated vehicles.

[8] See F Pizzetti, *Privacy e il diritto europeo alla protezione dei dati personali. Il Regolamento europeo 2016/679* (Turin, Giappichelli, 2016).

In administration, AI has been successfully employed in providing public services and exercising public policy.[9] As the processing skills of computers is progressing exponentially, it is hoped that discretionary public decision-making processes will not encounter, in principle, technological obstacles caused by the constant pressure of cyber processing on reproducing human analytical reasoning. Many believe that, given the processing skills of computers and the possibility that these instruments have to access an infinite amount of information in real time so as to find the best solution for a specific case, we could witness a transformation in public opinion.[10]

There are scholars who, by adapting the theory of balancing constitutional rights[11] to the activity of comparing personal interests in the exercise of discretion, formulate algorithms whose application would ensure the maximum satisfaction of primary concerns, with less attention paid to those of minor importance.[12] Other scholars are instead considering the possibility of an automated administrative decision when, through the use of software, valid criteria are introduced to pilot the exercise of power case-by-case.[13] In these instances, an administrator's discretion would be exercised on principle as well as on predisposed criteria; therefore, the computer processor should examine this information when making a decision.[14]

We are edging nearer to the so-called 'automated decision', with the wide use of AI that, by solving complex problems through 'reasoning' and knowledge, explains and justifies a chosen solution.[15] We are dealing with an 'automated legal consultant' that has overturned the classic scheme of human–machine interrogation and is capable of asking questions (as, for example, a public official does) in order to acquire the factual data and information necessary to identify applicable provisions, so as to come to a decision[16] which must be fully motivated and proposed for use to the owner of an entity.

The administrative network is the one that, at least in theory, best lends itself to computerisation and automation.[17] It is precisely this 'procedural' characteristic,

[9] For example, with reference to the use of automated information systems in the provision and management of public services in Australia, see G Sartor, *Sistemi basati sulla conoscenza giuridica e servizi pubblici* (Diritto dell'informazione e dell'informatica, 2008) 463ff.

[10] See S Civitarese Matteucci and L Torchia, *La tecnificazione dell'amministrazione* (Florence, Florence University Press, 2017) 36.

[11] See R Alexy, *On Balancing and Subsumption. A Structural Comparison* (Ratio Juris, 2003) 433ff.

[12] See PLM Lucatuorto and S Bianchini, *Discrezionalità e contemperamento degli interessi nei processi decisionali dell'Amministrazione digitale* (Cyberspazio e diritto, 2009) 41ff.

[13] See A Masucci, *Procedimento Amministrativo e nuove tecnologie* (Turin, Giappichelli, 2011) 93.

[14] See F Saitta, *Le patologie dell'atto amministrativo elettronico e il sindacato del giudice amministrativo* (Rivista di Diritto amministrativo elettronico, 2003) 19.

[15] See PLM Lucatuorto, *Intelligenza artificiale e diritto: le applicazioni giuridiche dei sistemi esperti* (Cyberspazio e diritto, 2006) 219ff.

[16] See F Morollo, *Documento elettronico fra e-government e artificial intelligence* (www.federalismi.it, 2015) 19.

[17] See VD Marongiu, *L'attività amministrativa automatizzata* (Rimini, Maggioli Editore, 2005).

along with its 'globally relevant function', that combines with the order of an algorithm and presents unusual similarities. Finally, although AI is growing exponentially, there is still a stumbling block between administrative activity and computerisation, which concerns its degree of discretion, that much cited 'administrative discretion'[18] considered by MS Giannini as an 'invariant' of administrative law.[19]

## III. The Electronic Administrative Measure

Administrative activity, like any other human activity, has undergone an important transformation in recent decades, due to an ever-greater use of new forms of technology in general and greater reliance on information technology, and telematics in particular. The use of new forms of technology in administration has given rise to two different worlds that have joined together with, on the one hand, the use of the computer as a database (a restrictive and minimalistic use, given its potential), and on the other, the use of the computer to process administrative documents electronically and through digital media.

I will examine the combination of IT and administrative activity, the electronic processing of administrative measures, the processors that prepare content and the implications that arise, considering the relative aspects and conditions, as well as the jurisdictional safeguards, where applicable.[20] It is the computer that, through inputting and programming, makes a decision.[21] What has been presented above can be described using the language of respected doctrine, that is, passing from 'computer-archive' to 'computer-official'[22] or substituting 'computer processing in documentation', for IT purposes aimed at collecting and organising specifically requested data for users, with 'meta-documentation', which instead tends to mechanically reproduce human mental processes, such as identifying solutions to specific problems.[23]

We are witnessing a profound and progressive change in administrative activity that brings jurists to doubly ponder the present, as regards the study and interpretation of the current uses and potential of IT devices, implemented by positive law and based on administrative decisions, with an eye towards a future which cannot

[18] See F Gorgerino, *Discrezionalità amministrativa ed ermeneutica giuridica* (Diritto e Processo Amministrativo, 2018) 1265ff.

[19] For MS Giannini, *Il Potere discrezionale della pubblica amministrazione*, the invariants are concepts that last longer than others, but are still drawn from the analysis of positive law (Milan, Giuffrè, 1939).

[20] See the definition given by Saitta (n 14).

[21] See A Masucci, *Atto amministrativo informatico* (Milan, Giuffrè, 1997) 221.

[22] See A Masucci, *L'atto amministrativo informatico. Prima lineamenti di una ricostruzione* (Naples, Jovene, 1993) 13.

[23] See M D'Angelosante, *La consistenza del modello dell'amministrazione 'invisibile' nell'età della tecnificazione: dalla formazione delle decisioni alla responsabilità per le decisioni* (Florence, Florence University Press, 2016).

take legislation by surprise.[24] It is legitimate to ask whether, at this point, information and communication technology will be used to codify the decision-making process so as to bring automated decisions (or rather, electronic processing) and, therefore, to pass from the 'archive computer' to the 'computer-official'. In order to draw up a measure that defines the structure of relationships and interests according to the provisions of the law, it is necessary to provide the electronic processor with appropriate instructions, that is, the logic-mathematical rules derived from a process of rationalisation of human activity, based on actual cases and specific legal conditions.

One idea of an electronically processed administrative measure, which is not very problematic and easily accessible, is the so-called non-discretionary act.[25] Such an experiment was presented as long ago as 1978 in a paper[26] by Duni, who analysed the close relationship between a non-discretionary act and the possibility of entrusting the processing of a measure to a computer. When speaking strictly of so-called non-discretionary acts there emerges a strong theoretical awareness and practical experience in the administrative practices of the time[27] which, therefore, determined the extent of computerisation in successfully enacting distinctively non-discretionary acts.

The introduction of IT systems into Italian public administration was presented in reconstructions by both Frosini in 1982[28] and Fantigrossi in 1993,[29] who reported on common issues brought up by the diversity of the systems being used in different facets of public administration, as well as by the lack of a common standard in use. Didactic development has permitted a more complete reconstruction, although limited to the electronic processing of the so-called non-discretionary acts. By way of example, a computer that has been programmed according to the technical parameters concerning the rules on speed limits in road traffic ascertains, through technology, that the speed limit has been exceeded, imposes the administrative sanction proposed for that instance and applies the relative measures. Once the data has been entered, the computer transforms the quantifiable data (input) into outgoing data (output), without carrying out any autonomous 'reasoning', using algorithms (human intelligible computational procedure), which subsequently transform it into a program (artificial intelligible computational procedure).

We are faced with the classic norm–fact–effect scheme,[30] as the decision may be automated only if the regulatory provision can be effectively and univocally

[24] See P Otranto, *Decisione amministrativa e digitalizzazione della p.a.* (www.federalismi.it, 2018) 27.

[25] See F Follieri, *Decisione amministrativa ed atto vincolato* (www.federalismi.it, 2017)4.

[26] See G Duni, *L'utilizzabilità delle tecniche elettroniche nell'emanazione degli atti e nei procedimenti amministrativi. Spunto per una teoria dell'atto emanato nella forma elettronica* (Rome, Rivista Amministrativa della Repubblica Italiana, 1978) 407ff.

[27] See A Ravalli, *Atti amministrativi emanati mediante sistemi informatici: problematiche relative alla tutela giurisdizionale* (TAR, 1989) 261–62.

[28] See V Frosini, *L'informatica e la p.a.* (Rivista trimestrale di diritto pubblico, 1983).

[29] See U Fantigrossi, *Automazione e pubblica amministrazione. Profili giuridici* (Bologna, Il Mulino, 1993) 33ff.

[30] *cf* E Capaccioli, *Manuale di diritto amministrativo* (Padova, Cedam, 1983) 267ff.

codified, so that there can be appropriate instruction in determining the content of a measure.[31] Therefore, only what is attributable to provisional judgement, whereby condition 'A' arises and effect 'B' is produced,[32] is relevant.

In order for an automated system to carry out the activities that a public official would carry out with uniformity, versatility and efficiency,[33] it must be, for any matter in question, free of administrative discretion and based on analytical legal concepts that are useful for quantifying reality.[34]

There can be two levels of administrative decision. The initial level is where there is a lack of legal provisions applied to mandatory administrative measures. In this case, the administration decides to exercise its function by adopting software that, through pre-established rules and in compliance with the law, transforms input into output. For the most part, in edict, the legal basis of an administration's power to use software for the automation of the binding activity is the result of an independent choice made by individual entities.[35] Such an organisational choice would still comply with the principles of reason and logic,[36] as the automated decision undoubtedly entails advantages in terms of reducing the risks of unequal treatment, compliance with the law, protection from corruption and thoroughness at a preliminary level.[37] What better tool could achieve impartiality and sound administration?

The second level of decision-making concerns the content of the commands structured in the algorithm that are translated into software. Non-analytical legal concepts are used to build norm-based cases so that an acceptable hermeneutical option can be identified. The result is a decision that, translated into software, produces a uniform effect on the combination of relationships and interests affected by the automated measures.[38] The transition to computer-based decision-making also depends on the need for an accurate language that renders relative statements more easily reduced to an algorithm, so much so that automation, along with stiff legal terminology, may eliminate the benefits that 'adaptive behaviours'[39] bring to the operation of complex organisations.[40]

[31] See Saitta (n 14) 17: 'Without doubt compatible with the logic of the electronic computer – given that the software translates the legal data (general principles, rules and jurisprudence) and the factual data into mathematical language, giving life to a formalized logical reasoning that combines a conclusion that given the initial elements, it is immutable – it is winning.'

[32] See Morollo (n 16) 17–18.

[33] See A Usai, *Le elaborazioni possibili delle informazioni. I limiti alle decisioni amministrative automatiche* (Rome, Istituto Poligrafico dello Stato, 1992).

[34] *cf* Follieri (n 25) 13.

[35] See Masucci, *Procedimento Amministrativo* (n 13) 86.

[36] See Saitta (n 14) 24.

[37] See F Costantino, *Autonomia dell'amministrazione e innovazione digitale* (Rome, Jovene, 2012) 171ff.

[38] See Follieri (n 25) 15.

[39] See V Frosini, *Informatica diritto e società* (Milan, Giuffrè, 1988).

[40] See Civitarese Matteucci and Torchia (n 10) 34–35.

The automated measure, despite having undeniable advantages in terms of efficiency, cost-effectiveness and successful action, as well as being a guarantee of uniform treatment and non-opposition, does not in itself entail legitimacy. It would be illegitimate if, for example, the instructions provided in computer software were incorrect, or if there were software issues[41] or malfunctioning hardware. In the event of an error by the administration or the private entity in preparing a program, all measures in a particular category would be affected and alternative solutions would be sidestepped, since the illegitimacy would depend not on the execution of the commands given on a case-by-case basis (and therefore by the processor), but from the choices made in the development of the algorithm and its translation into software.

In order to verify compliance with the cause–effect outline defined by the norm and, therefore, establish the presence of any flaws in the algorithm (or software), full knowledge of the commands that the administration has programmed into the digital processor is necessary. In a recent ruling, the Tribunale Amministrativo Regionale (TAR) Lazio[42] recognised the claimants' right to access the algorithm of the program used to carry out an entire procedure, but also affirmed the full legitimacy of the administration's option to manage procedures under the Electronic Processing Act.

However, despite the decisions of the administration, the rights of access of the interested parties must remain reserved. In response to a request for access, it is not enough for an administration to describe the algorithm used, since, in order benefit fully, the configuration and the so-called 'source code', or text, of the algorithm of a program, elaborated in specific code during the programming phase, must be included in a source file and accessible to the parties concerned.

The decision of an organisation to opt for digital processing in administrative procedures cannot interfere with safeguards and guarantees, since the use of technology must be balanced by constant reference to the principles and institutions of due process. Observance of, and reference to, the procedures in due process guarantee a citizen's rapport with the public authority in cases where a discretionary decision[43] is subject to digital processing. Although the principle in part tends

[41] For a more careful analysis on the appeal of the intra-procedural administrative acts that constitute the prerequisite for the electronic administrative act adopted at the end of the computerised procedure and, in particular, for the distinction between software and programming instructions provided by the administration, see Saitta (n 14) 24–27, who distinguishes the software (which cannot be classified as an administrative act and therefore inseparable from an independent appeal, but whose defects could determine the illegitimacy deriving from the final provision) from the 'software programming rules' (independently contestable as administrative acts). On the pathology of the electronic administrative act, see AG Orofino, *La patologia dell'atto amministrativo elettronico: sindacato giurisdizionale e strumenti di tutela* (Foro Amministrativo, 2002) 2257ff.

[42] TAR Lazio, section III-bis, judgment of 22 March 2017, n 3769.

[43] See MS Giannini, *Il potere discrezionale della pubblica amministrazione. Concetto e problemi* (Milan, Giuffrè, 1939); C Mortati, *Discrezionalità* (Turin, Utet, 1960) 1098ff; A Piras, *Discrezionalità amministrativa* (Milan, Enciclopedia del diritto, 1964) 65 ss.; V Cerulli Irelli, *Note in tema di*

to exclude any discretionary provision for electronic processing, it is undeniable that technology is making tremendous progress and advancing at such an incessant pace that it is disrupting consolidated relationships and interests. It should be noted that any repercussions on constitutional stability, and the administrative function itself, that result from the computerisation of administrative activity within the framework of the state are yet to be clearly identified.

## IV. Liability

Liability for claims resulting from an electronically processed administrative measure is rooted in the well-known adage *causa causae est causa causati*, that is, a logical procedure that ultimately holds accountable the administrative authority which had opted for the use of IT in issuing administrative measures. To verify that the intention of a computerised measure is traceable to an administrative authority, one must bear in mind the aforementioned *causa causae est causa causati*.

Thus, the will of the computer is the will of the authority. Through a computer program, an organisation may predispose 'decisions' for an indeterminate number of cases that, even when taken at a later stage, remain attributable to the authority.[44] However, attributing responsibility to an authority is not a solution to the problem, as it may be in other circumstances. Indeed, it is necessary to deal with the subjective element of the compensatory measure, and it is here that problems arise.

Eminent doctrine states that:

> It is certainly problematic to propose the accountability of a public authority for adopting and/or executing an unlawful digitally-processed administrative measure. If Civil Code Article 2043 requires that accountability be incurred when there is wilful misconduct or negligence within the powers granted, this is particularly difficult to carry out in the case of digitally processed administrative measures.[45]

Applying the terms provided by Italian Civil Code, Article 2043 in addressing the issue is somewhat difficult, if not impossible. This is because the context leading to the computerisation of the measure is characterised by the presence of multiple public and private entities (for example, the company that created the software), as well as the great difficulty in accurately identifying the causes of, and those responsible for, the disservice.

According to prominent doctrine, administrative power is not exercised by a single official, but by a computerised administrative system. The intentions of a digitally processed administrative measure, in fact, is not attributable to a single

*discrezionalità amministrativa e sindacato di legittimità* (Diritto Processuale Amministrativo, 1984) 463; L Benvenuti, *La discrezionalità amministrativa* (Padova, Cedam, 1986); G Barone, *Discrezionalità (diritto amministrativo)* (Rome, Enciclopedia Giuridica, 1989) 2ff.

[44] See Masucci, *L'atto amministrativo informatico* (n 22) 85.

[45] ibid 85.

person, but to a multitude of people. Databases which are autonomous from an organisational point of view satisfy the demands of decision-making authorities with a great amount of data and information. In this regard, an organisation entrusts the development of programs to software companies, which rely on the minimal collaboration of the public officials of the departments responsible for the activity at hand. It is for this reason that it is difficult to verify an administrator's wilful misconduct or gross negligence. Rendering the detection of negligence even more difficult is the mere element of recurrent computer error, which is in no way attributable to the administrative official.[46]

A further complication can be the statute on contextualising digitally processed administrative measures within the categories of the Digital Administration Code (CAD) (Legislative Decree 7 March 2005, n 82, CAD). This statute puts great pressure on the person supervising procedure, who must simultaneously consider:

1. the responsibilities assigned to the administrative official that develops the software and/or enters and/or transmits the data;
2. the responsibilities of the supervisor overseeing the computerised management of documents, document flow and the archives, who, pursuant to Article 61 of Presidential Decree 445 of 2000, must ensure a proper functioning of the system; and
3. the responsibilities of the person who drafts the internal procedural steps, subscribed by digital (as defined by Article 1 CAD).[47]

The application of the CAD in the digital processing of an administrative measure is also justified by Attachment 1 to the Presidential Decree (dpcm) of 13 November 2014, which defines the 'automatic generation' of an electronic document as one that is directly elaborated and executed by the computer system, meeting specific conditions and administrative requirements on the right of access to digital programming.[48]

Consequently, there may be a computer language used by the person in charge of the procedure which could further reduce the possibility of controlling the final result for the supervisor. Accordingly, it is undeniable that all of the issues stated above will tend to intensify as systems expand and become ever more complex. Precisely from this perspective, it is very often unrealistic to trust that the user of the processor knows exactly what his computer system (AS) will do. Discernment may be impeded by a series of factors: for example, unfamiliarity with the circumstances of the various settings in which the AS will operate, as well as the impossibility of replicating, at least with sufficiently complex factors, all the

[46] ibid; see also D'Angelosante (n 23) 169.
[47] See D'Angelosante (n 23) 170.
[48] ibid 170.

processing operations that the software (of the AS) may perform in each instance. Furthermore, the user does not have all the information that may be available to his AS.

Finally, it would be impossible for the user to foresee (at least in the case of a software assistant that is able to assimilate, and therefore automatically update) which data and instructions are comprised when the software is processing.[49] In practice, the problem remains the same, namely that of the safeguard restrictions that would derive from enforcing Article 2043 of the Italian Civil Code on the public administration, rather than imposing strict liability, as provided for in other legal systems.[50]

The only favourable solution that would avoid safeguard restrictions on the recipients of an administrative measure, while providing a new 'immunity for authority',[51] would be the possibility of specific legislation that would impose strict liability on the public authority for damages caused by the execution of administrative duties through digital processing.[52] Morollo has also commented on this point, observing how liability for damages brought on by digital processing, which is free of fault and based solely on objective elements, may be considered: for example, one benchmark could be risk, the so-called 'cyber risk'.[53]

Attempts towards strict liability have already been reported in Italian doctrine, which refers to the case cited in Article 2050 of the Civil Code (CC), according to which responsibility must be placed on whomever can avoid complications (or at least ensure against them). This is an unforeseeable responsibility, also applicable to circumstances that are beyond control, which may be placed on the developer, the owner or the user of a system.[54]

It is important to stress that a shift to strict liability does not necessarily imply the approval by a law[55] and that the same may be reached through interpretation; according to statutes, what is provided for by Article 2050 CC may also be applied to so-called 'atypical' activities, whose potential risk is assessed in practice, case by case, by a judge.[56] Ultimately, given the complexity of the matter, the complications to those who may in some way be affected and the 'risky' nature of using information technology and digital processing for administrative documents, what has been stated in rulings on the issue may be of great help, pending the unlikely intercession of legislators.

[49] See G Sartor, *L'intenzionalità dei sistemi informatici e il diritto* (Rivista trimestrale di diritto e procedura civile, 2003).
[50] See Masucci, *L'atto amministrativo informatico* (n 22) 140.
[51] ibid 140.
[52] ibid 139.
[53] See Morollo (n 16) 27.
[54] See Sartor, *L'intenzionalità dei sistemi informatici e il diritto* n 49).
[55] See Masucci, *L'atto amministrativo informatico* (n 22) 139ff.
[56] See C Salvi, *La responsabilità civile* (Milan, Giuffrè, 1998) 125.

## V. A Necessary Change of Perspective

The use of AI, given its intricate algorithmic development, poses a fascinating legal as well as cultural challenge, despite its uncertainties. In the collective consciousness, there are already numerous, in part fanciful, renderings of the implications that may arise with technological advancement. Public administration has already been overwhelmed by such forceful innovation, which will hereafter lead to the progressive computerisation of administrative procedure. There will be greater dynamic development in relations with the private sector and greater speed in processing, with improvement not only in the quality, but also in the quantity, of administrative activity. It is vital for public administration to technologically and professionally adapt to private standards, so as to avoid disservice to the community in general.

The Italian Council of State[57] has recently re-examined the use of algorithms in administrative procedures and delivered a new ruling.[58] The Council of State reiterated the importance of using computer algorithms in public administration in order to benefit in terms of greater efficiency and greater neutrality in administrative activity. The option of using computerised procedures must be encouraged, as it saves time in processing purely repetitive and discretionary transactions, while also preventing any interference or errors that may be made by a human operator. The use of AI in administrative procedures can be attributed to a practical and prevailing application of Article 97 of the Italian Constitution, which is able to implement good performance techniques by which public administration will succeed in performing with efficiency, efficacy and economy.

At present, there are no AI systems able to completely take over the role of a jurist. However, with minimal human effort, the systems available can produce simple or recurrent legal acts, draw out norms, judicial precedent, statutes and reasoning, or analyse documents regarding actuality and understand them as well as a human does, for the limited purposes in which that knowledge may be considered useful.

Despite the doubts that may arise in safeguarding 'against' those measures, adopted by an administration, that are 'technically set' to comply with the law, it must be taken into account that a computerised measure may render outstanding – or, rather, virtually nullify – any possible breaches in law or incompetence, since it will decide according to rules of logic, non-contradiction and equal treatment.[59]

The benefits that the state and its people will gain from the transition to a computerised administration have already been outlined. Nevertheless, it is also important to analyse what has been stated in Italian doctrine regarding the risks of such a process. Doctrine has emphasised the risks that may derive from an

[57] Council of State, judgment no 2270 of 2019.
[58] Council of State, judgment no 8472 of 2019.
[59] See D'Angelosante (n 23) 169.

impairment in the performance of a computerised system, as in a system crash, or from contracting private authorities (such as the owners and managers of IT equipment, who are very often removed from any form of supervision by the state) to carry out public duties, in addition to the potential misconceptions that may result from the storage of data, as in the case of cloud computing.[60]

Another issue concerns the possible damage that could result from assaults (including terrorist attacks) on the computer system. At present, the Italian government is recruiting IT consultants who are skilled in the development of AI to carry out public services. Furthermore, at the legislative level, discussion continues, albeit still at an early stage, on the impact of robotics and artificial intelligence.

Therefore, on the one hand, the jurist is called to reflect on the current and potential uses of IT procedures and tools, as endorsed by positive law, as well as on administrative decisions that are actually genuinely shared by citizens. On the other hand, it is important to look towards the future of administration, which, as has been heretofore emphasised, will require the current legal systems to change.

## VI. Conclusions

In conclusion, what has been discussed in this chapter certainly does not presume to have expanded on the variety of issues concerning the effects of AI on public administration. However, certain considerations can be made based on what has been discovered.

In everyday life, consumers deal with AI systems in widespread use. It is easy to predict that further expansion in use could curtail direct civil interaction. Given that the acquisition of products now takes place through intelligent machines, meals may be ordered online and home-delivered, and newspapers and books are read online on platforms that understand and influence preferences, more and more people will be telecommuting, with fewer and fewer present in the workplace.

Therefore, the social world will increasingly be mediated by machines with doubtless less direct social interaction. What has been noted so far clearly shows how the use of AI in public administration requires a re-examination (if not an amendment) of legal institutions and of the organisational principles and regulations of administrative activity.

Against this background and by way of example, attention should be focused on giving structure to procedural dynamics and the relationship between administrative procedure and legality. For this reason, and in light of what has been observed in the preceding paragraphs, a doubt remains. Can a system of principles and legal institutions, conceived and built around an individual, a 'human being',

[60] See ML Maddalena, *La digitalizzazione della vita dell'amministrazione e del processo* (Foro Amministrativo, 2016); see also F Cardarelli, *Amministrazione digitale, trasparenza e principio di legalità* (Il diritto dell'informazione e dell'informatica, 2015) 227ff.

be so easily transferable and adaptable to a world of algorithms and intelligent machines? Public administration will certainly become more efficient, but it may be completely deprived of that element of humanity that makes administrative activity acceptable to its beneficiaries, despite its elements of one-sidedness and imperative.

However, in order to answer this question fully, it is necessary to establish what, if any, room there is for AI in a context where administrative action is characterised by a right to good governance, as detailed in Article 41 of the EU Charter of Fundamental Rights, in a summary of the procedural rights of a citizen that is guided by an obligation to provide clarifications that leave no room for defined algorithmic systems.[61]

My personal opinion, in view of what has been analysed in this work, is optimistic. I am certain that AI is on the verge of such sophisticated evolution that it will easily interact with human intelligence. It appears necessary, instead, to establish the appropriate means of integrating AI and man, so that even where professional systems are in use, man may continue to provide those cognitive skills lacking in a machine, while maintaining control over the information that is transmitted and the process of its application.

[61] See DU Galetta, *Il diritto ad una buona amministrazione europea come fonte di essenziali garanzie procedimentali nei confronti della Pubblica Amministrazione* (Rivista Italiana di diritto pubblico comunitario, 2005) 819ff.

# PART V

# The Information and Technology Revolution and Its Impact on Data Protection, Privacy and Human Rights

# 13

# The Impact of the Information and Technology Revolution on the Constitutional Rights with Particular Attention to Personal Data Protection Issues

CARLO COLAPIETRO

## I. The Technology Revolution between Datafication and Artificial Intelligence

With the beginning of the twenty-first century, a new technological revolution began. This has led to a widespread digitalisation of the environment that surrounds us, as well as to the accumulation of a quantity of data significantly greater than what had been produced hitherto throughout human history. This refers to the central role achieved by personal data in any sector, the so-called datafication. It is the continuous datafication process of the surrounding world that is precisely likely to be reduced to information and represented by a set of data;[1] that is, the quantitative measurement of whatever phenomenon that is thus converted into data capable of being collected and analysed.[2]

[1] R D'Orazio, 'La tutela multilivello del diritto alla protezione dei dati personali e la dimensione globale' in V Cuffaro, R D'Orazio and V Ricciuto (eds), *I dati personali nel diritto europeo* (Turin, Giappichelli, 2019) 67.

[2] See V Mayer-Schönberger and K Cukier, *Big Data: Una rivoluzione che trasformerà il nostro modo di vivere e già minaccia la nostra libertà* (Milan, Garzanti, 2013) 19–20 and 109–15, in which, in an attempt to make visible the size of data produced until 2013, with reference to data, it is stated 'if it were all printed in books, they would cover the entire surface of the United States some 52 layers thick. If it were placed on CD-ROMs and stacked up, they would stretch to the moon in five separate piles'. In this regard, Garante per la protezione dei dati personali, Autorità Garante della Concorrenza e del Mercato and Autorità per le Garanzie nelle Comunicazioni, 'Final Report of the Big Data Survey', 10 February 2020, 5–6, point out that 'in 2018, worldwide a total volume of 28 zettabyte (ZB) of data was generated, recording an increase higher over ten times than in 2011'.

The capacity to transform any aspect of reality into data has been achieved through the combination of multiple factors. This includes, first of all, the increased computing power with which modern technological tools are equipped and, in parallel, the progressive reduction of the costs required for their development and fulfilment. Suffice it to say that most of the smartphones used nowadays can be purchased at a contained and widely affordable price, yet they have features more powerful and considerably more complex than the computers produced up until just a few years ago. This has resulted in the spread of technology into every aspect of daily life. It has also allowed each individual to have multiple devices available that make it possible to interact with the surrounding reality, thus contributing to the datafication process and the production of an ongoing data flow.[3]

The increasing quantity of data generated and the potential underlying its use has ensured that data is now of the utmost importance on the international scene, to the extent that it is extensively defined as the new digital oil. Nevertheless, data shows a characteristic that makes it even more precious than fossil fuel. Indeed, far from representing a limited and consumable wealth, data constitutes a resource capable of being freely shared, treated and reused multiple times, and its use by one person does not affect its use by anyone else.

Despite the importance data has acquired, data per se does not provide information, nor is it capable of producing value. To make this possible, data should be processed, treated and aggregated in the same way as crude oil, which must undergo a cleaning and refining process before it can actually be used as fuel. This is when the ways and tools by which data is processed are of crucial importance, so the use of artificial intelligence (AI) acquires a significant relevance, particularly with regard to machine learning systems.

Indeed, data represents the essential fuel to develop and train AI, which is understood to be a system that, given a complex objective, works either in the physical or digital dimension, perceiving the surrounding environment through the acquisition and interpretation of data and deciding accordingly the best action to be implemented in order to meet the target objective.[4]

Such technology originated in the middle of the twentieth century,[5] but, due to high calculation power it requires and the considerable amount of data currently available, it has only now become an integral part of the environment that surrounds us, representing a precious opportunity for social and economic

[3] L Floridi, *The Fourth Revolution: How the Infosphere Is Reshaping Human Reality* (Oxford, Oxford University Press, 2014) 6–14.

[4] High-Level Expert Group on Artificial Intelligence, 'A Definition of AI: Main Capabilities and Disciplines' (8 April 2019) 6.

[5] On this aspect, see AM Turing, 'Computing Machinery and Intelligence' in R Epstein, G Roberts and G Beber (eds), *Parsing the Turing Test* (Dordrecht, Springer, 2009); J McCarthy, ML Minsky, N Rochester and CE Shannon, 'A Proposal for the Dartmouth Summer Research Project on Artificial Intelligence, August 31, 1955' (2006) 4 *AI Magazine* 27.

growth at the international level, while imposing a careful reflection on the risks for personal rights and freedom that can derive from its use.[6]

## II. The Constitutional Dimension of Artificial Intelligence

The increasing penetration of AI into every aspect of our daily lives introduces significant questions for which constitutional law should necessarily take responsibility. This is because constitutional law enables an identification, as soon as possible, of an effective approach towards the use of intelligent systems that allows us to take full advantage of the technological innovation without leading to an unjustified compression of the rights of individuals.

Therefore, it is necessary to question the impact that AI might have on the constitutional rights of individuals with reference to the main areas of interest in the state–citizen relationship.[7]

One of the main sectors in which the first reflections about the use of AI has been raised is the labour market, and a double dimension of interest has been immediately identified. Above all, an opportunity has been detected to delegate specific task types to intelligent systems, with particular reference to mechanical and highly repetitive tasks, as well as to arduous jobs or activities characterised by a high level of risk for individuals. At the same time, the introduction of AI in this field necessarily leads to a major transformation of work, resulting, on the one hand, in the extinction of some of today's jobs and, on the other hand, in the birth of new and innovative professions.

In this respect, one factor to consider, since it is likely to determine multiple dimensions of concern, is that the aforementioned change will be extremely rapid. Since time will be required to acquire adequate skills, the vanishing in the short term of old jobs will not immediately correspond to a simultaneous creation of new professions and jobs. Constitutional law, according to Articles 4 and 35 of the Italian Constitution, should address its commitment to managing the transition phase in the field of work, which, at least initially, runs the risk of generating negative impacts in the employment dimension. At the same time, it is necessary to invest in the creation of new vocational training so that citizens can acquire the knowledge needed to appropriately meet the current and future labour market demand.

[6] The awareness of opportunities and risks related to AI strongly emerges within the strategy on this matter adopted by the European Union. See particularly European Commission, 'Artificial Intelligence for Europe', COM (2018) 237; European Commission, 'White Paper on Artificial Intelligence – A European Approach to Excellence and Trust', COM (2020) 65.

[7] In this regard, see C Casonato, 'Costituzione e intelligenza artificiale: un'agenda per il prossimo futuro' (2019) 2 *BioLaw Journal* 713, who proposes an investigation into the areas of the constitutional law that will be more involved in the spread of AI, highlighting for each of them the potential opportunities and the main concerns that deserve further contemplation.

The need to create new skills appears closely related to a contemporary change in the education sector, which should not remain indifferent to the changes deriving from the technological revolution and the spread of AI. In accordance with the combined provisions of Articles 9 and 34 of the Italian Constitution, the state should promote the development of culture and education. This should be made possible through the creation of high-level skills. For this purpose, there should be a careful coordination between university and postgraduate education, as well as between the different areas of knowledge that are needed, so that the training provided can be multidisciplinary. In the same way, it is appropriate to take initiatives within the first level of education, so that the individual, from childhood, develops an adequate familiarity with and comprehension of the new technologies and becomes aware of their intrinsic ability to permeate reality and transform the world.[8]

In parallel, pursuant to the provisions of Article 33 of the Italian Constitution, the state should invest in culture through the promotion of scientific and technological research. In this respect, AI can contribute by strongly fostering research, both by opening new topics of investigation and by itself becoming a tool to carry out the scientific research activity. This latter case is well represented by iCub, a humanoid robot equipped with AI that was created at the Istituto Italiano di Tecnologia, and is used by researchers to test algorithms aimed at the motor control of robots, as well as to study the cognitive development of human beings and human–machine interaction arrangements.[9]

The reflections regarding AI in the education sector appear closely linked to a further matter, in which the use of intelligent systems opens the doors to highly promising applications. Specifically, the healthcare sector benefits both from the renewed impulse of scientific and technological research and from the application of AI directly within healthcare and social-welfare activities. By ensuring the right to health laid down in Article 32 of the Italian Constitution, the state has the possibility of ensuring specific and potentially more effective treatments for citizens, combined with significant savings of time and economic resources. Thus, there is an opportunity to provide highly personalised medical treatment, tailored to the patient, who can be monitored in real time regarding any aspect of treatment at any time of day.[10]

[8] In this regard, despite not specifically referring to first-level education, the attempt made in Finland by the University of Helsinki and Reaktor to implement 'The Elements of AI', a free online course aimed at encouraging citizens to understand the nature of AI and the potential uses of such technology, appears creditable.

[9] See G Metta, G Sandini, D Vernon, L Natale and F Nori, 'The iCub humanoid Robot: An Open Platform for Research in Embodied Cognition' in *Proceedings of the 8th Workshop on Performance Metrics for Intelligent systems* (New York, Association for Computing Machinery, 2008); N Nosengo, *I robot ci guardano* (Bologna, Zanichelli, 2013) 77–83.

[10] See A Spina, 'La medicina degli algoritmi: Intelligenza artificiale, medicina digitale e regolazione dei dati personali' in F Pizzetti (ed), *Intelligenza artificiale, protezione dei dati personali e regolazione* (Turin, Giappichelli, 2018) 320–31.

With regard to social welfare, given the increase in life expectancy in the worldwide population, the need for the design of new forms of care for elderly people is becoming urgent. Such need, once again, may be met through the combined use of robotics and AI. The application of the latter in the health sector allows the achievement of benefits that do not remain restricted to a single individual but, more generally, represent an advantage for the collective whole. By way of example, reference can be made to the use of AI for the forecast, detection and management of epidemics, such as the hotbed of Ebola in Africa in 2014 and the spread of the Zika virus in Brazil in 2016, as well as what is happening today with the coronavirus.[11]

However, the usefulness that AI may have in the health field should be carefully balanced so that the introduction of intelligent systems does not integrally replace the involvement of the natural person. Indeed, were that to occur, there would be the risk of creating a dehumanisation effect in an activity, such as in the health and welfare area, in which care, empathy and human contact constitute extremely important aspects of the doctor–patient relationship.[12]

With the protection of human health comes the right to a good-quality environment, both as an individual subjective right and as a response to society's interest in environmental protection and sustainability.[13] In this field, AI also offers many opportunities due to an increased capacity to forecast and manage ecological disasters in a timely manner, as well as to effectively tackle global challenges related to climate and environmental protection.[14]

Notwithstanding the potential advantages, it is necessary also to consider the environmental impact that threatens to occur in the future because of the spread of AI and its integration with robotics. It is particularly desirable to take due account of the eco-sustainability of intelligent systems throughout their lifecycle, from the phase of data storing and algorithm training to the phase of disposal of the hardware on which they were implemented. Work is being undertaken to produce AI systems that require a lower energy consumption for their operation while, at the same time, considering the problem of how to manage the increasingly extending data centres designed for algorithm training, with regard to both the space

[11] In this regard, see A Vespignani, *L'algoritmo e l'oracolo. Come la scienza predice il futuro e ci aiuta a cambiarlo* (Milan, il Saggiatore, 2019), which describes the strategy used to forecast, map and manage, through the use of AI, the epidemics of Ebola and Zika which took place in 2014 and 2016, respectively. For the purpose of completeness, it should also be noted that the author, as the Director of the Laboratory for the Modelling of Biological and Socio-technical Systems at Northeastern University, together with his working group, has also initiated the above-mentioned activities in relation to the recent epidemic of COVID-19: see www.mobs-lab.org/2019ncov.html.

[12] On this, see L Zardiashvili and E Fosch-Villaronga, '"Oh, Dignity Too?" Said the Robot: Human Dignity as the Basis for the Governance of Robotics' (2020) 30 *Minds and Machines* 130; EA Ferioli, 'L'intelligenza artificiale nei servizi sociali e sanitari: una nuova sfida al ruolo delle istituzioni pubbliche nel welfare italiano?' (2019) 1 *BioLaw Journal* 169.

[13] C Colapietro and M Ruotolo, *Diritti e libertà* (Turin, Giappichelli, 2014) 109.

[14] In this respect, see European Commission, 'The European Green Deal', COM (2019) 640, 9–18. See also C Villani, *For a Meaningful Artificial Intelligence: Towards a French and European Strategy* (2018) 100.

occupied and the arrangements to recycle the heat they generate.[15] In the same way, for the purpose of preventing a negative ecological impact from the spread of AI, scientific research has focused its efforts on the study and realisation of biodegradable materials so that the artificial machines that will populate our future will be decomposable and, as such, eco-sustainable.[16]

Given that the development of algorithms is introducing the possibility of making some decision-making processes automated, at least in part, reflections on the integrability of AI within public administration,[17] as well as within the sector of justice, appear equally relevant.

In the justice sector, in particular, multiple uses have been hypothesised and have already been concretely applied in some countries. First, AI is used for predictive policing, for the definition of priorities and for strategic planning.[18] Secondly, it is for matching databases and information analyses aimed at strengthening the implementation of operational intelligence. Lastly, along with these applications is the introduction of AI for the assessment of risks regarding people, as well as for the implementation of automated decision-making processes.[19] In this context, algorithmic systems can be used to support – and even replace – court activity, as in the case of the COMPAS and HART software, employed in the USA and the UK, respectively, to forecast the risk of recidivism.[20]

[15] Again, see Villani (ibid) 105.

[16] For this, see R Cingolani, *L'altra specie. Otto domande su noi e loro* (Bologna, Il Mulino, 2019) 59 and 142–44.

[17] About the employment of algorithms to support the decision-making activity of the public administration, in the Italian experience, reference is particularly made to the mobility of teachers provided by the reform of the so-called Buona scuola in accordance with Law no 107/2015; indeed, on this matter, many judgments by the administrative court have concerned algorithmic decision-making processes: Tar Lazio, sez III-bis, n 3769 del 2017; Tar Lazio, sez III-bis, n 9230 del 2018; Cons Stato, sez VI, n 2270 del 2019; Cons Stato, sez VI, n 8472 del 2019. For further on the matter, see MC Cavallaro and G Smorto, 'Decisione pubblica e responsabilità dell'amministrazione nella società dell'algoritmo' (2019) 16 *Federalismi.it* 8, A Simoncini, 'L'algoritmo incostituzionale: intelligenza artificiale e il futuro delle libertà' (2019) 1 *BioLaw Journal* 73; G Avanzini, *Decisioni amministrative e algoritmi informatici. Predeterminazione, analisi predittiva e nuove forme di intellegibilità* (Naples, Editoriale Scientifica, 2019) 35.

[18] See C O'Neil, *Armi di distruzione matematica. Come i Big Data aumentano la disuguaglianza e minacciano la democrazia* (Milan, Bompiani, 2017) 125–30, where reference is made to the software processed by the Californian start-up PredPol and employed by police forces to organise and allocate the available resources within the territory.

[19] Such tripartition in the use of AI in the justice sector is proposed in M Oswald and J Grace, 'Intelligence, Policing and the Use of Algorithmic Analysis: A Freedom of Information-Based Study' (2016) 1(1) *Journal of Information Rights, Policy and Practice* 3.

[20] About the employment of COMPAS software, see H Liu, C Lin and Y Chen, 'Beyond *State v Loomis*: artificial intelligence, government algorithmization and accountability' (2019) 27 *International Journal of Law and Information Technology* 126; A Simoncini and S Suweis, 'Il cambio di paradigma nell'intelligenza artificiale e il suo impatto sul diritto costituzionale' (2019) 1 *Rivista di filosofia del diritto* 95. For the HART software, see House of Commons – Science and Technology Committee, *Algorithms in Decision-Making* (23 May 2018) 13–14; M Oswald, J Grace, S Urwin and GC Barnes, 'Algorithmic Risk Assessment Policing Models: Lessons from the Durham HART Model and "Experimental" Proportionality' (2018) 27 *Information & Communications Technology Law* 227.

In the same way as the sectors previously analysed, the application of AI in the fields of justice and public administration would seem to allow the development of a higher level of efficiency and effectiveness of the initiatives put in place, as well as ensuring, in the abstract, an increased impartiality of the activity performed. Moreover, AI opens the way to major biases for individuals, since it is capable of affecting any dimension of individuals, including their most intimate and delicate aspects, such as those concerning sexuality and the relationship with death. For example, initial questions are being raised about the opportunity to employ sex robots,[21] as well as about the acceptability of employing machine learning systems to produce new forms of commemoration of and contact with the deceased.[22]

Hence, AI represents a technology capable of shaping, for better or for worse, every field in which it is employed, from the sectors concerned with the state–citizen relationship to the individual sphere where everyone develops their own personality. For this reason, constitutional law must necessarily take a close interest in the management and application of AI, to ensure that in shaping reality, AI does not negatively affect the concept of human dignity itself, a supreme value that is the foundation of the entire constitutional framework.

## III. The New Forms of Algorithmic Discrimination

Technological innovation, together with the development of AI, definitely has the potential to determine a higher substantive equality between individuals than has been the case in the past. Indeed, new technologies can represent effective tools for the reduction of inequalities, acting, for example, on the provision of social benefits and on the activities to combat evasion, as well as on the ways in which people can engage with each other.[23]

Regarding this latter case, suffice it to say that the realisation of the most recent social networks (eg Instagram, TikTok), which structure their arrangements of interaction on the sharing of images and not written texts, represent user-friendly tools for everyone, including that part of the global population who are currently

[21] In this regard, C Casonato, 'Intelligenza artificiale e diritto costituzionale: prime considerazioni' [2019] *Diritto pubblico comparato ed europeo* 117 points out that the employment of sex robots may present both negative and positive effects. For the concerns related to the employment of sex robots, see R Mackenzie, 'Sexbots: Sex Slaves, Vulnerable Others or Perfect Partners?' (2018) 9 *International Journal of Technoethics* 6–9; otherwise, Zardiashvili and Fosch-Villaronga (n 12) highlight the possible beneficial applications of sex robots, such as their potential application to support and take care of disabled people.

[22] See G Ziccardi, *Il libro digitale dei morti. Memoria, lutto, eternità e oblio nell'era dei social network* (Milan, UTET, 2017) 189–93 and 243, who pointed out how the employment of machine learning systems jointly with the mind uploading might affect the relationship with the deceased, running the risk, particularly, of 'generat[ing] pathological situations, situations of addiction or, even wors[e], of confusion and lack of understanding of the real separation'.

[23] On this, see G Resta, 'Governare l'innovazione tecnologica: decisioni algoritmiche, diritti digitali e principio di uguaglianza' (2019) 2 *Politica del diritto* 218.

illiterate. In this respect, the social networks, although likely to be based on an economic interest more than an altruistic one, would ensure, at least prima facie, equal possibilities of access, exchange and debate for the benefit of those unable to read or write.

However, along with the introduction of innovative technological tools comes the danger of a renewed inequality of treatment to which an individual may be subjected, both in terms of the traditionally detected forms of abuse and the instigation of new mechanisms of discrimination.

There is, first, the risk that a strengthening will occur of the already recognised forms of discrimination – the eradication or, at least, reduction of which has been worked hard on for years. A good example of this are the most recent concerns related to the achievement of gender equality, which, although recognised by Article 3 of the Italian Constitution and despite the efforts made, has faced significant obstacles because of the spread and use of new technologies.

For a long time, many attempts have been made to bridge a gender inequality that now might be worsened by the development of AI and its employment for the implementation of voice assistants (eg Siri, Alexa and Cortana). In this context, it should be noted that voice assistants, designed to be fully available at any moment, are similar in that they are presented mainly by female names and voices, and are unlikely to be bestowed with masculine characteristics. Therefore, voice assistants eventually take on a female identity, and are given the task of addressing the interlocutor with condescendence and of granting any request received, however unpleasant, offensive or inappropriate the request might be. Thus, such a design choice at the basis of a technological tool can only perpetuate – and even strengthen – the existing discriminatory stereotypes towards the female gender, threatening to restrict women to a role of subordination and subjection, and rejecting the idea that they can be given positions of responsibility and leadership.[24]

Secondly, constitutional law is faced with new forms of discrimination, unexplored in respect to the traditional categories generally detected so far. Several parties have pointed out how anti-discrimination law is not fully capable of protecting individuals from inequalities of treatment which may derive from the use of AI.[25]

The new forms of discrimination appear to be extremely pervasive and dangerous, since they are founded on a quantity of data and arrangements of data processing that are unprecedented in human history. This is mainly due to the increase in personal data flow, produced whether consciously or not by each

[24] See UNESCO, EQUALS Skills Coalition, 'I'd Blush If I Could: Closing Gender Divides in Digital Skills through Education' (2019); NN Loideain and R Adams, 'From Alexa to Siri and the GDPR: The Gendering of Virtual Personal Assistants and the Role of Data Protection Impact Assessment' (2020) 36 *Computer Law & Security Review* 1.

[25] On this, see FZ Borgesius (ed), *Discrimination, Artificial Intelligence, and Algorithmic Decision-Making* (Strasbourg, Council of Europe, 2018) 18–2; L Giacomelli, 'Big Brother Is "Gendering" You. Il diritto antidiscriminatorio alla prova dell'intelligenza artificiale: quale tutela per il corpo digitale?' (2019) 2 *BioLaw Journal* 278.

individual at any moment of the day. These elements allow a deep analysis of any aspects of individuals and the profiling of people, both finding the characteristics that make them unique and identifying the aspects that allow the person to be matched with groups with common characteristics. In this way, an analysis is conducted of the actions of the person in multiple perspectives, as an individual and as part of a collective, giving rise to personalised and cross-cutting discriminatory treatments, according to the group with which the person is associated from time to time, and even though this association is unpredictable or incomprehensible for the interested party.

Therefore, if, in the past, discrimination has been dealt with based on rigid categories and pre-established protected groups, this may no longer be enough. An approach with greater flexibility is needed.

Along with the inequalities of treatment that affect the traditional protected groups – identified, for example, based on sex, ethnicity or religious belief – come inequalities concerning individuals because they belong to new groups with the most variable forms (eg those who do not practice physical activity, those who do not eat vegetables). Also, the new mechanisms of discrimination are capable of affecting individuals by taking advantage of their distinctive weaknesses and making use of the aspects that characterise their individuality. This is what happens, for example, with price discrimination,[26] through which it is possible to offer to any and each individual the product they need at the highest price, despite the fact that the same product can be purchased by others at a different and lower cost.

The renewal of discriminatory treatment, both traditional and new, seems to be tightly related to the introduction of AI within predictive and decision-making processes that tend, in this way, to convey the impression of replacing the intrinsic subjectivity of human reasoning with an objective and impartial procedure regulated by the algorithm.

Thus, it is necessary to focus attention on the functioning of AI to prevent its use resulting in illusory objectivity and reliability compared with the results it has produced. Indeed, it is necessary to take into consideration how the outcomes of an algorithmic process derive from multiple factors, first of all the one related to the quality of data involved in the automated procedure or in the training of AI. In addition to not being updated and correct, the data might reflect a partial image of reality, since it represents only a part of the population. Or, it might turn out to be intrinsically discriminatory itself since, as a historical representation of past events, it would crystallise pre-existing biases. It is essential to carefully evaluate the choices made for the purpose of the algorithm design, such as the purpose for which the AI system has been implemented, as well as the choice of the categories

[26] On this matter, see R Steppe, 'Online Price Discrimination and Personal Data: A General Data Protection Regulation Perspective' (2017) 33 *Computer Law & Security Review*; FZ Borgesius and J Poort, 'Online Price Discrimination and EU Data Privacy Law' [2017] *Journal of Consumer Policy*.

of data to be taken into consideration for a correct and effective achievement of the target purpose, together with the related configurable responsibilities of those who have developed the algorithmic code.[27]

Such complexity can hardly be identified and contrasted on account of the self-reference and lack of transparency that some AI systems may present: both through the consolidation of cycles of negative feedback, based on which the algorithm, by using its own results, self-legitimises the correctness and the reliability of its own functioning;[28] and due to the opacity of some intelligent systems, which does not always allow a look at the inside of the machine to understand what logical paths and motivations have led to a specific decision or forecast.[29]

In dealing with the topic of AI, therefore, it is necessary to adopt an approach that is particularly careful of the extent of discrimination that may derive from it, keeping in mind the design and implementation factors that can introduce discriminatory logic inside the algorithm, so that, on the basis of such awareness, it is possible to promote a development and employment of AI that is respectful of the human person.

## IV. The Role of the Right to the Protection of Personal Data: Concerns and Opportunities

In analysing the close connection between technological innovation and the actual protection of constitutionally recognised rights, it is necessary to note that AI boasts a special relation to the right to the protection of personal data, since, as has previously been pointed out, personal data constitutes the primary resource through which algorithms are trained. At the same time, they represent the main elements for the implementation of highly personalised and potentially discriminatory processing operations. In addition to this, inside EU Regulation 2016/679 (the General Data Protection Regulation, GDPR) is the meaning borne by the right to the protection of personal data which, not remaining restricted to the sole protection of the individual's information sphere, is aimed at offering a comprehensive protection of personal rights and freedoms, paying particular attention to the discriminatory consequences related to the application of AI.[30]

[27] On the algorithmic discrimination arrangements, see S Barocas and AD Selbst, 'Big Data's Disparate Impact' (2016) 104 *California Law Review*; Borgesius (n 25) 10–15; A Moretti, 'Algoritmi e diritti fondamentali della persona. Il contributo del Regolamento (UE) 2016/679' (2018) 4/5 *Diritto dell'Informazione e dell'Informatica* 801.

[28] The mechanism of the cycles of negative feedback is widely described in O'Neil (n 18).

[29] On the topic, see F Pasquale, *The Black Box Society. The Secret Algorithms that Control Money and Information* (Cambridge, MA, Harvard University Press, 2015).

[30] In this regard, B Goodman, *A Step towards Accountable Algorithms?: Algorithmic Discrimination and the European Union General Data Protection*, 29th Conference on Neural Information Processing Systems (Barcelona, NIPS Foundation, 2016) 1 notes how the GDPR represents the first legislation openly dealing with the topic of algorithmic discriminations.

A one-to-one relation is thus established between AI and data protection. It is characterised, first of all, by the relevant concerns introduced by the use of algorithmic systems in comparison with the core principles of data protection, such as the principle of data minimisation, of purpose and storage, and of transparency.[31]

The need to make AI models increasingly perform leads, in general, to the indiscriminate collection of a massive amount of data, with no verification that it is actually needed or relevant to the processing meant to be implemented. At the same time, the desire to have available an increasing amount of data causes the extension of data storage beyond the processing for which the data was collected. Thus, data may be reused more and more times for new purposes, including the training of further AI systems. In practice, data is stored for an unlimited time and reused for purposes different from the original ones, ignoring the restrictions imposed by the principle of minimisation and rendering the principles of both restriction of data retention and purpose limitation substantially meaningless.

The development of AI also risks the creation of considerable friction in relation to the need to make the ways in which data is processed knowable. While compliance with the principle of transparency can be ensured with regard to merely automated systems, for which it appears that the logic process can be fully inferred, it is not otherwise possible for some types of AI. Indeed, significant opacity issues are found in relation to machine learning systems, and it is not always possible to exactly understand the process followed by the algorithm to produce the final result. Such opacity tends to be further facilitated by the frequent reasoning on the trade secret and IP rights that are meant to ensure the secrecy of the logic code used, thereby preventing the algorithm from being made accessible, knowable and, therefore, verifiable by whoever is subjected to it.

Although the relation between AI and data protection is a subject of considerable concern, it is nevertheless characterised by the potential contribution that the protection of personal data could provide in achieving a first system of rules aimed at the proper use of intelligent systems. Focusing on GDPR legislation, support can be identified both in the general principles of the regulation and in specific provisions contained therein.

The attention paid by the GDPR to the accuracy of data is an element that is certainly applicable to AI.[32] In particular, the principle of data quality perfectly fits the algorithm training phase, which takes place initially at the moment of selection of data through which the AI system is to be implemented and, thereafter, throughout its cycle of employment, to ensure that the data used remains consistent with the purpose and processing for which it is meant. The principle of data quality, therefore, would allow from the outset the prevention of algorithmic

[31] See Art 5, para 1(a), (b), (c) and (e) of the GDPR. In this regard, see C Kuner, FH Cate, O Lynskey, C Millard, NN Loideain and DJB Svantesson, 'Expanding the Artificial Intelligence–Data Protection Debate' (2018) 8 *International Data Protection Law* 290; M Butterworth, 'The ICO and Artificial Intelligence: The Role of Fairness in the GDPR Framework' (2018) 34 *Computer Law & Security Review* 258.

[32] See Art 5, para 1(d) of the GDPR.

decisions that result ex ante in corruption, achieving discriminatory results caused by the incorrectness of the data or the crystallisation of pre-existing biases.[33]

Despite not being easily recognisable, the principles of transparency and privacy by design have a role in the partial weakening of the frictions created by the use of algorithms.[34] Indeed, the principle of privacy by design imposes a careful weighting of the risks that may derive for individuals, so as to promote from the outset the development of an algorithmic system that is respectful of the rights and freedoms of individuals. In the same way, the principle of transparency, despite the intrinsic opacity of some intelligent systems, represents a fundamental reference point to which any subject involved in the implementation of new technologies and the processing of personal data should be oriented, so that the use of AI does not open the way to unjust biases.

These general principles are mostly set up inside the GDPR through some specific provisions that, if adequately developed, seem to be capable of providing useful operational tools that can be used whenever an AI system is applicable.

Indeed, it is possible to note how Articles 13, 14, 15 and 22 of the GDPR make clear reference to fully automated processing operations of personal data, thus including the potential operations carried out through algorithmic systems. Despite the aforementioned difficulties for full compliance with the principle of transparency, the first three Articles aim to introduce the protection of information in favour of the data subjects, ensuring that they will be notified when subjected to processing that is fully implemented by an algorithm, and that they have the possibility of accessing its underlying logic.[35]

As well as these provisions, Article 22 of the GDPR recognises that individuals have the right not to be subjected to fully automated processing operations that are capable of significantly affecting the person. On this point, it must immediately be pointed out how the above-mentioned right takes the form of a proper general prohibition addressed to the controller, and does not result in a right to object recognised to the data subject. In this way, Article 22 obliges the controller, by default, to protect the data, while, for its application, the data subject is not required to have a proactive behaviour to be kept through a specific objection to the processing.[36]

It is appropriate to also highlight that the provision of Article 22 addresses decisions achieved through fully automated procedures, but is not applicable to procedures with detectable human involvement. This does not mean that the

[33] G D'Acquisto, 'Qualità dei dati e Intelligenza Artificiale: intelligenza dai dati e intelligenza dei dati' in Pizzetti (n 10) 266 points out how the lack of data quality in AI training may transform an occasional error into a systematic error and, therefore, into a permanent bias that is not easily fixable.

[34] See Art 5, para 1(a) and Art 25, para 1 of the GDPR.

[35] See Art 13, para 2(f), Art 14, para 2(g) and Art 15, para 1(h) of the GDPR.

[36] In this regard, see Article 29 Working Party, 'Guidelines on Automated Individual Decision-Making and Profiling for the Purposes of Regulation 2016/679' (17/EN WP 251 rev 01, 2018) 19–21; M Brkan, 'Do Algorithms Rule the World? Algorithmic Decision-Making and Data Protection in the Framework of the GDPR and Beyond' (2019) 27 *International Journal of Law and Information Technology* 98.

participation of a person in the automated process determines per se that the above referred rule is not applicable. In this regard, Article 22 adopts a highly substantive approach, so as to also include within its scope those automated processes in which there apparently exists human involvement, but that involvement is limited to a symbolic contribution, that is not substantially relevant to the outcome of the decision-making process.[37] Although significant attention is paid to ensure that automated processing operations are assigned not only to the algorithm but also to actual human involvement, the provision of Article 22 risks overlooking the practical power of AI systems. By this, reference is made to the concrete capacity of the algorithm to capture the entire process in which it is employed, leading the involved person to rely on it and to delegate to it the whole assessment and decision-making activities assigned, even when the use of AI was supposed to constitute just an instrumental element and a support for the human activity.[38]

Furthermore, the right not to be subjected to entirely automated processing operations bears obvious limits due to the exceptions provided in paragraph 2 of Article 22, with particular reference to the new derogation on agreement introduced by the GDPR and represented by the data subject's consent.[39] Indeed, a similar exception may not fully take into account the difficulties faced in having to ensure a positive expression of consent by individuals who, because of the requirements and complexity characterising AI systems, risk receiving either extremely generic information on the processing arrangements of their data or, conversely, highly technical and specific information that is hard to understand. Such concerns also apply to a very dynamic context in which the data subject is exposed to continuous data processing activities and subsequently receives a large number of policies that require willingness, time and concentration to be properly read and understood.

The arrangement of consent, therefore, would not appear to be totally appropriate to protect individuals inside the digital world, mainly with reference to complex processing operations like those performed through AI, so that the identification of consent as a derogation in Article 22 of the GDPR could, in fact, represent a breakthrough in the system of warranties that the data protection legislation offers to protect individuals.[40]

In order to ensure a higher level of protection for individuals, a long debate has also taken place about the possibility of clarifying within the GDPR, and

[37] On this, see Article 29 Working Party (ibid) 20–21.

[38] Regarding the practical power of the algorithm, see Simoncini (n 17).

[39] It should be noted that the derogation of the data subject's explicit consent, recognised in Art 22, para 2(c) of the GDPR, was not previously provided within the repealed Art 15 of Directive 95/46/EC concerning 'Automated individual decisions'.

[40] About the weakening of consent as an arrangement capable of ensuring an actual self-determination of the data subject, see A Mantelero, 'La gestione del rischio nel GDPR: limiti e sfide nel contesto dei Big Data e delle applicazioni di Artificial Intelligence' in A Mantelero and D Poletti (eds), *Regolare la tecnologia: il Reg. UE 2016/679 e la protezione dei dati personali. Un dialogo fra Italia e Spagna* (Pisa, Pisa University Press, 2018).

particularly with regard to Article 22, a right to explanation for data subjects that would give them the right to receive an explanation of any decision made in their regard through an entirely automated procedure.[41] The recognition of such a right would certainly contribute to an enrichment of the available tools for the person to understand the reasons that have led to a specific decision and to be able to ensure that the latter does not conceal any internal discrimination. Currently, the clarification of a right to explanation does not seem to be easily identified, not only in the substantive dimension, given the complexity of processing appropriate arrangements for the delivery of such an explanation, but also due to the literal extent of the GDPR, where explicit provisions on this matter are lacking. The sole reference to such an ex post explanation of the algorithmic decision is provided in Recital 71 of the GDPR, which, on one hand, although bearing an important interpretation value, does not present any legally binding power while, on the other hand, it contains some protection measures reported entirely in Article 22, paragraph 3 of the GDPR, except for the measure regarding the right to obtain an explanation of the decision achieved through the automated procedure. Therefore, in order to make it possible to identify the actual establishment of a right to explanation, it will be necessary to closely follow which operational solutions will be designed to support transparency in AI systems and, at the same time, what case law evolution will occur regarding the interpretation of Article 22 and Recital 71 of the GDPR.

The provisions thus far referenced represent, in their own way, expressions of the principle of transparency intended to remove the veil of secrecy that enshrouds the algorithm operation as well as to facilitate a background of trust of AI systems. In the same way, a similar objective is pursued through the risk-based approach that, beyond constituting a pillar of the entire GDPR order, finds a fundamental setup in the arrangement of the impact assessment introduced by Article 35, to be implemented when processing presents high risks concerning rights and freedoms of individuals, especially where innovative technologies, like AI, are used.

The impact assessment allows the examination of ex ante estimates of the potential biases to which a person is exposed because of the use of algorithmic systems. In this way, it permits the timely adoption of the required technical and organisational safety measures aimed at reducing the risk level. The arrangement provided in Article 35 of the GDPR is an extremely useful tool for the protection of individuals, but it might not always be easily usable with regard to AI. Impact assessment remains linked to a judgment performed by the controller who, therefore, in order to be able to ensure a correct weighting of the risks deriving

[41] About the existence in the GDPR of an actual right to explanation, see B Goodman and S Flaxman, 'European Union Regulations on Algorithmic Decision-Making and a "Right to Explanation"' (2017) 38(3) *AI Magazine*; on the contrary, see S Wachter, B Mittelstadt and L Floridi, 'Why a Right to Explanation of Automated Decision-Making Does Not Exist in the General Data Protection Regulation' (2017) 7(2) *International Data Protection Law*, who pointed out how, above all, a right to be informed can be identified inside the GDPR. Starting from these two opposite theses, a rich doctrinal debate has been developed on the possibility of setting up a right to explanation and on the possible meaning that should be ascribed to it.

from the use of algorithmic systems, must be able to rely on adequately ripe skills and competences, both on personal data protection and on the main operation arrangements of AI. In any case, the arrangement of the impact assessment provides the opportunity to extend the risk weighting set out in the GDPR beyond the sole field of data protection, achieving an assessment that, although increasing its own degree of complexity, is enriched with further analytical dimensions, both in respect to potential biases to which whatever fundamental right is subjected and with reference to the ethical and social-nature impacts that may concern the collectivity as a whole.[42]

Lastly, with the measures described above, comes the possibility of relying on specific accountability tools that have been provided to support the controller, such as the codes of conduct and certification mechanisms.[43] Despite a lack of extensive development in terms of data protection, such tools might allow the regulation of AI and make more fluid some of the steps related to the implementation of AI and the relevant types of use. Through the involvement of third parties with specific competences and audit powers, certifications would grant that algorithmic systems are developed in a manner that would avoid injurious or discriminatory processing operations, while codes of conduct would allow the identification, with respect to AI, of standard application arrangements, jointly assessed and evaluated as suitable to ensure the adequate protection of individuals.[44]

Therefore, the observation of the relation existing between AI and the right to the protection of personal data allows the significance of the concerns posed to individuals by this new technology to be recognised. Although aware of the limitation of data protection rules, it is possible to simultaneously and clearly detect the role that the same data protection rules might play in the legislative and cultural effort that should be made, at the international level, to define the main aspects of the correct use of AI.

## V. Final Reflections

The constitutional setup characterising EU Member States, including Italy, at present appears adequately structured to consider and protect those areas where AI will have the greatest impact, as well as to be able to point out the main principles to follow so that its development occurs in a way that is respectful of the human person. In view of the rapidity of technological innovation, it would not

[42] See Council of Europe, 'Artificial Intelligence and Data Protection: Challenges and Possible Remedies' (Strasbourg, 25 January 2019) 13–14; A Mantelero, 'AI and Big Data: A Blueprint for a Human Rights, Social and Ethical Impact Assessment' (2018) 34(4) *Computer Law & Security Review*.

[43] See Arts 40 and 42 of the GDPR.

[44] On this matter, see Council of Europe, 'Guidelines on Artificial Intelligence and Data Protection' (Strasbourg, 25 January 2019) 3; F Pizzetti, 'La protezione dei dati personali e la sfida dell'Intelligenza Artificiale' in Pizzetti (n 10) 142–50.

seem appropriate to provide, at the constitutional level of sources of law, for ad hoc reform measures aimed at establishing a specific regulation of algorithmic systems. In this regard, acting inside constitutional charts through the setup of specific provisions addressing AI might appear to be a measure that is not fully acceptable or, at least, is premature.[45]

What is instead necessary is to ensure that, once the fundamental principles that should be followed are identified, they are expressed adequately through a rule system that, based on the EU constitutional tradition, is coordinated and flexible enough to keep up with the pace of technological innovation. Therefore, the challenge faced is to concretely ensure that the fundamental principles already known at the constitutional level are innovatively set up so as to be fully operative inside the new digital world.

Such a purpose may be pursued by using soft law tools and sectoral legislation, in respect of which, as underlined in the previous section, the rules on the protection of personal data represent one of the most innovative and cutting-edge regulations.[46] Despite the existence of several dimensions of improvement, the GDPR embeds general principles and operational tools that provide first reference indications about the development and application arrangements of AI. Beyond promoting the use of soft law tools as the codes of conduct or certification mechanisms, such legislation has the merit of being able to pay close attention to technological innovations. At the same time, it reaffirms the centrality of the human person, and the protection of fundamental rights and freedoms recognised to them.

The objective for which to strive, therefore, is not to include technology inside constitutional charts, but instead to transpose constitutional values inside algorithmic systems.[47] With the path undertaken by the European Union, it is necessary to address a human-centric AI model that boosts citizens' trust rather than fear, and that, keeping means and ends clearly distinguished, does not subject individuals to AI but identifies in AI a precious tool made for the exclusive service of the human being.[48]

[45] Concerning the willingness to introduce, at a constitutional level, provisions specifically addressing AI, see the draft constitutional law no 2585 presented by the French Parliament on 15 January 2020, also regarding the integration of the first paragraph of the Constitution Recitals with the 'Charte de l'intelligence artificielle et des algorithmes'.

[46] It is not the case that the legislation on data protection is widely referred to in High-Level Expert Group on Artificial Intelligence, 'Ethics Guidelines for Trustworthy AI' (8 April 2019).

[47] See the notion of hybrid constitutional law in Simoncini and Suweis (n 20).

[48] The essence of a trustworthy and human-centric AI model is outlined in High-Level Expert Group on Artificial Intelligence (n 46).

# 14

# The Digital Revolution and the Constitutional Orders' Vertical and Horizontal Challenges to Protect Privacy

PATRICIA JONASON

> [A] democratic constitution has an important task in the age of big data: it must guarantee and promote privacy. In doing so, it protects not only the basic rights of its citizens. Far beyond this, it contributes to a functioning democracy, and the value of this cannot be overestimated.[1]

## I. Introduction

New information and communication technologies (NICTs) have revolutionised our lives, for better or for worse. For example, they allow unprecedented and unlimited access to a bank of global knowledge and all kinds of information, greatly facilitate remote communication with a large number of fellow citizens, and allow faster and more accurate medical diagnoses. On the other side of the coin, the use of NICTs also undeniably poses challenges to the right to privacy and in particular to the protection of personal data. Indeed, technologies such as the use of big data, the Internet of Things, web scraping, predictive modelling, profiling, biometrics, cryptocurrency, blockchain, RFID chip, drones, facial recognition, GPS and digital surveillance in general can potentially have a negative impact on privacy and in particular on the informational self-determination of individuals. Threats to privacy in the broad sense of the term have many names: aggregation,[2] distortion,[3] exclusion,[4] geolocalisation, a spatial and temporal panoptic that does

[1] V Boehme-Nessler, 'Privacy: A Matter of democracy. Why Democracy Needs Privacy and Data Protection' (2016) 6 *International Data Privacy Law* 222, 228.

[2] DJ Solove, *Nothing to Hide – The False Tradeoff between Privacy and Security* (Yale University Press, 2011) 27.

[3] ibid 28.

[4] ibid 27.

not forget,[5] exhaustive tracking, the impossibility of being anonymous, digital identity theft, harassment and lynching on social networks, the malaise of young people caught in the spiral of comparison with others caused by the use of social networks and the battle for likes, the 'nudging of interests', the 'filter bubble', etc.[6]

New technologies increase the scale of threats and damage in a dialectical relationship with the new societal behaviours they generate. In fact, 'the change in the scope and duration of invasion of privacy following from new technologies, as well as additional innovation and the resulting ways it can affect our behaviour, amount to novel forms of invasion of privacy'.[7]

The societal changes brought about by the digital revolution also increase the risks of intrusion into private life. In particular, the change in our modes of communication, expressed in the ever-increasing use of social media, further heightens the vulnerability of individuals with regard to their private lives. This situation contributes to, and is aggravated by, the concomitant and correlated blurring of the boundaries between private and public life.[8]

These threats are compounded by the ever-increasing use of technology, first and foremost in the public sector, but also in the private sector – in large and small companies, and even with individuals. As a result, while in the past the state has been considered as the primary source of threat to the privacy of citizens, it has now been joined, and even overtaken, in this position by private actors, in particular the GAFAM (Google, Amazon, Facebook, Apple and Microsoft) companies. In Orwellian terms, the *Big Brother* metaphor is these days supplemented by the metaphor of the *little brothers.*[9]

Privacy, in its many facets, ranging from the right to be left alone to the right to participate in society, including informational self-determination and the power of a person to behave as they choose,[10] has thus become one of the most fragile human rights of modern times. Now, 'infringing our privacy' does not only mean 'attacking our freedom, our personal autonomy and therefore our personal dignity';[11] it is also attacking the proper workings of democracy.[12] Indeed, the right

[5] See generally V Mayer-Schönberger, *Delete – The Virtue of Forgetting in the Digital Age* (Princeton and Oxford University Press, 2009).

[6] Not to mention the discrimination caused by the digital divide – which affects the most disadvantaged but also our elders and people suffering from mental difficulties – and by the scoring methods and discomfort caused by digital stress.

[7] A Schreiber, 'Cloud-Enabled Technologies and Privacy Paradigms: Israeli Challenges and Responses' (2016) 6(1) *International Data Privacy Law* 49, 50.

[8] Patricia Blanc-Gonnet Jonason (2015) 'Démocratie, transparences et Etat de droit – La transparence dans tous ses états' (2015) 27(1) *European Review of Public Law* 121, 128.

[9] See, eg R Whitaker, 'A Faustian Bargain? America and the Dream of Total Information Awareness' in K Haggerty and R Ericson (eds), *The New Politics of Surveillance and Visibility* (Toronto, University of Toronto Press, 2018) 142.

[10] P Kayser, *La protection de la vie privée par le droit*, 3rd edn (Aix-Marseille, Presses Universitaires Economica, 1995) 12.

[11] C Vallet, 'Le dévoilement de la vie privée sur les sites de réseau social: Des changements significatifs' (2012) 1 [80] *Droit et société* 163, 165, 222.

[12] See, eg Boehme-Nessler (n 1) 228. See also A Rouvroy and Y Poullet, 'The Right to Informational Self-Determination and the Value of Self-Development: Reassessing the Importance of Privacy for

to privacy does not only have individual value linked to individual self-realisation; it also has collective value in the protection of democratic values, such as pluralism. It follows that threats to privacy, as the European authorities in particular have pointed out, have a negative impact on freedom of expression.[13]

The change in the nature and extent of threats to privacy, in the broad sense of the term, arising from new digital technologies requires legal systems to provide a substantial response. The supranational European legal systems – the European Convention on Human Rights (ECHR),[14] the European Charter of Fundamental Rights[15] and European secondary legislation – are, of course, a common foundation for protection in European states.[16] The seriousness of the issue also calls for specific mobilisation of national legal systems. In my view, such mobilisation should involve normative reinforcement on three levels: robust constitutional entrenchment, protecting privacy vertically and horizontally; legislation that is more attuned to ethical issues, right from the initial stage of technological innovation; and a body of soft law. This chapter will focus on the constitutional mechanisms and the challenges they face in protecting privacy against NICTs. To examine the subject, I will start from two national constitutional systems: the French constitutional system and the Swedish constitutional system.[17]

First, I will examine what measures have been taken so far, in both countries, at constitutional level, to respond to the threats to privacy posed by new technologies (section II). Then I will examine the reasons for which constitutional protection is currently being strengthened in the two countries under review (section III). The chapter will conclude with concrete proposals for bolstering the right to privacy in these two constitutional systems (section IV).

## II. The State of Art in the Constitutional Protection of Privacy against New Technologies in Sweden and France

The two constitutional systems selected – the French Constitution of 1958 and the Swedish Constitution of 1974 (in this case, the Instrument of Government[18]) – are

Democracy' in S Gutwirth, Y Poullet, P de Hert, C de Terwangne and S Nouwt (eds), *Reinventing Data Protection?* (Berlin, Springer Verlag, 2009) 45–76.

[13] Joined Cases C-293/12 and C-594/12 *Digital Rights Ireland Ltd v Minister for Communications, Marine and Natural Resources and Others and Kärntner Landesregierung and Others* [2014] ECLI:EU:C:2014:238, para 28.

[14] Art 8, Right to respect for private and family life.

[15] Art 7, Respect for private and family life and Art 8, Protection of personal data.

[16] The legislation highly protective of personal data, in particular the GDPR General Data Protection Regulation (EU) 2016/679 [2016] OJ L119/59.

[17] The analysis contained in this article is, of course, intended to go further than the two national models selected.

[18] The Instrument of Government is one of four fundamental texts that together make up the Swedish Constitution.

examples of two different models of the development of constitutional protection of the right to privacy. These systems have each in their own way – through case law in France (section IIA) and through the constitutional route in Sweden (section IIB) – adapted the protection provided by the Constitution to protect privacy against the infringements it could suffer, particularly as a result of the use of new technologies. After reviewing the history of these developments, I will make some comparative remarks (section IIC).

## A. Protection of the Right to Privacy in France: Enshrinement by Case Law

The French Constitution does not expressly provide for the protection of the right to privacy.[19] However, the Conseil constitutionnel (Constitutional Council), the institution in charge of monitoring the conformity of laws with the Constitution, has enshrined this right through case law, which has developed in several stages.

First, the Constitutional Council linked the right to privacy to the 'individual liberty' guaranteed by Article 66 of the Constitution and protected by the judiciary courts (the jurisdictions of the *ordre judiciaire*). The first such decision on vehicle searches dates from 1977.[20] Although the right to privacy is not expressly referred to, it is, according to academic writings, 'the first step towards the recognition, under the guise of individual liberty, of the secrecy of private life as a constitutional principle'.[21]

The constitutional nature of the right to privacy was recognised expressly two decades later, in 1995, during the review of the law on security policy and programming.[22] The Constitutional Council concluded that 'Failure to respect the right to privacy may be such as to infringe on individual liberty', which is a 'constitutionally guaranteed' civil liberty. This initial express recognition, still on the basis of Article 66 of the Constitution, coincided with the recognition of the protection of privacy with regard to new technologies, since the legislative provisions, the review of which by the Constitutional Council led to express reference to the right to privacy, related to the installation of video surveillance systems.

Since a judgment[23] on universal health coverage in 1999, however, the Constitutional Council has changed the constitutional basis for the right to privacy. This protection is now based on Article 2 of the Declaration of the Rights of Man and the Citizen, a declaration mentioned in the preamble to the Constitution, and which therefore forms part of the *bloc de constitutionnalité* (constitutionality

[19] Redécouvrir le préambule de la Constitution – Rapport du comité présidé par Simone Veil (2008) La documentation Française 70.

[20] Cons Const, 12 January 1977, No 76-75 DC.

[21] V Mazeaud, 'La constitutionnalisation du droit au respect de la vie privée' (2015) 3(48) *Les Nouveaux Cahiers du Conseil constitutionnel* 5, 10.

[22] Cons Const, 18 January 1995, No 94-352 DC.

[23] Cons Const, 23 July 1999, No 99-416 DC.

bundle) to which the Constitutional Council refers. The authority guaranteeing compliance with the Constitution thus held that 'the freedom [proclaimed by Article 2 of the Declaration of the Rights of Man and the Citizen] implies "respect for privacy"'.[24] In this judgment, the potential infringement of the right to privacy, and *a contrario* its protection under the constitutional system, also related to the use of new technologies, namely a computerised system for the transmission of health information of electronic cardholders.

The change of constitutional basis has practical and legal implications in that it extends jurisdiction over the protection of the right to privacy to the administrative courts, whereas, under Article 66 of the Constitution, it was under the sole jurisdiction of the courts of the *ordre judiciaire*.[25] The fact remains that this transfer does not in any way alter the fact that it is a fictitious connection since, as Vincent Mazeaud points out, 'the right to privacy does not arise from the "liberty" proclaimed by Article 2 of the 1789 Declaration any more than it does from the "individual liberty" provided by Article 66 of the Constitution'.[26]

In parallel with this development by case law, several attempts were made – in 1977, 1992 and 2008 – to expressly enshrine the right to privacy within the body of constitutional legislation. None of them were successful.[27] In any event, the Constitutional Council has been able to set up constitutional mechanisms for protection against digital technologies that infringe on privacy.[28]

## B. Constitutional Protection of Privacy in Sweden: Constitutional Provisions under Constant Adaptation

The constitutional protection of privacy, including against new technologies, has followed a very different course in Sweden since the right to privacy is expressly enshrined in the Constitution.

Constitutional protection of the right to privacy is, moreover, twofold in Sweden: a general principle of the protection of privacy is provided in one chapter, in the form of a political declaration of intent, while, in a chapter that constitutes a catalogue of fundamental rights, some of the aspects of the right to privacy have been given enhanced constitutional protection.

The Swedish Constituent Assembly first reflected on the issue of privacy as such[29] during the first constitutional revision in 1976. The starting point for

[24] Mazeaud (n 21) 11.
[25] ibid 12.
[26] ibid.
[27] Redécouvrir le préambule, 16 and 69–77.
[28] See the case law of the Constitutional Council in MC Ponthoreau, 'Le droit au respect de la vie privée' 13–21.
[29] Some provisions protecting certains aspects of privacy (such as the protection against home searches) were nevertheless already to be found in the catalogue of rights in the first version of the Constitution, which entered into force on 1 January 1975.

discussion was the question of whether Article 8 of the ECHR could be a model to be followed.[30] Considering that the introduction into the Swedish Constitution of rules as general and imprecise in content as those provided in Article 8 was 'manifestly inadequate', the Constituent Assembly 'excluded' the idea of introducing general protection in the form of a mandatory (constitutional) rule.[31] Instead, a provision was introduced into the Constitution (in the form of a political declaration of intent)[32] setting out a general principle of the protection of privacy in chapter 1 thereof, which, under the heading 'Basic Principles of the Form of Government', provides a set of guidelines for public authorities. According to section 2 of this chapter, 'public institutions must … protect the privacy and family life of individuals'.

The primary function of this provision, which is in principle non-binding, but may have political significance,[33] is 'to oblige the State to act positively to ensure that the right [to privacy] is protected, promoted and enforced as widely as possible'.[34] In practice, this provision does not seem to have been particularly promoted by Swedish institutions responsible for constitutional review, and it is therefore difficult to gauge its effectiveness with respect to new technologies.

Such protection of privacy does, however, exist through the provisions included in the catalogue of human rights in chapter 2 of the Constitution, which are mandatory and entail negative obligations of the public authorities.[35] This chapter, which from the outset provided specific protection against certain invasions of privacy (against inter alia body searches and raids), was expanded in 1989, and then again in 2010, to include provisions for protection against new intrusive technologies.

The first alteration to the body of constitutional legislation to improve its effectiveness in mitigating risks to privacy potentially raised by new technologies was aimed at the growing threats to privacy due to the technical possibilities of centrally recording a large amount of information on individuals.[36] It has taken the form of the insertion in chapter 2, section 3 of the following provision: 'Every citizen shall be protected, to the extent set out in more detail in law, against any violation of personal integrity resulting from the registration of personal information by means of automatic data processing.'

This provision differed in several respects from the other provisions of the chapter into which it had been incorporated. Indeed, contrary to the other

[30] Prop 1975/76:209 *Om ändring i Regeringsformen* 72.

[31] ibid.

[32] ibid 131.

[33] SOU 2008:3 *Skyddet för den personliga integriteten – Bedömningar och förslag* 96.

[34] SOU 1975:75 *Medborgerliga fri- och rättigheter* 184.

[35] The two provisions overlap partially each other. SOU 2008:3 (n 33) 96.

[36] This issue, considered by many as an central privacy issue (Prop 1987/88:57 *Om grundlagsfäst integritetsskydd* 9), had already been discussed at the time of the constitutional revision of 1976. No provision was adopted, however, due to the ongoing reform at that time of the Personal Data Act.

provisions that oblige the legislator to be passive, this constitutional rule meant that the legislator had an active role to play by enacting legislation.[37] Unlike the other provisions of chapter 2, this provision could not be applied directly by public authorities.[38] It also had the specificity of referring to a certain technical process: automated data processing.

This provision came into force on 1 January 1989, but was repealed in 2011 in the wake of another constitutional reform which, by extending the scope of privacy protection to surveillance and mapping, had made the provision redundant.

This second constitutional reform resulted in the insertion into the catalogue of human rights of a provision protecting individuals against 'significant infringements [made by the State] on the individual's privacy if they occur without consent and consist in surveillance or the mapping of the personal circumstances of the individual'.

This provision, which broadened the physical scope of protection, was implicitly due to technological developments, since in practice the infringements against which the new provision is intended to provide protection are, to a large extent, made possible and/or exacerbated by the use of new technologies (automated files, signals intelligence, wiretapping).[39] The reason expressly advanced by the Constituent Assembly was its desire 'to express in the Constitution greater respect than currently exists for the right of individuals to their privacy'.[40]

The Swedish Constituent Assembly, abandoning the idea of placing positive obligations on the state (the adoption of a law) which had been applied in the protection against automated processing, reverted to the traditional idea of regulating the limitations on privacy by public authorities by way of negative obligations.

From the perspective of human rights, the right to privacy has been subject to successive changes towards ever-greater protection, reflecting the will of the Swedish Constituent Assembly to protect this right against the infringements generated by new technologies and raise the standing[41] of this right, which had for too long been kept in the shadow of the freedoms of opinion, and thereby give greater recognition to the value of private life.

[37] SOU 2008:3 (n 33) 117.

[38] ibid.

[39] Prop 2009/10:80 *En reformerad grundlag* 180–82.

[40] Furthermore, the Constituent Assembly aimed to adjust the protection of privacy to the standard established by the Court of Strasbourg (SOU 2008:3 (n 33) 247). In Sweden, where the emphasis has been placed on the imperative of having a democratic and free society, freedoms of opinion (right to information, freedom of expression and freedom of the press) have traditionally received a preferential treatment to the detriment of the right to respect for private life. In such a context, the right to privacy has been instrumentalised in the service of freedom of opinion and been deprived of intrinsic value. See E Reimers, 'Integritetsskyddet i regeringsformen' (2009) 4 *Svensk Juristtidning* 447.

[41] See Prop 2009/10:80 (n 39)176 and dir 2014:65 5.

## C. Comparative Remarks

Consequently, in France as well as in Sweden, notwithstanding their different approaches – through case law in France and through legislative additions in Sweden – the constitutional system has been established as a bulwark against the infringements that may arise from the use of new technologies. Notwithstanding the differences in the mechanisms of protection as such (section IIC(i)), the constitutionalisation of the right to privacy has had similar effects in both countries (section IIC(i)i).

### *(i) Differences in the Protective Mechanisms*

With regard to constitutionality review prior to legislation being passed, the differences relate to the kind of legislation that is the subject of referral (in France, a so-called small law, in Sweden, a draft law) and to the referral procedure (in France, launched at the request of 60 members of Parliament, 60 senators, the President of the Republic, the Prime Minister, the President of the National Assembly and the President of the Senate, and in Sweden, a systematic referral in the circumstances set out by the Constitution). There are also differences relating to the bodies in charge of examining constitutionality (in France it is the Conseil constitutionnel, composed of nine members appointed by political bodies – the President of the Republic and the Presidents of the Parliamentary Assemblies – and in Sweden it is the Council of Legislation, composed of four sitting or retired judges from the two supreme courts) and to the legal scope of the opinion of the competent body (mandatory in France, not so in Sweden).

As for the constitutionality review conducted post hoc, ie by a constitutional body, such procedure exists in France by means of the *question prioritaire de constitutionnalité* (priority preliminary ruling on the issue of constitutionality), which came into force in 2010, but has no equivalent in Sweden. The French system, which allows any litigant, in the course of proceedings, to challenge the constitutionality of a legislative provision applied in the relevant case, has the same legal effects as constitutionality review prior to legislation being passed: the Constitutional Council, after review by the Supreme Court with jurisdiction in the case (Cour de Cassation or Conseil d'Etat), repeals the provision or law it deems unconstitutional. In Sweden, the only action available – which is also available in France – is for the courts and administrative authorities to set aside a provision deemed contrary to the Constitution in a case submitted for their review.

Constitutionality review is conducted on the basis of similar criteria in France and in Sweden, which comprise the balance of interests to be protected applying the principle of proportionality. While in France the criteria have been developed by the case law, in Sweden, they are enshrined in the Swedish Constitution.[42]

[42] Ch 2, ss 20 and 21.

In both legal systems, the body responsible for constitutionality review must decide on the limitations placed on fundamental rights by the legislator – in this case, on limitations to the right to privacy as a result of the use of new technologies.[43]

### *(ii) Similar Effects in Both Countries*

The constitutional protection of privacy makes it possible, by way of a constitutionality review before legislation is enacted, both in France and in Sweden, to prevent enactment of legislation containing provisions that infringe the right to privacy. It also enables the non-application of such legislation already in force. Lastly, it provides protection to citizens with regard to acts committed by the public authorities. As it is guaranteed by the Constitution, the right to privacy can therefore be relied upon before the courts/defender of rights/Ombudsman by litigants claiming that the public authorities have infringed the right in question. In the latter cases, it is not the law itself, and hence the legislator, but the authorities applying the law that will be under review.

While the French and Swedish constitutional systems thereby provide protection against threats to privacy in a vertical relationship, in the current state of positive constitutional law in these two countries, it is less certain that they are fully capable of meeting the challenge of the ever-increasing 'privatisation' of these threats. Furthermore, one could well ask if these constitutional systems are sufficiently equipped to deal with threats which, beyond the personal dignity of individuals, are threats to the foundations of democracy.

## III. The Need to Reinforce the Constitutional Protection of Privacy for a Better Response to the Challenges Posed by New Technologies

As the primary national instrument for the defence of fundamental rights and freedoms, and as a compass and barometer of the values promoted in a given society, the Constitution should robustly enshrine the right to privacy which is essential for individuals and for the proper functioning of democracy (section IIIA). The constitutional system should also incorporate a horizontal effect that would allow for better protection of privacy in respect of private actors, to take into account the paradigm shift facing contemporary society (section IIIB).

[43] The two constitutional orders studied show some permeability to European law within the protection of a privacy field. This is particularly well illustrated by the preparatory works when it concerns Sweden (see especially SOU 2008:3 (n 33) and Prop 2009/10:80 (n 39)). For France, see, eg 'La protection des données à caractère personnel, domaine emblématique des interactions jurisprudentielles entre cours européennes et Conseil constitutionnel' (2019) 2 *Titre VII*, www.conseil-constitutionnel.fr/publications/titre-vii/la-protection-des-donnees-a-caractere-personnel-domaine-emblematique-des-interactions.

## A. The Importance of Robust Enshrinement of the Protection of Privacy in the Constitution

The right to privacy is, as already mentioned, fundamental in two respects: as a right protecting the private sphere of individuals and what constitutes a human being, and as a *sine qua non* for the exercise of democratic freedoms. Consequently, for it to feature in the Constitution, which 'is a matrix, the foundation of all legal norms in the domestic system, whether as a direct foundation or as a necessary stage in the normative procedure',[44] seems to be essential. In France, the right to privacy is not expressly mentioned in the constitutional bundle, whereas in Sweden, a *general* constitutional right to privacy worthy of the name is clearly lacking.

The enshrinement of the right to privacy at the highest level of the hierarchy of norms, which I am advocating, would also 'highlight the fundamental importance of [this right] for society'.[45] The symbolic value of constitutional inclusion, which would bolster the protection already provided by law, should not be overlooked, as pointed out by the Swedish Constituent Assembly when the provision on the protection of privacy in respect of automated processing was introduced into the Constitution. It 'was aware that such protection already existed, especially through the law on personal data protection and the law on secrecy', and emphasised that 'the provision proposed in the Constitution was not … intended to strengthen the physical protection of the right to privacy' but should be considered 'as an indication of the weight society has attached to this issue'. The advantage of adopting such a constitutional rule, in the committee's view, was 'precisely its symbolic value'.[46]

Such an approach is found in France's second unsuccessful attempt (in 1992) to enshrine the right to privacy in the Constitution: it seemed 'necessary' to the committee that initiated the proposal 'that these rights, already recognised in the law, be enshrined in the text of the Constitution'.[47]

The French Constituent Assembly, which expressed its views during the last attempt in 2008 to enshrine the right to privacy in the Constitution, was of another opinion. To the contrary, it dismissed the idea of 'the express reaffirmation, in the Preamble of the Constitution, of the right to privacy and the protection of personal data'[48] on the grounds that these rights were 'already enshrined … in two sources of law which, in the hierarchy of norms, are binding on the

[44] B Bonnet, 'Les rapports entre droit constitutionnel et droit de l'Union européenne, de l'art de l'accommodement raisonnable' (2019) 2 *Titre VII* 6, www.conseil-constitutionnel.fr/publications/titre-vii/les-rapports-entre-droit-constitutionnel-et-droit-de-l-union-europeenne-de-l-art-de-l-accommodement.

[45] As has been stated by the Swedish Data Protection Board during the reform leading to the introduction of a constitutional provision concerning data processing, Prop 1987/88:57 (n 36) 25.

[46] SOU 2008:3 (n 33) 281.

[47] Redécouvrir le préambule 16.

[48] ibid 74.

legislature' – constitutional case law and the international commitments of France. The doctrine of useful effect advocated by the committee in charge of the matter – meaning that a right need not be introduced where such introduction 'does [not] constitute a genuine innovation or provide a significantly superior protection of rights' – was, in the Constituent Assembly's view, applicable to this matter.[49] It should be pointed out that this position ran counter to the recommendations of the then Chairman of the Commission Nationale pour l'Informatique et les Libertés (National Commission for Data Processing and Liberties, the French data protection body).[50]

One may feel that the position of the French Constituent Assembly, like that of the Swedish Constituent Assembly, which did not propose the inclusion of a general right to privacy in the Swedish constitutional text, is regrettable – all the more so since enshrining the right to privacy within the Constitution would not run counter to the idea of leaving it to the legislature to provide 'fine-tuning'[51] for certain situations and to adapt the rules of law to technological and societal advances. The Constitution, like a compass, would simply set the course. Consequently, the argument raised in France against the constitutional inclusion of 'too rigid rules [that] could quickly become obsolete or, worse, severely restrict future development'[52] and the accusation made in Sweden that there would be a block on legislation 'that is needed in order to protect important interests or as part of ongoing social and economic reform activities, where the possibility of adaptation should be possible for rapid social development',[53] could, it seems, be dismissed. One only needs to observe the flexibility of Article 8 of the ECHR and the technological and social adaptations that a general principle of protection of the right to privacy has allowed.[54]

Greater visibility for this right, which would lead to an improvement in the quality of the law, militates in favour of the express constitutional enshrinement of a (general) principle of the protection of privacy. The legislature would thereby have to prepare the law most thoroughly, weighing up the choices carefully and including all the necessary guarantees, and would be obliged to 'give a clear account of the balance of interests struck in assessing [the proposed measures]'.[55]

Additionally, the actors involved in the law-making process would be provided with a more robust tool for assessing the constitutionality of a law that is being prepared. In the case of Sweden, the introduction into the Constitution of a provision on protection against surveillance and mapping has provided the opportunity

[49] ibid 71.
[50] ibid 70.
[51] ibid 77.
[52] ibid 75.
[53] SOU 2008:3 (n 33) 246.
[54] See eg K Grabarczyk, 'Vie privée et nouvelles technologies' (2011) 7 *RDLF*, http://rdlf.upmf-grenoble.fr/?p=704.
[55] Prop 2009/10:80 (n 39) 177.

for the bodies consulted on draft legislation (*remissinstanser*) to express their views on the conformity of the texts submitted with the conditions for restricting the right to privacy set out in the Swedish Constitution. Reinforcing the constitutional protection of the right to privacy at the level of the text itself would therefore have practical, and not just symbolic, consequences.

## B. The Enshrinement of Multidimensional Protection: Vertical and Horizontal Effect

Invasions of privacy are increasingly the result of private action, and in particular by information behemoths, where these actors both initiate the invention of new technologies and market or use them, challenging the assumption that the state is the sole source of threats to privacy. It therefore appears necessary to adjust the constitutional protection of privacy so that, going beyond any possible threat from the state, it could also protect individuals and society from threats from private actors.

Such protection from infringements by private actors would rely on what is commonly referred to in academic writings as the horizontal effect of fundamental rights. According to this 'doctrine', with its many interpretations and uncertain scope,[56] 'individuals would not only be beneficiaries of fundamental rights, in the form of freedoms guaranteed by constitutional or international norms, but also under the obligation to comply with them'.[57]

In simple terms, the concept of the horizontal effect of fundamental rights is applied in two scenarios. One is 'indirect horizontal effect through an obligation of protection', a situation in which 'the State has not only the (negative) obligation not to unduly limit the fundamental right, but also the (positive) obligation to protect this right, in particular against infringements by private persons'.[58] This idea of a horizontal effect as the result of positive obligations on the state is abundant in the case law of the European Court of Human Rights. The other is 'direct horizontal effect of fundamental rights' or, more precisely, their 'direct horizontal application'.[59] In this case, 'the obligations to respect fundamental rights are more simply directly *applicable* to private persons'.[60]

[56] 'To this day, the capacity of public law norms to affect the relationship between private individuals commonly known as horizontal effect, remains an unclear and inconsistent field of law. No universally accepted theory has so far emerged': JF Krahé, 'The Impact of Public Law Norms on Private Law Relationships Horizontal Effect in German English, ECHR and EU Law' (2015) 2 *European Journal of Comparative Law and Governance* 124, 124.

[57] T Hochmann and J Reinhardt, 'L'effet horizontal, la théorie de l'État et la dogmatique des droits fondamentaux' in T Hochmann and J Reinhardt (eds), *L'effet horizontal des droits fondamentaux* (Editions A Pedone, 2018) 7, 8.

[58] T Hochmann, 'Typologie des droits fondamentaux' in Hochmann and Reinhardt, *L'effet horizontal des droits fondamentaux* (n 57) 119, 129.

[59] ibid 139.

[60] ibid.

Developed by the writings of German academics[61] to protect the weak (workers) against the strong (employers) in the field of employment relations, the doctrine of horizontal effect is also of interest with regard to the right to privacy. In this area, too, the average man finds himself in a relationship of domination – in this case, a technical-economic one – with private sector actors. This domination is expressed in several ways. There is the fact that since technologies – invented, marketed and used mainly by the GAFAM companies – have invaded every sector of society, no one is able to escape them (digital abstinence being nearly impossible). Domination is also expressed in the imbalance of power. Thus, in cloud computing, for instance

> on all aspects of security and data protection, consumers are almost entirely at the whim of the provider; and providers generally are able to shift the entire risk loss to the consumer. On top of those, consumers have essentially no bargaining power to amend those weaknesses.[62]

In addition, there is a lack of informational self-determination, coupled with, and overlapping with, the existence of a digital, temporal and spatial panopticon,[63] made possible by the Internet and search engines. Beyond the aspiration to redress the imbalance between individuals and digital actors, a second justification for the establishment, in the area of the right to privacy, of obligations on private actors sanctioned by the Constitution is the spreading, liberticidal impact of NICTs on the functioning of democracy. The inclusion in the body of constitutional legislation of mechanisms with 'horizontal effect' would therefore clearly establish the duties of private digital actors towards individuals, as well as in respect of the democratic values that transcend them.

As for actual economic domination by digital actors, it paves the way for technological domination, the two being caught in an infernal dialectic.

In any event, the right to privacy is unquestionably a right that can be expressed both as a right entailing negative obligations and as a right entailing positive obligations of the state. This is confirmed by the interpretation given to Article 8 of the ECHR guaranteeing the right to privacy. Originally intended to protect individuals from state interference, it 'has the strongest (partly realised) potential for horizontal applicability'.[64]

In order to move beyond the traditional pattern of vertical state–individual constitutional protection, it might indeed be more appropriate to describe the

[61] See, eg A Seifert, 'L'effet horizontal des droits fondamentaux – Quelques réflexions de droit européen et de droit comparé' (2012) 48 *Revue trimestrielle de droit européen* 801, 802.

[62] A Schreiber, 'Cloud-Enabled Technologies and Privacy Paradigms: Israeli Challenges and Responses' (2016) 6(1) *International Data Privacy Law* 49, 50. The author even refers to AC DeVore, 'e-Legal: Privacy and Law Enforcement on the World Wide Web: Cloud Computing: Privacy Storm on the Horizon' (2010) 20 *Albany Law Journal of Science & Technology* 365, 371.

[63] On these concepts, see Mayer-Schönberger (n 5) 111–12.

[64] G Phillipson and A Williams, 'Horizontal Effect and the Constitutional Constraint' (2011) 74 *MLR* 878, 898.

matter in terms of the obligations imposed by fundamental rights to protect individuals and society against the harmful actions of private actors[65] rather than in terms of horizontal effect. The approach here is not theoretical, but pragmatic: it seeks solutions to protect privacy and democratic society against the infringements generated by NICTs, which either put liberticidal and dehumanising technical solutions on the market or cause such infringements directly through their own use of digital technologies.

It could therefore be possible to establish protection of privacy by the following protective mechanisms, it being understood that not all of these mechanisms would be appropriate for each constitutional system.

One such mechanism would be for the Constitution to include a positive obligation on the state to legislate in order to protect the privacy of citizens and democratic society by, for example, obliging private actors to respect a kind of code of ethics, and/or by establishing a body responsible for the ethical control of innovations.

The news is full of examples of technologies with liberticidal effects in the making, such as cryptocurrency, facial recognition tools, tracking applications and electronic chip implants. It is therefore vital that the legislature, as the representative of the people – and one that can have an overall view of the privacy-infringing technologies at work – should make societal choices that go beyond the freedom of each individual and set a course for the future of humanity.

The idea of introducing such a protective mechanism, in turn, raises questions about the responsibility of the state should it fail to satisfy its positive obligation to protect the right to privacy. Would it be possible to envisage a system of compensation by the state for harm caused by the passivity of public actors (in particular, the legislature)?

The positive obligation placed on public actors could be coupled with the inclusion in the Constitution of duties of private actors in relation to respect for privacy and even a sort of precautionary principle. This would require them to take privacy issues into account at the stage of innovation, as well as at the stage of manufacturing and pre-marketing of potentially privacy-invasive and/or dehumanising technologies, such as new algorithms or social networking features. The duty to respect privacy should also apply so that liberticidal practices could be avoided once the technology is on the market, as in the case of Cambridge Analytica, by way of an example that has had very far-reaching consequences.

In addition to taking into consideration the weight of private actors in the field of human rights and the violations that may ensue, expressly introducing into the constitutional text the right to privacy with horizontal effect could raise awareness among such actors of the value of this right and the need for it to be respected.

[65] Compare with the concept of *Grundrechtsbindungen Privater* proposed by Christoph Gusy and positively commented on by Olivier Beaud in 'Les obligations imposées aux personnes privées par les droits fondamentaux. Un regard français sur la conception allemande' (2013) 10 *Jus Politicum* 2.

Moreover, in addition to the solemnity afforded, constitutional enshrinement could also be expected to give greater visibility to this right.[66]

As with the positive obligations on states, the question of the enshrinement of the duties of private actors raises the question of sanctions in the event of non-compliance. Now, what would happen if such actors were not legally liable, ie where 'there is no remedy for the victim in the event of a violation', as Thomas Hochmann points out?[67] 'Such circumstances do not invalidate the obligations on private persons,' he argues, stating, however, that 'Legally, private persons are under an obligation to respect the rights that the Constitution guarantees to others.' The quoted author does, however, conclude that 'Quite simply, the breach of this obligation cannot give rise to a judicial sanction. There is a risk that direct horizontal application will remain dead letter law.'[68]

This examination has demonstrated, on the one hand, the importance of highlighting the right to privacy by expressly enshrining it in constitutional instruments, and, on the other hand, the relevance of enshrining (robustly) the 'horizontal effect' of the protection of privacy.

## IV. Proposals *de lege ferenda* to Meet the Challenges of Digital Society

As I suggested earlier in this chapter, I advocate the explicit enshrinement in constitutional instruments of a general and mandatory right to privacy, the effect of which would be not only vertical, but also horizontal. In concrete terms, this inclusion could take different forms from country to country. In what follows, I will consider solutions for the French and Swedish constitutional systems (section IVB). Before discussing and presenting these solutions, however, it is necessary to ensure that the national systems examined would be ready to undergo such transformations on a societal and technological level, and at the level of the legal system and the Constitution as such (section IVA).

### A. Are the Conditions Right?

It is clear that the galloping pace of development in all kinds of technology, with strong potential for the infringement of privacy and a dehumanising effect, has galvanised politicians and civil society in the broad sense of the term, including the scientific community, into action. The Constituent Assembly has a duty to listen to the opinions that are being expressed and to warn against the risk of

[66] See below section IVB.
[67] Hochmann and Reinhardt, *L'effet horizontal des droits fondamentaux* (n 57) 119, 143–44.
[68] ibid 144.

humanity becoming dehumanised in the future. It must also accept that, in view of the exponential nature of technological development, the assessments that it made a decade or two ago, on the adequacy of the mechanisms in place for the protection of privacy, have become obsolete.

As far as French law is concerned, constitutional jurisprudence may well be 'constructive and evolving', accompanying the 'enshrinement of new dimensions of fundamental rights and freedoms, and even altogether new rights',[69] but the fact remains that express enshrinement in constitutional texts would be welcome.

In Sweden, in the early 2000s, the lawmaker (in this case, the government) recognised the relevance of conducting regular and thorough analyses of the constitutional provisions guaranteeing the right to privacy,[70] and stated that the question of not introducing a general constitutional provision to protect privacy was not definitively closed.[71]

As to whether or not the French and Swedish systems are constitutionally capable of undergoing transformations towards stronger affirmation of the right to privacy, the question revolves mainly around the enshrinement of the horizontal effect of this right.

Of course, in France and Sweden, the discussion on the horizontal effect of fundamental rights is far from being as rich as it is, for example, in Germany. But does this mean that the legal and constitutional traditions of France and Sweden would prevent the insertion into the Constitution of horizontal provisions to protect the right to privacy?

In Sweden, this would prima facie be the case. The preparatory work for the 2011 reform asserts that extending the right to privacy to mandatory status 'to imply a positive obligation on the State, would lead to a strong differentiation of this right from other rights and freedoms guaranteed by the Constitution'.[72] The Constituent Assembly added, 'it is difficult to argue for placing the protection of privacy in such a special position in the Constitution'.[73]

However, in addition to the fact that I believe that the problems highlighted by violations of the right to privacy provide highly cogent grounds for a more protective and derogatory regime for this right, it should be recalled that in the past (1989–2011) a provision protecting privacy with indirect horizontal effect – on the protection against automated processing – had been included in the Swedish Constitution. At the time, several, and far from the least significant, bodies involved in the legislative procedure leading to the adoption of this provision hailed the application of the new constitutional rules between individuals.[74]

[69] J Bonnet and P Türk, 'Le numérique: un défi pour le droit constitutionnel' (2017) 57 *Nouveaux Cahiers du Conseil constitutionnel* 9.

[70] See dir 2004:51, quoted by SOU 2008:3 (n 33) 187.

[71] See dir 2004:51 and SOU 2008:3 (n 33) 187.

[72] SOU 2008:3 (n 33) 246.

[73] ibid.

[74] Such as the Data Inspection Board and the Law Faculty of Stockholm University, Prop 1987/88:57 (n 36) 25 and 27.

Swedish constitutional tradition does not, therefore, seem to constitute an irremediable obstacle to the establishment of protective mechanisms with horizontal effect. This is also the case in France, where the case law of the Constitutional Council already recognises certain horizontal applications of the rules it has identified on the protection of privacy,[75] and where, moreover, a constitutional provision in another area – the right to a good environment – has introduced duties owed by individuals.

In short, I consider that it is possible to conclude that the constitutional tradition of the two countries examined herein would not, as such, constitute an obstacle to inserting an express and general principle of the protection of privacy, and to establishing a right to privacy with horizontal effect. I propose hereunder solutions for France and Sweden to strengthen the constitutional protection of the right to privacy. These solutions differ to take into account the differences between the two countries in respect of positive law and constitutional traditions.

## B. Proposed Solutions for France and Sweden

Two solutions, or a combination of the two, could be offered to the French Constituent Assembly. One solution would be to insert a provision guaranteeing vertical and horizontal protection of the right to privacy into the Constitution itself. Another solution would be to adopt a charter on the right to privacy which, like the 2005 Charter for the Environment, would have a constitutional value by virtue of reference thereto in the preamble to the Constitution.

There would be several advantages to be gained by the use of such an instrument. More extensive than a single article, a charter would, as is the case with the Charter for the Environment in the field of environmental protection and sustainable development, make it possible to highlight the dangers posed by new technologies[76] and to set out the importance of the right to privacy and the issues involved in its protection – both from an individual and collective perspective.

Such a charter could have a pedagogical role in raising awareness. It could also serve as a legal and ethical compass for all the actors involved (private companies, individuals, the legislature, the Constitutional Council and courts), especially if it establishes a precautionary principle like the Charter for the Environment. Again, as with the Charter for the Environment,[77] such an instrument that would also provide the opportunity for expressly establishing the duties of private actors would thereby make it possible to emphasise the liability of these actors, notably

[75] See D Ribes, 'Atteintes publiques et atteintes privées au droit au respect de la vie privée dans la jurisprudence du Conseil constitutionnel' (2015) 3(48) *Les Nouveaux Cahiers du Conseil constitutionnel* 35.

[76] Note that a charter dedicated to artificial intelligence and algorithms was submitted in January 2020 to the French Parliament.

[77] Y Aguila, 'Les acteurs face à la constitutionnalisation du droit de l'environnement' (2014) 43 *Nouveaux Cahiers du Conseil constitutionnel* 43, 47–48.

with regard to the invention of new technologies. Why should we not contemplate that in the area of privacy protection, which is crucial to humanity as the environment, the 'constitutional innovation'[78] constituted by a charter would provide similar benefits?

Such benefits would be numerous and significant: in addition to the fact that the Charter for the Environment spurs a 'dynamic of reform',[79] in that 'some of its provisions, in order to reveal the full potential of [the Charter], require clarification through legislative or even regulatory provisions',[80] it is also a source of 'dynamism in the development of case law',[81] providing inspiration to the courts, before which 'the Charter may be invoked'.[82] Another particularly substantial effect of the Charter, which could well be transposed into the field of the right to privacy, is its impact on private actors. Thus, 'there is a growing awareness among economic actors of environmental issues and their impact on the company's image'.[83]

A third solution would be to combine the adoption of a charter with the express inclusion of the right to privacy in the body of the Constitution. Such a solution would increase the visibility and awareness of the provisions, particularly for private actors. While the more informed might know that a charter referred to in the preamble of the Constitution will form part of the constitutional bundle, most private actors are probably not aware of these subtleties of French constitutional law, and will be more attentive to a provision in the Constitution itself than to a charter.

For Sweden, where the constitutional mosaic is different to that of France – and where there is no example of a charter attached to the constitutional bundle – I propose three solutions. As with France, it is possible for them to be combined.

One solution would be to give more weight to the general provision on the protection of privacy in the chapter dedicated to a political declaration of intent in the Swedish Constitution, which, let us not forget, provides both horizontal and vertical protection. As also mentioned above, this provision forms part of a set of provisions that are a priori not mandatory. It would, however, appear that some of these provisions – and there is no reason not to include the provision enshrining privacy – are in the process of acquiring greater authority.[84] Evolution towards greater effectiveness of this provision depends on the proclivity of the courts and other supervisory bodies, such as the Ombudsman, to make use of it, but it also depends on the propensity of the legislature to refer to and draw inspiration from it.

[78] ibid 55.
[79] ibid.
[80] ibid 48.
[81] ibid 45.
[82] ibid.
[83] ibid 54.
[84] Bull and Sterzel noticed that sometimes the Council of Legislation or the courts use them. 'It is not excluded that the provision in the future will have an increase importance but it is not possible to foresee it today': T Bull and F Sterzel, *Regeringsformen – En kommentar* (Lund, Studentlitteratur, 2015) 51.

A second option, which could be considered in the light of the precedent of the provision on the protection against automatic processing, which had introduced an indirect horizontal effect, would be to introduce into the catalogue of human rights (chapter 2 of the Constitution) a provision of a general nature with indirect and/or direct horizontal effect.

A third, more radical, solution would be to enshrine the right to privacy, as is the case for the freedom of the press and the freedom of expression, in a specific constitutional law. Such specific constitutional document would also provide an opportunity for introducing provisions enshrining horizontal protection. While this could help to redress the imbalance between the freedom of opinion and the right to privacy, and give the right to privacy a completely different status in Swedish society, this solution seems more than theoretical, given that the principles of openness and transparency still reign supreme in Sweden.

## V. Conclusion

In a time of pandemic, as currently experienced, there is an understandable temptation for states, as well as a high degree of tolerance from the part of citizens, to produce and use digital tracking technology to monitor and constrain the disease. Meanwhile, we are seeing legal orders 'withdraw into themselves' in their responses to the crisis. Protective privacy mechanisms provided by domestic constitutions may therefore represent a crucial bulwark against the ill-considered adoption of liberticidal acts which may impair the humanity of tomorrow.

# PART VI

# Information and Technology Revolution and Health Related Rights

# 15

# Artificial Intelligence in Social and Health Services: A New Challenge for Public Authorities in Ensuring Constitutional Rights

GUERINO FARES

## I. Introduction

By taking advantage of the precious opportunities that technological development offers, national health and social services systems can improve their performance by reducing time and costs and simplifying actions and procedures rationally. There are numerous potential applications of artificial intelligence (AI) to the healthcare and social services sector. They produce benefits for patients, optimising their treatments, as well as for society, compensating the increasingly higher costs of treating new diseases and meeting increasingly more complex care needs. The use of predictive algorithms and techniques may be extremely valuable in several operational contexts: from the prevention to the diagnosis of diseases, from surgery to rehabilitation, from home-based care for elderly and disabled people to the organisation of social services in households. However, the desirable implementation of AI must respect the supreme principles of law and fundamental human rights on which modern democracies and contemporary constitutional orders are based: the principles of equality; equal treatment and access to services; the right to freedom of the individual; the principle of proportionality and the precautionary principle in risk management; the right to self-determination and the right to the protection of personal data; and the right to decision-making that is not fully automated but may include a contribution from AI that is managed by a human being.

## II. The Relationship between AI and Health and Social Services: The Opportunities Offered by the Technological Development

The social and healthcare sector is being impacted more and more by digital and artificial intelligence systems because of increasing developments of sophisticated machine learning and techniques that are able to find complex patterns in data. This chapter is focused mainly on the digitalisation of public action connected to the big data phenomenon and the algorithmic procedures (eg e-health, telemedicine, mHealth and smartphone apps for healthcare purposes, robotic surgery).

Meanwhile, the correct management of those technologies that are based on AI needs the legal framework related to the welfare state to be adapted, with the aim of guaranteeing citizens' constitutional rights to the greatest extent: from the effectiveness of care to equality in patients' access to medical treatment; from reasonableness of the administrative procedures to the application of data protection regulation.

The chapter aims to propose an analysis of the main constitutional and administrative issues with regard to artificial intelligence, covering the role of AI and digital technologies in both the design and the delivery of those types of services.[1]

Many different definitions of AI have been given over time. Some people talk about 'the science of making machines which do things that would require intelligence if done by men'.[2] Others talk about a 'cross-disciplinary approach to understanding, modelling, and replicating intelligence and cognitive processes by invoking various computational, mathematical, logical, mechanical, and even biological principles and devices'.[3]

The European Commission is also aware of how important the notion of artificial intelligence is,[4] which defines it as follows:

> Artificial intelligence (AI) refers to systems that display intelligent behaviour by analysing their environment and taking actions – with some degree of autonomy – to

[1] 'The health sector has been hailed by the Organisation for Economic Co-operation and Development (OECD) as the perfect platform for AI, due to the need for data to improve diagnostics and treatments and because of the volume of data generated by patients and professionals in electronic health records and the Internet of Things. AI can contribute to the improvement of decision-making in the diagnosis and treatment of patients and to the development of new treatments': see European Foundation for the Improvement of Living and Working Conditions – Eurofound, 'Research Report on "Public Services – Impact of Digitalisation on Social Services"' (Luxembourg, 2020) 14, http://eurofound.link/ef19043.

[2] J Copeland, *Artificial Intelligence: A Philosophical Introduction* (Hoboken, NJ, Blackwell Publishing, 1993) 1.

[3] K Frankish and WM Ramsey (eds), *The Cambridge Handbook of Artificial Intelligence* (Cambridge, Cambridge University Press, 2014) 7. The theory of the algorithm as a process to be applied to numbers is introduced in AM Turing, 'Rounding-Off Errors in Matrix Processes (1948)' in *Collected Works of AM Turing*, vol II (Amsterdam, DC Ince, 1992).

[4] Other definitions of AI have been formulated, such as, the ability of a digital computer or a computer-controlled robot to perform tasks that are usually associated with the highest intellectual

> achieve specific goals. AI-based systems can be purely software-based, acting in the virtual world (eg voice assistants, image analysis software, search engines, speech and face recognition systems) or AI can be embedded in hardware devices (eg advanced robots, autonomous cars, drones or Internet of Things applications). Many AI technologies require data to improve their performance. Once they perform well, they can help improve and automate decision-making in the same domain.[5]

The Commission itself offers clear examples of this innovative tool with enormous potential for public policies: 'AI is helping us to solve some of the world's biggest challenges: from treating chronic diseases or reducing fatality rates in traffic accidents to fighting climate change or anticipating cybersecurity threats.'[6]

However, all of the definitions given for AI are now dated; they need to be updated to reflect technological progress, especially considering the benefits and risks related to the new superintelligence, defined as 'any intellect that greatly exceeds the cognitive performance of humans in virtually all domains of interest'.[7]

AI and machine learning are constantly evolving areas of research and practice, and the discussions about transparency, proportionality and accountability are consequently increasing. The availability of computing power and the access to large pools of heterogeneous datasets have allowed researchers to develop even more demanding algorithms to analyse data and search for patterns, correlations and links that may be of significance.

Furthermore, we need specific information about the main issue of AI, namely the 'decision paradigm', which is linked, for instance, to the right not to be subjected to a decision based solely on automated processing in order to obtain social benefits.

Administrative procedural automation may set milestones in the interpretation and declination of the measures adopted through it and in the consequent profiles of administrative responsibility. The assignment of decision-making

processes characteristic of human beings (the ability to reason either to discover meanings or to learn from past experience); or as a scientific discipline that aims to develop programs or machines (software and/or hardware) that have behaviour that would be defined as intelligent if it were exhibited by a human being. Science and experience have also shown that important practical results are achievable in the context of decision-making processes, the understanding of natural language, and the recognition of models and images. The common assumption for these processes is that a machine can be considered as a child who, gradually educated, develops an adult brain: A Turing, 'Computing Machinery and Intelligence' (1950) 59 Mind 433.

[5] See Communication from the Commission to the European Parliament, the European Council, the Council, the European Economic and Social Committee of the Regions about 'Artificial Intelligence for Europe' (COM (2018) 237 Final, Brussels, 25 April 2018).

[6] AI includes tools with all the features if used in healthcare sector. So much so that on February 19th 2020 the European Commission has approved a set of documents called *Shaping Europe's digital future: European data strategy and AI White paper*, putting in evidence how much the classic areas of European wellbeing, first of all healthcare, will benefit from AI. This package is composed of the 'Commission Report on safety and liability implications of AI, the Internet of Things and Robotics', a 'White Paper on Artificial Intelligence', the Communication about 'A European Strategy for Data', and the Communication about 'Shaping a digital future for Europe'.

[7] N Bostrom, *Superintelligence. Paths, Dangers, Strategies* (Oxford, Oxford University Press, 2017) 11.

processes to an algorithm means that the result derived from this application must be considered as an 'administrative IT act'. This act must be in compliance with the general principles that govern the administrative activities' system, together with the relevant obligations of transparency and publicity.

The methodology to be used will be to connect the various aspects of a broader topic for the purpose of finding solutions related to the various problems.

In this context, big data plays a very important role in many ways within the health and pharmaceutical sectors, and has already transformed various facets of that sector. These huge datasets are leading to new drug discoveries and improving clinical trials more efficiently. For example, various devices allow researchers to monitor trial participants in real time, and healthcare professionals are enabled to predict and prevent illness in better ways.[8]

From personalised medicine to assisted diagnostics and to genetic engineering, the possibilities of AI are seemingly endless. However, legal and regulatory challenges remain, especially after the introduction of EU Regulation 2016/679 (the General Data Protection Regulation, GDPR), which takes into account that the digitalisation of processes can lead to issues regarding the privacy.

Moreover, patient-centred health data contributes to patient outcomes whilst reducing wasteful spending in healthcare.

An area where the potential benefits of big data have been particularly significant, but also where data quality constraints have been evident, is healthcare and medical research.[9] The possible sources of this kind of information are the most disparate: electronic health records, medical records, medical literature, clinical trials, insurance claims data, pharmacy prescriptions, data entered by patients or recorded on apps or fitness trackers, etc.[10]

After all, in this perspective the field of emergency medicine is fundamental, considering that there are three main areas of AI use in emergency medicine: AI in predictive modelling, AI in patient monitoring, and AI in emergency department operations.[11]

However, the potential benefits could be better-quality healthcare, with interventions more precisely tailored to individual patients' circumstances if their medical and other data can be matched to extensive datasets. In fact, big data benefits depend on the quality of the datasets being brought together. Medical professionals are often concerned about the quality of hospital data because the data collection process is out of date and no longer appropriate for big data analysis.

[8] These words are from AS Berne, 'Big Data in the Pharmaceutical Sector – between Protection and Transparency: Opportunities and Legal Challenges' (2019) 1 *European Pharmaceutical Law Review* 1.

[9] See House of Commons – Science and Technology Committee, 'The Big Data Dilemma. Fourth Report of Session 2015–16' (London, 12 February 2016) 23.

[10] See W Nicholson Price, 'Artificial Intelligence in Health Care: Applications and Legal Implications' (2017) 14 *The SciTech Lawyer* 10.

[11] See N Liu, Z Zhang, AF Wah Ho and ME Hock Ong, 'Artificial Intelligence in Emergency Medicine' (2018) 2 *Journal of Emergency and Critical Care Medicine* 82.

In some cases, premature conclusions are being drawn from the data because it is not rich enough. Moreover, the further away the interpretation of the health data is from the person who produced it, the more likely it is to be misinterpreted: this is why it would be appropriate to improve standardisation and the way we record things.

In practice, digitalisation is a major trend in healthcare, and the mining of health-related data is on the rise. Big data offers the possibility of deriving novel insights to support decision-making processes, but also brings together unknowns with regard to data quality and hence the robustness of the evidence generated. It is also possible to distinguish between four different types and origins of health-related data: voluntary (collected through devices and software), obligatory (from insurance and health cards), explored (through patient-originated research on the Internet) and inferred (through assumptions from existing health data).

Some scholars have successfully pointed out that

> there are many expectations and hopes for applying AI techniques in the medical field. First of all, the possibility of developing predictive models with obvious advantages in terms of prevention. Secondly, the ability to put in place early diagnosis, in order to guarantee a prompt reaction using the most appropriate care. Finally, the affirmation of chatbot-based environments promises to guarantee the right information for patients, accompanying them in their care processes. AI could be capable of solving many problems in several e-health contexts. Intelligent virtual assistants, now embedded in smartphones or dedicated home speakers, like Microsoft Cortana and Apple Siri, but increasingly present in people's home devices, such as voice assistants Amazon Alexa or Google Assistant, are supported by systems with powerful AI features. These tools represent today the most advanced and captivating frontier of the use of AI to facilitate everyday life'.[12]

The devices for healthcare can provide support for social assistance at the same time, this double utility reflecting the mixed needs that part of the population, especially the older one, has.

[12] See P Guarda, '"OK Google, Am I Sick?": Artificial Intelligence, e-Health, and Data Protection Regulation' (2019) 1 *BioLaw Journal* 362, who adds that 'particular conditions requiring elaborate treatment plans could benefit from AI tools during specific therapies. Incorporating an artificial intelligence system capable of automatically formulating plans based on specific conditions would provide value to both physicians and patients alike. This is the case of ecosystems designed to innovate the processes of interaction between physician and patient, with an evident impact also on the organizational models that regulate the performance of health services.[] These intelligent systems may look for inconsistencies, errors and omissions in an existing treatment plan or may be used to formulate a treatment based on a patient's specific condition and on accepted treatment guidelines. The intelligent agent can, furthermore, be used for finding information, for example on the Internet, relevant to a particular disease, integrating knowledge about user preferences and needs into such searches, or for automatically interpreting medical images (ie X-rays, angiograms, CT scans, etc), becoming a formidable tool especially with regard to mass screens where the system could signal potentially abnormal images for detailed human attention. Finally, expert systems and decision support systems, programmed to aggregate and store a large amount of data modelled for specific purposes, can be successfully used in the field of medical devices in applications for cardiac monitoring and automated ECG, medical imaging, clinical laboratory analysis, and so on'.

The term 'telecare', as a synonym of 'telehealth', explains this concept well. Telecare includes technical devices and assistive technology, as well as professional healthcare services to assist, monitor and care for people from a distance.[13]

Essentially, the general objectives of telecare services are as follows: (i) promoting the permanence and inclusion of dependent people in the context where they normally live; (ii) enhancing and keeping the degree of autonomy and independence of dependent persons at home; (iii) favouring the safety and trust of dependent persons; (iv) providing relief for dependent persons and their relatives; and (v) serving as support for carers living with the dependent person.

Therefore, healthcare and social assistance are just two combined factors in the perspective of digitalisation as a multitasking process: AI can contribute towards reducing the time spent on customer support and administrative tasks and increasing the involvement of citizens in the policymaking process. AI can also contribute towards better-informed decisions in the design of services and policies, for example, by fine-tuning the allocation of resources for health and social care services in different areas.[14] AI can also allow data to be pulled from various aspects of a person's assessments and care plans, searching and analysing unstructured text for key concepts to help social care and health service workers access information relevant to that individual. AI could also allow the reduction of costs by enabling care workers to optimise people's health and well-being through offering general practitioners preventative options, reducing visits to hospitals and emergency rooms, and driving competition among service providers.[15]

[13] Telecare includes a variety of services such as communication, monitoring, consultation, diagnostics and training: see Parliaments and Civil Society in Technology Assessment – Pacita, *Telecare Technology for an Ageing Society in Europe – Current State and Future Developments* (Brussels, Pacita, 2014) 9 http://wp6.pacitaproject.eu/wp-content/uploads/2014/02/Telecare-description-web.pdf.

[14] European Commission, 'Report of the Expert Panel on effective ways of investing in Health (EXPH)' (Luxembourg, 2019) 4, http://ec.europa.eu/dgs/health_food-safety/index_en.htm.

[15] 'Technology Enabled Care services are more and more designed to empower individuals to support themselves in their own homes and manage their own health conditions. For example, connected care services are able to detect smoke or gas or a person falling; the aim is ultimately to improve health outcomes. Many products and services are commercially available such as telecare devices, at-home alarms, activity monitoring, bed occupancy sensors (to notify possible falls), to allow users to live independently but receive social assistance when needed. The targets for these products include older people and people with disabilities. Such products enhance users' access to care services while also improving their inclusion since they can live independently instead of staying in hospitals or care homes. Introducing more monitoring services to provide 24/7 remote support via traditional and digital routes will create efficiencies of scale while helping older people to care for themselves. In other cases, the service enables online and video consultations for people with disabilities, child welfare services, psychosocial assistance for children and for families, support for child rights issues and other care services for children and multidisciplinary cooperation. The service combines various technologies for service providers, such as telepresence for consultations and other forms of co-working and information transfer forms for relaying confidential information, and allows communication between professionals and between professionals and users. Virtu.fi also provides services for citizens, such as online bookings, guidance and counselling (including via telepresence), and tools for measuring various personal health indicators. In social services the sectors of greatest development and perhaps of most interest are those related to teleassistance and the management of digital administration related to accessing social services. The traditional method of service delivery is changing, with greater emphasis now on how technology can support people through proactive alert monitoring rather than reactive response calls': see Eurofound (n 1) 16.

It is estimated that telecare in Europe includes a lot of technologies: sensors and monitoring devices, detectors, alarm systems, communication devices, video or imaging devices, smartphone apps and specialised medical devices connected to the Internet. In some countries, videoconferencing and other remote services are available on devices used by people with disabilities, child welfare services and services for families with children.[16] It is also estimated that demand for technology-enabled care services will increase with the ageing of the population and care budget constraints.[17]

The demographic changes are expected to increase the demand for telecare services thanks to population ageing, greater confidence with devices (people are starting to gain confidence in using new devices more and more), decreasing device costs and increased portability. Other factors also work as an incentive to develop the use of AI tools, such as service quality, efficiency, security and inclusion in the perspective of service users. From the technological side, the general increase of wearable devices in all areas of society will increase both acceptance and use of telecare devices. Moreover, the interaction between devices is predicted to improve over time. Barriers to further use of telecare do, however, remain, in the form of legal, ethical and data protection issues, and the need to train staff and users.

Healthcare and social assistance can also benefit from the use of robotics at the same time. In fact, robots can prepare people for their care appointments and encourage them to do things that they can still do themselves, like drinking an extra glass of water on a hot day or going for a walk. At the same time, they can help older people with rehabilitation exercises, or to take a medicine or receive healthcare.

In addition, data matching and data mining techniques are suitable for mixed use, such as to evaluate the eligibility for public benefits or to target sanitary inspections.

The digital technologies can also guarantee mixed advantages, including devices that can be used for both security alarms and health checks. Welfare technology reduces pressure on social and healthcare services by decreasing consultations, home nursing services and admissions to hospital. For example, the economic gains that could be achieved through the use of digitally supported training come from less commuting by therapists and fewer hours of therapy needed due to improvements in service users' condition.

Big data and AI are leading to radical changes in decision-making processes.[18] It would consequently be appropriate to analyse the paradigm shift that is occurring

[16] In particular regarding the Finnish experience, see T Kauppila, K Kiiski and M Lehtonen, 'Sähköhelmenkalastus – Sosiaalihuollon sähköisten palvelujen nykytila ja kehittämistarpeet' (2018) 25, http://julkaisut.valtioneuvosto.fi/handle/10024/160653.

[17] See Eurofound (n 1) 17.

[18] See DA Hashimoto, G Rosman, D Rus and OR Meireles, 'Artificial Intelligence in Surgery: Promises and Perils' (2018) 268(1) *Annals of Surgery* 70.

in the field of social and health services, along with its implications for constitutional and administrative law. The application of AI in administrative decisions regarding the sector at issue is very interesting. This overview will continue by reflecting on the radical transformations that are proceeding at great speed, underlining the main challenges that can be effectively addressed only through interdisciplinary approaches. In conclusion, some fundamental principles of a new constitutional and administrative law in the cybernetic era should be proposed.

Digital transformation of health promotion and disease prevention requires targeted oversight and safeguards for its full potential to be harnessed. Moreover, people who would most benefit from mobile health and other such digital tools may be the least likely to have easy access to it. More generally, health promotion and disease prevention pave the way for a more effective and efficient health system.[19]

As an eminent Italian scholar has pointed out,[20] today a growing number of decisions affecting human liberties are made by algorithms. This evidence raises a vast number of questions concerning the transparency of such tools, the legal and ethical framework for algorithmic decision-making, and the societal and cognitive impacts of such algorithmic automation. Therefore, the big challenges now are, on the one hand, to outline the inherent tension between AI and law and, on the other hand, to examine and critique the standards set by GDPR to provide effective protection for fundamental liberties.

AI uses algorithms. Consequently, it is important to focus first of all on the definition of algorithm, the most basic of which is 'an organised sequence of calculations'.

Algorithm is a word that derives from al-Khuwărizmĭ, the nickname of the Arab mathematician Muhammad ibn Mŭsà, who lived in the ninth century. It is an older concept than that of AI, which adopts and uses it.

According to a more innovative concept, algorithm is a mathematical system that answers a question or founds the solution to a problem. An algorithm that answers in terms of yes or no is called a 'decision procedure'. An algorithm that answers by providing a specific number is called a 'calculation procedure'.[21]

[19] The progress made thanks to AI shows how the programs have acquired most of their content for learning, rather than for the original input. As a result, hearing prostheses filtering environmental noise, support for the medical diagnosis of tumours, drafting of therapeutic plans and ECG interpretation are available today: Bostrom (n 7) 40.

[20] See A Simoncini, 'The Unconstitutional Algorithm: Artificial Intelligence and the Future of Liberties' (2019) 1 *BioLaw Journal* 63. The author talks about a new doctrine of 'precautionary constitutionalism' through which protection of fundamental rights and the rule of law should be granted within the designs of new technologies.

[21] Ultimately, the algorithm is a process characterised by two essential requirements: a finite number of steps, on the one hand, and the finalisation to a real and concrete result, on the other: 'Algorithm' in *Encyclopaedia Britannica, Micropaedia*, 15th edn (1985), www.britannica.com/science/algorithm. After algorithm and AI, blockchain technology has entered the economic and legal system since 2008, offering new opportunities for use to both public and private entities in the healthcare and welfare services sector. According to the Italian legislation, blockchain uses so-called distributed ledger technology (DLT) (see Italian Legislative Decree 14 December 2018 no 135, Article 8-ter). For doctrine, see F Votta, '"Distributed Ledger Technology" and "Blockchain": Considerations on the Possible

Therefore, any entity, public or private, that provides healthcare services can use the algorithm whenever it has to make a decision or answer a question from the patient. The algorithm has a growing usefulness, as it is used within standardised procedures that must answer a very high number of questions or make a lot of serial decisions. In such cases, the algorithm takes far less time to execute a decision than a man would need, and benefits from a memory that is much greater than that of a normal human being.

Nevertheless, the control of an enormous amount of data by a few companies puts people's confidentiality at risk. In more precise terms, for example, AI allows a profiling of the political preferences of people, which could be considered to represent a specific risk to the pluralism that must characterise every democratic regime. Therefore, it could be an unknown factor for the rule of democracy and for the freedom of expression on which this structure is based.

With the increase in computational calculation capacity and the connected growth in quantity and quality of data available today, the possibilities for profiling people can in fact be easily expanded to the field of political orientations. As often happens with Internet advertising, whereby people are increasingly receiving offers targeted to their tastes, such as information of a political nature – particularly electoral information – the risk is that people are exposed to very limited and specific information based on their presumed preferences. In this way, profiling can more easily include people's political leanings, which are increasingly being influenced by big data.

Moreover, we must consider that AI tools are not perfect machines. In fact, AI also makes mistakes. Therefore, it is impossible to completely delegate to the machine an administrative procedure regarding the assignment of social benefits to the citizens: it is a fault of the system.

Evolution of the Public Administrations Digitalisation' (www.giustamm.it, 2019) 11. As recently clarified by the Opinion of the European Economic and Social Committee on Blockchain and the EU Single Market: What Next? (Own-Initiative Opinion) (2020/C47/03), 'Blockchain (hereafter BC) and distributed ledger technology (DLT) has the potential to transform society. BC is a mathematical structure for storing data in a way that limits corruption and fake data'. In the meantime, 'BC is defined as both a code, ie a communication protocol, and a public register, in which all transactions between network participants are recorded one after the other, with a high degree of transparency and in a way that cannot be altered'. 'BC is a technology for promoting user trust. It makes it possible to share on-line information, agree on and record transactions in a verifiable, secure and permanent way.' 'This opinion focuses on BC as a technology, which can be applied to a whole host of areas and industries such as energy, finance, food and agriculture, medicine and healthcare, elections and governance.' As goal 3 'Good health and wellbeing and the opportunity in sharing patient healthcare records more securely and efficiently'. Moreover, 'these are self-executing contractual states stored on the blockchain which nobody controls and therefore everyone can trust. Examples are trade clearing and settlement, gift/loyalty coupons, electronic health records, royalty distribution, product provenance, peer-to-peer transactions, lending, insurance, energy credits, and voting.' As noted by European Commission, 'in the area of social welfare, blockchain has been used by pension providers in the Netherlands to set up a pension infrastructure that allows tax authorities, employers and employees to monitor the contributions made by individuals in different pensions funds': see European Commission, *Blockchain Now and Tomorrow: Assessing Multidimensional Impacts of Distributed Ledger Technologies* (Luxembourg, 2019).

The same warning must also be applied in other fields. Let us take the example of hiring procedures. Sometimes the hiring procedure is managed only by the AI system by means of an algorithm, which results in choices devoid of any justification without the identification of an administrative official, who assesses the individual situations or correctly outsources the related provisional decisions.

In an important case law,[22] regarding the hiring procedure specifically, the judge confirmed the plaintiff's perspective, according to which the algorithm arranged transfers in one province rather than another, in one type of job rather than another, without taking into account the preferences indicated in the respective transfer requests, and without any reason or the slightest transparency.[23]

Thanks to this kind of case, brought by some teachers for the assignment of their place of employment, the concept of algorithm captured the attention of interpreters and operators of the law and, consequently, of scholars.

The administrative judges highlight the pros and cons of applying digital technologies to administrative decisions. In his opinion, the following should be appreciated: (i) digitalisation is important for improving the quality of services provided to citizens and users; (ii) the algorithm certainly guarantees the compliance with the efficiency and cost-effectiveness of the administrative action and the good performance of the public administrations; and (iii) the advantages, in managing repetitive and discretionary activities, achievable by excluding interference due to negligent or malicious conduct by the official as a human being, with the greatest guarantee of impartiality. There are also doubts: (iv) the fact that the technical rule that governs the algorithm is still a general administrative rule, managed by man and not by machine, and as such is subject to general administrative principles (reasonableness, proportionality, publicity, transparency, judicial control, etc); and (v) the attempt to deprive the administrative judges of the ability to check the algorithmic rule, even though they are indeed obliged to verify the correctness of the automated procedures in all their phases and components.

In other words, the result of the application of the algorithm has been contested: consequently, in that case the IT administrative act was judged not to be correct

[22] Italian Consiglio di Stato, sez VI, 13 dicembre 2019 n 8472 has stated three fundamental principles: (i) the possibility for the recipient to be aware of the decision-making processes; (ii) the non-exclusivity of the automated decision; and (iii) the ban of discriminations due to the algorithmic decision. Similarly, see sez IV, 8 aprile 2019 n 2270 and Tar Lazio, sez III-bis,14 febbraio 2017 n 3769. For doctrine, see S Crisci, 'Evoluzione tecnologica e trasparenza nei procedimenti "algoritmici"' (2019) 2 *Law of Internet* 380; G Mancosu, 'Les algorithmes publics déterministes au prisme du cas italien de la mobilité des enseignants' (2019) 1 *Rivista Italiana di Informatica e Diritto* 75.

[23] For further analysis of the debate about how best to achieve algorithmic transparency, from which several approaches have emerged in order to ensure and demonstrate the data protection compliance of 'black box' big data processing activities such as machine learning, see Information Commissioner's Office, 'Big Data, Artificial Intelligence, Machine Learning and Data Protection' (Wilmslow, 2017) 86; JA Kroll, J Huey, S Barocas, EW Felten, JR Reidenberg, DG Robinson and H Yu, 'Accountable Algorithms' (2017) 165 *University Pennsylvania Law Review* 633. The theory of transparency as an antidote to opacity is supported, among others, by F Pasquale, 'Beyond Innovation and Competition: The Need for Qualified Transparency in Internet Intermediaries' (2010) 104 *Northwestern University Law Review* 160.

and to be against the law, due to the irrationality of its results compared to the provisions of the same law.

Public administrations must also be able to exploit the significant potential of the digital revolution.[24] In this context, the use of computer algorithms for making decisions that affect the public and private spheres must be justifiable in terms of efficiency and neutrality. In many fields, algorithms promise to become the tool used to correct the distortions and imperfections that typically characterise the cognitive processes of, and choices made by, human beings. These aspects, in particular the limits of human beings, have been highlighted in recent years by an impressive body of literature on behavioural economics and cognitive psychology. In this context, the decisions made by algorithms thus take on an appearance of neutrality, the result of aseptic, rational, data-based calculations.

What should be clear is that without human control, the defects of an automated device may produce effects that are contrary to the expected ones: complication instead of simplification, partiality of results instead of completeness, and irrationality of outcomes instead of equity and plausibility.[25] Thus, the more discretionary the nature of the activity to be performed, the more evident the limits of the automated procedure will become.[26]

## III. The European Regulatory Framework: Promoting the Use of AI

EU competencies in health protection have been increasing over the years, although without affecting the powers of the EU Member States, which remain responsible for the organisation and funding of health and social care.

Reaffirming the greater adequacy and incisiveness of its actions in certain fields, the European Union has acquired competence in social and health matters that is cross-sectoral and horizontal. As such, it is capable of justifying its influence on any other policy with the objective of 'ensuring a high level of human health protection' (Article 168 TFEU).

In particular, through its actions, the EU can complete the measures adopted by individual Member States: promoting public health and disease prevention, encouraging cross-border cooperation in their services and stimulating the technological innovation of national welfare systems.

[24] DK Citron and F Pasquale, 'The Scored Society: Due Process for Automated Predictions' (2014) 89 *Washington University Law Rev* 1 discusses 'technological due process'.

[25] See RC Lawlor, 'What Computers Can Do: Analysis and Prediction of Judicial Decisions' (1963) 49 *American Bar Association Journal* 337; R Keown, 'Mathematical Models for Legal Prediction' (1980) 2 *Computer Law Journal* 829.

[26] See M Bovens and S Zouridis, 'From Street-Level to System-Level Bureaucracies: How Information and Communication Technology is Transforming Administrative Discretion and Constitutional Control' [2002] *Public Administrative Review* 66.

Therefore, through a considerable set of soft law acts, the EU has supported the implementation of e-health projects, among them the realisation of health information networks, the use of electronic health records and digital health records, telemedicine services and portable monitoring systems.

Most recently, building on Articles 16 and 114 TFEU, in addition to Article 168 TFEU, the European Commission adopted a set of acts aimed at promoting the creation of a digital single market in the health and care sectors. The objective of these initiatives is to enhance digital health data to provide targeted and personalised treatments to citizens, making them active participants in the management of their health, as well as in a more efficient and effective use of the available resources.

The contents of the European Commission's *State of Health in the EU – Companion Report 2017*[27] are very interesting and can be summarised as follows:

- Patient-centred care and patient empowerment require general knowledge about self-care and self-management but also 'soft skills' such as communication and teamwork. Indeed, soft skills become increasingly important in conjunction with (and not separate from) the digital transformation of health and care, as patient-centeredness and patient empowerment are facilitated by, for instance, e-health, mobile health (mHealth) and individual access to electronic patient records;
- The spread of digital technology is currently revolutionising traditional clinical practice. Indeed, the expansion of eHealth is leading to new ways of care delivery, requiring a new mix of skills, such as information or interpretation for detailed genetic assessment so as to improve diagnosis and treatment;
- The implementation of the next stage of development in e-health infrastructure, such as electronic medical records in primary care, e-prescriptions and patient registries, will not only contribute to longer-term efficiency of healthcare spending but will also enhance the quality and continuity of care for patients. A digital strategy is necessary;
- Technology is also a strong driver of patient empowerment: tailored apps and smart portable devices provide effective support for healthy lifestyles and for involving the patient directly in the management of chronic conditions. Finally, strongly related to the Digital Single Market Strategy, advanced information and communication technologies will allow for the creation of large and interconnected databases of medical and health data. At the same time, new technologies are a key driver of health spending and its projected growth. It is therefore crucial to carefully evaluate the cost-effectiveness of new technologies and assess what works and does not work for patients and providers. In order to reap the benefits of technology and effectively enhance the quality of care, it requires adequate training of the health workforce, as well as a supportive environment in terms of professional culture, incentives and organizational arrangements.

[27] https://ec.europa.eu/health/sites/health/files/state/docs/2017_companion_en.pdf.

A comprehensive set of actions within the digital transformation of health and care, part of the Digital Single Market Strategy, has been provided in a specific Commission Communication.[28]

In particular, the 2017 Commission Communication on the mid-term review of the Digital Single Market Strategy recognises an advanced data infrastructure with citizens' secure access to their electronic health records and patient empowerment through interaction with healthcare providers as key features of the digital transformation of health and care.

The subsequent *State of Health in the EU – Companion Report 2019*[29] should be noted for its importance, and its highlights are worth reporting:

- Building on the 2018 Commission Communication enabling the digital transformation of health and care in the Digital Single Market, the new Report looks at its potential for health promotion and disease prevention. Digital solutions, such as apps, wearable technology and online fora, hold great potential for health promotion and disease prevention, with best practice examples emerging across the EU. These innovative approaches help raise awareness and empower citizens to take control of their healthy behaviour and lifestyle choices. Digital solutions should, however, always be seen as part of a broader, comprehensive health promotion and disease prevention strategy;
- Digital platforms and environments could become a new health promotion setting, requiring targeted oversight and safeguards, with a particular focus on stepping up digital health literacy. A host of associated barriers and risks require consideration at the European level, with a bearing on – inter alia – interoperability, privacy and reimbursement criteria. Policy efforts should also take into account digital health literacy so that mHealth can be used appropriately and by all. Harnessing the potential of digital solutions for health promotion and disease prevention will depend on an openness to these innovative technologies combined with a critical understanding of their success factors;
- A good health promotion strategy includes digital tools, services and platforms having great potential when it comes to health promotion and disease prevention. Such digital solutions, be it apps, wearable technology or online fora, may empower people to enjoy a healthy lifestyle and prevent them from developing illnesses. Some mHealth tools even highlight early symptom or disease indicators, provide feedback to health workers and assist in patient adherence to treatment programs. These digital solutions also open up new inter-sectoral avenues to health determinants, such as transport, urban planning and the environment.

[28] See the Commission, 'Communication on the Mid-term Implementation Review of the Digital Single Market Strategy', COM (2017) 228, https://eur-lex.europa.eu/legal-content/EN/TXT/?qid=1496330315823&uri=CELEX:52017DC0228.

[29] https://ec.europa.eu/health/sites/health/files/state/docs/2019_companion_en.pdf.

In other words, apps, wearable technology and online fora can all empower people to enjoy a healthy lifestyle and prevent them from developing illnesses.

However, digital solutions may give rise to new or increased inequalities between people who do and those who do not have the skills to harness their potential. Similarly, varying levels of national or regional support for the rollout of digital health solutions can have an impact on who is given the possibility of benefiting from these tools, thus exacerbating inequalities. Employing digital solutions to strengthen health and well-being will require equal digital opportunities, widespread digital literacy, strong digital security and well-designed, effective tools, services and platforms.[30] EU Member States are required to exchange experiences, transfer best practices and develop common approaches to support the uptake of mHealth solutions for better health promotion, disease prevention and chronic disease management.

No less significant is the 2018 'Communication from the Commission to the European Parliament, the European Council, the Council, the European Economic and Social Committee and the Committee of the Regions on enabling the digital transformation of health and care in the Digital Single Market; empowering citizens and building a healthier society'.[31]

This Communication:

- stresses that health information portals, smartphones and mHealth apps can empower citizens to take a more active role in looking after their health and changing their health behaviours. It also recognises that the uptake of digital solutions for health and care remains slow and varies greatly across Member States and regions, so that it is very important to promote a uniform level common to all countries;
- underlines that the WHO also acknowledges that mHealth can improve access to health information and promote positive changes in health behaviours to prevent the onset of acute and chronic diseases. In particular, the organisation sees the use of mHealth tools as a good opportunity for increasing awareness to bring about changes in the key risk factors for non-communicable diseases and for increasing patient, family and community involvement.

The same Communication undertakes the resolution of the problems presented by the presence of diversified national models and non-interoperable technologies. For this purpose, it offers support to Member States in terms of funding and actions aimed at promoting, on the one hand, the political cooperation and exchange of best practices across the different national health and care systems and, on the other hand, the sharing of genomic data or other health data needed for the progress of research and personalised medicine.

[30] See the 2019 OECD report 'How's Life in the Digital Age? Opportunities and Risks of the Digital Transformation for People's Well-Being', www.oecd.org/publications/how-s-life-in-the-digital-age-9789264311800-en.htm.

[31] https://eur-lex.europa.eu/legal-content/EN/TXT/?uri=COM%3A2018%3A233%3AFIN.

As rightly pointed out, thanks to this document,

> artificial intelligence is hereby introduced, for the first time, in the European documents that expressively address the digital health with reference to health data, as an essential technology that, operating on such data, opens new care perspectives, new forms of disease prevention and personalised treatments.[32]

Ultimately, health information portals, smartphones and mHealth apps can help citizens to take a more active role in looking after their health and changing their health behaviours.

However, the regulatory European framework within which the new AI technologies in the field of health and social care should be placed is not well-defined yet. Currently, the framework is composed of pieces of legislation that are focused on another primary matter but that are also applicable to the sector at issue on the basis of possible intersections with it: for example, the legislation on medical devices, electronic identification, the security of networks and information systems, as well as the protection of personal data.

In other respects, the only specifically and directly relevant act is the European Parliament Resolution of 16 February 2017, with recommendations on Civil Law Rules on Robotics. The Resolution is not limited to dealing with the dimensions regarding the civil liability for damage; it also provides valuable information on the principles that should drive the introduction and use of robotic technologies with social benefits for elderly and disabled people and national health services.[33]

As discussed in the next section, privacy issues, consent and access to personal data are some of the main issues identified in implementing digitalisation strategies and using digital technologies in social services; therefore, some mitigating measures are needed.

The difficulties of ensuring privacy could affect the development of digital services. This risk is higher when the trust of the service user is lacking: in some cases the state has kept the data of users illegally; and medical data has been stolen from devices that are connected to a record system or used to send targeted advertising messages and even to blackmail patients.

[32] See EA Ferioli, 'Artificial Intelligence in Social and Health Services: A New Challenge to the Role of Public Institutions in Italian Welfare?' (2019) 1 *BioLaw Journal* 168.

[33] E Macrì and A Furlanetto, 'Robots between Myth and Reality Interacting with People in Social Environments and Hospitals. An Approach through Risk Management and Law' (2017) 3 *Rivista italiana di medicina legale* 1045, which points out the first strong position adopted by a European authority on the need to introduce effective rules in the matter of robots and artificial intelligence, has highlighted all the legal, ethical and economic contradictions related to the massive introduction of such technologies in daily life. Regarding the main liability issues of a cutting-edge robotic surgery application, see G Guerra, 'Comparative Law, and Robotics: Reflections on American "Litigation" Regarding Robotic Surgery' (2016) 2 *Diritto dell'informazione e dell'informatica* 157, who argues that further studies on a tight relationship between law and the brain sciences is basically important in order to reach an authentic interpretation of new robotic functions and their legal implications. For an in-depth examination of the interaction between robots and human beings and its ethical and legal effects, see A Bertolini, 'Human–Robot Interaction and Deception' (2018) 2 *Osservatorio di Diritto Civile e Commerciale* 645.

Therefore, in principle, strong data protection safeguards should accompany increased use and analysis of data to ensure that the user consents to the use of their data and that the data is anonymised where possible.[34]

## IV. AI Tools and the Protection of Constitutional Rights: A Case Analysis

As already mentioned, AI has for a long time had a number of applications in the health sector, giving rise to many advantages in terms of, inter alia, tests, robotic surgery, remote diagnosis and medical care for elderly people and vulnerable groups: it is clear, then, that the promotional approach adopted by the European Commission on several occasions has underlined the benefits in terms of cost reduction related to the digital transformation of healthcare and social assistance.

Looking at these dynamics, the interpreter dutifully takes on the task, primarily ethical rather than legal, of subjecting the new devices to an assessment of compatibility with the system of guarantees and of the inviolable human rights constitutionally enshrined: personal freedom and its specific facets (Article 5 of the European Convention on Human Rights; Article 13 et seq of the Italian Constitution); the right to the protection of personal data (last protected by the GDPR); and the right to good administration (Article 41 of the Charter of Fundamental Rights of the European Union).

The last-mentioned right requires, in particular, that the decisions taken by a substantially public entity be adequately justified. This leads to the affirmation that, although human intelligence can be supported by AI, it cannot be entirely replaced by it (see Article 22 GDPR).[35]

[34] See Local Government Association, 'Transforming Social Care through the Use of Information and Technology' (London, LGA, 2017). For the healthcare sector, appropriate training and skills development in privacy and security measures for processing personal health data has been recommended. Adequate training and skills development are required for social services as well. It is a challenge for staff to ensure that data is collated, shared and used in a way that reassures service users that their data is protected; therefore, it is vital that training is provided to improve skills in this area. For further details, see OECD, 'Recommendation of the Council on Health Data Governance' (Paris, 2019).

[35] For more details on this general ban, see G Noto La Diega, 'Against the Dehumanization of Decision-Making – Algorithmic Decisions at the Crossroads of intellectual Property, Data Protection, and Freedom of Information' (2018) 9(3) *JIPITEC* 17; S Wachter, B Mittelstadt and C Russell, 'Counterfactual Explanations without Opening the Black Box: Automated Decisions and the GDPR' (2018) 31 *Harvard Journal of Law and Technology* 841; Data Protection Working Party, 'Guidelines on Automated Individual Decision-Making and Profiling for Purposes of Regulation 2016/679' (6 February 2018). Regarding the healthcare sector, see E Begoli, T Bhattacharya and DF Kusnezov, 'The Need for Uncertainty Quantification in Machine-Assisted Medical Decision-Making' (2019) 1(1) *Nature Machine Intelligence* 20. As noted by another author, although a rule any algorithmic decision, which has a significant effect on individual, is prohibited, nevertheless the scope of this provision is still narrow, since it refers to fully automated decision-making, and may be easily circumvented by including a merely formal human intervention in the decision process, with no influence on the outcomes of that process: see P Savona, 'Administrative Decision-Making after the Big Data Revolution', www.federalismi.it, no 19/2018, 32.

In the medical field, the risk of violation of the above-mentioned Article 22 is perhaps lower than in other sectors. As more advanced AI applications are used in the medical field, the human being's contribution is not entirely excluded. An example is provided by telemedicine, which is meant as a way of supplying health-care services through innovative information and communication technology that is capable of mitigating circumstances in which the health professional and the patient, or even two professionals, are not in the same location.[36] Therefore, in such cases, the human operator still has the main role, together with the responsibility for the interpretation of symptoms and reports, so that the technical progress is not exposed to the risk of failure and biases of calculation systems that end up breaching the most relevant freedoms of the individual, among which the right to the protection of health is paramount according to the relevant international, European and Member States laws.

At most, regarding informed consent, the problem arises of making the information's content clear when explaining the purposes of the processing. This is because the group of people who can use personal data could depend on the specific arrangement followed: telemonitoring and telerehabilitation usually involve the operator and the patient, while teleconsultation extends the scope by making contact possible between a remote facility and a specialised centre.

Another example is minimally invasive surgery. In this field, automated tools (such as the Da Vinci, Prebot, Star or Watson robots) perform surgeries under the control of the operator, whose contribution is therefore preserved.

Obviously, we should not disregard the importance of the predictive values of any algorithm that is able to forecast complex phenomena and to rapidly and simultaneously collect and process big quantities of data:[37] advancing a diagnosis, calculating the probability of the onset of a disease or the statistically relevant factors regarding the incidence and spread of an epidemic represent achievements beneficial for the future of human beings.

At the same time, support of the analysis of cases that are not otherwise easily solvable or the performance of a service with low technical complexity should not hide the fact that it is not acceptable to delegate everything to machines to the extent that the human being is completely excluded from the basic choices, thereby undermining his or her dignity.

[36] Regarding the general framework, see European Commission, 'Communication on Telemedicine for the Benefit of Patients, Healthcare Systems and Society', COM (2008) 689, whose aim is to support Members States in achieving large-scale and beneficial deployment of telemedicine services by building confidence in and acceptance of this new technology, taking into account that the level of telemedicine spread must be measured both on the demand side (citizens) and on the supply side (healthcare facilities). Therefore, Member States are warmly invited to assess and adapt their national regulations enabling wider access to telemedicine services, by addressing issues such as accreditation, liability, reimbursement, privacy and data protection.

[37] JM Balkin, 'The Three Laws of Robotics in the Age of Big Data', Yale Law School Faculty Scholarship Series no 5159 (2017), http://digitalcommons.law.yale.edu/fss_papers/5159, talks about the 'society of the algorithm'.

The mark of the natural person and, in this case, of the health operator cannot be suppressed: in fact, in considering the scope of any AI, the right to substantiation and review of the automated decision – and not only the logics applied in taking it – has increasingly been taking root.

It has been pointed out that even if a medical action does not benefit from a specific constitutional guarantee in terms of the obligation to state the reasons, 'it is possible to doubt the total legitimacy of a medicine that bases its decisions on computer operations for which none can ensure understanding and control'.[38]

In other words, the outcomes of robotic procedures must be in compliance with the legislative provisions and the purposes admitted therein; in addition, the arrangements and rules that are the bases for the setting up of a procedure must be clear and ex post verifiable.

Some very salient issues are the rights to freedom and the right to self-determination in particular: it is the right that is expressed through informed consent and that authorises third parties, for example, to subject the consenting person to a medical action or to personal data processing for various purposes.

From digital clinical records to paperless prescriptions and electronic health records, new problems emerge regarding the protection of a patient's information from interference that is undue and not authorised by the data owner.

The regulation of these cases suggests that a personalistic model should be followed that, on the one hand, enhances the relationships between patients and health professionals but, on the other hand, prefers a patient-focused approach to treatment in which the informed consent provided by the patient is a core element.

In the various scenarios described above – (i) computer-based storage and processing of data regarding people's health status in e-health forms, (ii) predictive or probabilistic analysis of the patient's clinical situation on the basis of algorithms in telemedicine and (iii) setting and execution of robotic surgery – the protection levels and the response instruments used to prevent the possible breach of human fundamental rights and guarantees should be shaped with regard to the circumstances in these scenarios.

In sectors in which subjective rights and constitutional values should be considered, the employment of cutting-edge technologies requires, in general, a careful updating, if not a real reshaping, of the regulatory principles of the sectors affected by scientific progress.

With regard to e-health, the most important type is represented by the electronic health record, which collects digital or digitalised data and documents regarding patients' health.

[38] See C Casonato, 'Constitution and Artificial Intelligence: An Organizer for the Next Future' (2019) 2 *BioLaw Journal* 718.

## V. Bringing Together Patient's Health and Social-Health Digital or Digitalised Data

In the context of the computerisation of health data to which Member States may introduce further conditions and limitations (see Article 9, paragraph 4 GDPR), the electronic health record has been subject, since the very beginning, to a set of restrictions concerning the establishment, subsequent inputting and access that is guaranteed only to the patient and the authorised health staff.

The electronic health record also requires the data subject's consent. In various Member States, including Italy, this consent has not been expressly retracted, not even after Article 75 of the Privacy Code – in its new formulation post Legislative Decree no 101/2018 and in compliance with the provisions of Article 9 GDPR – eliminated the necessity of consent for data processing for treatment and diagnosis purposes.

Regarding telemedicine and robotic surgery, the most relevant aspects are: principles of and rights to proper functioning in terms of quality of data and process; the responsible programming and execution of surgeries; the justification of the choices made and the possibility of contesting them before a judge;[39] equality and equal access to the new opportunities provided by technology; and the protection of dignity and freedom of self-determination of the individual.

The final topic which remains to be dealt with came to the fore in social and mass media chronicles after various governments expanded the range of measures required to face the health emergency caused by the spread of the virus known as COVID-19.

There are issues concerning the announced launch of the apps for contact tracing. These tools have valuable potential for tracking the spread of the virus, but their compatibility with the supreme principles of modern constitutional orders have yet to be verified.[40]

[39] A Soro, *Democrazia e potere dei dati* (Milan, Baldini+Castoldi, 2019) 181, highlights how, in the case of entirely automated decisions based on a contract or consent, the recipient has a power, no longer merely preventive but also responsive, that results in the right to: (i) obtain human action on the process by the owner; (ii) express his/her opinion; and (iii) contest the adopted decision. Similarly, with regard to the use of AI in the procedural field, it is worth mentioning the significant comments by D Pavli, Partly dissenting opinion in *Einarsson and others v Iceland* App no 39757/15 (CEDU Judgment, second section, 4 September 2019): 'Emerging practice in the Council of Europe area is in line with this general approach. Thus, courts in at least two jurisdictions (the United Kingdom and Ireland) have approved in recent years the use of technology-assisted review, employing a form of artificial intelligence known as predictive coding, for the purposes of electronic disclosure in high-stakes civil litigation. The rationale would apply with equal force in criminal cases of comparable complexity. Again, the underlying premise for the use of such advanced technology is, of course, that both sides are granted the fullest possible access to begin with. And, secondly, that criminal-law frameworks and investigative practices are organised in such a way as to facilitate adequate access for the defense at the appropriate (that is, early) stage of proceedings.'

[40] As stated in the Circular of the Italian Ministry of Health of 25 March 2020 – '[Updating of the organizational guidelines for hospital and territorial services during the COVID-19 emergency]', considering that the systemic use of the emerging technologies (data analytics, artificial intelligence)

In the framework of the AI–health protection relationship, there is vital interest in exploring any abstractly useful proposal to support the policies aimed at containing the spread of the pandemic. Policies regarding the use of the technology for purposes of monitoring and prevention of infections should be precisely delineated.

The health, social and economic emergency related to the recent and rapid large-scale spread of the coronavirus obliges policymakers and those responsible for institutions and the care of people to verify the effectiveness and sustainability of the measures that can be adopted for the eradication of the disease and to overcome its many negative effects in citizens' lives.

Some rightly point out that if the aim is to decisively take a path back to normality, it seems impossible to disregard the use of tracing systems that monitor movements and personal contacts, mainly by using specific apps that can be installed on users' or patients' smartphones. Indeed, it seems impossible to renounce mechanisms that allow concerned people to be informed about the presence of people who have tested positive or that facilitate the identification of asymptomatic people who should be subjected to quarantine.

In the debate, there is also strong defence of the following scheme. Citizens going outside should know if there are virus-positive individuals among those with whom they have been in contact; once at home, they should know if they, in turn, have been infected; if they have symptoms but are not able to go to a hospital or first aid facilities because of restrictions by authorities, they should receive prompt and adequate diagnoses and treatment care by the operators who receive their phone requests.[41]

Given these circumstances, apps can complement the other measures – swabs and protective devices (gloves, masks, etc) – capable of containing the spread of the virus and limiting its reproduction capacity.

The identification of infected individuals, their isolation and retrospectively reconstructing their interpersonal contacts should be considered as the basic steps in the operational chain.

and of telemedicine (teleconsultation, telecare) in other countries in the world has already proven to give very effective contributions to monitoring of and containing the infections from coronavirus SARS-CoV-2, it is appropriate to select the technological solutions of telecare for home-based patients (both for COVID-19-related diseases and for other diseases, including chronic ones), the best technologies and solutions for continuous tracing, alerting and prompt control of the level of exposure of people to the risk and, subsequently, of the epidemic's evolution across the territory. This is to allow the Ministry of Health and the Istituto Superiore di Sanità, in collaboration with the World Health Organization, to evaluate the best digital solutions available with respect to telemedicine and home-based care apps, and technology-based tools and strategies for the 'active' monitoring of the infection risk, and to coordinate at the national level the adoption and use of these technological solutions in order to improve the results in terms of monitoring and contrast of the spread of COVID-19.

[41] In the list of the recommendations contained in the Circular of the Italian Ministry of Health of 27 March 2020 for the management of immunosuppressed patients during the COVID-19 emergency, it should be pointed out in particular the following: (g) activate, whenever possible, telemedicine examinations, except for clinic and/or treatment needs, to prevent as much as possible the access to hospital first aid facilities.

From the perspective of safeguarding of human fundamental rights, which have to be balanced with the effectiveness of the instrument adopted, it is necessary to be aware that to identify the legal basis legitimising the use of an app, mandatory or voluntary, the app's specific functionality should be considered as a dependent variable.

In this regard, the potential of an app is very broad, as demonstrated by experience: mass screening; the provision to users of useful telephone numbers or updated information and insights about the epidemic's trend; the regular detection and control of clinical parameters; geolocalisation; remote medical support; remote monitoring of virus-positive and/or isolated patients; the transmission of alerts or warnings to individuals who present suspicious symptoms or who have been in contact with infected patients; verifications of compliance with the measures of social distancing and the obligation to stay at home; and the transmission of information to police forces in order to facilitate the execution by them of institutional purposes. All these objectives are abstractly compatible with the multifunction purposes of an app designed for contact tracing. And, in all likelihood, the app could perform a variety of other functions.

The app is one of the significant examples of devices specifically intended for tracing health and pharmaceutical products, able to dialogue with IT company systems and to interface with clinical records, to drive the dynamics of home-based care or guide the correct administration of drugs and treatments, to perform predictive analyses about patients' health status or even to rationalise the expenditure processes for the supply and storage of materials purchased.

In its evolution, the multilevel legal order has been including the development of protections in the case of the processing of health data with the use of computer technologies. The purpose is to make the processing of sensitive data lawful.

Among others, examples are provided by the following rules:

- In Recitals 6 and 7 of the GDPR, it is respectively underlined that 'Rapid technological developments and globalisation have brought new challenges for the protection of personal data' and the technological developments 'require a strong and more coherent data protection framework in the Union, backed by strong enforcement, given the importance of creating the trust that will allow the digital economy to develop across the internal market. Natural persons should have control of their own personal data. Legal and practical certainty for natural persons, economic operators and public authorities should be enhanced'; and
- Article 35, paragraph 1 of the same EU Regulation states that where the data processing uses new technologies likely to produce a high risk to the maintenance of rights and freedoms of individuals, there should be an assessment of the impact of the same processing on the protection of personal data, with the arrangements described in detail in the following paragraph (paragraph 2) of the same Article and in line with Article 32 regarding the responsibilities borne by the controller (or the processor, if delegated by the latter) in order to

set up the most suitable and appropriate technical and organisational measures (in the case of telemedicine, for example, the major issue is to ensure the safety of the health information that is processed).

At the national level, many legal orders have established similar and very significant rules. The Italian privacy code, for example, provides that: (i) the measure to safeguard the processing of health, genetic and biometric data must take account of the scientific and technological developments in the sector addressed by the same measures; (ii) the principles of the continuous application of protection measures to data regarding health must always be expressly safeguarded; (iii) the data subject's consent is still required for the processing operations related to the use of medical apps through which autonomous controllers collect personal data, as well as health data, for purposes other than telemedicine or when, regardless of the purpose of the application, the data subject's information can be accessed by subjects other than the health professionals or other individuals bound to professional secrecy; and (iv) sensitive data that could reveal a person's health status can be processed only through organisational arrangements that make the data subject not identifiable, such as encoding or encryption techniques.

As mentioned above, the legal basis for the lawfulness of the processing should consider the specific characteristics of the assessed device's purposes. The prediction of virus-positive cases and/or the prevention of infection outbreaks may require measures that limit personal freedoms for the benefit of public health.

Given the sensitivity of the matter and the legal and social effects of contact tracing through an app, it seems reasonable to affirm that the functional characteristics of the app be validated at its origin and controlled throughout its employment by the policymaker who provides or promotes its adoption and who subsequently must manage it, guiding its use by the masses responsibly.

The topic of health apps was addressed during the application of legislation prior to EU Regulation 2017/745 on medical devices, namely Directive 93/42/CEE. This earlier legislation concerned software embedded in a device or constituting a medical device regardless of the technological support used.

In general, in regulating a single application of AI, the assessment of the impact on privacy is crucial, so it is important to put the need for personal data protection at the centre of the human–science and freedom–technological progress relationships.

The specific informed consent as a tool can, however, prove to be a restriction that limits in a disproportional way the concrete benefits achievable by AI: the sharing and processing of a huge quantity of data – as shown in the example of precision medicine or scientific research based on the use of genetic data and samples stored in biobanks[42] – may generate considerable treatment benefits for

[42] See JE Lee, 'Artificial Intelligence in the Future Biobanking: Current Issues in the Biobank and Future Possibilities of Artificial Intelligence' (2018) 7(3) *Biomedical Journal of Scientific & Technical Research* 1.

people, provided that a rigid imposition of the voluntary scheme does not substantially frustrate its potential.[43]

If it does, then the consent required for the creation, inputting and updating of an electronic health record may not be vital in the case of apps like the ones at issue. In the case of electronic health records, the consent means accepting the purposes of a data processing that is likely to essentially affect the personal sphere of the consenting subject. In the case of apps for contact tracing, the debate is mainly about public health purposes. In this perspective, the legislative act may represent the lawfulness condition of the processing, especially if the collected data is processed in a basically anonymous and aggregated form, as well as if its confidentiality and integrity are preserved across the transmission procedure through the relative infrastructures.

Therefore, alternatives to the consent-centred perspective are not absent. Indeed, the ability to ensure the effective anonymity of data goes beyond the outreach of the GDPR (see Recital 26) and the urgent and absolute obligation of ensuring the maximum level of privacy. The enactment of a legal act authorising the data processing for public interest reasons in the field of public health (Articles 6, 9, paragraph 2(*i*), 23, paragraph 1(*e*) and Recitals 41, 46 and 50) is a sufficient justification for the processing.

Furthermore, the consent, in addition to being technically unnecessary, sometimes may also prove to be counterproductive:[44] suffice it to say that providing for its acquisition at all costs corresponds to the exercise of the rights under Article 7 GDPR, among which is the right to the withdrawal of the same consent, with the high probability of deleting the data previously collected and enhanced, which would have easily deducible detrimental effects at the expense of the planned public health purposes.

On the contrary, statutory coverage can prevent this type of effect to the extent that Article 9, paragraph 2(*i*) GDPR allows data retention by the manager, still without prejudice to the appropriate and specific measures to protect the data subject's rights and freedoms, particularly professional secrecy.

Nevertheless, it should be clear that if privacy consent is not necessary in cases such as the one at issue, the voluntary aspect seems unlikely to be disregarded in the overall architecture of a contact-tracing policy via smartphones; in fact, quite the contrary.

At this point, the above-mentioned legal basis for personal data processing is no longer relevant. What is relevant, upstream, is the legal basis of any obligation to participate in the mass screening. Such an obligation, from time to time and depending on the features of each app, can be detected in the constitutional

[43] See C Casonato, 'Artificial Intelligence and Constitutional Law: First Considerations' in DPCE (2019) special booklet, 108.

[44] See P Quinn, 'The Anonymization of Research Data – a Pyric Victory for Privacy that Should Not Be Pushed Too Hard by the EU Data Protection Framework?' (2017) 24 *European Journal of Health Law* 14.

provisions that legitimise mandatory health treatments and limits to personal freedom and to the freedom of movement, to stay and to meet people.

The assumed obligatory nature of joining the contact-tracing project might undermine its success anyway, given that the achievement of a minimum but high threshold of participants (for example, 70 or 80 per cent) seems essential for this purpose.

The difficulty of enforcing such an obligation, although formally justified and theoretically complemented by sanctions, would lead to the highly predictable circumstance that a project that has an inspiring rationale that is not accepted or shared by the target people may be easily obstructed. People may avoid downloading the app, switch off their mobile devices, deactivate their network connections, enable the aeroplane mode or simply not carry it. It is also not certain that all eligible individuals for the project would have a smartphone.

With reference to the effectiveness of the operation, the initial input should logically originate from the reporting of the doctor who, having correctly detected and interpreted the symptoms, shall be required to record the infection case in order to initiate the contact chain that allows identification of the areas with a potentially higher risk.

Therefore, the preferable and most successful approach seems to be encouraging the free and voluntary participation of the citizen in installing and using the app, perhaps by providing incentives for this purpose. Such incentives could include data anonymity and a guarantee of non-reidentification; excluding the processing of such data for secondary and different purposes, eg police controls; the assurance that the data will be deleted at the end of the programme; a commitment to respecting the privacy of the participant's family; the adoption of technologies compatible with data encryption (eg Bluetooth); the assurance that data will be stored in the user's device rather than in an external facility; the prior definition of actions to be taken in the case of data breach or of risk that data is unlawfully processed; the promise of appropriate privacy protection training of the staff that will use the concerned equipment; scientific evidence of the real effectiveness of the initiative from an epidemiological perspective; prohibition of the transfer of the owned data outside the European Union; renunciation of processing genetic data; and various material rewards (eg phone top-up, fiscal bonuses or other measures that do not breach the principles of equality, equal treatment and non-discrimination in the access to essential provisions and services or basic economic provisions).

It is not conceivable to reserve access to information channels or special treatment programmes only to those who join the app programme, or to provide swabs or protection devices only to the participants. It may be possible to allow the programme volunteers a higher freedom of movement and participation in public life – including the use of services that are not considered essential and are particularly prohibited because of the spread of the virus – precisely because of the tracing done by those managing the system.

Throughout this programme, only data strictly needed to fulfil the intended purposes will be collected, reducing as much as possible the risk of improper uses of, or possible external attacks on, a system that, in any transmission between its various users (patient, doctor, health facility, data manager), is able to make the app user's IP address unintelligible and, in any case, not associable to the user's personal details.

Focusing on the confidence element also means building trust regarding the fact that the public subject is responsible for the entire range of management, storage, ownership and responsibility reports of the processing of the data collected. This should be done upon an appropriate exploration of the different competencies of states and regions in this specific matter.

At the same time, a stable and balanced mix of personal freedoms and social aspects, of rights of individuals and the general duty of solidarity towards anyone, and of the individual and collective dimensions of the right to health protection, represents the most solid foundation for any effective emergency legislation.

Ultimately, if the aim is to promote an extensive public health programme inspired by noble prevention, diagnosis and care purposes, it is necessary to boost citizens' confidence that, by cooperating with the management of the emergency system, a civic duty is carried out, and personal and egoistic interests are served. Such a programme can be enhanced by fair incentives, and the risks of abuses and aggression should be curtailed.

The element of citizens' confidence in institutions remains the keystone of the system, as shown by other experiences (eg the electronic health record).[45] Otherwise, if based on an obligation to participate, the initiative would be unsuccessful and compromised, since there is no legal and especially practical basis for such an obligation.

In addition, confidence in the proposing authority could lead the patient to urge the connection and updating of the clinical record and electronic health record with COVID-19 information, or to request, through the inputting of the required data, a feature that provides local assistance, along with the assurance of self-distancing.

In conclusion, to defeat COVID-19, it is necessary to take a further step forward in the universe of potential offered by new technologies, expertly regulate the law–science relationship and take on responsible risk management.

In a context where the evolution of the epidemic and the setting up of treatments addressing the disease are unknown factors, the backward mapping of the contacts by those who have been infected is increasingly essential.

First, it is necessary to detail the functions that such a software must guarantee, taking into account three primary criteria for contact tracing: (i) who (detection of

[45] The experience gained in blockchain technologies also shows how important the element of trust is: if, in a public registry, a series of data are annotated with a high degree of transparency and in a non-modifiable form, the data processing is made safe and the trust of the participants in the validation process grows. In this way, blockchain technology ensures the security of digital transaction operations and the legal regulation reduces the level of risks in artificial intelligence.

the health status); (ii) where (geolocalisation); and (iii) with whom (relationships with others).

Actions intended to really mitigate and prevent the spread of infection cannot disregard the identification of potential risks, defining the most exposed areas and subjects (in terms of symptoms, pre-existing diseases, age and others) and aiming to provide indications about what behaviours to adopt (asking for a test, staying in self-isolation, etc).

Tracing the interrelations between individuals at risk, wherever they happen (on means of transport, in shops and retail establishments, companies and public places, etc), allows us to optimally define the sanitisation operations necessary and places to be made inaccessible.

The legal basis, however, depends on the type of app and the function that it develops.

The principle of self-determination can manifest in a number of multifaceted forms. On the one hand, there is the informed consent to the health treatment that facilitates the joint realisation of the patient's right to health protection and to personal freedom. On the other hand, the informed consent to personal data processing does not necessarily correspond to the purpose of the data subject's health protection, since it might be used for other objectives.

The case of an app to be used for contact tracing does not properly identify the first type of consent, since the issue does not concern coercive health treatments in the strict sense. At most, it concerns a call for detection of parameters and data that are useful for the reconstruction of the clinical status for any voluntary treatment measures aimed at the solution of the health problem.

The same applies to the second type of consent (the privacy consent), which can be terminated upon the assurance that data is managed so that anonymity is ensured and/or on the basis of a legislative act that, inspired by the fulfilment of primary public health purposes, provides measures for the suitable protection of citizens' fundamental rights.

A third type of consent is highly relevant, or better yet, an expression of willingness should be encouraged through incentives for boosting awareness that participation in the prevention and contrast programme is right, effective and guaranteed to keep the basic principles of our legal order.

Respect of the intangible legal principles means following the paths of equality, proportionality, temporariness, recognition of protection against any abuse, identity safeguards, privacy and recognising the human being's dignity.

In order for the monitoring system results to be acceptable to the public, it is necessary, among others, to screen and make the flow of the collected data impermeable to the public security authority, above all police forces.

A software credibly aimed at supporting the anticipation of the end or weakening of restrictions, thanks to the pandemic containment measures, is not particularly suitable for purposes having a high impact on the personal freedom that would require legal restraints (ie other and more guaranteed instruments, like the reasoned acts of the judicial authority).

The processing of personal data belonging to particular categories according to the definitions in Article 9 GDPR per se gives rise to problems of compatibility with the constitutional framework; in view of this, further uses for the purposes of the police, for the investigations of crimes or for general responsibilities are absolutely not recommended, just because they are of doubtful constitutionality.

At the same time, incentives for the downloading of the app are admissible upon compliance with the standards of reasonableness and proportionality. Therefore, basically, a reasonable and constitutionally lawful incentive cannot have the exercise of the right to freedom as a counterpart.

A correct scaling of the incentives strengthens the voluntary basis and the personalist principle by providing a valid alternative for the hard path of mandatory participation in the tracing programme.

A radical renouncement of fundamental freedoms is not a viable objective, and it should not be sacrificed in the name of a massive assessment of individuals' infection risk.

The humanisation of processes is undoubtedly required: it is necessary to convey to the citizens the message that on the other side of the device there is not merely an algorithmic calculation, but a doctor or another health operator in person who is available for dialogue and personal support in their case; at the same time, citizens must be ensured that their sensitive data will be capable of being identified again only if they test positive for the virus. Unnecessary information (subjective limits) or information no longer required over time (time limits) should be deleted. In any case, care should be taken to prevent individuals other than the health professionals taking care of a patient's clinical path from knowing the patient's identity (subjective limits).

# 16

# Gene Editing e-Machine Learning: The International and EU Legal Framework

NADINA FOGGETTI

## I. Introduction

Gene editing may be used in order to modify an embryo or a gamete to generate a healthy individual. In particular, CRISPR-Cas9 is a technique that was developed to verify the possibility to prevent in the future some genetic hereditary diseases.[1] In this specific context, gene editing issues will be analysed in the field of data protection, human rights, bioethics and bioinformatics.

Gene editing activity often requires the use of machine learning techniques in order to guarantee the most accurate result possible.[2] Machine learning technologies to perform algorithm training use genomic data databases, also exploiting the potential of cloud technology. The machine learning activity can use databases containing real genomic data. A group of researchers in China announced the birth of children with genomes edited by CRISPR-Cas9 technology, opening an ethical-legal debate on the problems connected with the protection of genomic identity and legitimacy in the light of the international law of the mentioned techniques.

## II. Legal Framework Concerning Gene Editing in International Law

The development of new genome editing technologies, such as CRISPR-Cas9, has provoked an important reaction in particular within the scientific community. Gene modification methods are not new, but have played an essential role

[1] A Plaza Reyes and F Lanner, 'Towards a CRISPR View of Early Human Development: Applications, Limitations and Ethical Concerns of Genome Editing in Human Embryos' (2017) 144 *Development* 3, doi:10.1242/dev.139683.

[2] www.weareworldquant.com/en/thought-leadership/machine-learning-meets-genome-editing/.

in biomedical research for several decades. The new genome editing technologies have made possible simple and precise modifications in a wide variety of species. For this reason, gene editing at the regional level has been analysed by the Council of Europe, and in particular by the Council of Europe's Committee on Bioethics (DH-BIO).

The Convention on Human Rights and Biomedicine (ETS No 164, 1997), hereinafter referred to as the Oviedo Convention, is the only international legally binding instrument addressing human rights in the biomedical field. The Oviedo Convention represents the outcome of an in-depth discussion at European level on developments in the biomedical field, in particular in the field of genetics. This work was guided by the acknowledgement of the positive perspectives of genetic modification with the development of knowledge of the human genome; but also by the greater possibility to intervene in and control the genetic characteristics of human beings, raising concern about possible misuse and abuses, in particular the intentional modification of the human genome to produce individuals or groups endowed with particular characteristics and required qualities. Article 13 of the Oviedo Convention addresses these concerns about genetic enhancement, or germline genetic engineering, by limiting the purposes of any intervention on the human genome, including in the field of research, to prevention, diagnosis or therapy. Furthermore, it prohibits any intervention with the aim of introducing a modification in the genome of any descendants. These expectations and concerns both remain very relevant today with regard to the new genome editing technologies.

The DH-BIO reiterated the relevance of the principles enshrined in the Oviedo Convention and the need to reflect on the ethical and legal implications deriving from the implementation of the new approaches (DH-BIO/INF (2015) Final).[3] The DH-BIO is convinced that the Oviedo Convention provides principles that can be used as a reference for the debate called for on an international level, on the fundamental questions raised by these recent technological developments, and recalls that the need for such debates was foreseen by the Convention in its Article 28. As part of its mandate, the DH-BIO examines the ethical and legal challenges raised by the emerging genome editing technologies in the light of the principles laid down in the Oviedo Convention.

The International Summit on Human Gene Editing in 2015 drafted a declaration excluding the possibility of applying DNA modifications to embryos intended for implantation.[4] Following the second International Summit on Human Genome Editing, in 2018, and the announcement of the birth of two babies in China

[3] Committee of Bioethics (DH-BIO) 8th meeting, 1–4 December 2015, Strasbourg, 'Statement on Genome Editing Technologies', https://rm.coe.int/168049034a.

[4] Meeting in Brief of the Committee on Science, Technology and Law Policy and Global Affairs, December 1–3, 2015, 'International Summit on Human Gene Editing: A Global Discussion', https://www.ncbi.nlm.nih.gov/books/NBK343651/.

following genome intervention, the DH-BIO considered it important to reiterate its statement on genome editing technologies adopted during its eighth plenary meeting (1–4 December 2015). The second International Summit released a press release entitled 'Ethics and Human Rights Must Guide Any Use of Genome Editing Technologies in Human Beings'.[5] According to this statement by the Council of Europe Committee on Bioethics, modification methods are not new but have for several decades been playing an essential role in biomedical research. New genome editing technologies such as CRISPR-Cas9 have made possible simple and precise modifications in a wide variety of species. For this reason, there is strong support from the DH-BIO for better understanding of the causes of diseases and their future treatment, and these technologies have considerable potential for research in this field and to improve human health. Moreover, the DH-BIO highlights that the application of genome editing technologies to human gametes or embryos raises many ethical, social and safety issues, particularly from any modification of the human genome that could be passed on to future generations, and it considers that these expectations and concerns 'remain very relevant today with regard to those new genome editing technologies. Addressing these issues is the objective of the work carried out by the DH-BIO.'

The DH-BIO, in the definition of its terms of references for 2020–2021 (DH-BIO/INF (2019) 12),[6] has introduced, in the context of priority in the protection of human rights, the task of examining the ethical and legal issues raised by development in genome editing technologies in relation to Article 13 of the Oviedo Convention.

In 2010, the Steering Committee on Bioethics of the Council of Europe (CDBI) drafted a document concerning pre-implantation diagnosis in order to provide information on the new diagnostic technique, which had legal and ethical implications in several European Countries.[7] Article 13 of the Oviedo Convention states that 'An intervention seeking to modify the human genome may only be undertaken for preventive, diagnostic or therapeutic purposes and only if its aim is not to introduce any modification in the genome of any descendants'.

The application of gene editing to germinal cellules is prohibited in the USA because there is a specific prohibition introduced by Food and Drug Administration to use public funds in order to finance studies in which 'a human embryo is deliberately created or modified to take on a heritable genetic modification'. According to Italian law no 40 of 2014, 'any form of eugenic selection of embryos and simulations or interventions aimed at altering the genetic heritage of the embryo or gamete' is also forbidden. The DH-BIO reiterated the relevance of the principles

[5] DH-BIO, 'Ethics and Human Rights Must Guide Any Use of Genome Editing Technologies in Human Beings' (DC 169(2018)).

[6] DH-BIO, 'Terms of Reference of the DH-BIO for 2020–2021' (DH-BIO/INF (2019) 2), https://rm.coe.int/inf-2019-12-tor-dhbio-20-21-e/16809c82ce.

[7] Steering Committee on Bioethics of the Council of Europe, 'Background Document on Preimplantation and Prenatal Genetic Testing: Clinical Situation, Legal Situation' (CDBI/INF (2010)).

enshrined in the Oviedo Convention and the need to reflect on the ethical and legal implications arising from the implementation of new approaches.

The balance between the need to preserve the genetic heritage of the embryo or the gamete and the protection of the right to health that requires medical and genetic editing has been analysed in the light of international law by the European Court of Human Rights (ECtHR). The case law of the ECtHR states that EU Member States are afforded a wide margin of appreciation in this area, in the absence of a common international legal framework in this field. In App no 54270/10, the judgment of Costa and Pavan v Italy of 28 August 2012, the ECtHR ruled that, by forbidding the recourse of couples with a genetic defect to medically assisted procreation (MAP) and pre-implantation genetic diagnosis (PGD), whilst simultaneously permitting abortion in cases where the foetus is suffering from such an illness, Italy had, due to this alleged inconsistency, violated Article 8 of the Oviedo Convention – which guarantees the right to respect of private and family life.[8] The Italian Government raised concern over the risks of recognising the right to a 'healthy child', but the Court, in admitting that the 'desire' of couples carrying a genetic illness to resort to MAP and PGD constituted a right under Article 8 of the Convention, excluded the consideration of this perspective. This case further demonstrates the increasing willingness of the ECtHR to limit the margin of appreciation of the states in this field, in other words, the space to manoeuvre that the Strasbourg organs are willing to grant national authorities in fulfilling their obligations under the European Convention on Human Rights, including in the most ethically controversial areas. The ECtHR jurisprudence affirmed the absence of a right to have a 'healthy child'. Moreover, this Court decision represents an important step in the recognition of a right to a genetically healthy child – that is to say, to eugenics: the Court recognises the right to bring into the world a child who is not affected by the illness that they carry.

This decision of the ECtHR is different from the consolidate jurisprudence of the same court. In particular, in the *Dickson v United Kingdom*, the ECtHR recognised neither a right to MAP nor a positive obligation to assure access to this biotechnology.[9]

The *Costa and Pavan v Italy* decision represents the first step to the affirmation of the right to eugenics practices. This judgment in fact illustrates the ECtHR's increasing tendency to enlarge the scope of Article 8 of the Oviedo Convention. In this perspective, Article 8 of the European Convention on Human Rights (ECHR) aims to guarantee the individual's personal autonomy, the right to 'personal development' or even its right to auto-determination. The consequence of this judgment is the extension of Article 8 ECHR, and it should be analysed in the light of the extraordinary development of biotechnologies.[10]

[8] *Costa and Pavan v Italy* App no 54270/10 (ECtHR, 28 August 2012).

[9] *Dickson v United Kingdom* App no 44362/04 (ECtHR, 4 December 2007).

[10] M Castellaneta, 'Fecondazione, la norma europea prevale su quella italiana' [2012] *Il sole 24 ore* 1.

## III. Legal Framework at EU Law Level

The legal framework for gene editing at the EU level is based on Directive 2004/23/EU,[11] which aims to define standards of quality and safety, in order to ensure a high level of protection of human health. The scope of this Directive is to provide harmonisation of national laws in this matter. In the application of Article 7, the Directive should apply to tissues and cells, including reproductive cells, foetal tissues and cells, and embryonic and adult stem cells. The same Directive should not interfere with decisions made by Member States concerning the use or non-use of any specific type of human cell, including embryonic cells. The EU legislation aims to protect the margin of appreciation of Member States; moreover, it requires the application of all provisions necessary to protect public health, given the specific risks of these cells based on the scientific knowledge of their particular nature, and to guarantee the respect of fundamental rights. The EU Directive is compliant with the Charter of Fundamental Rights of the European Union and with the international legal framework conserving the protection of human rights and dignity of the human being with regard to the application of biology and medicine, in particular the Oviedo Convention.

Within the EU legal framework, it is necessary to also include Directive 2001/20/CE[12] and Regulation no 536/2014.[13] These EU legal acts provide that no gene therapy trials may be carried out which results in modification of the subject's germline genetic identity.

In this context, the European Commission has provided that gene editing technologies like CRISPR could, in principle, be used in several areas of healthcare, such as in vitro fertilisation, and for manufacturing medicinal products offering cures or treatments for patients affected by life-threatening diseases. The Commission defines that it is thus important to support the development of these products while protecting citizens, and that modification of the subject's germline genetic identity are prohibited under the EU clinical trial legislation.[14] The EU Commission moreover suggests that the use of such techniques for in vitro fertilisation would be a national decision and that, were a Member State to allow such a technique, it would need to comply with the EU requirements on safety and quality as laid down in Directive 2004/23/EC.

[11] Directive 2004/23/EC of the EU Parliament and of the Council of 31 March 2004, on setting standards of quality and safety for the donation, procurement, testing, processing, preservation, storage and distribution of human tissues and cells [2004] OJ L102/48–57.

[12] Directive 2001/20/EC of the European Parliament and the Council of 4 April 2001 on the approximation of the laws, regulation and administrative provision of the Member States relating to the implementation of good clinical practice in the conduct of clinical trials on medicinal products for human use [2001] OJ L121/34–44.

[13] Regulation EU 536/2014 of the European Parliament and of the Council of 16 April 2014 on clinical trials on medicinal products for human use, and repealing Directive 2001/20/EC [2014] OJ L158/1.

[14] Answer given by Mr Andriukaitis on behalf of the European Commission, 29 January 2019, EN P-006073/2018, https://www.europarl.europa.eu/doceo/document/P-8-2018-006073-ASW_EN.html.

In the field of the use of genetically modified organisms, the European Court of Justice (ECJ), in a judgment of 25 July 2018, decided that organisms obtained by the new technique of directed mutagenesis are genetically modified organisms[15] within the meaning of Directive 2001/18/EC, and that they are subject to the obligations laid down by the GMO Directive.[16] The objective of this Directive is to approximate the laws, regulations and administrative provision of the Member States and to protect human health and the environment when carrying out the deliberate release into the environment of a genetically modified organism for any purpose other than placing it on the market within the EU Community. It is important to note that the Directive's definition of 'genetically modified organisms' does not include human beings.

The GMO Directive and the ECJ decision invoke the application in this field of the precautionary principle in order to balance the use of gene editing techniques and the protection of human beings. As outlined by a statement of the Group of Chief Scientific Advisors of the European Commission, new techniques of directed mutagenesis include gene editing such as CRISPR-Cas9 methodologies. The legal status of the products of such technique is uncertain, because it is unclear whether they fall within the scope of the GMO Directive.[17]

## IV. The Protection of Genomic Data and the Right to Privacy

Gene editing requires the use of machine learning technology in order to guarantee a precise result. The machine learning activity uses databases containing real genomic data. It shows a high level of risk from the point of view of data protection. The use of these databases allows an ever-greater power of genetic profiling in the context of work and insurance, and may improve the risk of discrimination based on the genetic characteristics.

A first issue that it is necessary to analyse relates to the right to privacy. Data protection principles and rules can be found at the international level in several international conventions, such as in Article 8 of the European Convention on Human Rights and Fundamental Freedoms[18] and Article 17 of the International

[15] Judgment of Court of Justice of 25 July 2018, Case C-528/16 *Confédération paysanne contre Premier minister* EU:C:2018:583.

[16] Directive 2001/18/EC of the European Parliament and of the Council of 12 March 2001 on the deliberate release into the environment of genetically modified organism and repealing Council Directive 90/220/EEC [2001] OJ L106/1–39.

[17] Statement by the Group of Chief Scientific Advisor, 'A Scientific Perspective on the Regulatory Status of Products Derived from Gene Editing and the Implications for the GMO Directive', https://ec.europa.eu/info/sites/info/files/2018_11_gcsa_statement_gene_editing_1.pdf.

[18] European Convention on Human Rights and Fundamental Freedom, Rome, 4 November 1950, www.echr.coe.int/documents/convention_eng.pdf.

Covenant on Civil and Political Rights.[19] In the context of the Council of Europe, the major conventions codifying the principles of data protection are the Convention for the Protection of Individuals with regard to Automatic Processing of Personal Data[20] and the Convention on Human Rights and Biomedicine.[21] At the European Union level, the most important act is Regulation 2016/679.[22]

This Regulation introduces the specific protection of genetic data. In Whereas no 34, it establishes that

> Genetic data should be defined as personal data relating to the inherited or acquired genetic characteristics of a natural person which result from the analysis of a biological sample from the natural person in question, in particular chromosomal, deoxyribonucleic acid (DNA) or ribonucleic acid (RNDA) analysis, or from the analysis of another element enabling equivalent information to be obtained.

Article 4, paragraphs 13 and 14 defines genetic and biometric data. Moreover, EU Regulation 2016/679 introduces in Article 9 a specific rule for the same categories of data, including genetic and biometric data. The processing of particular categories of personal data is prohibited because of the risk of illicit use of this data. The prohibition of processing shall not apply if the cases are regulated by paragraph 2 of Article 9, in particular if the data subject has given explicit consent to the processing and if the principle of necessity applies with respect to the fulfilment of obligations or the exercise of specific rights, insofar as it is authorised by EU law and by the national law.

At the Council of Europe level, the notion of privacy does not have a unique and restrictive definition, because in ECtHR case law regarding Article 8 of the ECHR the term 'privacy' may include many aspects of physical and social identity. Among these, the name and any other means of personal identification are suitable to establish the connection of a person in a family group.[23] The ethnic identity is included in the term 'private life' or 'privacy'. Specifically, deoxyribonucleic acid (DNA) samples and DNA profiles are personal data, because they refer to identified or identifiable persons. There is no information more personal and private

[19] International Covenant on Civil and Political Rights, adopted and opened for signature, ratification and accession by General Assembly Resolution 2200A (XXI) of 16 December 1966, entry into force 23 March 1976, in accordance with Article 49, www.ohchr.org/en/professionalinterest/pages/ccpr.aspx.

[20] Convention of the Council of Europe for the Protection of Individuals with regard to Automatic Processing of Personal Data, Strasbourg, 28 January 1981, http://conventions.coe.int/Treaty/EN/Treaties/Html/108.htm.

[21] Convention of the Council of Europe for the Protection of Human Rights and Dignity of the Human Being with regard to the Application of Biology and Medicine: Convention on Human Rights and Biomedicine, Oviedo, 4 April 1997, http://conventions.coe.int/Treaty/EN/Treaties/Html/164.htm.

[22] EU Regulation 2016/679 of EU Parliament and Council, of 27 April 2016 on the protection of natural persons with regard to the processing of personal data on the free movement of such data, and repealing Directive 95/46/EC [2019] OJ L119/1–88.

[23] *Unal Tekeli c Turchia* App no 29865/96 (EctHR, 16 November 2004).

than an individual's genetic information. DNA is the information that defines who we are as individuals both physically and mentally; it is the building block of life.[24]

Once this genetic information becomes available to the mass public, there is a great likelihood that employers, the government and insurance companies will be able to gain access to an individual's genetic code. With access to an individual's genetic information, companies may begin to discriminate against individuals predisposed to develop cancer or another disease. Insurance companies may be able to deny individuals coverage simply because they know that a certain individual has the possibility of developing a genetic disease.[25]

By comparing these findings, there is an effective risk of discrimination with regard to ethnic groups. It is possible to identify a specific form of discrimination, that is based on genetic and ethnic characteristics. The distribution of genetic polymorphisms, in fact, may vary from one group to another, and employers or insurance companies could discriminate groups with increased susceptibility to pathogens. For this reason, if we limit the analysis of the legal issues related to privacy, we cannot provide a concrete answer to the problem. The effective protection of genetic data may be considered a key element in the contest between protection of the right to health and the principle of equality and non-discrimination. The effectiveness of principles stated in international and European law is related to the national provisions concerning the right to privacy.[26]

In the USA, several cases have occurred in which persons have not given their consent for a genetic test in order to prevent violation of their right to privacy. In this case, the right to health has been compromised.[27]

[24] WS Klug, MR Cummings, CA Spencer, A Palladino and D Killian, *Essentials of Genetics*, 10th edn (London, Pearson, 2019). Cells are the fundamental units of living organisms. Within cells are nuclei, which serve as the 'life force' of the cells. The nucleus contains the genetic material in eukaryotic organisms, organisms which have true nuclei and membranous organelles. In prokaryotes and viruses, organisms which lack true nuclei, their genetic information is stored in a nucleoid region or in their protein coat of their cell membrane. DNA and RNA are the nucleic acids found in an organism's cells. DNA serves as the molecule that stores genetic material. A molecule of DNA is organised into units called genes. Genes are the functional units of heredity, composed of a linear array of nucleotides, which are the building blocks of DNA and RNA. Genes are organised into chromosomes, and the chromosomes serve as the vehicle through which genetic information is transmitted. Within a person's cell is a nucleus, the nucleus houses the DNA molecule, DNA is the building block of genes, the genes make up chromosomes, and the chromosomes serve as the transmitter of genetic information. Therefore, DNA serves as the structural building blocks, which define an organism's life. Genetic information 'directs cellular function, determines an organisms external appearance, and serves as the link between generations in every species'. Art 11 of the Oviedo convention, prohibits any form of discrimination.

[25] DL Mclochlin, 'Whose Genetic Information Is It Anyway? A Legal Analysis of the Effects that Mapping the Human Genome Will Have on Privacy Rights and Genetic Discrimination' [2001] *Marshall Journal of Computer & Information Law* 610.

[26] M Hyun-Myung Tan, 'Advancing Civil Rights, the Next Generation: The Genetic Information Non-discrimination Act of 2008 and Beyond' (2009) 19 *Health Matrix: The Journal of Law-Medicine* 63; MI Torres Cazorla, 'Legislación interna española y biomedicina: una aproximación a los recientes avances experimentados respecto al derecho a ser/no ser informado' in JM Sanchez Patron (ed), *Bioderecho internacional y europeo. Desafíos actuales* (Valencia, Editorial Tirant Lo Blanch, 2014).

[27] Working Group Concerning the Protection of Genetic Data of 17 March 2004, n 12178/03/IT WP 91, http://ec.europa.eu/justice/policies/privacy/docs/wpdocs/2004/wp91_it.pdf.

At the regulatory level, the situation across the EU appears to be uneven. Indeed, while some Member States have explicitly listed genetic data as sensitive data in their data protection law, with all the safeguards and restrictions associated, in most Member States the issue of the processing of genetic data is not as such regulated by specific legislation.[28]

A central issue that must be examined is the principle of non-discrimination based on genetic characteristics. In the context of the established framework of the prohibition of discrimination, a fundamental issue concerns the discriminatory potential that could result from improper use of genetic information.

## V. Gene Editing and the Prohibition of Discrimination

The genetic characteristics are related to the health of a person, even in the absence of an actual pathology or symptomology. The real potentiality of genetic tests resides in their scope. Genetic tests generally have not only a diagnostic scope, but also predictive purposes.[29] Genetic tests may underline a specific predisposition to develop certain diseases, but they do not reveal certainty. It is common to use genetic tests in order to achieve different ends, for example for a socioeconomic purpose. The improper use of genetic tests may in many cases cause discrimination based not on the actual possibility of contracting a disease, but on the mere probability of developing a pathology.[30]

The first act in this sector is the Resolution of European Parliament of 16 March 1989 on 'The Ethical and Legal Problems of Genetic Engineering'.[31] Subsequent acts are the European Parliament Resolution on 'The Protection of Human Rights and Dignity of the Human Being with regard to the Application of Biology and Medicine', adopted on 20 September 1996, and the European Parliament Resolution on 'Respect for Human Rights in the European Union', adopted on 16 March 2000.

In this field, the most important act that establishes the principle of non-discrimination for genetic characteristics is Article 21 of the Charter of Fundamental Rights of European Union of 2000, which states that

> Any discrimination based on any ground such as sex, race, colour, ethnic or social origin, genetic features, language, religion or belief, political or any other opinion,

[28] BA Sokhansanj, 'Beyond Protecting Genetic Privacy: Understanding Genetic Discrimination through Its Disparate Impact on Racial Minorities [2012] *Columbia Journal of Race and Law* 279.

[29] PR Billings, 'Discrimination as a Consequence of Genetic Testing' [1992] *American Journal of Human Genetics* 476.

[30] JA Robertson, 'Privacy Issues in Second Stage Genomics' (1999) 40 *Jurimetrics Journal* 59; LB Andrews and AS Jaeger, 'Confidentiality of Genetic Information in the Workplace' [1991] *American Journal Law and Medicine* 175; LO Gostin and JGJ Hodge, 'Genetic Discrimination: The Use of Genetically Based Diagnostic and Prognostic Tests by Employers and Insurers' [1991] *American Journal Law and Medicine* 109.

[31] Resolution of European Parliament of 16 March 1989 on 'The Ethical and Legal Problems of Genetic Engineering, www.codex.vr.se/texts/EP-genetic.html.

> membership of a national minority, property, birth, disability, age or sexual orientation shall be prohibited.[32]

After the entry into force of the Lisbon Treaty, this principle is compulsory because the Charter has the same authority as the Treaties of the EU.

At the Council of Europe level, the prohibition of discrimination on genetic bases is established in Article 11 of the Oviedo Convention. Article 11 states that 'any form of discrimination against a person on grounds of his or her genetic heritage is prohibited'. The content of Article 11 is not clear, and offers only partial protection against the discriminatory use of genetic information by insurance companies and employers. In the Explanatory Report, there are some indications regarding the concept of 'discrimination', but there is no definition of 'genetic heritage'.[33]

The principle of non-discrimination, as stated in Article 14 of the ECHR, is enriched with a new hypothesis of discrimination.[34] It is necessary to evaluate the scope of the prohibition of this discrimination also in the light of the ECtHR case law concerning Article 14.[35] The discrimination based on the genetic heritage regards the situation of people who have been denied equal opportunity on the basis of an alleged risk that has not yet occurred.[36] These persons are not yet ill, so in this regard are equal to all others. A difference, however, may arise in the future due to hereditary factors. The most part of the doctrine qualifies the aforementioned conduct in the context of the prohibition of discrimination.[37] But there is a part of the doctrine that affirms the application of the data protection law and principles.[38] On the basis of the last interpretation, the protection against the

[32] Charter of Fundamentals Rights of the European Union in Official Journal of the European Community [2000] OJ C364/01, www.europarl.europa.eu/charter/pdf/text_en.pdf.

[33] HDC Roscam Abbing, 'The Convention on Human Rights and Biomedicine. An Appraisal of the Council of Europe Convention' [1998] *European Journal Health Law* 377.

[34] E Draper, 'The Screening of America: The Social and Legal Framework of Employers' Use of Genetic Information' [1999] *Berkeley Journal of Employment & Labor Law* 286; DM Studdert, 'Direct Contracts, Data Sharing and Employee Risk Selection: New Stakes for Patient Privacy in Tomorrow's Health Insurance Markets' [1999] *American Journal Law and Medicine* 233; MA Pagnattaro, 'Genetic Discrimination and the Workplace: Employee's Right to Privacy v Employer's Need to Know' [2001] *American Business Law Journal* 139; KA Steinforth, 'Bringing Your DNA to Work: Employers' Use of Genetic Testing under the Americans with Disabilities Act' [2001] *Arizona Law Review* 965; PT Kim, 'Genetic Discrimination, Genetic Privacy: Rethinking Employee Protections for a Brave New Workplace' [2002] *NW University Law Review* 1497; PA Roche, 'The Genetic Revolution at Work: Legislative Efforts to Protect Employees' [2002] *American Journal Law and Medicine* 271; NJ King, S Pillay and GA Lasprogata, 'Workplace Privacy and Discrimination Issues Related to Genetic Data: A Comparative Law Study of the European Union and the United States' [2006] *American Business Law Journal* 79.

[35] M De Salvia, *Compendium Della Cedu* (Naples, Editoriale Scientifica,1998).

[36] A Santosuosso and A Tamburini (eds), *Malati di Rischio. Implicazioni Etiche, Legali e Psico-Sociali dei Test Genetici in Oncologia* (Milan, Masson, 1999).

[37] MA Hall and SS Rich, 'Laws Restricting Health Insures' Use of Genetic Information: Impact on Genetic Discrimination' [2000] *American Journal of Human Genetics* 293.

[38] A Rogers and D Durand de Bousinger, *Une Bioéthique Pour L'europe* (Strasbourg, Conseil d'Europe, 1995); F Francioni, *Biotechnologies and International Human Rights* (Oxford, Hart Publishing, 2007).

genetic discrimination may be founded on the protection against the unauthorised use of data.[39] Moreover, Article 10 of the Oviedo Convention introduces the right to protect privacy regarding the health information. This article does not recall the principles stated in Article 11, nor does it suggest a link between Article 10 and Article 11.

The most significant risks related to the use of genetic information concern possible violation by private companies.[40] The Oviedo Convention regulates the relationship between persons and states (vertical effect). Paragraph 25 of the Explanatory Report explains that Article 11 'is not intended to impose a general positive obligation on the Parties to take measures to prevent or remedy all instances of discrimination in relations between private persons'. States have the faculty to introduce legislative measures concerning genetic discrimination in the private context, but there are no specific obligations in this field. Hence, Article 11 poses several issues regarding the scope of the principle of non-discrimination.

A first consequence is that the Oviedo Convention does not introduce the obligation for Member States to protect individuals against genetic discrimination. This principle is not applicable in the relations between private persons. For this reason, it is not applicable in the case of genetic discrimination in the private sector. Article 11 does not provide any protection against the unlawful use of genetic data in the workplace or in an insurance context. In this case, there will be an additional form of discrimination based of the area in which the genetic discrimination occurs: public or private. In the case of public discrimination, it is possible to apply Article 11 of the Convention; on the contrary, in discrimination concerning the private sector, the same article is not applicable. The Explanatory Report that completes the Convention defines the concept of 'discrimination', but it does not clarify the meaning of genetic discrimination.

Article 12 of the Oviedo Convention states that the tests which are predictive of genetic diseases or which serve either to identify the subject's predisposition as a carrier of a gene responsible for a disease or to detect a genetic predisposition or susceptibility for a disease may be performed only for health purposes or for scientific research linked to health purposes, and subject to appropriate genetic counselling. These are, in fact, the principles that must be respected in genetic research. The health purpose is also needed for scientific research, as too is genetic counselling. It is necessary, moreover, to respect the principle of proportionality (between the scope and the measure adopted).[41] One of the risks

[39] IR Pavone, *La Convenzione Europea Sulla Biomedicina* (Milan, Giuffrè, 2009).

[40] C Campiglio, 'Il Principio Di Non Discriminazione Genetica Nella Recente Prassi Internazionale' [2008] *Diritti Umani e Diritto Internazionale* 513; IR Pavone, 'Diritti Dell'uomo e Genetica' in *Enciclopedia Giuridica* (Milan, Treccani, 2007).

[41] L Lattanzi, *Il trattamento dei dati genetici, in Genetica e medicina predittiva: verso un nuovo modello di medicina*? (Milan, Giuffrè, 2000) 280–95; J Motoc, 'The International Law of Genetic Discrimination: The Power of Never Again' in T Murphy (ed), *New Technologies and Human Rights* (Oxford, Oxford University Press, 2009).

associated with genetic analysis related to bioinformatics and the human genome project is the danger of stigmatisation of populations and ethnic groups or parents with certain types of genes or genetic risks. The concept of stigma precedes and accompanies that of discrimination.

## VI. The Principle of Non-stigmatisation

Often the genetic characteristics identified through genetic tests conducted as part of the human genome project and in the context of bioinformatics do not concern particular individuals, but an ethnic group. In this regard, we pass from the protection of an individual right to the need to protect the rights of an ethnic group. Non-discrimination, non-stigmatisation and equality are fundamental human rights principles and components of the right to health. Article 2 of the Universal Declaration of Human Rights states that everyone 'is entitled to all the rights and freedoms set forth in this Declaration, without distinction of any kind, such as race, colour, sex, language, religion, political or other opinion, national or social origin, property, birth or other status'. Before the Oviedo Convention, the Committee of the Council of Europe had instructed the CDBI to develop a Protocol with the aim to taking into account questions relating to the use and protection of the results of predictive genetic tests for purposes other than health or scientific research linked to health. In 1997, the Working Party on Human Genetics submitted the first report, and then in 2003 the first draft of the Protocol was elaborated.[42] In Article 4, the Protocol established the principle of non-discrimination. First in 2004 and then in 2006, the Committee limited the scope of the Protocol, and excluded applications of predictive testing with labour or assurance aims. The final version of the Protocol contains in Article 4 the principle of 'Non-discrimination and non-stigmatisation'. It states also that 'appropriate measures shall be taken in order to prevent stigmatisation of persons or groups in relation to genetic characteristics'.

Also, the UNESCO International Declaration on Human Genetic Data of 2003 clarifies in Article 7 that every effort should be made to ensure that human genetic data and human proteomic data are not used for purposes that discriminate in a way that is intended to infringe, or has the effect of infringing, the human rights, fundamental freedoms or human dignity of an individual, or for purposes that lead to the stigmatisation of an individual, a family, a group or communities.[43] In this

[42] Steering Committee on Bioethics (CDBI) Working Party on Human Genetics (CDBI-CO-GT4), Strasbourg, 27 October 1997, DIR/JUR (97) 13 Bis, www.coe.int/t/dg3/healthbioethic/activities/07_human_genetics_en/DIR-JUR(97)13Genetics.pdf.

[43] The International Declaration on Human Genetic Data was adopted unanimously and by acclamation at UNESCO's 32nd General Conference on 16 October 2003, www.unesco.org/new/en/social-and-human-sciences/themes/bioethics/human-genetic-data/. This Declaration and the Universal Declaration on the Human Genome and Human Rights are the only international points of reference in the field of bioethics.

regard, appropriate attention should be paid to the findings of population-based genetic studies and behavioural genetic studies and their interpretations. In order to prevent discrimination, The UNESCO Declaration on Human Genetic Data states in Article 14 that human genetic data, human proteomic data and biological samples linked to an identifiable person should not be disclosed or made accessible to third parties, in particular employers, insurance companies, educational institutions and the family. The issue has been analysed in the elaboration of the Preliminary Draft Declaration on Universal Norms on Bioethics of 2005, and Article 11 of the Declaration states that no individual or group should be discriminated or stigmatised on any grounds, in violation of human dignity, human rights and fundamental freedoms.[44] The stigmatisation generally does not infringe on personal rights, because it consists in a psychological approach characterised by hostility in front of a person perceived as 'different'.[45]

The stigmatisation is also related to the social, educational and work-related exclusion of a group. It reinforces inequalities and contributes to the worsening of the inequities and vulnerabilities of certain individuals or groups. Stigmatisation generally consists in words or behaviour that tags or labels someone on the basis of his actual or alleged characteristics. The fight against this attitude concerns, at the social and cultural levels, the awareness campaign concerning the human genome or about the informatics use of the genetic data. Stigmatisation is the first step to discrimination.

For this reason, the most important act at the universal level requires states to introduce at the national level specific measures to prevent discrimination.[46] The Oviedo Convention does not introduce a principle of non-stigmatisation, and there is a lack of protection in this area. The stigmatisation of groups is linked to the screening programs that target at subset of the population. These screening tests are designed to search for or exclude pathologies. A misperception of pathologies or a misinterpretation of the scope of screening may lead to the stigmatisation of persons or groups involved in the research. At this level, the awareness of the population regarding the scope of the screening is important, in order to prevent the stigmatisation. The use of characteristics for a composite drawing or description of the perpetrator of a crime may lead to the stigmatisation of certain groups within society. Information on ethnic origin is the prototypical

[44] Preliminary Draft Declaration on Universal Norms on Bioethics, SHS/EST/CIB-EXTR/05/CONF.202/2, Paris, 9 February 2005, www.ordemenfermeiros.pt/legislacao/Documents/Legislacao-Saude/Declaracao_Universa_Bioetica_%20UNESCO.pdf.

[45] 'Being labelled as having "bad genes" can have serious social and psychological consequences for individuals, and this stigmatization may be stronger and more common where levels of education and understanding of genetics is low': R Who, Regional Office for the Western Pacific, 'Ethical Issues Related to New Developments in the Health Sector' (Doc WPR/RC53/INF.DOC./1, 30 August 2002) 17.

[46] International Convention on the Elimination of All Forms of Racial Discrimination (CERD) Adopted and opened for signature and ratification by General Assembly resolution 2106 (XX) of 21 December 1965, entry into force 4 January 1969, in accordance with Article 19, www.ohchr.org/EN/ProfessionalInterest/Pages/CERD.aspx.

example of information that may have such an effect, especially if the ethnic group constitutes a minority in society. The prohibition of genetic discrimination has not been imposed on the international community. At the EU level, since the entry into force of Lisbon Treaty, the European Charter of Fundamental Rights has the same legal authority as the Treaties, and it provides protection against the violation of the rights established in the constitutive Treaties.[47]

The Oviedo Convention states that Member States must establish appropriate judicial protection to prevent or put a stop to unlawful infringement (Article 23) and apply appropriate sanctions in the event of infringement of the Convention (Article 25). The Oviedo Convention has, moreover, introduced an innovative dispute resolution system, which involves the ECtHR. On the basis of Article 29 of the Oviedo Convention, the ECtHR may give, without direct reference to any specific proceedings pending in a court, advisory opinions on legal questions concerning the interpretation of the Convention, at the request of: the government of a party, after having informed the other parties; or the committee set up by Article 32, with membership restricted to the representatives of the parties to the Oviedo Convention, by a decision adopted by a two-thirds majority of votes cast. This rule is the first and only example of advisory competence of the ECtHR in the context of conventions promoted by the Council of Europe. It represents an integration of national systems of protection which must respond quickly to prevent violation of the Convention and in the event of a threat.

The Oviedo Convention does not give individuals a right to initiate proceedings before the ECtHR. However, facts which are infringement of the rights contained in the Convention may be considered in proceedings under the ECHR if they also constitute a violation of one of the rights contained in the ECHR. The Explanatory Report the Oviedo Convention specifies that the ECtHR, through an innovative interpretation of the ECHR, may also analyse cases that represent violations of rights established in the Oviedo Convention.[48] Moreover, it is possible to refer a matter

[47] Regarding the entry into force of the Lisbon Treaty and the effect regarding the Charter of EU Fundamental Rights, see U Villani, *Istituzioni di diritto dell'unione Europea* (Bari, Cacucci, 2019); G. Tesauro, *Diritto dell'Unione europea* (Padova, Cedam, 2012); E Adam and A Tizzano, *Lineamenti diritto dell'Unione europea* (Turin, Giappichelli, 2014); L Daniele, *Diritto dell'Unione europea* (Milan, Giuffrè, 2018).

[48] The report regarding the Oviedo Convention suggests that 'Under Article 14 of the European Convention on Human Rights, the enjoyment of the rights and freedoms set forth in the Convention must be secured without discrimination on any ground such as sex, race, color, language, religion, political or other opinion, national or social origin, association with a national minority, property, birth or other status. Article 11 adds to this list a person's genetic heritage. The prohibition of discrimination set out thus applies to all areas included in the field of application of this Convention. This notion also includes non-discrimination on grounds of race as understood by the 1965 United Nations Convention on the Elimination of all Forms of Racial Discrimination and as it has been interpreted by the Convention Committee (CERD). In particular, it cannot prohibit positive measures which may be implemented with the aim of re-establishing a certain balance in favor of those at a disadvantage because of their genetic inheritance.' The Explanatory Report to the Convention on Human Rights and Biomedicine was drawn up under the responsibility of the Secretary General of the Council of Europe, on the basis of a draft prepared, at the request of the Steering Committee on Bioethics (CDBI),

concerning genetic discrimination to the ECtHR in case of violation of Article 14 of the ECHR (which now includes the principle of genetic discrimination). A part of doctrine affirms that it is possible to consider genetic discrimination in Article 14 of the ECHR, in the context of 'other status'.[49] This interpretation is compliant with the Explanatory Report's annexes to the Convention of Oviedo. Finally, it is necessary to highlight that genetic discrimination in the sectors of assurance and employment does not fall within the scope of the Oviedo Convention, and for this reason the ECtHR cannot accept cases regarding this issue.[50]

## VII. Concluding Remarks

In conclusion, it is possible to affirm that the use of gene editing systems, in the context of the EU and international legal frameworks concerning bio-law, is possible only if it aims to improve the health conditions of the individual and does not aim to carry out eugenics experiments.

The ECtHR has outlined the necessity to implement Article 8 of the ECHR in order to include the right to use eugenics techniques in field of the PGD. The ECtHR invokes the application of the non-discrimination principle in the use of genetic information in the PGD technique concerning embryos.

In the light of the definition of the new right to use gene editing techniques, it is necessary to reconcile this new emerging right with the protection of fundamental rights, such as the prohibition of genetic discrimination. Finally, the close interconnection between the right to science[51] in the context of human rights must

by Mr Jean Michaud (France), Chairman of the CDBI. It takes into account the discussions held in the CDBI and its Working Group entrusted with the drafting of the Convention; it also takes into account the remarks and proposals made by delegations. The Committee of Ministers authorised the publication of this Explanatory Report on 17 December 1996. The Report is available at http://conventions.coe.int/Treaty/en/Reports/Html/164.htm.

[49] MA Hall and S Rich, 'Laws Restricting Health Insurers' Use of Genetic Information: Impact on Genetic Discrimination' (2000) 66 *American Journal of Human Genetics* 293.

[50] BA Lenox, 'Genetic Discrimination in Insurance and Employment: Spoiled Fruit of the Human Genome Project' [1997] *University of Dayton Law Review* 198; ME Ashley, 'Genetic Discrimination by Employers and Insurance Companies Based on Predictive Genetic Information' [2003] *The School of Law Texas Tech University* 1071.

[51] This right found further recognition in 1966, in the International Covenant on Economic, Social and Cultural Rights (ICESCR), a multilateral treaty adopted by the United Nations General Assembly. The combined reading of these two provisions provides the legal foundations of what is now commonly referred to as the 'right to science' or, less succinctly, the right to enjoy the benefits of scientific and technological progress and its applications'. Art 15(1)(b) ICESCR recognises the right of everyone 'to enjoy the benefits of scientific progress and its applications'. Part of the corpus of economic, social and cultural human rights, the so-called 'right to science' has long been overlooked, with the result that its legal development is rudimentary at best. However, given its growing contemporary relevance, legal academics and practitioners have turned their attention to the study and elaboration of the right to science with a view to bringing further conceptual clarity to this universal human rights norm. Aspects of the right to science are also recognised in other international and regional human rights instruments.

be highlighted. As clearly emerges from the ECtHR's case law and from the international legal framework, the use of eugenic and gene editing techniques must be oriented to the protection of human rights, such as the right to health, the right to life and the prohibition of discrimination. In this perspective, a precautionary approach is important in regulating science and the emerging technologies, because this approach is often applied to situations where a potential risk of an activity may be anticipated or identified, often using traditional risk assessment or scientific evaluation, but where scientific data is insufficient to fully demonstrate or quantify the risk or causal relationships.[52]

The precautionary principle is detailed in Article 191 of the Treaty on the Functioning of the European Union and it aims to ensure a higher level of environmental protection through preventative decision-making in the case of risk. In practice, however, the scope of this principle is far wider and also covers consumer policy, together with EU legislation concerning food and human, animal and plant health.[53] The definition of the precautionary principle should also have a positive impact at the international law level, ensuring the appropriate level of environmental and health protection in international negotiations.[54] It has already been introduced in various international agreements, notably in the Agreement on the

Notably, Art 27(1) of Universal Declaration of Human Rights recognised the right of everyone 'to share in scientific advancement and its benefits'. In a regional context, Art 14 of the Additional Protocol to the American Convention on Human Rights in the Area of Economic, Social and Cultural Rights and Art 42 of the Arab Charter on Human Rights both adopt language substantially similar to the ICESCR. The right to science is also recognised and elaborated upon in soft law instruments, notably, the UN Declaration on the Use of Scientific and Technological Progress in the Interests of Peace and for the Benefit of Mankind (UN Declaration on Scientific and Technological Progress), proclaimed by the UN General Assembly in 1975. UNESCO has also adopted several instruments relating to science and technology, including the Universal Declaration on the Human Genome and Human Rights, the Universal Declaration on Bioethics and Human Rights, the Recommendation on the Status of Science and Scientific Researches and the Declaration of Ethical Principles in Relation to Climate Change. In 2012, the HRC Special Rapporteur in the field of cultural rights reported on the Right to Enjoy the Benefits of Scientific Progress and its Applications with a view 'to catalys(ing) a robust discussion among states, scientific researchers and practitioners, civil society groups, and the private sector to further elucidate the right to science'. In October 2018, the Committee on Economic Social and Cultural Rights commenced a consultative process with a view to clarifying the interpretation of this right through the drafting of a general comment on Art 15 ICESCR on the right to enjoy the benefit of scientific progress and its applications. L Vinuales, 'Legal Techniques for Dealing with Scientific Uncertainty in Environmental Law' [2010] *Vanderbilt Journal of Transnational Law* 437; A Boyle, 'Some Reflections on the Relationship of Treaties and Soft Law' [1999] *ICLQ* 901; AM Hubert, 'The Human Right to Science and Its Relationship to International Environmental Law' [2019] *European Journal of International Law* 33.

[52] HS Burnett, 'Understanding the Precautionary Principle and Its Threat to Human Welfare' [2009] *Social Philosophy* 379; HI Miller and G Conko, 'Precaution without Principle' [2001] *Nature Biotechnology* 302; C Star, 'The Precautionary Principle versus Risk Analysis' [2003] *Risk Analysis* 1; C Munthe, *The Principle of Precaution and the Ethics of Risk* (New York, Springer, 2011); RV Percival, 'Who's Afraid of the Precautionary Principle?' [2005] *Pace Environmental Law Review* 21.

[53] SM Gardier, 'A Core Precautionary Principle' [2006] *Journal of Political Philosophy* 33; SO Hansson, 'Decision-Making under Great Uncertainty' [1996] *Philosophy of the Social Sciences* 369.

[54] J Koplin, C Gyngell and J Saveluscu, 'Germline Gene Editing and the Precautionary Principle' [2019] *Bioethics* Special Issue: Human Germline Editing 49.

Application of Sanitary and Phytosanitary Measures concluded in 1995 within the framework of the World Trade Organization.[55]

The principle was explicitly recognised during the UN Conference on Environment and Development in Rio de Janeiro in 1992 and was included in the so-called Rio Declaration. Since then, the precautionary principle has been implemented in various environmental instrument, and in particular in biodiversity conservation. The application of the precautionary principle may, in general, be invoked when a phenomenon, product or process may have a dangerous effect, identified by a scientific and objective evaluation, if this evaluation does not allow the risk to be determined with sufficient certainty.[56] The application of the principle involves a risk analysis on the basis of the proportionality between the measure taken and the chosen level of protection, the non-discrimination in the application of the measure, the consistency of the measure with similar measures already taken in similar situations or using similar approaches, an examination of the costs and benefits of the action or its lack of adoption, and a review of the measure in the light of scientific development.[57] The precautionary principle is relevant only in the event of a potential risk, even if this risk cannot be fully demonstrated or quantified or its effects determined because of the insufficiency or inclusive nature of the scientific data. In the field of gene editing, it may be possible to apply the precautionary principle, in particular concerning the principle of non-discrimination.

One of the most important issues concerning the application of gene editing is the possible discrimination or stigmatisation. In the application of the precautionary principle, any measures taken should not be discriminatory.

[55] IM Goklany, *The Precautionary Principle: A Critical Appraisal of Environmental Risk Assessment* (Washington DC, Cato Institute, 2001).

[56] S Clarke, 'The Precautionary Principle and the Dual-Use Dilemma' in B Rappert and M Selgelid (eds), *On the Dual Uses of Science and Ethics: Principles, Practices and Prospects* (Canberra, Australian National University, 2018); J Herington, 'Health Security and Risk Aversion' [2016] *Bioethics* 479.

[57] P Harremoes, D Gee, M MacGarvin, A Stirling, J Keys, B Wynne and S Guedes Vaz, *The Precautionary Principle in the 20th Century: Late Lessons from Early Warnings* (London, Earthscan Publication, 2013).

# INDEX

**Introductory Note**

References such as '178–79' indicate (not necessarily continuous) discussion of a topic across a range of pages. Wherever possible in the case of topics with many references, these have either been divided into sub-topics or only the most significant discussions of the topic are listed. Because the entire work is about the 'IT revolution', the use of this term (and certain others which occur constantly throughout the book) as an entry point has been minimised. Information will be found under the corresponding detailed topics.

www.ingramcontent.com/pod-product-compliance
Ingram Content Group UK Ltd.
Pitfield, Milton Keynes, MK11 3LW, UK
UKHW020237290926
15470UKWH00002B/594

9 781509 940875